Lecture Notes in Computer Science 12093

More information about this series at http://www.springer.com/series/7409

Wanling Gao · Jianfeng Zhan · Geoffrey Fox ·
Xiaoyi Lu · Dan Stanzione (Eds.)

Benchmarking, Measuring, and Optimizing

Second BenchCouncil International Symposium, Bench 2019
Denver, CO, USA, November 14–16, 2019
Revised Selected Papers

 Springer

Editors
Wanling Gao (iD)
Institute of Computing Technology,
Chinese Academy of Sciences
Beijing, China

Geoffrey Fox
School of Informatics, Computing,
and Engineering
Indiana University
Bloomington, IN, USA

Dan Stanzione
Texas Advanced Computing Center
The University of Texas at Austin
Austin, TX, USA

Jianfeng Zhan
Institute of Computing Technology,
Chinese Academy of Sciences
Beijing, China

Xiaoyi Lu
Department of Computer Science
and Engineering
The Ohio State University
Columbus, OH, USA

ISSN 0302-9743   ISSN 1611-3349 (electronic)
Lecture Notes in Computer Science
ISBN 978-3-030-49555-8   ISBN 978-3-030-49556-5 (eBook)
https://doi.org/10.1007/978-3-030-49556-5

LNCS Sublibrary: SL3 – Information Systems and Applications, incl. Internet/Web, and HCI

This Springer imprint is published by the registered company Springer Nature Switzerland AG
The registered company address is: Gewerbestrasse 11, 6330 Cham, Switzerland

Preface

This volume contains a selection of revised papers presented at Bench 2019: the Second BenchCouncil International Symposium, held in November, 2019, in Denver, CO, USA. To advance the state of the art of AI and other benchmarking, the International Open Benchmark Council (BenchCouncil) has three fundamental responsibilities. First, it releases influential benchmarks and index to prevent from chaotic competitions within AI, computer, finance, education, medical, and other technological industries. Second, it encourages data-driven, intelligence-inspired, and benchmark-based quantitative approaches to tackling multi-disciplinary challenges. Finally but not least, BenchCouncil incubates benchmark projects and hosts the BenchCouncil benchmark projects, and further encourages reliable and reproducible research using the BenchCouncil benchmark projects or incubator benchmark projects.

This year, BenchCouncil released four top level AI benchmarking projects, including AIBench – a scenario-distilling benchmarking methodology and an AI benchmark suite, HPC AI500 – a benchmark suite for HPC AI systems, Edge AIBench – an end-to-end edge AI benchmark Suite, and AIoTBench – an AI benchmark suite for benchmarking mobile and embedded device intelligence. Using AIBench as baseline, BenchCouncil hosted the 2019 AI System and Algorithm Challenge (http://www.benchcouncil.org/competitions.html) and organized the 2019 BenchCouncil International Symposium on Benchmarking, Measuring and Optimizing (Bench 2019) (http://www.benchcouncil.org/bench19/index.html). The 2019 AI Challenge consists of four challenge tracks: International AI System Challenge based on RISC-V, International AI System Challenge based on Cambricon Chip, International AI System Challenge based on X86 Platform, and International 3D Face Recognition Algorithm Challenge. The Bench 2019 symposium solicits papers that address hot topic issues in benchmarking, measuring, and optimizing systems. This book includes 31 regular papers from the Bench 2019 conference, which were selected from 79 submissions, yielding an acceptance rate of 39%. The tutorials about AI benchmarks for datacenter (AIBench), edge (Edge AIBench), and HPC (HPC AI500) were presented at the conference, but are not included in this book.

The call for papers for Bench 2019 attracted a number of high-quality submissions. During a rigorous review process, in which each paper was reviewed by at least three experts. In addition, we invited five keynote speakers, including Dr. Dan Stanzione from The University of Texas at Austin; Prof. Dhabaleswar K. (DK) Panda from The Ohio State University; Mr. Gilad Shainer from Mellanox; Prof. Geoffrey Fox from Indiana University; and Prof. Felix Wolf from TU Darmstadt in Germany. Bench 2019 also hosted five invited talks, including Dr. Zheng Cao from Alibaba; Dr. Dong Li from ICT, Chinese Academy of Sciences, and Seaway Technology Co., LTD.; Prof. Bo Wu from Colorado School of Mines; Dr. Weijia Xu from The University of Texas at Austin; and Dr. Gabriel Antoniu from Inria.

During the conference, BenchCouncil sponsored two awards to recognize important contributions in the area of benchmarking, measuring, and optimizing. The BenchCouncil Achievement Award recognizes a senior member who has made long-term contributions to benchmarking, measuring, and optimizing. Prof. Dr. Tony Hey, the Chief Data Scientist at Rutherford Appleton Laboratory STFC, was named the 2019 recipient of the International Open Benchmark Council (BenchCouncil) Achievement Award. The BenchCouncil Best Paper Award is recognizes a paper presented at the Bench conferences, which demonstrates potential impact on research and practice in benchmarking, measuring, and optimizing. Khaled Ibrahim, Samuel Williams, and Leonid Oliker from Lawrence Berkeley National Laboratory received the Bench 2019 Best Paper Award for their paper: "Performance Analysis of GPU Programming Models using the Roofline Scaling Trajectories." In addition, 13 challenge teams from Georgia Institute of Technology, The Ohio State University, Google, etc., were honored with the 2019 AI Challenge Awards.

We are very grateful to the efforts of all authors related to writing, revising, and presenting their papers at Bench 2019 conference. We appreciate the indispensable support of the Bench 2019 Program Committee and thank them for their efforts and contributions in maintaining the high standards of the Bench 2019 symposium.

February 2020

Wanling Gao
Jianfeng Zhan

Organization

General Chairs

Dan Stanzione   Texas Advanced Computing Center,
The University of Texas at Austin, USA
Xiaoyi Lu   The Ohio State University, USA

Program Chairs

Jianfeng Zhan   ICT, Chinese Academy of Sciences,
University of Chinese Academy of Sciences, China
Geoffrey Fox   Indiana University, USA

Program Committee

Haiying Shen   University of Virginia, USA
Woongki Baek   UNIST, South Korea
Zheng Cao   Alibaba, China
Piotr Luszczek   University of Tennessee Knoxville, USA
Khaled Ibrahim   Lawrence Berkeley National Lab, USA
Li Zha   ICT, Chinese Academy of Sciences, China
Lei Wang   ICT, Chinese Academy of Sciences, China
Vladimir Getov   University of Westminster, UK
Gwangsun Kim   POSTECH, South Korea
Hyogi Sim   Oak Ridge National Laboratory, USA
Zhen Jia   Princeton University, USA
Weijia Xu   The University of Texas at Austin, USA
Bin Ren   Pacific Northwest National Laboratory, USA
Nikhil Jain   Lawrence Livermore National Laboratory, USA
Lucas Mello Schnorr   UFRGS, Brazil
Shantenu Jha   Rutgers University, USA
Bo Wu   Colorado School of Mines, USA
Jungang Xu   College of Computer and Control Engineering,
University of Chinese Academy of Sciences, China
Saliya Ekanayake   Virginia Tech, USA
Zujie Ren   Zhejiang University, China
Ryan E. Grant   Sandia National Laboratories, USA
Zhihui Du   Tsinghua University, China
Guang R Gao   Computer Architecture and Parallel Systems
Laboratory, University of Delaware, USA

Award Committee

Lizy Kurian John   The University of Texas at Austin, USA
Dhabaleswar K. (DK) Panda   The Ohio State University, USA
Geoffrey Fox   Indiana University, USA
Jianfeng Zhan   ICT, Chinese Academy of Sciences,
                                     University of Chinese Academy of Sciences, China

Keynote Speech and Invited Talks

BenchCouncil Achievement Award

Tony Hey

Rutherford Appleton Laboratory STFC

Tony Hey has a doctorate in particle physics from the University of Oxford. After a career in physics that included research positions at Caltech, MIT and CERN, and a professorship at the University of Southampton, he became interested in parallel computing and moved into computer science. His group was one of the first to build and explore the development of parallel software for message-passing distributed memory computers. He was one of the authors of the first draft of the MPI message-passing standard. Tony led the UK eScience initiative in 2001 before joining Microsoft in 2005 as Vice-President for Technical Computing. He returned to work in the UK in 2015 as Chief Data Scientist at the Rutherford Appleton Laboratory and leads the 'Scientific Machine Learning' group. Tony is a fellow of the Association for Computing Machinery, the American Association for the Advancement of Science, and the Royal Academy of Engineering.

Prof. Hey was honored for foundational contributions to distributed memory parallel machines, message-passing systems, and AI for sciences. Prof. Hey devised the first parallel benchmark suite – the 'Genesis' benchmarks – for performance evaluation of distributed memory parallel machines, and recently launches a large-scale data science benchmark.

Benchmarking Supercomputers in the Post-Moore Era

Dan Stanzione

The University of Texas at Austin

Abstract: In this talk, we will cover the increasing gaps between headline performance and application performance on Frontera and the last several generations of TACC supercomputers. We will also discuss the challenges of developing a new benchmark suite for the upcoming Leadership-Class Computing Facility, and solicit community input on capability benchmarks.

Bio: Dr. Dan Stanzione, Associate Vice President for Research at The University of Texas at Austin since 2018 and Executive Director of the Texas Advanced Computing Center (TACC) since 2014, is a nationally recognized leader in high performance computing. He is the principal investigator (PI) for a National Science Foundation (NSF) grant to deploy Frontera, which is the fastest supercomputer at any U.S. university. Stanzione is also the PI of TACC's Stampede2 and Wrangler systems, super-computers for high performance computing and for data-focused applications, respectively. For six years he was co-PI of CyVerse, a large-scale NSF life sciences cyberinfrastructure. Stanzione was also a co-PI for TACC's Ranger and Lonestar supercomputers, large-scale NSF systems previously deployed at UT Austin. Stanzione received his bachelor's degree in electrical engineering and his master's degree and doctorate in computer engineering from Clemson University.

Benchmarks and Middleware for Designing Convergent HPC, Big Data and Deep Learning Software Stacks for Exascale Systems

Dhabaleswar K. (DK) Panda

The Ohio State University

Abstract: This talk will focus on challenges in designing benchmarks and middleware for convergent HPC, Deep Learning, and Big Data Analytics Software stacks for Exascale systems with millions of processors and accelerators. For the HPC domain, we will discuss about the OSU Micro-Benchmarks (OMB) Suite and associated middleware for designing runtime environments for MPI+X programming models by taking into account support for multi-core systems (x86, OpenPOWER, and ARM), high-performance networks, and GPGPUs (including GPUDirect RDMA). Features and sample performance numbers from the MVAPICH2 libraries (http://mvapich.cse.ohio-state.edu) will be presented. An overview of RDMA-based designs for Hadoop (HDFS, MapReduce, RPC, and HBase), Spark, and Memcached, together with the OSU HiBD benchmarks (http://hibd.cse.ohio-state.edu) will be presented for Big Data Analytics. For the Deep Learning domain, we will focus on a set of different benchmarks and profiling tools to deliver scalable DNN training with Horovod and TensorFlow using MVAPICH2-GDR MPI library (http://hidl.cse.ohio-state.edu).

Bio: Dhabaleswar K. (DK) Panda is a Professor and University Distinguished Scholar of Computer Science and Engineering at The Ohio State University. He has published over 450 papers in the area of high-end computing and networking. The MVAPICH2 (High Performance MPI and PGAS over InfiniBand, Omni-Path, iWARP, and RoCE) libraries, designed and developed by his research group (http://mvapich.cse.ohio-state.edu), are currently being used by more than 3,025 organizations worldwide (in 89 countries). More than 600,000 downloads of this software have taken place from the project's site. This software is empowering several InfiniBand clusters (including the 3rd, 5th, 8th, 15th, 16th, 19th, and 31st ranked ones) in the TOP500 list. The RDMA packages for Apache Spark, Apache Hadoop, and Memcached together with OSU HiBD benchmarks from his group (http://hibd.cse.ohio-state.edu) are also publicly available. These libraries are currently being used by more than 315 organizations in 35 countries. More than 31,300 downloads of these libraries have taken place. High-performance and scalable versions of the Caffe and TensorFlow framework are available from https://hidl.cse.ohio-state.edu. Prof. Panda is an IEEE Fellow. More details about Prof. Panda are available at http://www.cse.ohio-state.edu/ panda.

InfiniBand In-Network Computing Technology for Scalable HPC/AI

Gilad Shainer

Mellanox

Abstract: The ever-increasing demands for higher computation performance drive the creation of new datacenter accelerators and processing units. Previously CPUs and GPUs were the main sources for compute power. The exponential increase in data volume and in problems complexity, drove the creation of a new processing unit the I/O processing unit or IPU. IPUs are interconnect elements that include In-Network Computing engines, engines that can participate in the application run time, and analyze application data as it being transferred within the data center, or at the edge. The combination of CPUs, GPUs, and IPUs, creates the next generation of data center and edge computing architectures. The first generations of IPUs are already in use in leading HPC and Deep learning data centers, have been integrated into multiple MPI frameworks, NVIDIA NCCL, Charm++, and others, and have demonstrated accelerate performance by nearly 10X.

Bio: Gilad Shainer serves as Mellanox's Senior Vice President of Marketing, focusing on high-performance computing. Mr. Shainer joined Mellanox in 2001 as a design engineer and later served in senior marketing management roles since 2005. Mr. Shainer serves as the chairman of the HPC-AI Advisory Council organization, he serves as the president of UCF and CCIX consortiums, a board member in the OpenCAPI and OpenFabrics organizations, a member of IBTA and contributor to the PCISIG PCI-X and PCIe specifications. Mr. Shainer holds multiple patents in the field of high-speed networking. He is a recipient of 2015 R&D100 award for his contribution to the CORE-Direct In-Network Computing technology and the 2019 R&D100 award for his contribution to the UCX technology. Gilad Shainer holds MSc degree and BSc degree in Electrical Engineering from the Technion Institute of Technology in Israel.

Benchmarking Perspectives on Emerging HPC Workloads

Geoffrey Fox

Indiana University

Bio: Geoffrey Charles Fox (https://www.engineering. indiana.edu/, http://www.dsc.soic.indiana.edu/, gcf@indiana.edu). Fox received a PhD in Theoretical Physics from Cambridge University where he was Senior Wrangler. He is now a distinguished Professor of Engineering, Computing, and Physics at Indiana University where he is director of the Digital Science Center. He previously held positions at Caltech, Syracuse University, and Florida State University after being a postdoc at the Institute for Advanced Study at Princeton, Lawrence Berkeley Laboratory, and Peterhouse College Cambridge. He has supervised the PhD of 73 students and published around 1,300 papers (over 500 with at least 10 citations) in physics and computing with an hindex of 78 and over 35,000 citations. He is a Fellow of APS (Physics) and ACM (Computing) and works on the interdisciplinary interface between computing and applications. Current work is in Biology, Pathology, Sensor Clouds and Ice-sheet Science, Image processing, Deep Learning, and Particle Physics. His architecture work is built around High-performance Computing enhanced Software Defined Big Data Systems on Clouds and Clusters. The analytics focuses on scalable parallel machine learning. He is an expert on streaming data and robot-cloud interactions. He is involved in several projects to enhance the capabilities of Minority Serving Institutions. He has experience in online education and its use in MOOCs for areas like Data and Computational Science.

Lightweight Requirements Engineering for Exascale Co-design

Felix Wolf

Department of Computer Science of TU Darmstadt, Germany

Abstract: Given the tremendous cost of an exascale system, its architecture must match the requirements of the applications it is supposed to run as precisely as possible. Conversely, applications must be designed such that building an appropriate system becomes feasible, motivating the idea of co-design. In this process, a fundamental aspect of the application requirements are the rates at which the demands for different resources grow as a code is scaled to a larger machine. However, if the anticipated scale exceeds the size of available platforms this demand can no longer be measured. This is clearly the case when designing an exascale system. Moreover, creating analytical models to predict these requirements is often too laborious especially when the number and complexity of target applications is high. In this paper, we show how automated performance modeling can be used to quickly predict application requirements for varying scales and problem sizes.

Bio: Felix Wolf is Full Professor at the Department of Computer Science of TU Darmstadt in Germany, where he leads the Laboratory for Parallel Programming. He works on methods, tools, and algorithms that support the development and deployment of parallel software systems in various stages of their life cycle. Prof. Wolf received his PhD degree from RWTH Aachen University in 2003. After working more than two years as a postdoc at the Innovative Computing Laboratory of the University of Tennessee, he was appointed research group leader at Jülich Supercomputing Centre. Between 2009 and 2015, he was head of the Laboratory for Parallel Programming at the German Research School for Simulation Sciences in Aachen and Full Professor at RWTH Aachen University. Prof. Wolf has published more than a hundred refereed articles on parallel computing, several of which have received awards.

FloraBench: An End-to-End Application Benchmark Suite for Datacenter

Zheng Cao

Alibaba

Abstract: The topic is FloraBench: an end-to-end application benchmark suite for datacenter. This talk abstracts the realistic application scenario of Alibaba and provides an application benchmark for datacenter computing – FloraBench. This Benchmark aims to identify the characteristics and bottlenecks of business E-commerce applications, and further optimize the performance of large-scale clusters.

Bio: Dr. Zheng Cao is a Senior Staff Engineer of the Alibaba Group and leads the architecture team of Alibaba Infrastructure Service BU. He received his PhD from ICT, Chinese Academy of Sciences. Before joining Alibaba Group, he served as a Professor at the Institute of Computing Technology, CAS and was one of the core architects of Dawning 5000, Dawning 6000 (ranked the 2nd in the TOP500 list), and Dawning 7000 supercomputer systems. His team is working on the Alibaba's workload analysis, software-hardware codesign, and datacenter architecture. He is a member of Advanced Computing Expert Committee, and Blockchain Expert Committee of China Computer Federation.

Towards Benchmarking AIOT Device Based on MCU

Dong Li

ICT, Chinese Academy of Sciences Seaway Technology Co., Ltd.

Abstract: The topic is "Towards Benchmarking AIOT Device based on MCU". This talk introduces MCU-based AIOT device and discusses the benchmarking requirements and goals. Seaway RTOS for AIOT devices provide KB-level Seaway RTOS kernel, KB-level runtime, and KB-level EdgeStack, and allow only one application for the whole end-Edge-cloud system.

Bio: Dr. Dong Li is an Associate Professor at Wireless Sensor Network Laboratory, ICT, Chinese Academy of Sciences and Seaway Technology Co., Ltd.

Harmonizing High-Level Abstraction and High Performance for Graph Mining

Bo Wu

Colorado School of Mines

Abstract: Graph mining algorithms that aim at identifying structural patterns in graphs are typically more complex than graph computation algorithms such as breadth first search. Researchers have implemented several systems with high-level and flexible interfaces customized for tackling graph mining problems. However, we found that for triangle counting, one of the simplest graph mining problems, such systems can be several times slower than a single-threaded implementation of a straightforward algorithm. In this talk, I will reveal the root causes of the severe inefficiency of state-of-the-art graph mining systems and the challenges to address the performance problems. I will describe AutoMine, a system we developed to automatically generate both specialized algorithms and high-performance low-level code for arbitrary patterns.

Bio: Bo Wu is an Associate Professor in the Department of Computer Science at Colorado School of Mines. His research focuses on leveraging compiler and runtime techniques to build efficient software systems for large-scale graph analytics and machine learning applications on heterogeneous platforms. He received the Best Paper Award at SC'15, an NSF CRII Award, an NSF Early Career Award, and an NSF SPX Award.

Deep Learning on HPC: Performance Factors and Lessons Learned

Weijia Xu

The University of Texas at Austin

Abstract: In this talk, we report several ongoing efforts for deploying and running deep learning applications using high performance computing clusters at Texas Advanced Computing Center. From both lessons learned through practices and designed experiments, we discuss several factors affecting the deep learning performances, both accuracy and execution time, at various stages of analysis pipeline from low level data storage to high level deep learning framework. The talk will end with discussions and future outlooks on development, deployment, and benchmark deep learning applications at scale.

Bio: Dr. Weijia Xu is a research scientist and lead the Scalable Computational Intelligence group at Texas Advanced Computing Center at The University of Texas at Austin. He received his PhD from Computer Science Department at UT Austin and has been an experienced data scientist. Dr. Xu's main research interest is to enable data-driven discoveries through developing new computational methods and applications that facilitate the data-to-knowledge transfer process. Dr. Xu leads the group that supports large scale data driven analysis and machine learning applications using computing resources at TACC. His projects have been funded through various federal and state agencies including NIH, NSF, City of Austin, and USDA. He has served in Program Committees for several workshops and conferences in Big Data, Cloud Computing, and HPC areas.

Towards a Methodology for Benchmarking Edge Processing Frameworks

Gabriel Antoniu

Inria

Abstract: With the spectacular growth of the Internet of Things, edge processing emerged as a relevant means to offload data processing and analytics from centralized Clouds to the devices that serve as data sources (often provided with some processing capabilities). While a large plethora of frameworks for edge processing were recently proposed, the distributed systems community has no clear means today to discriminate between them. Some preliminary surveys exist, focusing on a feature-based comparison. We claim that a step further is needed, to enable a performance-based comparison. To this purpose, the definition of a benchmark is a necessity. In this talk, we make this step by discussing the definition of a methodology for benchmarking Edge processing frameworks.

Bio: Dr. Gabriel Antoniu is a Senior Research Scientist at Inria, Rennes. He leads the KerData research team, focusing on storage and I/O management for Big Data processing on scalable infrastructures (clouds, HPC systems). His main current interests regard HPC-Big Data convergence for data storage and processing aspects. He currently serves as Vice Executive Director of JLESC – Joint Inria-Illinois-ANL-BSC-JSC-RIKEN/AICS Laboratory for Extreme-Scale Computing on behalf of Inria. He received his PhD degree in Computer Science in 2001 from ENS Lyon. He leads several international projects in partnership with Microsoft Research, IBM, Argonne National Lab, the University of Illinois at Urbana Champaign, and Huawei. He served as program chair for the IEEE Cluster conference in 2014 and 2017 and regularly serves as a Program Committee member of major conferences in the area of HPC, Cloud Computing and Big Data (SC, HPDC, CCGRID, Cluster, Big Data, etc.). He has acted as advisor for 19 PhD theses and has co-authored over 140 international publications in the aforementioned areas.

Contents

Best Paper Session

Performance Analysis of GPU Programming Models Using the Roofline
Scaling Trajectories. 3
  Khaled Z. Ibrahim, Samuel Williams, and Leonid Oliker

GraphBench: A Benchmark Suite for Graph Computing Systems 20
  Lei Wang and Minghe Yu

Early Experience in Benchmarking Edge AI Processors
with Object Detection Workloads 32
  Yujie Hui, Jeffrey Lien, and Xiaoyi Lu

AI Challenges on Cambricon Using AIBench

XDN: Towards Efficient Inference of Residual Neural Networks
on Cambricon Chips 51
  Guangli Li, Xueying Wang, Xiu Ma, Lei Liu, and Xiaobing Feng

Performance Analysis of Cambricon MLU100 57
  Jiansong Li and Zihan Jiang

Exploring the Performance Bound of Cambricon Accelerator
in End-to-End Inference Scenario 67
  Yifan Wang, Chundian Li, and Chen Zeng

Improve Image Classification by Convolutional Network on Cambricon 75
  Peng He, Ge Chen, Kai Deng, Ping Yao, and Li Fu

AI Challenges on RISC-V Using AIBench

RVTensor: A Light-Weight Neural Network Inference Framework Based
on the RISC-V Architecture 85
  Pengpeng Hou, Jiageng Yu, Yuxia Miao, Yang Tai, Yanjun Wu,
  and Chen Zhao

AIRV: Enabling Deep Learning Inference on RISC-V 91
  Yangyang Kong

AI Challenges on X86 Using AIBench

PSL: Exploiting Parallelism, Sparsity and Locality to Accelerate Matrix
Factorization on x86 Platforms 101
    Weixin Deng, Pengyu Wang, Jing Wang, Chao Li, and Minyi Guo

The Implementation and Optimization of Matrix Decomposition
Based Collaborative Filtering Task on X86 Platform 110
    Tianshu Hao and Ziping Zheng

An Efficient Implementation of the ALS-WR Algorithm on x86 CPUs 116
    Maosen Chen, Tun Chen, and Qianyun Chen

Accelerating Parallel ALS for Collaborative Filtering on Hadoop 123
    Yi Liang, Shaokang Zeng, Yande Liang, and Kaizhong Chen

AI Challenges on 3D Face Recognition Using AIBench

Improving RGB-D Face Recognition via Transfer Learning
from a Pretrained 2D Network 141
    Xingwang Xiong, Xu Wen, and Cheng Huang

An Implementation of ResNet on the Classification of RGB-D Images 149
    Tongyan Gong and Huiqian Niu

Utilization of Resnet in RGB-D Facial Recognition Problems 156
    Xi Xiong

Benchmark

Building the DataBench Workflow and Architecture 165
    Todor Ivanov, Timo Eichhorn, Arne Jørgen Berre,
    Tomás Pariente Lobo, Ivan Martinez Rodriguez, Ricardo Ruiz Saiz,
    Barbara Pernici, and Chiara Francalanci

Benchmarking Solvers for the One Dimensional Cubic Nonlinear Klein
Gordon Equation on a Single Core 172
    B. K. Muite and Samar Aseeri

AI

Deep Reinforcement Learning for Auto-optimization of I/O
Accelerator Parameters. 187
    Trong-Ton Pham and Dennis Mintah Djan

Causal Learning in Question Quality Improvement 204
    Yichuan Li, Ruocheng Guo, Weiying Wang, and Huan Liu

SparkAIBench: A Benchmark to Generate AI Workloads on Spark   215
   Zifeng Liu, Xiaojiang Zuo, Zeqing Li, and Rui Han

Big Data

Benchmarking Database Ingestion Ability with Real-Time Big
Astronomical Data   225
   Qing Tang, Chen Yang, Xiaofeng Meng, and Zhihui Du

A Practical Data Repository for Causal Learning with Big Data   234
   *Lu Cheng, Ruocheng Guo, Raha Moraffah, K. Selçuk Candan,
   Adrienne Raglin, and Huan Liu*

Datacenter

LCIO: Large Scale Filesystem Aging.   251
   Matthew Bachstein, Feiyi Wang, and Sarp Oral

BOPS, A New Computation-Centric Metric for Datacenter Computing   262
   Lei Wang, Wanling Gao, Kaiyong Yang, and Zihan Jiang

Anomaly Analysis and Diagnosis for Co-located Datacenter Workloads
in the Alibaba Cluster   278
   Rui Ren, Jinheng Li, Lei Wang, Yan Yin, and Zheng Cao

Performance Analysis and Workload Generator

SSH-Backed API Performance Case Study.   295
   *Anagha Jamthe, Mike Packard, Joe Stubbs, Gilbert Curbelo III,
   Roseline Shapi, and Elias Chalhoub*

NTP: A Neural Net Topology Profiler   306
   *Pravin Chandran, Raghavendra Bhat, Juby Jose, Viswanath Dibbur,
   and Prakash Sirra Ajith*

MCC: A Predictable and Scalable Massive Client Load Generator.   319
   Wenqing Wu, Xiao Feng, Wenli Zhang, and Mingyu Chen

Scientific Computing and Metrology

Apache Spark Streaming, Kafka and HarmonicIO: A Performance
Benchmark and Architecture Comparison for Enterprise
and Scientific Computing.   335
   Ben Blamey, Andreas Hellander, and Salman Toor

Benchmark Researches from the Perspective of Metrology   348
    Kun Yang, Tong Wu, Qingfei Shen, Weiqun Cui, and Guichun Zhang

Author Index   361

Best Paper Session

Performance Analysis of GPU Programming Models Using the Roofline Scaling Trajectories

Khaled Z. Ibrahim[✉], Samuel Williams, and Leonid Oliker

Lawrence Berkeley National Laboratory, One Cyclotron Road,
Berkeley, CA 94720, USA
{kzibrahim,swwilliams,loliker}@lbl.gov

Abstract. Performance analysis is a daunting job, especially for the rapid-evolving accelerator technologies. The Roofline Scaling Trajectories technique aims at diagnosing various performance bottlenecks for GPU programming models through the visually intuitive Roofline plots. In this work, we introduce the use of the Roofline Scaling Trajectories to capture major performance bottlenecks on NVIDIA Volta GPU architectures, such as warp efficiency, occupancy, and locality. Using this analysis technique, we explain the performance characteristics of the NAS Parallel Benchmarks (NPB) written with two programming models, CUDA and OpenACC. We present the influence of the programming model on the performance and scaling characteristics. We also leverage the insights of the Roofline Scaling Trajectory analysis to tune some of the NAS Parallel Benchmarks, achieving up to 2× speedup.

Keywords: Roofline model · Performance analysis · Parallel scaling · GPU · OpenACC · CUDA

1 Introduction

Accelerator technologies are nowadays prevalent in HPC computing. The top two machines in the top500 list [17] of June 2019 are based on NVIDIA Volta GPUs. The trend of using accelerator stems from the difficulty to improve the performance of general-purpose cores based on CMOS technologies. The introduction of GPU to general-purpose computing, although almost being more than a decade old, is still a complex endeavor for many application developers. Part of the difficulty is due to the architectural model, which impact how data should be layed out for optimal performance, the memory consistency model which affects handling data dependencies, the control-flow with its impact on lock-step execution, and the tradeoffs between doing recomputation or loading precomputed data.

Performance analysis for accelerator architectures is a daunting process. Performance tools, such as NVIDIA nvprof or Intel Vtune, could provide access to

© Springer Nature Switzerland AG 2020
W. Gao et al. (Eds.): Bench 2019, LNCS 12093, pp. 3–19, 2020.
https://doi.org/10.1007/978-3-030-49556-5_1

numerous hardware events capturing various events that could correlate to the observed performance. They may always not provide a notion of performance optimality, needed to assess whether further optimizations are needed.

For GPUs, metrics such as warp efficiency and occupancy are known to influence the observed performance, but there no agreed-upon method to assess the dependency of the observed performance on these metrics, or how impactful are these metrics on performance.

To this end, this paper introduces the use of Roofline Scaling Trajectories [10] to analyze the performance of GPU architectures. Specifically, we show how the Roofline Scaling Trajectory method stresses various architectural features as we change the number of GPU SMs involved in the computations. As such, these trajectories reveal the efficiency of GPU warp execution, the level of occupancy while changing the GPU SM count, and the efficiency in handling the temporal locality of the shared last level cache. The scaling trajectories shows the impact of the above inefficiencies against the GPU performance limits that is a function of the arithmetic intensity of the algorithm. We perform the analysis for several NAS Parallel Benchmarks [2] ported to the GPU architecture using the CUDA programming model and the pragma-based OpenACC model.

We proposed the use of the Roofline Scaling Trajectories to reveal the root cause of various performance inefficiencies. We show how to visually associate the scaling trajectories to various sorts of warp inefficiencies, including those due to branch divergence and those related to latency divergence, and occupancy degradation due to the lack of thread block parallelism. Moreover, the Roofline Scaling Trajectories has been shown [10] to reveal cache thrashing effects and its impact on temporal locality as we scale applications. Identifying the performance bottleneck of applications, we leveraged these insights in tuning the performance of two of the NAS benchmarks, achieving up to a 2× improvement.

The rest of this paper is organized as follows. Section 2 presents the motivation of this study. We summarize the performance influencing factors for GPU programming in Sect. 3. The programming model used for offloading computation to GPU accelerator and experimental setup are presented in Sect. 4 and Sect. 6, respectively. We introduce our novel performance analysis technique based on scaling trajectories in Sect. 5. We show the effectiveness of the proposed analysis technique in studying various NPB in Sect. 7, and our tuning efforts based on the introduced analysis in Sect. 8. We finally present related work in Sect. 9 and conclude in Sect. 10.

2   Motivation

The performance of two GPU ports of NPB 3.3, detailed in Sect. 6.1, is shown in Fig. 1. The first is based on OpenACC directives [15], and the other is based on the CUDA programming model [6]. We run the problem sizes, or classes, that could fit in the GPU memory for each implementation. We present strong scaling behavior while changing the number of SMs involved in the computation for multiple problem sizes. To conduct these experiments, we leveraged a new feature of the Volta architecture to enable Multi-Process Service (MPS) [14]. The hardware support for MPS allows dedicating a subset of the compute resources to a particular process or an application, thus achieving performance isolation (or QoS) and address space isolation.

We could easily recognize various suboptimal performance trends. For the OpenACC port of the NPB [19], we observe that LU and FT do not significantly improve with the increase in SM count, while MG improves and then drop in performance at high SM count. The performance does not improve significantly with the increase of problem size from Class A to B or C. For the CUDA variant of NPB [9], LU has a significant improvement with SM count. Increasing the problem size from Class A to B further improves the performance, but the trend is reversed when changing from Class B to C.

Unfortunately, the strong scaling curves show that there is room for improvement, but they do not shed light on the causes of the observed behavior or where

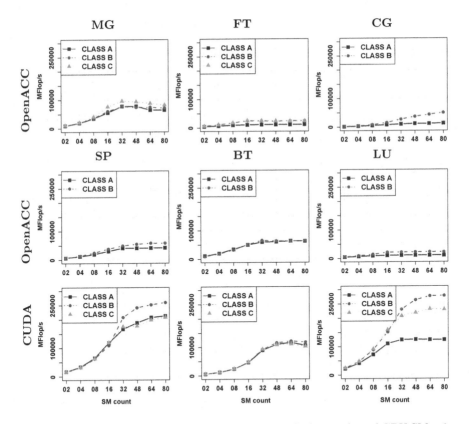

Fig. 1. Strong scaling of various NPB applications with the number of GPU SM using two programming models, CUDA and OpenACC. We observe various suboptimal scaling trends without a clear cause. The largest Class that could fit on a single GPU depends on the programming model.

the tuning effort of these GPU applications should be steered. Several profiling tools tries to address this challenge by showing hotspot analysis, hardware metrics for various architectural activities, communication, or access pattern. These tools include nvprof [13], TAU [16], etc. This paper extends the Roofline Scaling Trajectory technique [10] to demystify some of the observed performance trends.

3   Performance on GPU Architecture

The performance on a GPU is typically correlated to the efficiency of leveraging various architectural features. The NVIDIA GPU architectures have multiple levels of parallelism [14]: threads within a warp, warps sharing an SM, and multiple SMs within a GPU. Threads within a warp use the SIMT execution model. The execution of a warp of threads is typically more efficient when all threads choose the same execution path and create coalesced memory access. Earlier generations of GPUs use a single program counter for a warp of threads, as such the impact of a branch divergence is severe on performance. Volta GPUs provide a program counter and stack per thread, which alleviates the need for frequent re-convergence, but the execution remains more efficient when branch divergence is minimized. A CUDA thread block is a software abstraction that uses multiple warps and provides low-overhead synchronization primitives and communication through the shared memory. All warps of a thread block are scheduled and executed on the same SM. The hardware scheduler could schedule multiple thread warps (and possibly blocks) within an SM, assuming sufficient hardware resources are available, including registers, shared memory, etc. All warps co-scheduled within an SM use the same set of function units, 64 FP32 for Volta. The number of SMs in Volta is 80. Volta can schedule up to 64 warps per SM. Volta provides the multiprocess service (MPS) facility to allow multiple kernels to run concurrently on the GPU and to control the number of SM assigned to a kernel. We leveraged the MPS support in this study to control the number of SMs used concurrently.

The efficiency of performing computation on NVIDIA GPU requires careful consideration for the following dimensions.

– Warp efficiency within a group of threads, or SIMT efficiency, i.e., all threads follow the same path of execution or have the same latency to execute an instruction.
– SM Occupancy, i.e., the ability to schedule as many warps per SM as possible to hide the long latency of accessing the memory system. This also involves keeping GPU busy most of the time.
– Data locality, i.e., effective memory request coalescing and temporal L2 cache access.

These objectives could be conflicting. For instance, GPU occupancy would require pipelining small kernels, but one must provide enough parallelism to saturate the SMs. Efficient use of the cache hierarchy may also conflict with providing enough independent thread warps.

Ideally, a performance tool or technique would identify the performance sub-optimality and link it to one of the above performance dimensions.

4 GPU Programming Models in This Study

The benchmarks examined in this paper are written in two popular approaches for programming accelerators: directive-based offloading, and vendor-specific programming model (specifically CUDA for NVIDIA GPUs). The directive-based approach is a more productive approach for porting code to GPUs, but it may not leverage all vendor-specific architectural features. It allows for an incremental approach for porting codes to GPUs. The use of the CUDA model provides full control of vendor-specific hardware features, such as shared memory across threads, texture cache, etc. As such, it could provide a performance advantage while sacrificing some portability and productivity.

The OpenACC code parallelization of the NPB relies on maintaining the loop structure of the code, where the outer level of the loop nest is assigned to gangs, the second level to workers, and the third to vectors. For loop nest levels beyond three, some of the inner levels are unrolled manually. The objective of this programming style for accelerators is to strike a balance between the achieved performance and the coding effort to port the code. The OpenACC directive-based approach generally preserves the code structure and data layout.

The CUDA version uses an explicit mapping of each level of the loop into a dimension of the thread block or grid of threads. Because some of the inner loops have small trip counts, the developer used one of the thread dimensions to serve multiple levels of the loop nest. The developers also leveraged the GPU shared memory for efficient communication between threads sharing an SM.

5 GPU Roofline Scaling Trajectories

In this paper, we leverage the Roofline Scaling Trajectory technique for analyzing the performance and scalability of GPU-accelerated parallel applications. We aim to leverage this analysis technique to identify various kinds of performance bottlenecks that an application may experience on a GPU architecture. The Roofline Scaling Trajectory visualizes the scaling behavior and identifies the effects of cache and memory access locality, warp efficiency, and SM and GPU occupancy on application performance.

Figure 2 shows an example of Roofline Scaling Trajectories curves. Nominal machine-specific Rooflines are constructed for both the lowest and the highest level of concurrency (2 SMs and 80 SMs on Volta). The trajectory is a trend line of application performance and arithmetic intensity at each level of concurrency. One may apply this analysis for the full application or individual kernels. We use the empirical measurement technique laid out in earlier GPU Roofline studies [4, 12] to characterize the machine characteristics. Our focus is mainly on the DRAM Roofline model, where one must measure dram_read_transactions and dram_write_transactions metrics through the NVIDIA nvprof profiling tool.

We use the FLOPs reported by the application for all concurrency level to ensure that throughput reflects the application performance. We calculate the application arithmetic intensity as follows:

$$AI \leftarrow \frac{cannonical\ flop\ count}{(dram\_read\_trans + dram\_write\_trans) \times 32} \qquad (1)$$

The model could be easily extended to other levels of the hierarchy as presented in [4]. We rely on the application canonical FLOP count, estimated by the application developer rather than on relying on the profiling tool measurements. This allows consistent performance comparison because the number of FLOPs could change with the run configuration due to the use of data replication and reduction operations within a thread block, especially in the CUDA version. This method allows for a fair comparison across programming models.

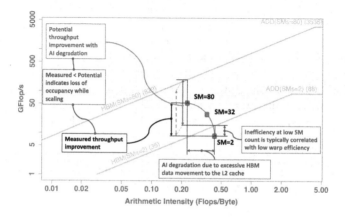

Fig. 2. The Roofline Scaling Trajectory on GPU architectures. Each point represents the throughput at a certain SM concurrency level. We use the Roofline Scaling Trajectories to diagnose various performance scaling bottlenecks, including warp execution inefficiency, loss of occupancy while scaling, excessive data movement to the cache hierarchy, etc.

Ideally, the performance should improve linearly with the increase of computational resources without degrading the arithmetic intensity. On a Roofline plot, this translates into a vertical change of throughput proportional to the increase of computational resources while changing concurrency. In practice, an application may experience a suboptimal change in throughput, or a change of the arithmetic intensity while scaling, e.g., a scaling curve pending to the left.

The dominant bottleneck typically changes when strong scaling the application. For instance, at low concurrency, it is typically difficult to saturate the bandwidth to shared levels of the memory hierarchy. In such case, the warp efficiency becomes the main limiting factor for an application to reach the Roofline. Although lower occupancy could result in a similar effect at low concurrency, for a kernel with non-trivial size, this is unlikely. Additionally, the lack of occupancy is easily distinguishable, as will be discussed later. As we strong-scale the application run, observing a loss of arithmetic intensity implies some cache thrashing at the shared cache levels. The potential of throughput improvement is typically impacted by the loss of arithmetic intensity for memory-bound applications. An occupancy reduction while scaling further lowers the observed performance gains.

Identifying the performance bottleneck is typically the first step to steer the optimization effort to the right problem. For instance, a warp efficiency issue occurs due to divergent branches or inefficient data indexing that results in a non-coalesced memory access across a thread warp. It would require particular code refactoring techniques, while loss of occupancy would require different remedies. The occupancy issue involves dealing with two conflicting constraints. First, improving parallelisms within a kernel requires a coarse-grained kernel to improve the GPU occupancy. Second, reducing stalls to launch a kernel requires pipelining kernel invocations by assigning a smaller task for each kernel. Balancing the two conflicting requirements requires some tuning for each target architecture. The code should ideally be structured to handle different task granularities.

6 Experimental Setup

6.1 Benchmark Suite

The NAS Parallel Benchmarks (NPB) [2] represent a broad set of computational patterns. The suite uses FT for spectral methods, CG for sparse linear algebra, LU for solving a regular-sparse lower and upper triangular system, and MG for multigrid PDE solver using a hierarchy of meshes. In addition, the suite contains two mini-apps, SP and BT, which carry key computational fluid dynamics (CFD) calculations on a structured grid. They involve the solution of independent systems of block tridiagonal equations with a 5×5 block size. The inner block dimensions are not friendly to warp sizes and different approaches are taken by the CUDA [9] and OpenACC [19] implementations. The OpenACC implementation assigns the full block to a single thread, while the CUDA version split these blocks between threads within a block. The first improves the efficiency of warp execution, while the second enhances the level of parallelism. Unfortunately, the CUDA authors only ported the SP, BT, and LU benchmarks.

6.2 System Setup

We conducted our experiments on the OLCF Summit supercomputer. Each summit node has two clusters of an IBM Power9 CPU and three NVIDIA Volta GPUs. Each cluster is connected through high-speed NVLink. Each node has a half-terabyte of coherent memory, and nodes are connected using dual-rail Mellanox EDR InfiniBand interconnect. Our experiments focused on the performance of a single Volta GPU. Each Volta GPU has 80 SMs each with a 256 KB register file and 96 KB of unified cache/shared memory. The SMs shared 6 MB of L2 cache and 16 GB of HBM2 memory, and each GPU has a theoretical peak of 7.8 TFLOP/s in double precision.

7 Scaling Trajectory Analysis for Computational Kernels

Before presenting the Roofline Scaling Trajectory, we show the wrap efficiency of various kernels for the studied set of benchmarks. The warp efficiency is defined as the ratio of the average active threads per warp to the maximum number of threads per warp [13]. This metric captures thread execution divergence and

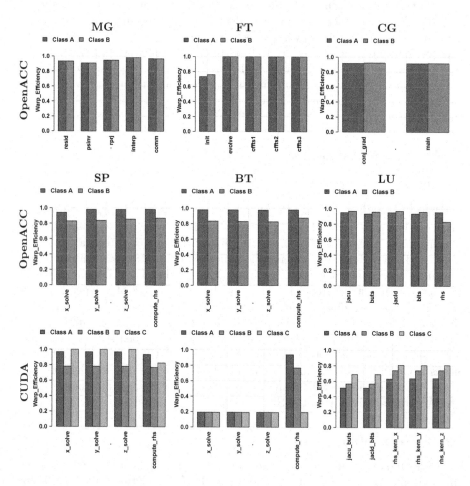

Fig. 3. Warp efficiency for various kernels of the NPB benchmarks. Generally, we observe higher warp efficiency for the OpenACC version compared to the CUDA version, specifically for the BT and LU benchmarks. Warp efficiency remains constant while changing the SM count and could change with the problem size.

typically does not change with the workload distribution across SMs. Latency divergence for application with irregular memory access [5] has the same impact on performance.

Figure 3 shows the warp efficiency for various kernels of each NPB application. Generally, the OpenACC port has a higher warp efficiency compared with the CUDA port, especially for the BT and LU. Changing the dataset size (i.e., the Class) could result in improvement of the warp efficiency, such as in the case of CUDA LU, or reduction in efficiency as in the case of OpenACC BT, or may have irregular change as with the CUDA SP. We will show that warp efficiency, as well as the indexing scheme of the arrays, influences the performance at low SM concurrency.

Figure 4 shows the Roofline line scaling behavior of the NPB applications. First, we observe that all applications are memory-bound based on their arithmetic intensity. As such, we simplified the Roofline architectural limits by removing the fused multiply-add ceiling for the compute-bound region as it is unattainable. The CUDA LU and OpenACC MG show the most noticeable change in AI, during strong or weak scaling. For BT, we notice a better efficiency at low concurrency for the OpenACC implementation compared with the CUDA variant due to the better warp efficiency, but the CUDA variant has a better occupancy when scaling. Except for CG and LU, OpenACC implementations have a high starting efficiency, due to the better warp efficiency. The OpenACC CG warps have a low efficiency at low concurrency that is due to the latency divergence [5], which reduces the warp efficiency. Importantly, this sort of warp inefficiency is typically not captured by the nvprof metric, but is captured by the Roofline Scaling Trajectory. The CUDA BT low warp efficiency manifests at low SM count in the Roofline scaling plot. For applications where both OpenACC and CUDA implementation exist, the arithmetic intensity is higher for the CUDA implementation, i.e., less data movement to the L2 cache is involved, which is critical for achieving a higher performance for memory-bound applications.

For CUDA LU and SP, we observe the loss of arithmetic intensity as we change the problem class (size). For LU, increasing the problem size improves the GPU occupancy, as such change from Class A to B results in performance improvement. For Class C, the reduction in arithmetic intensity, due to excessive data movement, reduced the overall gains. We observe a similar but less profound trend for SP. For OpenACC MG, we observe a performance exceeding the memory bound at low concurrency due to the efficient reuse of the L2 data. This results in arithmetic intensity improvement with weak-scaling at low concurrency. As one strong scales, the arithmetic intensity is reduced, especially at high concurrency.

For the OpenACC LU, we notice both low efficiency at small scale and suboptimal occupancy improvement as one strong scales. There is a slight improvement with the change of SM count. This application has a GPU occupancy problem that manifests at low SM count, as will be discussed later. For the CUDA LU, we notice the improvement at low concurrency while increasing the problem size, which correlates with the warp-efficiency improvement.

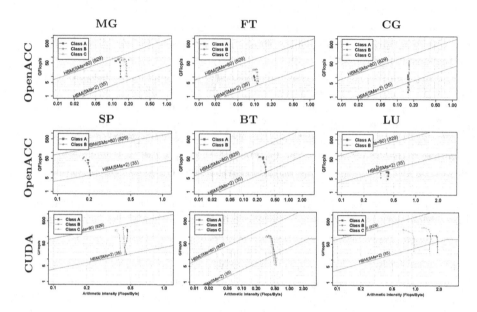

Fig. 4. Roofline Scaling Trajectories for Volta GPUs. CUDA BT and OpenACC LU application are limited by warp efficiency, while CUDA LU, OpenACC SP, BT, FT are limited by GPU occupancy. The arithmetic intensity of CUDA LU and OpenACC MG is noticeably affected by strong and weak scaling.

The change in occupancy affects the strong scaling behavior of applications. An application needs enough parallelism to saturate all available SMs to achieve optimal performance. As discussed in Sect. 5, the occupancy term affects the potential improvements while increasing the SM count. In Fig. 5, we consider the detailed SM occupancy behavior for CUDA BT and CUDA LU. For BT, we observe a constant occupancy during both weak and strong scaling. The scaling trajectory shows a high correlation with the measured SM occupancy behavior.

The occupancy of CUDA LU degrades with strong scaling. Increasing the problem size improves the occupancy, and the impact is not uniform across kernels. The jacld_blts kernel is the most affected by the loss of occupancy. The Roofline Scaling Trajectories for individual kernels captures such behavior precisely as shown in Fig. 6, both for loss of occupancy for the jacld_blts kernel, and the maintenance of good occupancy for the rhs_kernel_*. We notice that the rhs_kernel_x has a small change in arithmetic intensity during weak scaling compared with the rhs_kernel_y, z. Inspecting the code, we found a unit strided access in the x-direction and strided jumps for the y and z direction. Applying data transposes could typically be used to tackle such bottleneck, but require an efficient transpose that is lower overhead than embedding the strided access.

In general, there are two sources of loss of occupancy. One is reported by the nvprof profiling tool as achieved occupancy during the course of executing a kernel, and is defined as the ratio of the average active warps per active cycle to

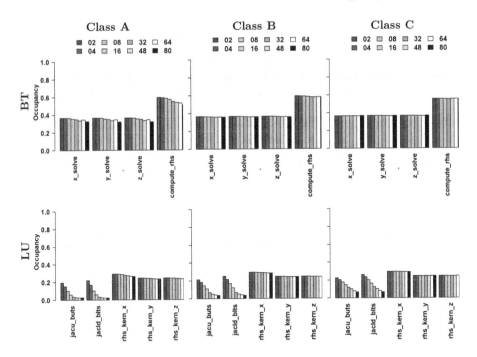

Fig. 5. Occupancy of CUDA Kernels with various Classes. LU suffers occupancy loss as we change the SM count, while BT has a stable occupancy for all concurrency levels.

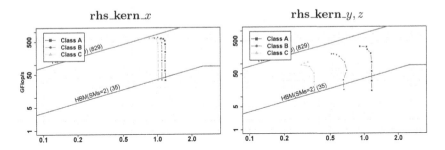

Fig. 6. CUDA LU scaling trajectories for individual kernels. The potential for performance scaling is significantly influenced by the change in arithmetic intensity for rhs_kernel_y, z, caused by strided access, compared with rhs_kernel_x.

the maximum number of warps supported on a multiprocessor [13]. We refer to this type as SM occupancy. The second is due to the idle time between launching kernels due to kernel invocation overhead, waiting for data movement between the host and the GPU, etc. We refer to this type as GPU occupancy. Ideally, we need to minimize the second type of occupancy loss because an idle GPU results in no use for all the SMs. Sources of this loss of occupancy include launch overhead and CPU pre-processing to launch a kernel. To quantify the CPU overhead to invoke a kernel on the GPU, we multiply the number of invocations by the uncontended latency for an invocation. We estimate the uncontended latency using the minimum observed at run time. We account not only for kernel invocation but also for other CUDA routines, such as cudaMemcpy. Our aim is to avoid considering the contention due to busy activity on the GPU as part of the GPU idle time.

Depending on the programming model, the number of device invocations could be significant. In general, we observed higher kernel invocation count in the OpenACC port compared with the CUDA port due to the incremental approach for porting each kernel. To preserve the loop structure for the CPU and device offload case when porting a routine with multiple loops using OpenACC, developers must individually annotate each of the loops, and the compiler must generate a kernel for each loop. The application most impacted by the invocation count is OpenACC LU. The OpenACCimplementation does not leverage the shared memory and as such can achieve high occupancy at low concurrency.

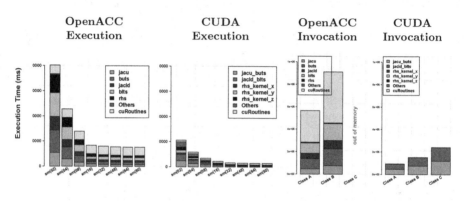

Fig. 7. Left two figures: execution time decomposition for both OpenACC and CUDA for the LU benchmark - Class B. Right two Figures: Kernel invocation count for different Classes. The OpenACC invocation is roughly 5× the CUDA version, leading to smaller granularity for kernels, which affects the occupancy and exacerbates the impact of CUDA runtime overheads.

Figure 7 depicts the invocation count for both the CUDA and the OpenACC port. Both have high invocation count with the OpenACC port is about 6× the CUDA invocation count. As such, the percentage of execution time spent in these overheads could be a significant time of the total execution time, as shown in Fig. 7. The time for overhead for the OpenACC version is more than 5× the overhead for the CUDA version. To distinguish the two kinds of loss of occupancy, we augment the scaling trajectory with an Amdahl shadow curve, which shows the maximum attainable throughput if all CUDA overheads are removed. The remaining loss of occupancy is due to limited concurrency during the kernel scaling. As shown in Fig. 9 for LU application, when the shadow curve hits the roofline, like the CUDA case, the application is suffering solely from GPU occupancy issue (no GPU activity due to overheads). When the shadow curve does not hit the roofline, like the OpenACC case, the application is suffering from active SM occupancy issue in addition to the inactive GPU issue.

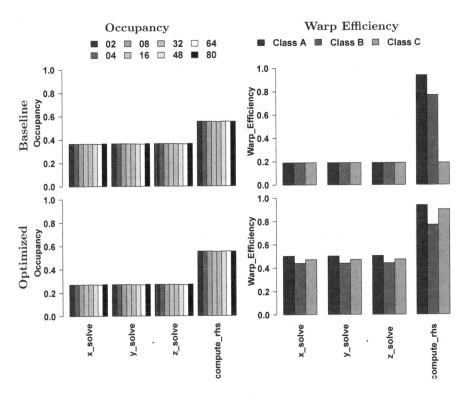

Fig. 8. Tuning tile size for BT and its impact on occupancy and warp efficiency. The best performing variant at the bottom sees improved warp efficiency at the cost of reduced occupancy, but the occupancy does not degrade with SM count.

7.1   GPU Cache Impact on Scaling Trajectories

We note that the overall capacity of the L1/shared memory[1] exceed the L2 capacity starting with a concurrency level of 48 SMs. Similarly, the register file capacity[2] exceed the L2 capacity starting with a concurrency level of 24 SMs. As such, leveraging the L2 temporal locality becomes hard to achieve beyond a certain concurrency level, unless the compiler or the programmer annotates memory accesses with appropriate cache hints to distinguish streaming memory accesses from accesses likely to leverage temporal locality. Moreover, while L2 could be effective in filtering traffic to the memory at low concurrency, the L1 surpass

---

[1] Volta configurable L1 cache/shared memory capacity is 128 KB per SM.
[2] Volta register file is 256 KB per SM.

the L2 in filtering effect at high concurrency leading to the improved arithmetic intensity applications with high SM concurrency. This arithmetic intensity trajectory reversal appears in multiple kernels including the Class C LU rhs_kernel_y routine, which we initially thought to be a performance anomaly.

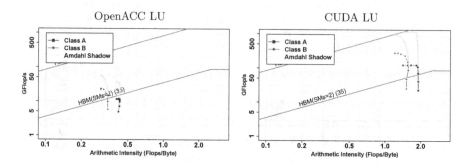

Fig. 9. Scaling trajectories with occupancy limits due to Amdahl's law serialization factor for LU using OpenACC and CUDA. Hitting the roofline with Amdahl shadow curve indicates inactive GPU occupancy issue (CUDA LU-Class B), otherwise active SM occupancy is an additional factor in the observed performance degradation.

8   Performance Tuning

While the main focus of this study is to develop a performance diagnostic technique, we explored the performance tuning for a couple of cases of the studied kernels, the CUDA BT and OpenACC FT. For the CUDA BT, the scaling trajectories reveal inefficiency at low concurrency, a symptom of a warp inefficiency issue. Inspecting the code, we found that a tuning parameter controls the number of 5×5 blocks that are assigned to a thread block and could be loaded into the shared memory. Increasing the block count leads to a reduced occupancy, as fewer threads blocks could share an SM, but it increases the efficiency. We explored different value for this parameter, and we found the best blocking value at $4\times$ the default value. The performance improvement ranged from 32–41% at full concurrency for the three problem sizes. In Fig. 8, we present the change in occupancy and warp efficiency before and after changing the blocking factor. Improving warp efficiency is key to performance. The reduction in occupancy does not hurt the performance as long there is no drop in occupancy as we change the SM count. This reduction in occupancy in this particular case is due to the decrease in thread block count and warps sharing an SM. The improvement in efficiency is $2.47\times$, while the drop in occupancy is $1.33\times$.

The second example is the OpenACC FT implementation, which is one of the applications that did not show efficient scaling due to poor GPU occupancy. Analyzing the kernel-wise scaling trajectory, we found that the bottleneck is part of the initialization routine, which is included in the benchmark execution time. On earlier generations of GPUs, the overhead of this phase is small compared with the rest of the execution time. On Volta, parallelization of the initialization part provided a 2× speedup for the whole benchmark. Overall, identifying the source of the performance degradation is half the road to tuning the application. The main limitation of the proposed technique is that it is mainly applicable at the kernel-level granularity.

9   Related Work

Performance analysis techniques can be categorized into two complementary classes: microscopic analysis, which relies on hardware events associated with a kernel invocation or a line of the source code, and macroscopic analysis, which focuses on system utilization or use efficiency.

Attributing hardware events—such as cycle count, cache misses or vectorization efficiency—to the source code steers the optimization efforts to hotspots within the program. Numerous tools, such as Intel Vtune [11] the CrayPAT [7], HPCToolkit [1] Tau [16] Scalsca [3], provide effective communication of underlying events and typically rely on sampling techniques to reduce overhead. These tools may not assess the potential for performance improvement.

The roofline technique can be classified as a macroscopic analysis technique that compares the application performance relative to realistic architectural limits that vary with the application arithmetic intensity. It identifies when the performance hits the machine limits. Various methods are typically used to characterize the application arithmetic intensity, including DRAM-based roofline technique [18] and the cache-aware roofline Model (CARM) [8], which considers the data movement to the L1 cache. The roofline method has been extended to different cache levels, incorporated into production quality tools such as Vtune [8], and is recently extended to the GPU architectures [4], but the main focus of these efforts is for the performance at the full node concurrency.

The roofline scaling trajectory [10] has recently been introduced for CPU-based architectures, where it is used to study the interaction with the cache hierarchy. In this work, we extend its use to the performance analysis for GPU architectures and show its effectiveness in exposing various performance bottlenecks such as warp efficiency and SM occupancy. We also show the influence of the programming model on various performance bottlenecks.

10   Conclusions

In this paper, we introduce the use of the Roofline Scaling Trajectory technique for analyzing GPU-accelerated workloads. The technique leverages a new NVIDIA Volta capability that allows controlling the number of SMs. The introduced method intuitively visualizes various performance bottlenecks such as warp inefficiency, suboptimal SM occupancy, in addition to characterizing the efficiency of utilizing the cache hierarchy for capturing locality. We used this analysis technique to study two implementations of NAS benchmarks using the

CUDA and the OpenACC programming models. Our analysis reveals the performance bottlenecks of the studied applications and the influence of the programming model on warp efficiency, SM occupancy, and memory access. We leveraged these insights to tune two of the studied applications, achieving up to a 2× improvement in run time.

Acknowledgment. This material is based on work supported by the Advanced Scientific Computing Research Program in the U.S. Department of Energy, Office of Science, under award number DE-AC02–05CH11231. This research used resources of the Oak Ridge Leadership Computing Facility at the Oak Ridge National Laboratory, which is supported by the Office of Science of the U.S. Department of Energy under Contract No. DE-AC05-00OR22725.

References

1. Adhianto, L., et al.: HPCToolkit: tools for performance analysis of optimized parallel programs. Concurr. Comput. Pract. Exp. **22**(6), 685–701 (2010). http://hpctoolkit.org
2. Bailey, D., Harris, T., Saphir, W., Van Der Wijngaart, R., Woo, A., Yarrow, M.: The NAS parallel benchmarks 2.0. Technical report NAS-95-010, NASA Ames Research Center (1995)
3. Calotoiu, A., Hoefler, T., Poke, M., Wolf, F.: Using automated performance modeling to find scalability bugs in complex codes. In: SC 2013 Proceedings of the International Conference on High Performance Computing, Networking, Storage and Analysis, pp. 1–12 (2013)
4. Yang, C., Kurth, T., Williams, S.: Hierarchical Roofline analysis for GPUs: accelerating performance optimization for the NERSC-9 Perlmutter system. Cray User Group (CUG), May 2019
5. Chatterjee, N., O'Connor, M., Loh, G.H., Jayasena, N., Balasubramonia, R.: Managing DRAM latency divergence in irregular GPGPU applications. In: SC 2014 Proceedings of the International Conference for High Performance Computing, Networking, Storage and Analysis, pp. 128–139 (2014)
6. Cook, S.: CUDA Programming: A Developer's Guide to Parallel Computing with GPUs, 1st edn. Morgan Kaufmann Publishers Inc., San Francisco (2013)
7. Cray: The Cray Performance Measurement and Analysis Tools. https://pubs.cray.com/content/S-2376/6.4.0/cray-performance-measurement-and-analysis-tools-user-guide-640/craypat
8. Ilic, A., Pratas, F., Sousa, L.: Cache-aware Roofline model: upgrading the loft. IEEE Comput. Archit. Lett. **13**(1), 21–24 (2014)
9. Dümmler, J.: A CUDA version of NPB 3.3.1. https://www.tu-chemnitz.de/informatik/PI/sonstiges/downloads/npb-gpu/index.php.en
10. Ibrahim, K., Williams, S., Oliker, L.: Roofline scaling trajectories: a method for parallel application and architectural performance analysis. In: International Conference on High Performance Computing & Simulation (HPCS) (2018)
11. Marowka, A.: On performance analysis of a multithreaded application parallelized by different programming models using Intel VTune. In: Malyshkin, V. (ed.) PaCT 2011. LNCS, vol. 6873, pp. 317–331. Springer, Heidelberg (2011). https://doi.org/10.1007/978-3-642-23178-0_28

12. Measuring Roofline Quantities on NVIDIA GPUs: Portability Across DOE Office of Science HPC Facilities. https://performanceportability.org/perfport/measurements/gpu/

13. nVidia: CUDA Profiler Users Guide. https://docs.nvidia.com/cuda/pdf/CUDA_Profiler_Users_Guide.pdf

14. nVidia: NVIDIA Tesla V100 GPU Architecture. https://images.nvidia.com/content/volta-architecture/pdf/volta-architecture-whitepaper.pdf

15. OpenACC STANDARD Organization: OpenACC Application Programming Interface. https://www.openacc.org

16. Shende, S.S., Malony, A.D.: The tau parallel performance system. Int. J. High Perform. Comput. Appl. **20**(2), 287–311 (2006)

17. Top 500 Supercomputers. http://www.top500.org

18. Williams, S., Watterman, A., Patterson, D.: Roofline: an insightful visual performance model for multicore architectures. Commun. ACM **52**(4), 65–76 (2009). https://doi.org/10.1145/1498765.1498785

19. Xu, R., Tian, X., Chandrasekaran, S., Yan, Y., Chapman, B.: NAS parallel benchmarks for GPGPUs using a directive-based programming model. In: Brodman, J., Tu, P. (eds.) LCPC 2014. LNCS, vol. 8967, pp. 67–81. Springer, Cham (2015). https://doi.org/10.1007/978-3-319-17473-0_5

GraphBench: A Benchmark Suite for Graph Computing Systems

Lei Wang[✉] and Minghe Yu

Institute of Computing Technology, Chinese Academy of Sciences, Beijing, China
{wanglei_2011,yuminghe}@ict.ac.cn

Abstract. In the Big data and IoT era, graph data processing is widely used. The graph data is a kind of structural data that defined entities as vertices and described dependencies between different entities as edges. Today, a lot of graph computing systems emerge with massive diverse graph applications deployed, evaluating graph computing systems become a challenge work. Existing graph computing benchmarks are constructed with prevalent graph computing applications. However, the graph micro-benchmark is lacking, which is a key for the system fine-grained evaluation and obtaining the upper bound performance of the system. In this paper, we take graph computing applications as the combination of basic operations and user-defined operations. Then, we build the GraphBench benchmark suite with micro-benchmarks (basic operations) and component benchmarks (graph computing applications). At last, we evaluates the current mainstream graph computing frameworks with GraphBench. We found that there is no one-size-fits-all solution for the graph computing system. Using GraphBench, we can evaluate the graph computing system at the fine-grained level and get more insights.

Keywords: Graph computing · Performance evaluation · Benchmark

1 Introduction

In the Big data and IoT era, more and more information is linked together as the large-scale graph data. The graph data is a kind of structural data that defined entities as vertices and described dependencies between different entities as edges. Processing large-scale graph data has been a major challenge for industry and academia communities. For example, Facebook needs to push advertisements to more than nine hundreds million users based on its graph analysis results. The PageRank algorithm of Google determines the index quality of more than one trillion Web pages. Today, lots of graph processing frameworks keep emerging, such as Gstore [5], Neo4j [6], OrientDB [7], GraphDB [8], PowerGraph [9], PowerLyra [10], GraphX [11], and Gemini [12]. Graph data processing frameworks can be divided into graph data management frameworks and graph computing frameworks. Graph data management framework is similar with the data management frameworks. Gstore, Neo4j, OrientDB and GraphDB are typical graph data management frameworks. On the other hand, graph computing

W. Gao et al. (Eds.): Bench 2019, LNCS 12093, pp. 20–31, 2020.
https://doi.org/10.1007/978-3-030-49556-5_2

frameworks process the graph data with different graph algorithms, such as page ranking, shortest path finding and so on. PowerGraph, PowerLyra, GraphX and Gemini are typical graph computing frameworks. In this paper, we focused on the graph computing systems , which are the computer systems equipped with graph computing frameworks and graph computing workloads.

Today, several graph computing benchmark suites are emerged, such as GraphBIG [1], LDBC [2], CRONO [3], and so on. These graph computing benchmark suites are all constructed with prevalent graph computing applications, the fine-grained micro-benchmark is lacking, which is a key for the system fine-grained evaluation and obtaining the upper bound performance of the system. From our observations, the public basic operations, such as loading data, counting the number of vertices, and so on, take a large proportion of the execution time of the graph workload. For example, the basic operations take more than 53% execution time of the PageRank workload. We define the graph computing workload as the combination of basic operations and user-defined operations. The basic operations are the public basic operations for the graph computing, whatever workloads or frameworks. The user-defined operations are the specific operations for the specific workloads. For example, loading graph data into the memory is the basic operation for all of graph workloads, and the weight calculating of the Web page is the user-defined operation for the PageRank workload. Based on this idea, we proposed GraphBench, which is the benchmark suite for graph computing system. Our contributions are three-fold as follows:

First, we proposed eight basic operations for graph computing, which are loading graph data(Load), counting the number of vertices(VerticeNum), counting the number of edges(EdgesNum), counting the out-degree of the specific vertex(VertexOutDegree), counting the in-degree of the specific vertex (VertexInDegree), obtaining the source vertex of the specific edge(EdgeSource), obtaining the destination vertex of the specific edge (EdgeDestination), and storing graph data(Store).

Second, we construct the GraphBench benchmark suite for the graph computing system. The GraphBench includes five component benchmarks and eight micro-benchmarks. The component benchmarks are chosen from eighteen typical graph computing applications and the micro-benchmarks are original from the graph basic operations. We chose five typical graph computing frameworks to implement the GraphBench, now the GraphBench benchmark suite includes 65 workloads.

Third, we evaluated five current mainstream graph computing frameworks with GraphBench. We found that CPU utilization, computation intensity and branch prediction are correlated with the user-observed performance of graph computing system, and the IPC (Instructions per cycle) does not totally conform with the user-observed performance. There is no one-size-fits-all solution for the optimization of the graph computing system, and we can evaluate the graph computing system at the fine-grained level and get more insights.

2   Related Work

GraphBIG [1] is a graph computing benchmark suite, which designed for evaluating the performance of graph computing systems. GraphBIG includes four
categories and thirteen typical graph applications. LDBC [2] is a benchmark
suite for evaluating different graph computing frameworks, which includes six
graph applications, and its data sets include real data sets and synthetic data
sets. CRONO [3] is a graph computing benchmark suit for multi-core processor,
which can be applied for multi-core simulators or the real multi-core computers.
CRONO includes four categories and ten typical graph applications. Yong' work
[4] focuses on evaluating the graph computing performance of the GPU platform, they do the performance evaluation on the three typical GPU platform
with nine different graph data sets and three typical graph applications.

   Existing graph computing benchmarks are all constructed with prevalent
graph computing algorithm workloads, and take graph computing algorithm
workloads as a whole for evaluation. We cannot fine-grained analyze the graph
computing system. For example, what is the critical path of the graph workload
and what is the upper bound performance of the graph computing system?

3   The Methodology of GraphBench

The methodology of GraphBench is shown in the Fig. 1. GraphBench is composed
with workloads and data sets. The workloads are Component Benchmarks and
Micro Benchmarks. We choose eighteen typical graph computing algorithms to
represent the graph computing applications. Component benchmarks are representative workloads which chosen from eighteen graph computing algorithm workloads, and Microbenchmarks are the basic operations set of graph computing.

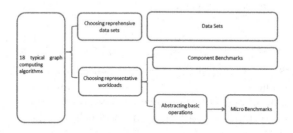

Fig. 1. The methodology of GraphBench

   The eighteen typical graph computing algorithms are shown in the Table 1.
We divided graph computing algorithms into five categories, which are path
planning, search, social analysis, network analysis and graph analysis. Then, we
chose the representative workloads from each category. They are Single-Source
Shortest Path (SSSP) of path planning, Breadth-first search algorithm (BFS)
of search, Connected Components (CC) of social analysis, K-core algorithm
(K-core) of network analysis and PageRank algorithm (PageRank) of graph
analysis.

Table 1. Eighteen graph computing algorithms

Categories	Algorithms
Path planning	Single source shortest path
	All pairs shortest path
	Minimum spanning tree
Search	Breadth-first search
	Depth-first search
	The traveling salesman problem
Social analysis	Connected component
	Strongly connected component
	Weakly connected component
	Community detection
	Triangle counting
Network analysis	K-core
	Degree centrality
	Closeness centrality
	Betweenness centrality
Graph analysis	PageRank
	Graph coloring
	Topological sort

4   Basic Operations of Graph Computing

For graph computing workloads, there are a lot of basic operations in the execution of graph computing algorithm. Such as: graph import, return an edge source (head) vertex, return an edge destination vertex and other basic operations, and these basic operations in the graph calculation algorithm regardless of proportion and frequency are very important. Therefore, the graph computing workload can be described as the combination of graph basic operations (GBOs) and user-defined operations (UDOs). We selected five representative graph computing algorithms for analysis. The Fig. 2 shows the PageRank algorithm flow : 1) Importing of graph data; 2) Counting the number of edges and vertices; 3) Setting vertex values as 1; 4) Obtaining the vertices' corresponding edges; 5) Calculating the outliers of the edges; 6) Returning new value to each vertex, and the value is the source vertex value obtaining from step 4 over the corresponding vertex degree value of step five; 7) Obtaining the new vertex value and calculating the value through the absolute value of the difference of above values; 8) if the absolute value is less than the threshold, the algorithm end, Otherwise, go to step four.

The graph computing workload can be described as the combination of graph basic operations (GBOs) and user-defined operations (UDOs). Figure 3 is the

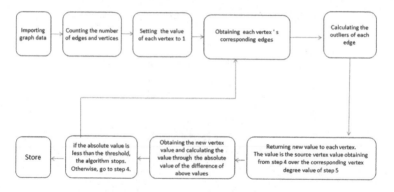

Fig. 2. The algorithm of PageRank

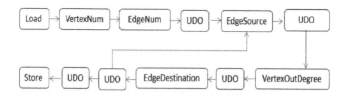

Fig. 3. The combination of GBOs and UDOs, taking PageRank as an example

description of the PageRank algorithm, which includes seven GBOs and five UDOs. The combination of GBOs and UDOs for other representative algorithms are shown on Fig. 4. We finally abstract eight basic operations of graph computing, which are described as following:

1) Loading graph data (Load). Load is the operation that imports the data into memory to build the specific graph data structure. This is the first step that all of graph computing applications need to do.
2) Counting the number of vertices (VerticeNum). VerticeNum is the operation that counts the number of imported vertices of the graph data.
3) Counting the number of edges (EdgesNum). EdgesNum is the operation that counts the number of imported edges of the graph data.
4) Counting the out-degree of the specific vertex (VerticeOutDegree). VerticeOutDegree is the operation that counts the Out-degree of the specific vertex.
5) Counting the in-degree of the specific vertex (VerticeInDegree). VerticeInDegree is the operation that counts the In-degree of the specific vertex.
6) Obtaining the source vertex of the specific edge (EdgeSource). EdgeSource is the operation that returns the source vertex of the specific edge.
7) Obtaining the destination vertex of the specific edge (EdgeDestination). EdgeDestination is the operation that returns the destination vertex of the specific edge.
8) Storing graph data(Store). Store is the operation that exports the result to the file on the disk.

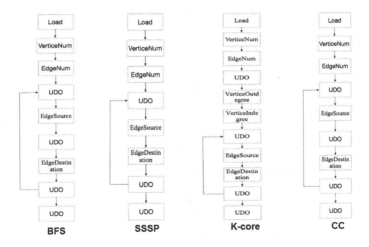

Fig. 4. The combination of GBOs and UDOs, for other algorithms

5 The Implementations of GraphBench

5.1 Component Benchmarks

Component benchmarks are representative workloads of eighteen graph computing algorithm workloads:

1) Single-Source Shortest Path (SSSP) of path planning [17]. The Single-Source
   Shortest Path algorithm is finding the shortest path from a specified source
   vertex to other vertices.
2) Breadth-first search algorithm (BFS) of search [18]. Breadth-First Search, is
   one of the commonly used algorithms for traversing the graph.
3) Connected Components (CC) of social analysis [19]. A connected component
   is a subgraph of an undirected graph, in which any two vertices are connected
   to each other by paths, and which is connected to no additional vertices in
   the supergraph [19]. CC is a algorithm to find the subgraphs.
4) K-core algorithm (K-core) of network analysis [20]. K-Core is a algorithm to
   identify smaller interconnect areas in the graph.
5) PageRank algorithm (PageRank) of graph analysis [21]. The PageRank algorithm is an algorithm used by Google to rank pages in the searching results
   of their search engine.

5.2 Micro Benchmarks and Fine-Grained Analysis

We implement graph basic operations as micro-benchmarks of GraphBench.
micro-benchmarks of GraphBench are independent workloads and process the
same data sets with component benchmarks. In order to do the fine-grained

analysis, we can break down the execution time of the component benchmark, through counting the execution time and times of the base operation's micro-benchmarks. And the execution time and times of each basic operation is obtained by insert counting codes into the component benchmark. As show on the Fig. 5, the Top five operations of PageRank workload are UDOs, Load, VertexOutDegree, VerticeNum and EdgeSource.

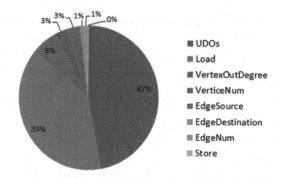

Fig. 5. The execution time breakdown of PageRank

5.3 Data Sets

We chose the data sets based on two principles. First, considering the power law characteristic of the data. The power law of the graph data is a very important factor for graph computing [9,10], and we chose the average clustering coefficient as the metric to evaluate the power law of the graph data. Second, considering graph data structure diversity. There are two types of data structure, one is the directed graph structure, another is the un-directed graph structure. At last, we choose four typical data sets:

1) EU email graph data set (Email) [13]
   The Email data set was the email data from October 2003 to May 2005 of a large European research institution. The Email data set is a directed graph data set, it has 265,214 vertices and 420,045 edges, and the average clustering coefficient of Email data set is 0.07.
2) Wikipedia graph data set (Wikipedia) [14]
   The Wikipedia graph data set is a data set from Wikipedia. The Wikipedia data set is a directed graph data set, it has 2,394,385 vertices and 5,021,410 edges, and the average clustering coefficient is 0.05.
3) Pokec social network data set (Pokec) [15]
   Pokec is a popular social network in the Slovak Republic. The Pokec data set is a directed graph data set, it has 1,632,803 vertices and 30,622,564 edges, and the average clustering coefficient is 0.1.

4) Live Journal graph data set (LJ) [16]

Live Journal is a free online blog community. Live Journal also allows users to form groups, and other members can join this group. The Live Journal dataset is a un-directed graph data set, it has 3,997,962 vertices and 34,681,189 edges, and the average clustering coefficient is 0.3.

5.4   Software Stacks

We chose four typical graph computing frameworks with the consideration of different partitioning strategies and execution models, which are PowerGraph, PowerLyra, GraphX and Gemini. We also implement all of GraphBench workloads with native C++ programs.

5.5   Summary

The GraphBench benchmark suite includes 65 implementations, which is summarized on the Table 2.

Table 2. The summary of the GraphBench

Types	Workloads	Data sets	Frameworks
Component	SSSP	Pokec	PowerGraph, PowerLyra, Gemini, GraphX, C++
	BFS	LJ	PowerGraph, PowerLyra, Gemini, GraphX, C++
	CC	LJ	PowerGraph, PowerLyra, Gemini, GraphX, C++
	K-core	LJ	PowerGraph, PowerLyra, Gemini, GraphX, C++
	PageRank	Wikipedia	PowerGraph, PowerLyra, Gemini, GraphX, C++
Micro	Load	LJ	PowerGraph, PowerLyra, Gemini, GraphX, C++
	VerticeNum	LJ	PowerGraph, PowerLyra, Gemini, GraphX, C++
	EdgesNum	LJ	PowerGraph, PowerLyra, Gemini, GraphX, C++
	VertexOutDegree	Email	PowerGraph, PowerLyra, Gemini, GraphX, C++
	VertexInDegree	Email	PowerGraph, PowerLyra, Gemini, GraphX, C++
	EdgeSource	Email	PowerGraph, PowerLyra, Gemini, GraphX, C++
	EdgeDestination	Email	PowerGraph, PowerLyra, Gemini, GraphX, C++
	Store	LJ	PowerGraph, PowerLyra, Gemini, GraphX, C++

6   Evaluations

6.1   Experimental Configurations and Methodology

Experimental Configurations. The experimental platform is equipped with the Intel Xeon E5645 processor and 96 GB memory, the operating system is Linux Ubuntu 16.04. The detailed configurations are summarized in Table 3.

Table 3. The configuration of the server node

CPU	Intel(R) Xeon(R) E5645 2.40G
Memeory	96 GB DDR3 1333 MHz bandwidth:8 GB/s
Network	Ethernet 1 G bandwidth:943 Mbits/s
Disk	SATA 1T bandwidth:154.82MB/s
OS	Ubuntu 16.04 and the kernel is 4.13.0-43-generic
GCC	4.3
Redis	4.2.5

We use GraphBench as the experimental workloads. In the experiments, we evaluate the current mainstream graph computing frameworks, which include PowerGraph, PowerLyra, GraphX, Gemini and C++.

6.2 Experiment Results and Observations

The User-Observed Metric. At the user-observed level, we choose the execution time as the metric. Figure 6 shows the execution time of the five component benchmarks of GraphBench. First, component benchmarks of GraphX have the longest average execution time. The main reason is that GraphX is implemented based on the Spark (which have a deep software stacks), other graph computing frameworks are implemented based on the C++. Furthermore, GraphX's micro-benchmarks also have the longest average execution time, which also proof that the deep software stacks result in the longest execution time of GraphX's workloads. Second, except the PageRank workload, Gemini's workloads have the highest performance among four graph computing frameworks (Gemini, GraphX, PowerGraph and PowerLyra). The main reason is that Gemini uses an adaptive push-pull model, which is a simple but high efficiency partition model. Gemini's push-pull model can improve the data importing efficiency

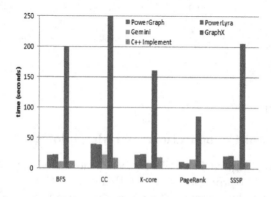

Fig. 6. The user-observed metric of GraphBench's component benchmarks

dramatically. So, the performance of Gemini's 'Load' workload is also out performance than others. Third, Gemini's PageRank workload execution time is slightly higher than PowerGraph and PowerLyra workload. This is because the average clustering coefficient of the Wikipedia data set, which used by the PageRank, is only 0.05. This resulted that PageRank needs more EdgeSource and EdgeDestination operations, and the perforamcne of EdgeSource and EdgeDestination of PowerGraph and PowerLyra are out performance than those of Gemini.

The System Level Metrics for the System. At the system level, we choose CPU utilization, I/O wait ratio, and computation intensity as metrics. The CPU utilization is defined as the ratio of the execution time of the CPU in the system level or user level to the total running time of the workload. The I/O wait ratio is defined as the ratio of the time the CPU waits for DISK I/O to the total system time of the CPU. The computation intensity is defined as the total number of floating point and integer instructions divided by the total number of memory accesses in terms of bytes in a run of the workload. For example, in a run of program A, it has n computation (floating point and integer) instructions and m bytes of memory accesses, so the computation intensity of program A is (n/m).

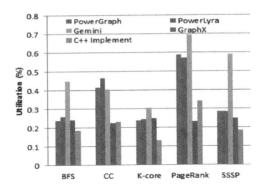

Fig. 7. The CPU utilization of GraphBench's component benchmarks

As shown in Fig. 7, first, the CPU utilization of the five component benchmarks of GraphBench. The average CPU utilization of the Gemini's workloads is 49%, those of PowerLyra, GraphX, PowerGraph and C++ are 37%, 24%, 35%, and 25% respectively. Gemini's workloads have the highest CPU utilization. Second, the average I/O wait ratio of GraphBench is not more than 4%, which implied that IO is not the bottleneck of GraphBench workloads. This is reasonable, as most of graph workloads do the operations on the memory, and Loading data to the memory is the first step for graph workloads. Third, the computation intensity of GraphBench also variant. The higher computation intensity of the workload implied that better locality of the workload. The average computation intensity of the Gemini workloads is 3.5, which is larger than others.

The Architecture Level Metrics for the System. At the architecture level, we chose IPC (Instructions per cycle), cache behaviors, and branch prediction behaviors as metrics. First, as shown in Fig. 8, the average IPC of the GraphX workload is 1.3, those of C++, PowerGraph, PowerLyra and Gemini are 1.2, 1.0, 1.0, and 1.0 respectively. The GraphX graph computing system is based on the Spark system, and the IPC of other the Spark system's workloads are also higher. Therefore, although the user-observed performance of GraphX is the lowest in the four graph computing frameworks, it is still a higher IPC. Second, the average L1I Cache MPKIL2 Cache MPKIL3 Cache MPKI are 9.2, 9.4 and 2.0 respectively. Third, the average branch miss ratio of GraphBench is 0.7%. The branch miss ratio of Gemini is only 0.6%, but that of GraphX is 1.3%.

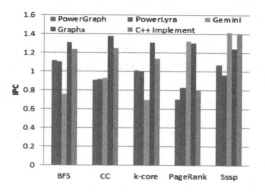

Fig. 8. The IPC of GraphBench's component benchmarks

From the above experimental results, we can see that there is no one-size-fits-all solution for the graph computing system. Using GraphBench, we can evaluate the graph computing system at the fine-grained level and get more insights. For example, we find that for the graph computing workload, the CPU utilization, the computation intensity and the branch prediction are correlated with the user-observed performance of graph computing system, and the IPC does not totally conform with the user-observed performance.

7   Conclusion

We build the graph computing benchmark suite–GraphBench, which includes micro-benchmark (graph basic operations) and component benchmarks (graph computing applications). Then, we evaluates the current mainstream graph computing frameworks with the GraphBench, experiments show that GraphBench can help people to better understand the graph computing system at the fine-grained level.

Acknowledgment. This work is supported by the National Key Research and Development Plan of China Grant No. 2016YFB1000201.

References

1. Nai, L., Xia, Y., et al.: GraphBIG: understanding graph computing in the context of industrial solutions. In: SC 2015: Proceedings of the International Conference for High Performance Computing, Networking, Storage and Analysis. IEEE (2015)
2. Erling, O., Averbuch, A., Larriba-Pey, J., et al.: The LDBC social network benchmark: interactive workload. In: Proceedings of the 2015 ACM SIGMOD International Conference on Management of Data. ACM (2015)
3. Ahmad, M., Hijaz, F., Shi, Q., et al.: Crono: a benchmark suite for multithreaded graph algorithms executing on futuristic multicores. In: 2015 IEEE International Symposium on Workload Characterization. IEEE (2015)
4. Guo, Y., Varbanescu, A.L., Iosup, A., et al.: An empirical performance evaluation of gpu-enabled graph-processing systems. In: 2015 15th IEEE/ACM International Symposium on Cluster, Cloud and Grid Computing. IEEE (2015)
5. Zou, L., Mo, J., Chen, L., Özsu, M.T., Zhao, D.: gStore: answering SPARQL queries via subgraph matching. Proc. VLDB Endow. **4**(8), 482–493 (2011)
6. Webber, J., Robinson, I.: A Programmatic Introduction to Neo4j. Addison-Wesley Professional, Boston (2018)
7. Developers O. OrientDB: Hybrid Document-Store and Graph NoSQL Database (2012)
8. Güting, R.H.: GraphDB: modeling and querying graphs in databases. VLDB **94**, 12–15 (1994)
9. Gonzalez, J.E., Low, Y., Gu, H., et al.: Powergraph: distributed graph-parallel computation on natural graphs. In: Presented as Part of the 10th USENIX Symposium on Operating Systems Design and Implementation (OSDI 2012) (2012)
10. Chen, R., Shi, J., Chen, Y., et al.: Powerlyra: differentiated graph computation and partitioning on skewed graphs. In: Proceedings of the Tenth European Conference on Computer Systems. ACM (2015)
11. Gonzalez, J.E., Xin, R.S., Dave, A., et al.: Graphx: graph processing in a distributed dataflow framework. In: 11th USENIX Symposium on Operating Systems Design and Implementation (OSDI 2014) (2014)
12. Zhu, X., Chen, W., Zheng, W., et al.: Gemini: a computation-centric distributed graph processing system. In: 12th USENIX Symposium on Operating Systems Design and Implementation (OSDI 2016) (2016)
13. Eu email communication network. http://snap.stanford.edu/data/email-EuAll.html
14. Wikipedia talk network. http://snap.stanford.edu/data/wiki-Talk.html
15. Pokec social network. https://snap.stanford.edu/data/soc-Pokec.html
16. Livejournal social network and ground-truth communities. https://snap.stanford.edu/data/com-LiveJournal.html
17. Shortest path problem. https://en.wikipedia.org/wiki/
18. Breadth-first search. https://en.wikipedia.org/wiki/
19. Connected component. https://en.wikipedia.org/wiki/
20. K-core. https://en.wikipedia.org/wiki/
21. Pagerank. https://en.wikipedia.org/wiki/

Early Experience in Benchmarking Edge AI Processors with Object Detection Workloads

Yujie Hui[1]([⊠]), Jeffrey Lien[2], and Xiaoyi Lu[1]

[1] Department of Computer Science and Engineering,
The Ohio State University, Columbus, OH, USA
{hui.82,lu.932}@osu.edu
[2] NovuMind Inc., Santa Clara, CA, USA
jlien@novumind.com

Abstract. Nowadays, GPGPU plays an important role in data centers for Deep Learning training. However, GPU might not be suitable for many Deep Learning inference applications, especially for Edge Computing scenarios, due to its high power consumption and high cost. Thus, researchers and engineers have spent a lot of effort on designing edge-side artificial intelligence (AI) processors recently. Because of different edge-side application requirements, edge AI processors are designed with different approaches, which make these processors very diversified. This scenario makes it hard for customers to decide what kind of processors may be more beneficial for their requirements. To provide a selection guidance, this paper proposes a three-dimensional benchmarking methodology and shares the early experience of evaluating three different kinds of edge AI processors (i.e., Edge TPU, NVIDIA Xavier, and NovuTensor) with object detection workloads (i.e., Tiny-YOLO and YOLOv2 with Microsoft COCO dataset). We also characterize a GPU platform (i.e., GTX 1080 Ti) from the three dimensions of accuracy, latency, and energy efficiency. Based on our experimental observations, we find that edge AI processors are able to deliver better energy efficiency (e.g., Edge TPU has the highest energy efficiency in our experiments.), while NovuTensor and Xavier, can also provide comparable performance in latency as GPU. Further, all these edge AI processors can achieve similar accuracy as GPU. The differences among these processors and GPU are less than 3%.

Keywords: Benchmarking · Edge Computing · AI Processor · Deep Learning

1 Introduction

The advancement of Deep Learning has been significantly taking advantage of high-performance computing technologies, such as multi-/many-core processors

This research is supported in part by National Science Foundation grant CCF# 1822987.

and accelerators, high-speed interconnects, etc. General Purpose GPUs (GPG-PUs) recently have become the most popular platforms for Deep Learning training workloads. Many modern data centers in the world provide efficient solutions for Deep Learning training with GPUs. However, Deep Learning infrastructures in data centers might not be suitable for Deep Learning inference workloads, due to the high power consumption and high cost of modern data centers, especially with many of the GPGPUs on cloud servers. Thus, Edge Computing based AI platforms are replacing GPGPUs for many Deep Learning inference applications [29]. The convergence of AI and Edge Computing provides more opportunities to businesses by efficiently running Deep Learning inference applications on edge-side AI platforms.

Edge-side AI platforms are typically equipped with specialized edge AI processors, which can support diverse Deep Learning inference applications, eliminate the high response time from data centers, and provide much cheaper solutions than GPU-based solutions for end users. Thus, more and more research and development activities have been spent on designing edge-side AI processors for Deep Learning inference applications and scenarios [11].

Due to different requirements from diversified Deep Learning applications, edge AI processors are typically designed with different approaches. For example, an edge AI processor may have a larger design space to have more memory. Or an edge AI processor may be designed to support only some specific Deep Learning operations in different requirements of performance, accuracy, and cost. Different designs of edge AI processors may lead to different performances. Thus, it is hard for customers to select an edge AI processor that may be most beneficial for their requirements. This scenario implies that the Deep Learning community needs more standard benchmarks, data-sets, and open research studies to evaluate and compare different edge AI processors for diverse applications.

However, we find that such kind of benchmark-oriented studies for edge AI processors are still not yet prevalent in the community. For example, the study in [1] has run several deep learning models on multiple edge devices, but the work mainly measures the latencies of running object detection workloads on those devices, which does not cover other important aspects for evaluating edge-side AI processors, such as accuracy and energy efficiency.

In order to provide more guidance to the community about how to select more appropriate edge AI processors for end users, this paper proposes a three-dimensional benchmarking methodology (i.e., accuracy, latency, and energy efficiency) on evaluating and comparing different edge AI processors. Deep Learning inference applications are usually customer-facing, which means the inference response time (i.e., latency) and the response accuracy may be more important than other performance metrics. In addition, since these AI processors are designed for Edge Computing platforms, energy efficiency will also be a very important factor for customers in selecting a device.

Based on our benchmarking methodology, we deploy Tiny-YOLO and YOLOv2, which are two popular object detection applications, on three different edge AI platforms (i.e., Edge TPU, NVIDIA Xavier, and NovuMind's NovuTensor). Accurate object detection is one of the most essential challenges for the

Deep Learning community to solve. YOLO-based Deep Learning solutions are extremely fast one-stage object detection systems in the Convolutional Neural Networks (CNN) architecture to detect objects efficiently from an image [37]. To mimic real object detection scenarios, we choose an open data-set from industry, i.e., Microsoft COCO [30] , which provides both training and validation images. We also compare these edge AI processors with a GPU platform (i.e., GTX 1080 Ti) from the three dimensions. These edge AI processors and GPUs typically support different machine learning frameworks and provide deployment tools individually. Note that Edge TPU and NovuTensor do not support some Deep Learning operations (e.g., leaky ReLU) in YOLO's neural network. We retrain a neural network model that is fully supported by these processors in our experiments.

Through our benchmarking experience, the major observations we find include: 1) All edge AI devices can provide similar-accuracy inference results with only 1% to 3% accuracy differences due to lower precision arithmetic. 2) All edge AI processors have better energy efficiency than the GTX 1080 Ti GPU. 3) NovuTensor and Xavier have good and comparable performance in latency as well as energy efficiency. 4) Edge TPU can achieve 6.7X higher energy efficiency but may be 14.79X slower than the GTX 1080 Ti GPU.

Overall, this paper makes the following specific contributions:

- We successfully deploy Tiny-YOLO and YOLOv2 inference applications on multiple edge AI platforms by leveraging deployment tools and modifying standard models to be hardware friendly. Then we compare multiple edge AI processors' performance through running representative object detection workloads (Sect. 5).
- Through our experimental results and observations (Sect. 5.4), we provide guidance to select edge AI platforms for consumers with our proposed three-dimensional benchmarking methodology.
- We share our early experience in benchmarking edge AI processors to the community and encourage more benchmarking efforts to promote the evolution of edge AI processors.

The rest of this paper is organized as follows. Section 2 provides the necessary background for this paper. Section 3 gives a high-level overview of modern edge AI processors. The benchmarking methodology is stated in Sect. 4. Section 5 gives our experiments results and observations. Section 6 introduces related work. Section 7 concludes the paper.

2   Background

In this section, we introduce inference and object detection task in deep learning as well as the edge AI platforms in our experiments.

2.1 Inference in Deep Learning

Training and inference are two important steps in Deep Learning. A Deep Learning model usually has millions of parameters to train. Modern GPGPUs can execute billions of floating-point operations per second (FLOPS), which has made GPGPUs the most popular training platforms for deep learning models. Deep Learning models are usually trained with Big Data in tens of hours to even hundreds of hours. Using multiple GPUs with large training batch sizes can accelerate training time. Trained models can be loaded on edge AI processors or GPUs to do real-time inference. Inference takes new input data to infer results using trained models. Deep Learning training requires high throughput while inference requires low latency. Thus, GPU-based clusters are used to train models because of their parallel computing capabilities, while a single edge device can be used to do inference. Inference brings Deep Learning models to many aspects in our real life. For example, a face recognition system takes a small batch of face images as input each time and infers the identities of the images in a short response time.

2.2 Object Detection and YOLO-Based Systems

Object detection is a typical inference workload that combines localization and classification tasks. For example, an autonomous driving system needs to detect objects in a short time using deep learning models. An object detection system can correctly infer several bounding boxes, which contain the object's location and category in the input image. Each training image is labeled with rectangular bounding boxes that annotate the locations and categories of the objects. Inference will predict multiple bounding boxes. A predicted bounding box with location and category information represents an inferred object. Gradient-based learning approach is used in CNNs to solve object detection tasks [27]. CNN has stronger expressive capability since it has deeper architecture compared with traditional models [41]. Multiple methods on object detection tasks have been proposed in these years such as R-CNN [19], Fast R-CNN [18], YOLO [36], YOLOv2 [37], and SSD [31].

YOLOv2 is a state-of-the-art object detection system [37]. Tiny-YOLO is a lite version of YOLOv2. Tiny-YOLO is faster but less accurate than YOLOv2, since YOLOv2 has more convolutional layers than Tiny-YOLO. Applications of YOLO are able to predict the location and category of objects from any input images. YOLOv2 has two main training components. The first pre-trained model has trained on ImageNet [16] dataset for the classification task. The second component is trained from the previous pre-trained model in the first component. The output of YOLO's neural networks is a feature map with multiple grid cells. Each grid cell predicts five bounding boxes with the probabilities of each class.

3   Overview of Edge AI Processors

This section provides a high-level overview of three different kinds of modern Edge AI processors.

3.1   Edge TPU

Edge TPU from Google provides an end-to-end edge AI solution. Edge TPU integrates onboard TPUs to execute neural networks (e.g., CNNs). TPU consists of Matrix Multiplier Unit (MXU), Unified Buffer (UB), and Activation Unit (AU) to execute convolutional calculations [25]. The key technology in TPU is called Systolic Array. Multiple ALUs are combined together in the systolic array and input data can be reused from one single register. But TPU can only execute a few

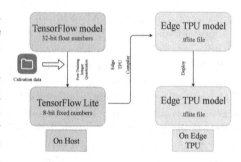

Fig. 1. Workflow to Create an Edge TPU Model

specific operations in a trade-off between performance and energy efficiency. The workflow to create an Edge TPU compatible model is shown in Fig. 1. A quantized TensorFlow Lite model is converted from a TensorFlow model using some calibration data. TensorFlow Lite is a lightweight version of TensorFlow designed for mobile and embedded devices. Then this quantized model needs to be compiled to a hardware compatible model via the Edge TPU compiler before deployment on the board. Edge TPU only supports INT8 or INT16 based quantization models and the quantization method can be found in this paper [24]. Some pre-trained and pre-compiled models for image classification and object detection tasks are provided in this project [5], which can be deployed on Edge TPU directly.

3.2   NVIDIA Xavier

NVIDIA Jetson AGX Xavier is an embedded system on a module, containing a Volta GPU, dual Deep Learning accelerators, a Carmel ARMv8.2 CPU, and 16GB memory [7]. Jetson AGX Xavier is an edge computing device for deploying AI applications and providing end-to-end AI solutions. Xavier allows users to configure operating modes at 10 W, 15 W, and max 30 W. Xavier supports AI software libraries like CUDA [35], cuDNN [12], and TensorRT to improve the inference performance. With the speeding up by TensorRT, Xavier can achieve high performance according to our experiments. NVIDIA TensorRT is a runtime for high-performance Deep Learning inference. Developers can use TensorRT to optimize their Deep Learning models and deploy them on any platforms that have TensorRT runtime from NVIDIA. TensorRT supports INT8 and FLOAT16 optimizations for Deep Learning models as well as the original FLOAT32 data type. TensorRT supports almost all the popular frameworks like TensorFlow, PyTorch, and Caffe. TensorRT takes trained models from those popular frameworks, optimizes the neural network models, and generates light-weight runtime engines for GPUs. Developers only need to deploy the generated runtime engines on the NVIDIA platforms like Jetson Xavier. Figure 2 illustrates the workflow to deploy a model on an NVIDIA platform using TensorRT.

Fig. 2. Deployment using TensorRT

3.3 NovuTensor

NovuMind's NovuTensor uses domain specific architecture focusing on performing 3D tensor computations. Traditional tensor processors like TPU implement convolution layer using 2D matrix multiplication. TPU and GPU calculate 3D convolution multiplication by unfolding the matrix into a 2D matrix and then multiplying the 2D matrix with convolution kernels. NovuTensor's architecture includes a patented design that natively performs 3D tensor computations on the chip, which can avoid the overhead of unfolding 3D tensors into 2D matrices that is inherent in other chips [32]. Processing natively 3D tensor computations achieves high performance and less memory usage. The native tensor processors inside NovuTensor chip convolve 3D tensors of input feature maps with 3×3 convolution kernels. 3×3 convolution kernels are very common in CNNs in previous work [13]. Thus, native tensor processors in NovuTensor can gain much bigger performance improvements for CNN models.

4 Benchmarking Methodology

This section presents workload, platform, and metric selection in our three-dimensional benchmarking methodology.

4.1 Workload Selection

A representative workload for benchmarking AI systems needs a real dataset. Microsoft COCO [30] (MS COCO) is one of the most popular open dataset in the community, which has been widely used in the computer vision field. MS COCO contains hundreds of thousand images from the real world for training, validation, and testing. The training and validation images are labeled with segmentation and bounding boxes. Annotations of MS COCO are arranged in the JSON format. MS COCO mainly contains three tasks (i.e., object detection, key-point detection, and segmentation). MS COCO has 80 categories, which is larger than other datasets like PASCAL VOC [17]. Object instances in MS COCO are also annotated more than those in PASCAL VOC. Developers can use C++ or Python APIs provided by MS COCO to load images and calculate the accuracy [6]. Based on these advantages of MS COCO, this paper chooses it to construct our object detection workloads with YOLOv2 and Tiny-YOLO.

4.2 Platform Selection

We choose GTX 1080 Ti, which is a general-purpose GPU, as our baseline to compare with Edge TPU, Xavier, and NovuTensor, which are edge-side AI platforms using application-specific integrated circuit (ASIC) for inference. These platforms are popular in the industry and use innovative technologies in their designs. Developers can deploy Deep Learning applications on these platforms. They have similar low power consumption (e.g., 20 W for NovuTensor and 30 W for Xavier). We also consider the software support when we select platforms in our experiments. These platforms support different Deep Learning frameworks (e.g., Caffe, TensorFlow, TensorFlow Lite, and PyTorch).

4.3 Metrics and Dimensions

To evaluate the performance of different edge AI processors, we record real-time statistics in our experiments. These statistics help us compare and explore characteristics of these platforms from the three dimensions we have selected in this paper, which include:

- Accuracy: This is typically the most important factor (i.e., how well the processor can infer correct answers) to consider for end users to select appropriate edge AI processors for their applications. We take the accuracy into account since the accuracy may be influenced by different hardware restrictions on Deep Learning operations, such as supporting lower-precision data types. A standard metric for the accuracy dimension is called mean Average Precision (i.e., mAP). mAP has been popularly used to evaluate the accuracy with object detection workloads [17]. mAP is the mean value of Average Precision (AP). One AP value is calculated for one category of images. To introduce mAP further, we first introduce the basic concepts of precision and recall in the following equations.

$$Precision = \frac{TruePositives}{TruePositives + FalsePositives} \tag{1}$$

$$Recall = \frac{TruePositives}{TruePositives + FalseNegatives} \tag{2}$$

Based on Eq. 1 and Eq. 2, we can draw a precision-recall curve for all predictions from validation dataset. In the curve, we can choose 11 points in the axis of recall, ranging from 0, 0.1, 0.2 until to 1.0. Then the corresponding 11 precision values will be used to calculate the Average Precision value. Equation 3 calculates an AP value for one category of images based on the 11 interpolated precision values, where $\dot{P}_r$ is the interpolated precision value in Eq. 1 and r corresponds to the recall in Eq. 2.

$$AP = \frac{1}{11} \sum_{r \in \{0, 0.1, \dots 1.0\}} P_r \tag{3}$$

$$mAP = \frac{\sum_{i=1}^{N} AP}{N} \tag{4}$$

Then, mAP can be calculated by Eq. 4, where N is the total number of categories. The MS COCO dataset contains 80 categories, which means N equals 80 in Eq. 4. The mAP for MS COCO is the mean value of these 80 average precision values.

– Latency: The time to complete an inference on the input images in one batch is defined as latency. Latency is one of the most important and critical dimension for inference since Deep Learning inference applications are usually customer-facing.
– Energy Efficiency: This means the number of input images can be fully processed per unit-power, which is usually expressed as performance/watt or images/second/watt. Energy efficiency is another key factor to be considered for choosing edge AI devices, since Edge Computing environments usually need lower energy-consumption technologies.

The dimensions and corresponding metrics mentioned above can help us benchmark different edge AI processors. Through these metrics, we are able to evaluate the performance of these edge AI processors and provide selection guidance for end users.

4.4   Experimental Methodology

To capture the real inference execution time on hardware, our experiments split the whole execution flow of running an inference application into three steps:

– Pre-processing time: is the time of the pre-processing step (e.g., normalization of input images).
– Execution time: measures the time of transferring the input feature maps into devices, execution, and receiving the output feature maps from devices.
– Post-processing time: is the time of the post-processing step (e.g., parse the output tensors to get readable prediction results).

To evaluate the performance of edge AI processors, only the execution time should be accounted. As for YOLO-based applications, the pre-processing step includes getting input images and normalization. The post-processing step gets a 3-dimensional tensor from neural network's output and decodes this tensor to get the prediction results.

5   Experiments

This section presents our experimental configuration and setup to perform the benchmarking on edge AI processors.

5.1 Hardware Configuration

The specifications of edge AI processors in our experiments are shown in Table 1. Table 1 illustrates the theoretical metrics for comparing these edge AI processors. Tera Operations per Second (TOPs) is a common metric for evaluating the throughput of AI processors, which represents the processing capability of an AI processor.

5.2 Setup

We deploy Tiny-YOLO and YOLOv2 applications on three edge AI platforms as shown in Table 1. The YOLO-based applications include three components, which are image pre-processing, trained CNN models, and inference post-processing. We select five thousands images in MS COCO's 2014 validation dataset as the inference workload for all AI platforms. We evaluate the AI devices with input images of both regular and large sizes. Thus, input images will be re-sized to 416 × 416 and 1024 × 1024 before feeding them into the neural network models. Every edge AI platform processes the same five thousands validation images and generates a JSON file with all the inferred bounding boxes. We use MS COCO API to parse the JSON file and calculate the mAP, which is the common accuracy evaluation metric for object detection task [6].

Edge TPU: We first convert Tiny-YOLO and YOLOv2 applications from Darknet framework to TensorFlow framework using DarkFlow [2], as Egde TPU only supports TensorFlow Lite. Darknet is the framework that supports original YOLO-based applications [3]. A model in Darknet includes two components, a configuration file and a binary file. The configuration file defines the architecture of the neural network and the binary file is the trained weights of convolutional kernels. We combine the configuration file and binary file into a TensorFlow SavedModel format file via DarkFlow. TensorFlow provides two ways to do quantization (i.e., post-training quantization and quantization-aware training). Post-training quantization creates a small model by using 8-bit values, but during inference, it is converted back to 32-bit floats. Quantization-aware training creates fake quantization nodes containing the minimum and maximum values of layers' weights during training. Edge TPU utilizes the quantized values to do inference. However, developers have to modify the training source code to do training-aware quantization. We use a new quantization toolkit without modifying training source code [8]. We feed 80 calibration images into the models, which can quantize and generate a TensorFlow Lite model. Then we compile the TensorFlow Lite model to an Edge TPU model that has instructions supported by Edge TPU.

Edge TPU does not support dynamic tensor sizes and only supports 3-dimensional tensors. If a tensor has more than three dimensions, only the three innermost dimensions can have a size greater than one. In this case, the batch size for inference could only be one when the input image has three channels.

YOLOv2 and Tiny-YOLO use leaky rectification (leaky ReLU) [26] as the activation function for all the convolutional layers. But leaky ReLU is not supported by Edge TPU. We replace leaky ReLU with ReLU and retrain the models, using four GTX 1080 Ti GPUs. Reorganization and route layers are also not supported by Edge TPU. Before deploying the models on Edge TPU, it is necessary to make sure that all the operations are supported with INT8 data type, because operations that do not have quantized implementations will not work with Edge TPU.

In addition, Edge TPU only supports 8-bit input data. As a consequence, the input image's pixels can not be normalized to Float32 data type between 0 and 1. So we modify the weights of the first convolutional layer to additionally transform input tensors to appropriate forms without normalization, which can match with the input requirements of Edge TPU.

Table 1. Specifications of platforms

Specification	Edge TPU	Xavier	NovuTensor	1080 Ti
Precision	INT8	INT8/FP16/FP32	INT8	FP32
TOPS	4	22.6/11.3/1.3	15	11.3
Memory	1 GB 32-bit LPDDR4	16 GB 256-bit LPDDR4X	2 GB 128-bit DDR4	11 GB 352-bit GDDR5X
Power (watt)	–	10/15/30	20	250
Process (nm)	–	12	28	16

Note that TOPS stands for Tera Operations per Second. We found or calculated from official specifications according to the corresponding precision. The power and process of Edge TPU are not reported by Google. We approximate the power as 2.5 W by our experimental devices.

Xavier: Our experiments deploy NVIDIA's deepstream reference applications [4], which contain YOLO-based applications implemented by TensorRT, on Xavier platforms. TensorRT 5.0.3 is installed in our experimental Xavier device. TensorRT is able to parse Deep Learning models and deploy optimized models on Xavier. TensorRT provides a plugin layer for developers to implement customized operations that are not supported by TensorRT (e.g., leaky ReLU). Using the plugin layer, we are able to deploy the original YOLO-based application on Xavier without modifying and retraining the model. We evaluate Xavier in both 15-W and 30-W modes. We set the INT8 data type in the deepstream application to compare with other hardware devices.

NovuTensor: NovuMind's NovuTensor is a special-purpose processor for AI inference applications. Designed for convolutional neural networks, it achieves high throughput and low latency for convolution computations. NovuTensor convolves the feature map with 3 × 3 kernels using the native tensor processors.

In our experiments, we deploy Tiny-YOLO and YOLOv2 applications on NovuTensor using NovuSDK. Hardware-friendly YOLOv2 and Tiny-YOLO models are deployed on NovuTensor by replacing the activation functions by ReLU and removing reorganization and route layers. NovuSDK provides APIs for developers to control the hardware.

5.3 Results

Figure 3 illustrates the mAPs of Tiny-YOLO and YOLOv2 applications running on different edge AI processors with 416 × 416 resolution input images. After quantization, the accuracy of YOLOv2 drops 2% to 3% and the accuracy of Tiny-YOLO drops 1% to 2% on all edge AI processors compared to the accuracy on GPU. Low precision arithmetic like INT8 reduces accuracy but accelerates the execution time [22]. The differences of accuracy degradation among different edge AI processors are varied, which is because these edge AI processors implement the quantization in different ways.

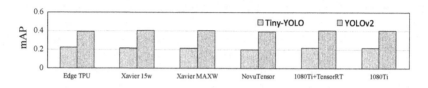

Fig. 3. Accuracy of YOLOv2 and Tiny-YOLO with 416 × 416 image size

Figure 4 shows the latency of processing a batch of input images. Edge TPU is slower than other edge AI processors, which are 28.74 ms and 94.37 ms for Tiny-YOLO and YOLOv2 applications, respectively. The architecture of YOLOv2 is more complex than Tiny-YOLO. The latency of Edge TPU increases more than other edge AI processors, when the neural network's architecture becomes complex. NovuTensor can achieve 14.08 ms and 24.78 ms for one batch of input images, which is faster than Xavier in the 15-W mode (i.e., 16.68 ms and 38.39 ms) and similar with (i.e., 14.16 ms for Tiny-YOLO) or slower than (i.e., 17.85 ms for YOLOv2) Xavier in the 30-W mode, respectively.

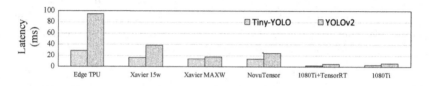

Fig. 4. Latency of YOLOv2 and Tiny-YOLO with 416 × 416 image size

Figure 5 illustrates the energy efficiency by taking the energy consumption into account. Edge TPU achieves relatively higher energy efficiency considering its very low power usage and GTX 1080 Ti seems not very energy-efficient since its large power consumption. NovuTensor has better energy-efficiency than Xavier in both 15-W and 30-W modes for the YOLOv2 application. NovuTensor also shows better energy-efficiency than Xavier in the 30-W (max) mode and comparable energy-efficiency as Xavier in the 15-W mode for the Tiny-YOLO application.

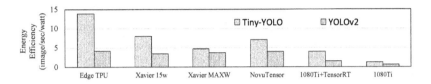

Fig. 5. Energy Efficiency of YOLOv2 and Tiny-YOLO with 416 × 416 image size

We also evaluate the performance of these edge AI processors with larger input images (i.e., 1024 × 1024), as shown in Fig. 6. All the devices can provide similar-accuracy inference results compared with GPU, thus the accuracy results are not shown here. Through our experiments, Xavier and NovuTensor can achieve comparable low latency and high energy efficiency.

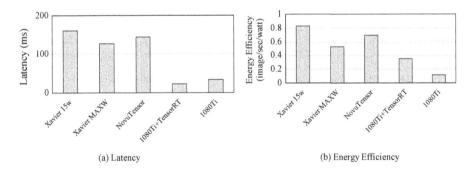

(a) Latency   (b) Energy Efficiency

Fig. 6. Performance of YOLOv2 with 1024 × 1024 image size

5.4   Observations and Summary

We combine all the measured results in our experiments and demonstrate them in three-dimensional charts as shown in Fig. 7. In order to compare edge AI processors clearly, we normalize the experimental results into these three dimensions. Performance, one of the three dimensions, is defined as the reciprocal of latency. In this way, if an edge AI processor can achieve a bigger score in the three-dimensional charts, it means the edge AI processor can be a better choice in the corresponding dimension. Through these two radar charts, we obtain some interesting observations as follows:

– All these edge AI processors are able to provide similar-accuracy inference results compared with the GTX 1080 Ti. Quantization from FP32 to INT8 data type during inference causes an accuracy drop around 1% to 3%.
– These edge AI processors are slower than GTX 1080 Ti GPU due to less computing cores and less power consumption. Edge TPU is **9.5X** and **14.79X slower** than GTX 1080 Ti with running Tiny-Yolo and YOLOv2, respectively. Despite Xavier and NovuTensor are slower than the GPU, Xavier is **2X** and **5.28X faster** than Edge TPU in the max power mode, and NovuTensor is **2.04X** and **3.8X faster** than Edge TPU, respectively, when running with Tiny-Yolo and YOLOv2 applications.
– Edge TPU exceeds other edge AI processors in energy efficiency, and it delivers **2.9X** and **1.13X higher** energy efficiency than Xavier as well as **1.96X** and **1.04X higher** energy efficiency than NovuTensor for Tiny-Yolo and YOLOv2, respectively.

As specified by our observations, these edge AI processors can perform Tiny-YOLO and YOLOv2 applications within a 3% accuracy drop. NovuTensor and Xavier achieve low latency and relatively high energy efficiency for object detection workloads. Edge TPU has the advantage of energy efficiency.

6   Related Work

This section presents related work about benchmarking AI processors.

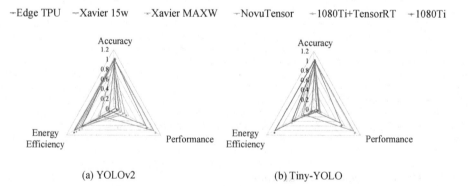

Fig. 7. Comparison of factors on YOLOv2 and Tiny-YOLO with 416 × 416 image size

6.1 Modern AI Processors

Deep learning especially neural networks have been proven in many state-of-the-art application systems to solve classification and object detection tasks [23,28]. The opportunity to design AI processors with high performance and efficiency attracts more and more researchers and engineers [10]. Multiple methods can execute deep learning workloads on modern AI processors, such as GPUs [14], FPGAs [9], or ASICs [11,20,25]. Some customized AI processors have been effectively studied such as k-NN accelerator on FPGA [39], k-NN classifier of IP cores design [34,38].

6.2 Edge AI Benchmarking

Due to the emergence of different edge AI processors for inference, we do see the effort of benchmarking these devices in the community. AIoT Bench [33] contains benchmarks for image classification, speech recognition, transformer translation, and micro workloads on Android-based systems and Raspberry Pi. The urgent requirements of edge AI benchmarking are also discussed in this paper [33]. The study in [1] runs several Deep Learning models on multiple edge devices and it mainly measures the latency of object detection workloads. A survey on different Deep Learning benchmarks summarizes multiple popular available benchmarks in the community [40]. EdgeAI Bench [21] contains four different benchmarking frameworks. These frameworks aim at benchmarking four specific scenarios using Deep Learning technologies in Edge Computing environments. EdgeBench [15] compares two serverless edge computing services on a standard Raspberry Pi 3B model. Compared to these related studies, this paper focuses on benchmarking three modern edge AI processors (i.e., Edge TPU, NVIDIA Xavier, and NovuTensor) with object detection workloads.

7 Conclusion and Future Work

We propose a benchmarking methodology to systematically evaluate three different kinds of edge AI processors (i.e., Edge TPU, NVIDIA Xavier, and NovuTensor) from the three dimensions of accuracy, latency, and energy efficiency. Based on our experimental results, we observe that NovuTensor and Xavier can provide comparable performance in latency and energy efficiency, which satisfy the major requirements for Deep Learning inference applications. They also have comparable performance in latency compared with GTX 1080 Ti. Edge TPU consumes less energy but is much slower for inference, which may influence the consumers' usage experience. Accuracy is important but seems not a major factor to make a selection on these edge AI processors, since they all can provide similar inference accuracy.

In the future, we will evaluate more combinations of different neural networks and edge AI platforms. We plan to propose an easy-to-use benchmarking toolkit for different edge AI processors.

References

1. Benchmarking Edge Computing. https://medium.com/@aallan/benchmarking-edge-computing-ce3f13942245
2. DarkFlow. https://github.com/thtrieu/darkflow
3. Darknet. https://github.com/pjreddie/darknet
4. Deepstream Reference Applications. https://github.com/NVIDIA-AI-IOT/deepstream_reference_apps
5. Models Built for Edge TPU. https://coral.withgoogle.com/models/
6. MS COCO API. https://github.com/cocodataset/cocoapi
7. NVIDIA Jetson AGX Xavier. https://developer.nvidia.com/embedded/jetson-agx-xavier-developer-kit
8. Post-Training Integer Quantization. https://medium.com/tensorflow/tensorflow-model-optimization-toolkit-post-training-integer-quantization-b4964a1ea9ba
9. Chakradhar, S., Sankaradas, M., Jakkula, V., Cadambi, S.: A dynamically configurable coprocessor for convolutional neural networks. In: ACM SIGARCH Computer Architecture News, vol. 38, pp. 247–257. ACM (2010)
10. Chen, T., et al.: BenchNN: on the broad potential application scope of hardware neural network accelerators. In: 2012 IEEE International Symposium on Workload Characterization (IISWC), pp. 36–45. IEEE (2012)
11. Chen, Y., Chen, T., Zhiwei, X., Sun, N., Temam, O.: DianNao family: energy-efficient hardware accelerators for machine learning. Communi. ACM **59**(11), 105–112 (2016)
12. Chetlur, S., et al.: cuDNN: efficient primitives for deep learning. arXiv preprint arXiv:1410.0759 (2014)
13. Ciresan, D.C., Meier, U., Masci, J., Gambardella, L.M., Schmidhuber, J.: Flexible, high performance convolutional neural networks for image classification. In: Twenty-Second International Joint Conference on Artificial Intelligence (2011)
14. Coates, A., Huval, B., Wang, T., Wu, D., Catanzaro, B., Andrew, N.: Deep learning with COTS HPC systems. In: International Conference on Machine Learning, pp. 1337–1345 (2013)
15. Das, A., Patterson, S., Wittie, M.: Edgebench: benchmarking edge computing platforms. In: 2018 IEEE/ACM International Conference on Utility and Cloud Computing Companion (UCC Companion), pp. 175–180. IEEE (2018)
16. Deng, J., Dong, W., Socher, R., Li, L.J., Li, K., Fei-Fei, L.: Imagenet: a large-scale hierarchical image database. In: 2009 IEEE Conference on Computer Vision and Pattern Recognition, pp. 248–255. IEEE (2009)
17. Everingham, M., Gool, L.V., KI Williams, C., Winn, J., Zisserman, A.: The pascal visual object classes (VOC) challenge. Int. J. Comput. Vis. **88**(2), 303–338 (2010)
18. Girshick, R.: Fast R-CNN. In: Proceedings of the IEEE International Conference on Computer Vision, pp. 1440–1448 (2015)
19. Girshick, R., Donahue, J., Darrell, T., Malik, J.: Rich feature hierarchies for accurate object detection and semantic segmentation. In: Proceedings of the IEEE Conference on Computer Vision and Pattern Recognition, pp. 580–587 (2014)
20. Han, S., et al.. EIE: efficient inference engine on compressed deep neural network. In: 2016 ACM/IEEE 43rd Annual International Symposium on Computer Architecture (ISCA), pp. 243–254. IEEE (2016)
21. Hao, T., et al.: EdgeAI bench: towards comprehensive end-to-end edge computing benchmarking. In: 2018 Bench Council International Symposium on Benchmarking, Measuring and Optimizing (Bench 2018) (2018)

22. Hashemi, S., Anthony, N., Tann, H., Bahar, I.R., Reda, S.: Understanding the impact of precision quantization on the accuracy and energy of neural networks. In Design, Automation & Test in Europe Conference & Exhibition (DATE), 2017, pp. 1474–1479. IEEE (2017)
23. Hinton, G.E., Srivastava, N., Krizhevsky, A., Sutskever, I., Salakhutdinov, R.R.: Improving neural networks by preventing co-adaptation of feature detectors. arXiv preprint arXiv:1207.0580 (2012)
24. Jacob, B., et al.: Quantization and training of neural networks for efficient integer-arithmetic-only inference. In: Proceedings of the IEEE Conference on Computer Vision and Pattern Recognition, pp. 2704–2713 (2018)
25. Jouppi, N.P., et al.: In-datacenter performance analysis of a tensor processing unit. In: 2017 ACM/IEEE 44th Annual International Symposium on Computer Architecture (ISCA), pp. 1–12. IEEE (2017)
26. Krizhevsky, A., Sutskever, I., Hinton, G.E.: Imagenet classification with deep convolutional neural networks. In: Advances in Neural Information Processing Systems, pp. 1097–1105 (2012)
27. Wick, C.: Deep learning. Informatik-Spektrum **40**(1), 103–107 (2016). https://doi.org/10.1007/s00287-016-1013-2
28. LeCun, Y., Bottou, L., Bengio, Y., Haffner, P., et al.: Gradient-based learning applied to document recognition. Proc. IEEE **86**(11), 2278–2324 (1998)
29. Lee, Y.-L., Tsung, P.-K., Wu, M.: Techology trend of edge AI. In: 2018 International Symposium on VLSI Design, Automation and Test (VLSI-DAT), pp. 1–2. IEEE (2018)
30. Lin, T.-Y., et al.: Microsoft COCO: common objects in context. In: Fleet, D., Pajdla, T., Schiele, B., Tuytelaars, T. (eds.) ECCV 2014. LNCS, vol. 8693, pp. 740–755. Springer, Cham (2014). https://doi.org/10.1007/978-3-319-10602-1_48
31. Liu, W., et al.: SSD: single shot multibox detector. In: Leibe, B., Matas, J., Sebe, N., Welling, M. (eds.) ECCV 2016. LNCS, vol. 9905, pp. 21–37. Springer, Cham (2016). https://doi.org/10.1007/978-3-319-46448-0_2
32. Lu, C.P., Tang, Y.-S.: Native Tensor Processor, and Partitioning of Tensor Contractions. https://patentscope.wipo.int/search/en/detail.jsf?docId=US225521272&tab=NATIONALBIBLIO
33. Luo, C., et al.: AIoT bench: towards comprehensive benchmarking mobile and embedded device intelligence. In: 2018 Bench Council International Symposium on Benchmarking, Measuring and Optimizing (Bench 2018) (2018)
34. Manolakos, E.S., Stamoulias, I.: IP-Cores design for the kNN classifier. In: Proceedings of 2010 IEEE International Symposium on Circuits and Systems, pp. 4133–4136. IEEE (2010)
35. Nickolls, J., Buck, I., Garland, M.: Scalable parallel programming. In: 2008 IEEE Hot Chips 20 Symposium (HCS), pp. 40–53. IEEE (2008)
36. Redmon, J., Divvala, S., Girshick, R., Farhadi, A.: You only look once: unified, real-time object detection. In: Proceedings of the IEEE Conference on Computer Vision and Pattern Recognition, pp. 779–788 (2016)
37. Redmon, J., Farhadi, A.: YOLO9000: better, faster, stronger. In: Proceedings of the IEEE Conference on Computer Vision and Pattern Recognition, pp. 7263–7271 (2017)
38. Stamoulias, I., Manolakos, E.S.: Parallel architectures for the kNN classifier-design of soft IP cores and FPGA implementations. ACM Trans. Embedded Comput. Syst. (TECS) **13**(2), 22 (2013)

39. Yeh, Y.-J., Li, H.-Y., Hwang, W.-J., Fang, C.-Y.: FPGA implementation of kNN classifier based on wavelet transform and partial distance search. In: Ersbøll, B.K., Pedersen, K.S. (eds.) SCIA 2007. LNCS, vol. 4522, pp. 512–521. Springer, Heidelberg (2007). https://doi.org/10.1007/978-3-540-73040-8_52
40. Zhang, Q., et al.: A survey on deep learning benchmarks: do we still need new ones? In: 2018 Bench Council International Symposium on Benchmarking, Measuring and Optimizing (Bench 2018) (2018)
41. Zhao, Z.-Q., Zheng, P., Xu, S.-T., Wu, X.: A review. IEEE Transactions on Neural Networks and Learning Systems, Object Detection with Deep Learning (2019)

AI Challenges on Cambricon Using AIBench

XDN: Towards Efficient Inference of Residual Neural Networks on Cambricon Chips

Guangli Li[1,2], Xueying Wang[1,2], Xiu Ma[1,3,4], Lei Liu[1(✉)],
and Xiaobing Feng[1,2]

[1] State Key Laboratory of Computer Architecture,
Institute of Computing Technology, Chinese Academy of Sciences, Beijing, China
{liguangli,wangxueying,maxiu01,liulei,fxb}@ict.ac.cn
[2] School of Computer Science and Technology,
University of Chinese Academy of Sciences, Beijing, China
[3] College of Computer Science and Technology, Jilin University, Changchun, China
[4] MOE Key Laboratory of Symbolic Computation and Knowledge Engineering,
Jilin University, Changchun, China

Abstract. In this paper, we present XDN, an optimization and inference engine for accelerating residual neural networks on Cambricon chips. We leverage a channel pruning method to compress the weights of ResNet-50. By exploring the optimization opportunities in computational graphs, we propose a layer fusion strategy, which dramatically decreases the number of scalar computation layers, such as Batch Normalization, Scale. Furthermore, we design an efficient implementation of XDN, including data preprocessing, hyper-parameter auto-tuning, etc. The experimental results show that the ResNet-50 model can achieve significant speedup without accuracy loss by using our XDN engine.

Keywords: Artificial intelligence systems · Residual neural networks · Cambricon chips · Performance optimization

1 Introduction

Recent years, neural networks have been achieved remarkable performance in various areas, including image classification [12,17,21], object detection [7,8,20], etc. However, the deep neural networks with increasing computational complexity are inefficient on traditional general-purpose hardware such as CPU. Accordingly, research on machine learning specific processors becomes an inevitable trend to satisfy the ever-increasing demand on computation capability in artificial intelligent domains [9]. A batch of domain-specific processors have been developed, such as Cambricon chips [1–3]. *2019 BenchCouncil International AI System and Algorithm Challenges* include the system challenges on

---

Li, G., Wang, X., Ma, X.—These authors contributed equally to this work.

© Springer Nature Switzerland AG 2020
W. Gao et al. (Eds.): Bench 2019, LNCS 12093, pp. 51–56, 2020.
https://doi.org/10.1007/978-3-030-49556-5_4

Cambricon [18], X86 [4,11], RISC-V [13] and a 3D face recognition algorithm
challenge [22], which poses challenges to the optimization of artificial intelligence
algorithms and systems.

2   Our Approach

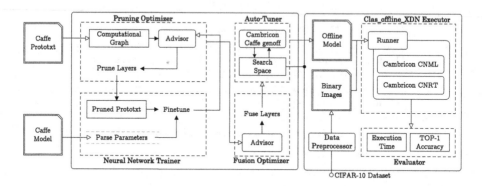

Fig. 1. Overview of XDN Engine

In this paper, we focus on optimizing the performance of ResNet-50 [12], a
widely used residual neural network architecture, on Cambricon chips. An optimization and inference engine, namely XDN (XiaoDianNao), is presented, which
is composed of a channel pruning approach, fusion strategies, hyper-parameters
tuning, data preprocessing, and an efficient executor. Figure 1 demonstrates the
approach of our XDN engine.

2.1   Pruning Optimizer and Trainer

The original Caffe prototxt is converted to a computational graph. An Advisor
is used to guide the channel pruning and the pruned model is re-trained by the
Trainer. The pruning approach by Optimizer and Trainer is iteratively performed
until all layers are optimized or unless the accuracy of model is not satisfied.

2.2   Fusion Optimizer

The layers of pruned neural network are fused by an Advisor. The main fusion
strategies including: 1) fusing convolution layers with correlative batch normalization layers and scale layers; 2) fusing convolution layers in different branches
of building blocks. Then, a fused and pruned neural network model is obtained.

2.3   Auto-tuner

Cambricon chips supports multi-core parallel execution and have several hyper-parameters, such as the number of threads, model_parallel, and data_paralell. The Auto-Tuner performs all options in the search space and the best option of hyper-parameters, which has minimum execution time, is recorded. The final offline model with the best option is generated by the "genoff" command of the Cambricon Caffe.

2.4   Executor and Evaluator

In order to decrease the time of reading data, the images of CIFAR-10 dataset are preprocessed and converted to a binary file by the Data Preprocessor. We design a Clas_offline_XDN Executor, which executes the final offline model with best hyper-parameters using Cambricon CNML and Cambricon CNRT. Finally, the execution time and the accuracy are calculated by the Evaluator.

3   Experimental Evaluation

3.1   Environmental Setting

We use Cambricon Caffe, a modified BVLC Caffe [14], as the development framework to train, test and generate neural network models. All experiments are performed on a server node of the BenchCouncil New Technology Testbed[1], which is equipped with an Intel i7-4770K CPU and a Cambricon MLU100 accelerator. The Cambricon MLU100 is a multi-core machine learning accelerator which contains 32 cores. The 32 cores are connected to 4 DDR controllers through network-on-chip (NOC) and each DDR controller is connected with 8 cores. In addition, Cambricon also provides the Cambricon Neuware Machine Learning Library (CNML) and the Cambricon Neuware Runtime Library (CNRT) for users to develop deep learning applications.

3.2   Overall Performance

We evaluate the performance by using the ResNet-50, which is a widely used neural network model, on the AIBench [5,6,10,15,19] and the dataset is CIFAR-10 [16]. The source code of AIBench is publicly available from http://www.bench\discretionary-council.org/benchhub/AIBench/ (Sign up to get access). Table 1 illustrates the performance of the ResNet-50 model with different optimization options of XDN.

OPT-0 denotes the baseline model and the original executor, which provided in Cambricon Caffe with default hyper-parameters of generation and parallelization.

---

[1] http://www.benchcouncil.org/testbed/index.html.

Table 1. Performance of ResNet-50 with XDN Engine

Optimization		Speedup	Accuracy
OPT-0	Baseline	1×	0.8439
OPT-1	OPT-A-1	4.48×	0.8439
	OPT-B-1	5.04×	0.8462
	OPT-C-1	5.29×	0.8191
OPT-2	OPT-A-2	4.67×	0.8441
	OPT-B-2	**7.44×**	**0.8455**
	OPT-C-2	7.62×	0.8203

OPT-1 denotes the optimized model by channel pruning and our XDN executor. OPT-A, OPT-B, OPT-C represent the model without pruning, the model with pruning of 17 layers which without accuracy loss, and the model with pruning of 25 layers which is faster but has slightly accuracy loss, respectively. The results of OPT-1 show that the efficiency of our channel pruning method.

OPT-2 denotes the optimized model by OPT-1 and layer fusion. The denotations of A, B, and C are similar to OPT-1. The results of OPT-2 show that the efficiency of our layer fusion strategy. As can be seen, OPT-B-2 is the best optimization without accuracy loss, which improves the performance by 7.44× over the baseline model with the original executor.

3.3   Analysis and Discussion

The experiment results prove the efficacy of our XDN engine. Firstly, OPT-A-1, which uses the original ResNet-50 model provided by the organizer, illustrates the efficiency of the XDN executor and auto-tuner. For the same model, the XDN executor is faster than original executor by using data preprocessing. The parallel hyper-parameters, such as the number of threads, are selected by an auto-tuning approach in the auto-tuner. Then, the performance improvement of the channel pruning optimizer can be proved by OPT-A, OPT-B, and OPT-C, which with different pruning degrees. As can be seen, the speed increases with more pruned layers. However, the pruned layers also lead to the accuracy loss. OPT-B is the best model without accuracy loss and OPT-C is the faster model which drops about 2% accuracy loss. Finally, OPT-2 confirms the efficacy of layer fusion optimizer. As can be seen, the performance of fused models (OPT-2) are better than the un-fused models (OPT-1).

We analyze the contributions of each optimization for OPT-B-2 performance, as shown in Table 2. The performance of first row is the baseline, which uses the original model and the default Cambricon Caffe executor, and the performance of last row the OPT-B-2, which is our best optimization method. As can be seen, each optimization method has necessity and effectiveness, which contributes the final performance in the XDN engine.

Table 2. Analysis of OPT-B-2 performance

Optimizations of XDN				Speedup
Pruning	Fusion	Data preprocess	Auto-tuning	
×	×	×	×	1×
✓	×	×	×	1.75×
✓	✓	×	×	2.72×
✓	✓	✓	×	3.03×
✓	✓	✓	✓	**7.44×**

4 Conclusion

In this paper, we presented an optimization and inference engine, namely XDN, for accelerating deep neural networks on Cambricon chips. The experimental results show that the optimized model can achieve high speedup without accuracy loss. The optimization methods of the XDN can not only be used to optimize residual neural networks, such as ResNet-50, but also other deep neural networks, such as GoogLeNet. In the future work, we plan to formalize our approach and test more deep neural network models.

Acknowledgment. This work is supported by the National Key R&D Program of China under Grant No. 2017YFB1003103, the Key Program of National Natural Science Foundation of China under Grant No. 61432016, and the Science Fund for Creative Research Groups of the National Natural Science Foundation of China under Grant No. 61521092.

References

1. Chen, T., et al.: Diannao: a small-footprint high-throughput accelerator for ubiquitous machine-learning. In: ACM Sigplan Notices, pp. 269–284. ACM (2014)
2. Chen, Y., Chen, T., Xu, Z., Sun, N., Temam, O.: Diannao family: energy-efficient hardware accelerators for machine learning. Communi. ACM **1**, 105–112 (2016)
3. Chen, Y., et al.: Dadiannao: a machine-learning supercomputer. In: Proceedings of the 47th Annual IEEE/ACM International Symposium on Microarchitecture, pp. 609–622. IEEE Computer Society (2014)
4. Deng, W., Wang, P., Wang, J., Li, C., Guo, M.: PSL: exploiting parallelism, sparsity and locality to accelerate matrix factorization on x86 platforms. In: International Symposium on Benchmarking, Measuring and Optimization (Bench 2019). Springer (2019)
5. Gao, W., et al.: AIBench: towards scalable and comprehensive datacenter AI benchmarking. In: Zheng, C., Zhan, J. (eds.) Bench 2018. LNCS, vol. 11459, pp. 3–9. Springer, Cham (2019). https://doi.org/10.1007/978-3-030-32813-9_1
6. Gao, W., et al.: AIBench: an industry standard internet service AI benchmark suite. arXiv preprint arXiv:1908.08998 (2019)

7. Girshick, R.: Fast R-CNN. In: Proceedings of the IEEE International Conference on Computer Vision, pp. 1440–1448 (2015)
8. Girshick, R., Donahue, J., Darrell, T., Malik, J.: Rich feature hierarchies for accurate object detection and semantic segmentation. In: Proceedings of the IEEE Conference on Computer Vision and Pattern Recognition, pp. 580–587 (2014)
9. Guo, K., Zeng, S., Yu, J., Wang, Y., Yang, H.: A survey of FPGA-based neural network inference accelerators. ACM Trans. Reconfigurable Technol. Syst. (TRETS) **12**(1), 1–26 (2019)
10. Hao, T., et al.: Edge AIBench: towards comprehensive end-to-end edge computing benchmarking. In: Zheng, C., Zhan, J. (eds.) Bench 2018. LNCS, vol. 11459, pp. 23–30. Springer, Cham (2019). https://doi.org/10.1007/978-3-030-32813-9_3
11. Hao, T., Zheng, Z.: The implementation and optimization of matrix decomposition based collaborative filtering task on x86 platform. In: International Symposium on Benchmarking, Measuring and Optimization (Bench 2019). Springer (2019)
12. He, K., Zhang, X., Ren, S., Sun, J.: Deep residual learning for image recognition. In: Proceedings of the IEEE Conference on Computer Vision and Pattern Recognition, pp. 770–778 (2016)
13. Hou, P., Yu, J., Miao, Y., Tai, Y., Wu, Y., Zhao, C.: RVTensor: a light-weight neural network inference framework based on the risc-v architecture. In: International Symposium on Benchmarking, Measuring and Optimization (Bench 2019). Springer (2019)
14. Jia, Y., et al.: Caffe: convolutional architecture for fast feature embedding. In: Proceedings of the 22nd ACM International Conference on Multimedia, pp. 675–678. ACM (2014)
15. Jiang, Z., et al.: HPC AI500: a benchmark suite for HPC AI systems. In: Zheng, C., Zhan, J. (eds.) Bench 2018. LNCS, vol. 11459, pp. 10–22. Springer, Cham (2019). https://doi.org/10.1007/978-3-030-32813-9_2
16. Krizhevsky, A., Hinton, G., et al.: Learning multiple layers of features from tiny images. Technical report, Citeseer (2009)
17. Krizhevsky, A., Sutskever, I., Hinton, G.E.: Imagenet classification with deep convolutional neural networks. In: Advances in Neural Information Processing Systems, pp. 1097–1105 (2012)
18. Li, J., Jiang, Z.: Performance analysis of cambricon MLU100. In: International Symposium on Benchmarking, Measuring and Optimization (Bench 2019). Springer (2019)
19. Luo, C., et al.: AIoT bench: towards comprehensive benchmarking mobile and embedded device intelligence. In: Zheng, C., Zhan, J. (eds.) Bench 2018. LNCS, vol. 11459, pp. 31–35. Springer, Cham (2019). https://doi.org/10.1007/978-3-030-32813-9_4
20. Ren, S., He, K., Girshick, R., Sun, J.: Faster R-CNN: Towards real-time object detection with region proposal networks. In: Advances in Neural Information Processing Systems, pp. 91–99 (2015)
21. Szegedy, C., et al.: Going deeper with convolutions. In: Proceedings of the IEEE Conference on Computer Vision and Pattern Recognition, pp. 1–9 (2015)
22. Xiong, X., Wen, X., Huang, C.: Improving RGB-D face recognition via transfer learning from a pretrained 2D network. In: Gao, W., et al. (eds.): Bench 2019, LNCS, vol. 12093, pp. 141–148. Springer, Cham (2019)

Performance Analysis of Cambricon MLU100

Jiansong Li[1,2] and Zihan Jiang[1,2(✉)]

[1] University of Chinese Academy of Sciences, Beijing, China
[2] Institute of Computing Technology, Chinese Academy of Sciences, Beijing, China
{lijiansong,jiangzihan}@ict.ac.cn

Abstract. In recent years, domain-specific hardware has brought significant performance improvements in deep learning (DL). Many frequently-used optimization techniques, such as data parallelism, model parallelism, data pipeline, weights pruning and quantization have been proposed to accelerate the inference phase of DL workloads. However, there is still lack of a comparison of these optimization techniques to show their performance difference on dedicated accelerators. This paper evaluates these frequently-used optimization techniques on a commercial accelerator, namely Cambricon MLU100. Considering the requirement of accuracy of DL nature, our metric not only measures the inference throughput but also has an accuracy constraint. Based on our analysis methodology and performance numbers, we have some key observations and implications that are valuable for the future DL hardware and software co-design. Furthermore, we explore the upper bound of MLU100 inference performance under the standard ResNet-50 model and CIFAR-10 dataset.

Keywords: Deep learning · Domain specific hardware · Performance analysis

1 Introduction

Deep learning (DL) has revolutionized many challenge AI domains, such as image recognition [14,23] and natural language processing [28,29]. However, the large quantity of numerical operations and parameters induced by deep neural networks (DNNs) pose a signicant challenge to general-purpose processors. To keep pace with the growing computational demand in modern DL workloads, hardware specialization has become a popular way [3,5,15,21,25]. Therefore, many dedicated accelerators are gaining popularity for their performance efficiency. They have been deployed in edge devices, servers, and datacenters. For example, Huawei Meta10 and P20 cellphones integrated Cambricon-1A DL processor

---

J. Li and Z. Jiang—Equal contribution.

© Springer Nature Switzerland AG 2020
W. Gao et al. (Eds.): Bench 2019, LNCS 12093, pp. 57–66, 2020.
https://doi.org/10.1007/978-3-030-49556-5_5

core [27]. Cambricon released MLU100 [1], which is a custom ASIC deployed in datacenter to accelerate the inference phase of morden DL workloads. And likewise, Google proposed Tensor Processing Unit to accelerate distributed machine learning [20].

Meanwhile, there are many frequently-used optimization techniques which enable the acceleration of the inference phase of modern DL workloads. These optimization techniques include but not limited to data parallelism, model parallelism, data pipeline, weights pruning and quantization [9,10,17,32]. The performance variance among these optimization techniques poses a challenge for the future DL hardware and software co-design. Design or select appropriate optimization techniques on the dedicated DL accelerators is important and not easy. Moreover, there is still lack of a comparison of these optimization techniques to show their performance variance on dedicated accelerators. In this paper, we evaluate these frequently-used optimization techniques on a commercial DL accelerator—Cambricon MLU100. To systematically evaluate the platform, we sweep these frequently-used optimization techniques as hyperparameters. We take the standard ResNet-50 [13] model and CIFAR-10 [22] dataset as our benchmark, which is provided by BenchCouncil 2019 International AI system and Algorithm Challenges (Cambricon Track[1]). Our workload is from AIBench [6,7], which is an AI benchmark for datacenter. The source code of AIBench is publicly available from http://www.benchcouncil.org/benchhub/AIBench (Sign up to get access). BenchCouncil organizes the international AI system challenges based on RISC-V [16], Cambricon chips [24,30] and X86 platforms [2,4,12], and the international 3D face recognition algorithm challenges [8,31]. BenchCouncil also provides AI benchmark for Edge [11], AIoT [26] and HPC [19]. Based on our analysis methodology and performance numbers, we conclude our observations and implications as following:

- Data pipeline and data parallelism significantly reduce the inference time while maintain the qualified accuracy.
- Compared with data parallelism, the impact of model parallelism on end to end inference throughput is not so significant.
- Weight pruning leads to a decline in accuracy although it may bring faster inference.
- High hardware throughput does not mean high end to end throughput.

Our observations and implications should help other researchers and practitioners to better the future DL hardware and software co-design. Furthermore, we explore the upper bound of MLU100 inference performance under the standard benchmark and reach an inference time of 384ms while preserving the target accuracy.

The rest of this paper is organized as follows: Sect. 2 introduces the background. Sect. 3 presents the evaluation methods and result is shown in Sect. 4. Section 5 concludes and discusses the future work.

---

[1] http://www.benchcouncil.org/competition/index.html.

2   Background

2.1   Hardware Characteristics

Cambricon MLU100 [1] is a DL accelerator deployed in datacenter to accelerate the inference phase of modern DL workloads. Its ISA is based on Cambricon [25]. The general architecture of MLU100 is shown in Fig. 1. Cambricon MLU100 is based on the multi-core architecture. It includes four channels connected via a network on chip (NOC). Each channel contains one DDR and eight computational cores. For example, Channel0 contains one DDR memory controller (DDR0) and eight computational cores, namely C0, C1, ..., C7. *DDR* is responsible for the storage of DNN model, input and output of DL workloads. While those computational cores perform the execution of DNN computation tasks.

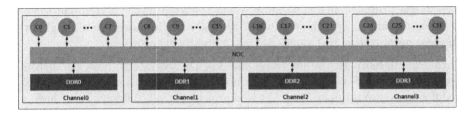

Fig. 1. Architectural information of Cambricon MLU100. Note that this picture is from Cambricon Caffe V0.9.7 documentation.

2.2   Software Stack

Figure 2 shows the software stacks of Cambricon MLU100. As we all know, Caffe [18] is an open-sourced software framework used for DL training and inference. It is written in C++ and widely adopted in research experiments and industry deployments. Cambricon MLU100 provides Caffe as its high-level programming framework. Application programmers can simply deploy their applications via Cambricon Caffe. CNRT is the runtime toolkit of Cambricon MLU100. It provides some common low-level utility APIs, such as device and memory management, kernel launch, task queue scheduler and etc. CNML is a wrapper of CNRT. It provides some helper functions for DNN models' loading and execution and common highly-tunned DNN operators at MLU100, e.g., convolution and pooling operators. Driver and kernel is responsible for the handling of memory management and interrupts of MLU100.

2.3   Optimization Techniques

Cambricon Caffe provides some common utilities for optimization, such as data parallelism, model parallelism and data pipeline. These optimization techniques

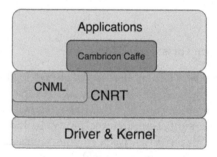

Fig. 2. Software Stacks of Cambricon MLU100. Note that this picture is from Cambricon Caffe V0.9.7 documentation.

usually improves the execution performance and preserves the final top-1 accuracy of DNN models during the inference phase. Besides, Cambricon Caffe supports weight pruning and quantization. While these optimization techniques usually have side effects over the final top-1 accuracy but improves the throughput. All these optimization techniques are not mutually exclusive.

Data Parallelism. In the inference phase of DL workloads, data parallelism means that given a CNN model, the input data is partitioned and assigned to different computational cores. As is shown in Fig. 3a, different cores have a complete copy of the DNN model. Each core simply gets a different part of the input data, and results from each core are somehow combined to get the final output. Data parallelism can greatly improve the throughout, since different parts of the input data can be executed concurrently.

Model Parallelism. As is shown in Fig. 3b, model parallelism means that different cores are responsible for the computations of different parts in a single network. For example, each layer in the neural network may be assigned to a different core. In the DL domain, we can take use of model parallelism by dividing a neural network into several subnets, and then putting each subnet into different cores of MLU100. Model parallelism can also improve the throughout, since for a single input, different parts of the DNN model can be executed concurrently.

Data Pipeline. In the inference phase of DL workloads, the input data flow will be fetched into host memory of CPUs from the disks, and then they will be uploaded into the device memory of MLU. Finally they will be fed to the computational cores of MLU. In this case, data pipeline can improve the workload balance of data prefetching, transfering and infeeding (Fig. 4).

Weights Pruning and Quantization. As the large amounts of synaptic weights incur intensive computation and memory accesses in the inference phase of DL workloads, researchers have proposed a number of effective techniques to explore the sparsity of DNN, including weight pruning, model compression and quantization [9,10,17,32]. Cambricon MLU100 tries to exploit the sparsity and irregularity of DNN models for the performance and power efficiency. It provides tools for weights pruning by setting the sparsity of the weights of input

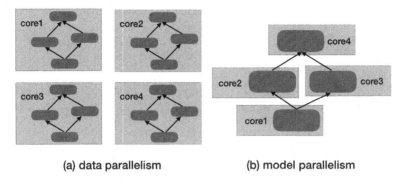

(a) data parallelism   (b) model parallelism

Fig. 3. Illustration of data parallelism and model parallelism.

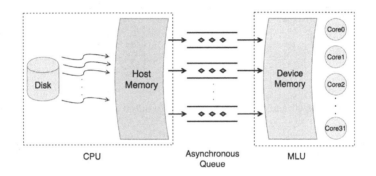

Fig. 4. Illustration of data pipeline. Note that to improve the throughput, we can launch multiple threads to read data from disks into the CPU memory and then dispatch the computational tasks into a queue that will be executed asynchronously. For those computational tasks within the same queue, they will be executed by their dispatching FIFO order. While those inter-queue tasks will be executed concurrently.

DNN model. Besides it provides tools to quantize the weights of DNN models into low-precision fixed-point numbers, e.g., INT8. We will discuss the effects of these optimization techniques over execution performance and top-1 accuracy in Sect. 4.

3   Evaluation Methods

Our experiments run on a heterogeneous environment. The host CPU is a 2.10 GHz Intel(R) Xeon(R) CPU E5-2620 v4 machine and 16 cores/32 threads and 20 MB of L3 cache per socket and 128 GB of memory, running Ubuntu 16.04.10 LTS and GCC 5.4.0. The device accelerator is Cambricon MLU100 [1]. For Cambricon MLU100, its device memory is 8GB, whose bandwidth is 102.4 GB/s. The peak performance of MLU100 is 16 TFLOPS.

Table 1. The ranges of the hyperparameters chosen in this paper.

Variable	Batch size	Data parallelism	Model parallelism	Thread number	Sparsity
Min	1	1	1	1	0.10
Max	1024	32	32	128	0.90
Inc	*2	*2	*2	*2	+0.01

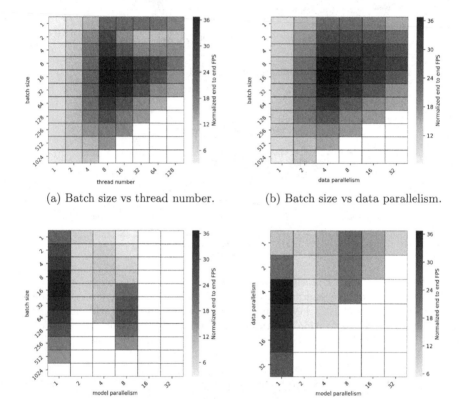

(a) Batch size vs thread number.   (b) Batch size vs data parallelism.

(c) Batch size vs model parallelism.   (d) Data parallelism vs model parallelism.

Fig. 5. The effects of batch size, thread number, data parallelism and model parallelism over execution performance. Note: the blank space means NaN. The FPS values are normalized to the speedup ratio over the end to end case where batch size, data parallelism, model parallelism and thread number are 1, 1, 1, 1 respectively.

Table 1 summarizes the hyperparameters chosen in this paper and how they are swept. Cambricon Caffe provides tools to set the *data parallelism* and *model parallelism* for the inference task. *Thread number* is the number of threads to be launched to read data from disks. *Batch size* is a hyperparameter that defines the number of image samples to be loaded in current iteration of inference tasks.

Sparsity is a hyperparameter that specifies the degree of zeros of the weights. For example, if its value is 0.3, that means 30% of the weights data will be zero. We evaluate the performance of Cambricon MLU100 under the standard ResNet50 [13] model and CIFAR-10 [22] datasets. The programming framework in this paper is Cambricon Caffe. For all workloads, we run 20 times and calculate the average.

4   Performance Numbers

All these hyperparameters in Table 1 are not mutually exclusive, we group these hyperparameters based on whether they affect the final top-1 accuracy. In this section, we discuss the effects of these hyperparameters over the final accuracy and execution performance.

4.1   Optimizations Preserving Accuracy

Hyperparameters like *batch size, thread number, data parallelism and model parallelism* usually have no side effects over the final top-1 accuracy. By sweeping the first four hyperparameters in Table 1, we find that the final top-1 accuracy of ResNet-50 over CIFAR-10 datasets at MLU100 preserves at 84.39%. In the terms of end to end FPS, the best configuration for the first four hyperparameters in Table 1 is 16, 4, 1, 8. To demonstrate the effects of *batch size, thread number, data parallelism and model parallelism* over execution performance, we choose this best configuration as guideline. For each case in Fig. 5, we sweep the corresponding two hyperparameters by fixing the other twos. As we can see from Fig. 5a and Fig. 5b, data pipeline and data parallelism significantly improve the end to end throughput. Meanwhile, we can see from Fig. 5c and Fig. 5d that the impact of model parallelism on end to end throughput is not so significant. For ResNet-50, best model parallelism is 1 in the terms of end to end throughput.

4.2   Optimizations Affecting Accuracy

As we mentioned in Sect. 4.1, the best configuration for the first four hyperparameters in Table 1 is 16, 4, 1 and 8 separately in the terms of end to end FPS. To demonstrate the effects of weight pruning over execution performance and top-1 accuracy, we choose this best configuration as guideline. We sweep the *sparsity* hyperparameter from 0.1 to 0.9 by fixing the other fours to the best configuration. As we can see from Fig. 6, weights pruning significantly affects the end to end and hardware throughput. In Fig. 6a, the hardware FPS increases when the input weight sparsity increases, since higher sparsity means more zeros in the weights data and higher throughput of the device accelerators. However, as is shown in Fig. 6b, with the increase of weights sparsity, the end to end FPS improvement slows down. That means high hardware throughput does not mean high end to end throughput, because of the load imbalance of data feeding between host CPUs and device accelerators. Besides, the top-1 accuracy drops

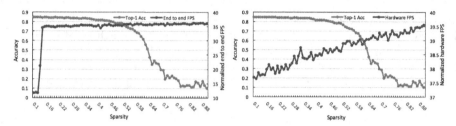

(a) Sparsity over accuracy and end to end FPS.

(b) Sparsity over accuracy and hardware FPS.

Fig. 6. The effects of weight pruning over execution performance and top-1 accuracy. Note that the x-axis is the sparsity of weights; the left y-axis is the global top-1 accuracy; the right y-axis is normalized FPS (frame per second), which can be treated as a proxy of FLOPS. The FPS values are normalized to the speedup ratio over the end to end case where batch size, data parallelism, model parallelism and thread number are 1, 1, 1, 1 respectively.

significantly with the increase of weights sparsity. In the real production environment, although weights pruning brings higher end to end throughput, a very low accuracy may not be acceptable. For the quantization optimization techiniques, the top-1 accuracy of MLU100 maintains at a qualified level.

5   Conclusion and Future Work

In this paper, we investigate many frequently-used optimization techniques including but not limited to *data parallelism, model parallelism, data pipeline, weights pruning* and *quantization*. And compare these optimization techniques to show their performance difference at throughput and top-1 accuracy on Cambricon MLU100. Based on our analysis methodology and performance numbers, we conclude our observations and implications which will help to better the future DL hardware and software co-design. As future work, we are planning to evaluate more DNN models on more DL accelerators.

Acknowledgement. This work is partially supported by the National Key R&D Program of China(under Grant No. 2017YFB1003103).

References

1. Cambricon: Cambricon MLU100. http://www.cambricon.com/index.php?c=page&id=20
2. Chen, M., Chen, T., Chen, Q.: HYGON-ALSWR: an efficient implementation of the ALS-WR algorithm on hygon x86 CPUS. In: Gao, W., et al. (eds.) International Symposium on Benchmarking, Measuring and Optimization (Bench 2019). LNCS, vol. 12093, pp. 116–122. Springer, Heidelberg (2020)

3. Chen, T., et al.: Diannao: a small-footprint high-throughput accelerator for ubiquitous machine-learning. In: ACM Sigplan Notices. vol. 49, pp. 269–284. ACM (2014)
4. Deng, W., Wang, P., Wang, J., Li, C., Guo, M.: PSL: exploiting parallelism, sparsity and locality to accelerate matrix factorization on x86 platforms. In: Gao, W., et al. (eds.) International Symposium on Benchmarking, Measuring and Optimization (Bench 2019). LNCS, vol. 12093, pp. 101–109. Springer, Heidelberg (2020)
5. Du, Z., et al.: Shidiannao: shifting vision processing closer to the sensor. In: ACM SIGARCH Computer Architecture News, vol. 43, pp. 92–104. ACM (2015)
6. Gao, W., et al.: AIBench: towards scalable and comprehensive datacenter AI benchmarking. In: Zheng, C., Zhan, J. (eds.) Bench 2018. LNCS, vol. 11459, pp. 3–9. Springer, Cham (2019). https://doi.org/10.1007/978-3-030-32813-9_1
7. Gao, W., et al.: AIBench: an industry standard internet service AI benchmark suite. arXiv preprint arXiv:1908.08998 (2019)
8. Gong, T., Huiqian, N.: An implementation of resnet on the classification of RGB-D images. In: Gao, W., et al. (eds.) International Symposium on Benchmarking, Measuring and Optimization (Bench 2019). LNCS, vol. 12093, pp. 149–155. Springer, Heidelberg (2020)
9. Han, S., et al.: EIE: efficient inference engine on compressed deep neural network (2016)
10. Han, S., Mao, H., Dally, W.J.: Deep compression: compressing deep neural networks with pruning, trained quantization and huffman coding (2016)
11. Hao, T., et al.: Edge AIBench: towards comprehensive end-to-end edge computing benchmarking. In: Zheng, C., Zhan, J. (eds.) Bench 2018. LNCS, vol. 11459, pp. 23–30. Springer, Cham (2019). https://doi.org/10.1007/978-3-030-32813-9_3
12. Hao, T., Zheng, Z.: The implementation and optimization of matrix decomposition based collaborative filtering task on the hygon x86 platform. In: Gao, W., et al. (eds.) International Symposium on Benchmarking, Measuring and Optimization (Bench 2019). LNCS, vol. 12093, pp. 110–115. Springer, Heidelberg (2020)
13. He, K., Zhang, X., Ren, S., Sun, J.: Deep residual learning for image recognition. CoRR abs/1512.03385 (2015). http://arxiv.org/abs/1512.03385
14. He, K., Zhang, X., Ren, S., Sun, J.: Deep residual learning for image recognition. In: Proceedings of the IEEE Conference on Computer Vision and Pattern Recognition, pp. 770–778 (2016)
15. Hennessy, J.L., Patterson, D.A.: A new golden age for computer architecture. Commun. ACM **62**(2), 48–60 (2019)
16. Hou, P., Yu, J., Miao, Y., Tai, Y., Wu, Y., Zhao, C.: RVTensor: a light-weight neural network inference framework based on the risc-v architecture. In: Gao, W., et al. (eds.) International Symposium on Benchmarking, Measuring and Optimization (Bench 2019). LNCS, vol. 12093, pp. 85–90. Springer, Heidelberg (2020)
17. Hubara, I., Courbariaux, M., Soudry, D., El-Yaniv, R., Bengio, Y.: Quantized neural networks: training neural networks with low precision weights and activations. J. Mach. Learn. Res. **18**(1), 6869–6898 (2017). http://dl.acm.org/citation.cfm?id=3122009.3242044
18. Jia, Y., et al.: Caffe: convolutional architecture for fast feature embedding. arXiv preprint arXiv:1408.5093 (2014)
19. Jiang, Z., et al.: HPC AI500: a benchmark suite for HPC AI systems. In: Zheng, C., Zhan, J. (eds.) Bench 2018. LNCS, vol. 11459, pp. 10–22. Springer, Cham (2019). https://doi.org/10.1007/978-3-030-32813-9_2

20. Jouppi, N.P., et al.: In-datacenter performance analysis of a tensor processing unit. In: Proceedings of the 44th Annual International Symposium on Computer Architecture, pp. 1–12. ISCA 2017, ACM, New York (2017). https://doi.org/10. 1145/3079856.3080246, https://doi.org/10.1145/3079856.3080246

21. Jouppi, N.P., et al.: In-datacenter performance analysis of a tensor processing unit. In: 2017 ACM/IEEE 44th Annual International Symposium on Computer Architecture (ISCA), pp. 1–12. IEEE (2017)

22. Krizhevsky, A.: The CIFAR-10 dataset. http://www.cs.toronto.edu/~kriz/cifar. html

23. Krizhevsky, A., Sutskever, I., Hinton, G.E.: Imagenet classification with deep convolutional neural networks. In: Advances in Neural Information Processing Systems, pp. 1097–1105 (2012)

24. Li, G., Wang, X., Ma, X., Liu, L., Feng, X.: XDN: towards efficient inference of residual neural networks on cambricon chips. In: Gao, W., et al. (eds.) International Symposium on Benchmarking, Measuring and Optimization (Bench 2019). LNCS, vol. 12093, pp. 51–56. Springer, Heidelberg (2020)

25. Liu, S., et al.: Cambricon: an instruction set architecture for neural networks. In: ACM SIGARCH Computer Architecture News, vol. 44, pp. 393–405. IEEE Press (2016)

26. Luo, C., et al.: AIoT bench: towards comprehensive benchmarking mobile and embedded device intelligence. In: Zheng, C., Zhan, J. (eds.) Bench 2018. LNCS, vol. 11459, pp. 31–35. Springer, Cham (2019). https://doi.org/10.1007/978-3-030-32813-9_4

27. Medium: Huawei 7nm Kirin 810 Beats Snapdragon 855 and Kirin 980 on AI Benchmark Test. https://medium.com/syncedreview/huawei-7nm-kirin-810-beats-snapdragon-855-and-kirin-980-on-ai-benchmark-test-af31996fb10e

28. Sutskever, I., Vinyals, O., Le, Q.V.: Sequence to sequence learning with neural networks. In: Advances in Neural Information Processing Systems, pp. 3104–3112 (2014)

29. Vaswani, A., et al.: Attention is all you need. In: Advances in Neural Information Processing Systems, pp. 5998–6008 (2017)

30. Wang, Y., Zeng, C., Li, C.: Exploring the performance bound of cambricon accelerator in end-to-end inference scenario. In: Gao, W., et al. (eds.) International Symposium on Benchmarking, Measuring and Optimization (Bench 2019). LNCS, vol. 12093, pp. 67–74. Springer, Heidelberg (2020)

31. Xiong, X., Wen, X., Huang, C.: Improving RGB-D face recognition via transfer learning from a pretrained 2D network. In: Gao, W., et al. (eds.) International Symposium on Benchmarking, Measuring and Optimization (Bench 2019). LNCS, vol. 12093, pp. 141–148. Springer, Heidelberg (2020)

32. Zhang, S., et al.: Cambricon-x: an accelerator for sparse neural networks. In: The 49th Annual IEEE/ACM International Symposium on Microarchitecture, pp. 20:1–20:12. MICRO-49, IEEE Press, Piscataway (2016). http://dl.acm.org/citation.cfm?id=3195638.3195662

Exploring the Performance Bound of Cambricon Accelerator in End-to-End Inference Scenario

Yifan Wang[1,2(✉)], Chundian Li[1,2], and Chen Zeng[1,2]

[1] SKL of Computer Architecture, Institute of Computing Technology, CAS,
Beijing, China
{wangyifan2014,lichundian,zengchen}@ict.ac.cn
[2] University of Chinese Academy of Sciences, Beijing, China

Abstract. Deep learning algorithms have become pervasive in a broad range of industrial application scenarios. DianNao/Cambricon family is a set of energy-efficient hardware accelerators for machine learning, especially for deep learning, covering from edge embedded devices to cloud data centers. However, in the real application scenario, the complicated software stack and the extra overhead (memory copy) hinder the full exploitation of the accelerator performance. In this paper, we try to explore the performance bound of Cambricon accelerator MLU100 in end-to-end deep learning inference scenarios (from data/model load to inference results store). We leverage the offline model to bypass the general deep learning framework, use the multiple threads programming to fully exploit the parallelism of the multi-core accelerator and apply specific data structure to decrease the memory copy overhead. The evaluation results show that, for RetNet-50 on CIFAR-10 dataset, our optimization methods are 32.09× faster than the baseline of the optimized batch size (64), and achieve 85% of the performance upper-bound on the Cambricon MLU100 board.

Keywords: DianNao/Cambricon accelerator · End-to-End Optimization · RetNet-50 on CIFAR-10

1 Introduction

Deep learning algorithms have become pervasive in a broad range of industrial application scenarios, such as autonomous driving, natural language processing, and advertisement recommendation. To meet the explosive growth of deep learning application requirements, many machine learning accelerators have been designed both from the academic and the industry, such as DianNao/Cambricon accelerators [3,4], Google TPU systolic architecture [15], and IBM TrueNorth neuromorphic processor [19].

© Springer Nature Switzerland AG 2020
W. Gao et al. (Eds.): Bench 2019, LNCS 12093, pp. 67–74, 2020.
https://doi.org/10.1007/978-3-030-49556-5_6

These hardware accelerators achieved high performance to process machine learning workloads in ideal evaluation environments. However, in the real application environments, developers usually utilize the hardware accelerators via machine learning frameworks, which are too high-level to handle the specific operator-level optimization on hardware [2,24], hindering the full exploitation of the accelerator performance. To address this problem, we focus on a specific end-to-end inference scenario, using a Cambricon MLU100 board [1] to process the image classification task over 10,000 images. This task is the Cambricon track on BenchCouncil AI Challenges, the other three tracks are AI system challenge of RISC-V [13] and X86 platform [7], and 3D face recognition algorithm challenge [23]. AIBench provides the workloads, datasets, and the baseline for the AI challenges [9,10]. The source code of AIBench is publicly available from http://www.benchcouncil.org/benchhub/AIBench/ (Sign up to get access).

To explore the performance bound of the Cambricon board over the specific end-to-end inference scenario, we adopt three optimization methods. Firstly, we use the serializing tool provided by Cambricon to generate a offline model, which bypasses the deep learning framework, accessing the hardware accelerator via runtime library. Secondly, we use the multiple threads programming to maximize the memory bandwidth of the external DRAM on the Cambricon board, fully exploiting the parallelism of the multi-core accelerator. Thirdly, we convert the image data to the expected input data structure of the Cambricon chip to decrease the memory copy overhead. According to evaluation results, our optimization methods are 32.09× faster than the baseline of the optimized batch size (64), and achieve 85% of performance upper-bound on the Cambricon MLU100 board.

The rest of this paper is organized as follows. In Sect. 2, we introduce the background. Section 3 presents our optimization methods. Section 4 illustrates the evaluation results. Finally, we conclude our work in Sect. 5.

2   Background

In this section, we briefly introduce the specific deep learning task, including the hardware accelerator, the neural network model and the input dataset.

DianNao Family and Cambricon MLU100 Accelerator. DianNao [3] is a high-throughput and energy-efficient accelerator for the deep neural network proposed in 2014. A large neural network can be split into small workloads to reuse the NFU (Neural Functional Unit) and SRAM buffers efficiently, so DianNao can execute neural networks on different scales. To support more machine learning algorithms and application scenarios, they have proposed various accelerator architectures, such as PuDianNao [18] for polyvalent machine learning algorithms and ShiDianNao [8] for computer vision algorithms on edge. Cambricon MLU100 is a commercial product based on DaDianNao [5] architecture, which is a multi-core supercomputer for machine learning. Cambricon MLU100 boards have been widely deployed in cloud servers to accelerate numerous machine learning applications.

Residual Neural Network and CIFAR-10 Dataset. Residual Network (ResNet) [12] is a classic deep neural network for image classification, which has been adopted in a lot of deep learning benchmarks as the evaluation workload [6,10,11]. ResNet leverages the residual blocks to address the degradation problem and achieves the lowest error on the ImageNet test set in 2015, and wins the ILSVRC classification competition [20] in 2015. And the deep residual learning framework has been one of the main trends in designing the deep neural networks [14,21,22]. CIFAR-10 dataset consists of 60,000 32 × 32 colour and labeled images in 10 classes [16], which is a standard dataset to evaluate the algorithm performance [12,17]. And CIFAR-10 also has been used in lots of deep learning benchmarks as the standard input [6,10].

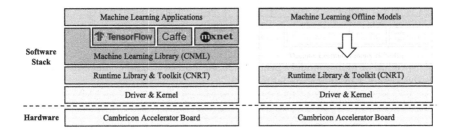

Fig. 1. Online (left) and offline (right) deployment.

3 Design and Implementation

In this section, we present the detailed optimization methods of the end-to-end inference workload mentioned above. Meantime, we illustrate the optimization results for each step.

3.1 Offline Model

Cambricon accelerators provide two programming libraries for users, the CNML (Cambricon Neuware Machine Learning) library and the CNRT (Cambricon Neuware Runtime) library. These two libraries allow developers to leverage the machine learning acceleration engine in the Cambricon board with the user-friendly programming framework and interface.

The libraries support online and offline approaches to deploy the machine learning algorithms on Cambricon accelerators, as shown in Fig. 1. The online method is a traditional way to deploy the machine learning model. The model is managed by the CNML framework, or other general machine learning frameworks (e.g. Caffe and TensorFlow). The offline method usually serializes the compiled computing graph and operators to a new file, generating a new model file (offline model), which can be loaded directly by the CNRT library. The online or offline approach decides whether the system will load the machine learning framework when executing the machine learning applications. The offline method makes the machine learning model bypass the machine learning framework and achieves higher performance than the traditional way in the end-to-end inference scenario.

The performance of the offline deployment method is shown in Fig. 2. Compared with the online deployment method, the offline method is 1.58× faster on average and 1.52× faster on the optimal bath size (64).

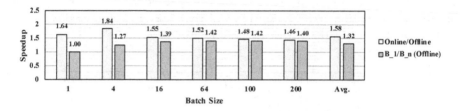

Fig. 2. Speedup of offline model optimization method over online, and $batch\_size = n$ over $batch\_size = 1$ in offline model method.

3.2   Multiple Threads

The Cambricon MLU100 provides n machine learning acceleration cores and m memory controllers (channels), $n \bmod m = 0$. Each channel manages an external DRAM and creates a hardware-queue (HQ) in the OS kernel. For a single thread program, the n acceleration cores access the data from 1 external DRAM, which will cause the bandwidth contention and degrade the accelerator performance. To exploit the parallelism of the memory controller, we create a m-thread program and bind each thread to a different channel (hardware-queue in OS), to maximize the data access bandwidth between the acceleration cores and external DRAMs.

There are two methods to leverage multiple acceleration cores on MLU100, model parallel and data parallel. The model is partitioned into n cores in the model parallel method, and the n cores will process 1 image collaboratively. In the data parallel method, each core is allowed to access the whole model, and the n cores will process n images concurrently and independently. The model parallelism introduces extra overhead because of the intermediate result copy and fusion. To exploit the parallelism of the multi-core, we set model parallelism to 1 and data parallelism to n (number of cores).

As shown in Fig. 3 after exploiting the parallelism of the MLU100, compared with the single-thread method, the parallel programming method is 11.83× faster on average and 12.17× faster on the optimal bath size (64).

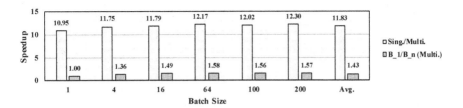

Fig. 3. Speedup of multiple-thread optimization method over single-thread, and $batch\_size = n$ over $batch\_size = 1$ in multiple-thread method.

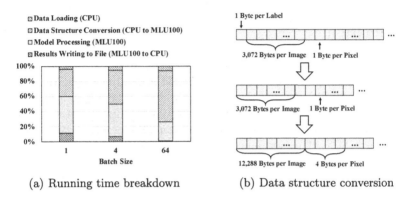

(a) Running time breakdown   (b) Data structure conversion

Fig. 4. Running time breakdown and data structure conversion.

3.3 Data Structure Conversion

To fully understand the bottleneck of the program, we collect the running time of each step in the program, and the running time breakdown is shown in Fig. 4(a). While leveraging the two optimization methods mentioned above, the data loading, model processing, and results writing to file only cost 6.06%, 25.74%, and 0.81% of the total processing time, respectively, while the image data type conversion costs 67.39% of the total time. The data structure conversion overhead is caused by the mismatch problem. The loaded images are formatted according to the data structure in the CIFAR-10 dataset, each image has 1 byte label data and 3,072 bytes pixel data. However, the MLU100 takes contiguous address space of the image data as the input, and each pixel is represented by a `float32` value. The data type conversion process is illustrated in Fig. 4(b).

To reduce the extra processing time caused by the data type mismatch, we reformat the image data according to the MLU100 input data structure, and the performance is shown in Fig. 5. After eliminating the data type mismatch problem, the performance is 1.60× faster on average and 1.73× faster on the optimal bath size (64).

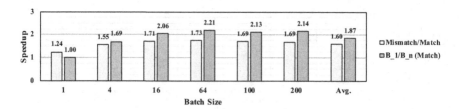

Fig. 5. Speedup of data structure matching optimization method over mismatch, and $batch\_size = n$ over $batch\_size = 1$ in matching method.

4 Evaluation

As we presented above, our optimization methods are 32.09× faster than the baseline. The peak performance of Cambricon MLU100 board is 64 TeraFlops (half-precision, 16-bit) [1], and the I/O bandwidth of the 4 channels PCIe is 8 GB/s, the Roofline Model of Cambricon MLU100 board is illustrated in Fig. 6. The Opt.3 is the final performance after we adopt three optimization methods, which achieve 85% of performance upper-bound on the Cambricon MLU100 board.

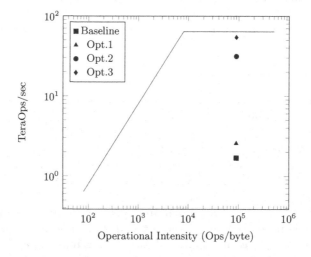

Fig. 6. Roofline model of Cambricon MLU100 board

5 Conclusion

Even though some hardware accelerators are energy-efficient in micro-benchmarks, a lot of potential is under the performance upper-bound while the end-to-end applications are executed on accelerators. To explore the performance bound of Cambricon board over the specific end-to-end inference scenario, we adopt three optimization approaches, while reducing the memory copy overhead and speeding up by utilizing better parallelism. The evaluation results show our optimization methods reveal 32.09× faster than the baseline on the optimal batch size (64). In addition, we achieve 85% of performance upper-bound of the Cambricon MLU100 board.

References

1. Cambricon Technologies: Cambricon MLU100 (2019). https://en.wikichip.org/wiki/cambricon/mlu/mlu100/
2. Chen, T., et al.: TVM: an automated end-to-end optimizing compiler for deep learning. In: 13th USENIX Symposium on Operating Systems Design and Implementation (OSDI), pp. 578–594 (2018)
3. Chen, T., et al.: DianNao: a small-footprint high-throughput accelerator for ubiquitous machine-learning. In: Proceedings of the 19th International Conference on Architectural Support for Programming Languages and Operating Systems (ASPLOS), pp. 269–284. ACM (2014)
4. Chen, Y., Chen, T., Xu, Z., Sun, N., Temam, O.: DianNao family: energy-efficient hardware accelerators for machine learning. Commun. ACM **11**, 105–112 (2016)
5. Chen, Y., et al.: DaDianNao: a machine-learning supercomputer. In: Proceedings of the 47th Annual IEEE/ACM International Symposium on Microarchitecture (MICRO), pp. 609–622. IEEE (2014)
6. Coleman, C., et al.: DAWNBench: an end-to-end deep learning benchmark and competition. Training **100**(101), 102 (2017)
7. Deng, W., Wang, P., Wang, J., Li, C., Guo, M.: PSL: exploiting parallelism, sparsity and locality to accelerate matrix factorization on x86 platforms. In: Gao, W., Zhan, J., Fox, G., Lu, X., Stanzione, D. (eds.) Bench 2019. LNCS, vol. 12093, pp. 101–109. Springer, Cham (2019)
8. Du, Z., et al.: ShiDianNao: shifting vision processing closer to the sensor. In: Proceedings of the 42nd International Symposium on Computer Architecture (ISCA), pp. 92–104. ACM (2015)
9. Gao, W., et al.: AIBench: towards scalable and comprehensive datacenter AI benchmarking. In: Zheng, C., Zhan, J. (eds.) Bench 2018. LNCS, vol. 11459, pp. 3–9. Springer, Cham (2019). https://doi.org/10.1007/978-3-030-32813-9_1
10. Gao, W., et al.: AIBench: an industry standard internet service AI benchmark suite. arXiv preprint arXiv:1908.08998 (2019)
11. Gao, W., et al.: Data motifs: a lens towards fully understanding big data and ai workloads. In: The 27th International Conference on Parallel Architectures and Compilation Techniques (PACT) (2018)
12. He, K., Zhang, X., Ren, S., Sun, J.: Deep residual learning for image recognition. In: Proceedings of the IEEE Conference on Computer Vision and Pattern Recognition (CVPR), pp. 770–778. IEEE (2016)
13. Hou, P., Yu, J., Miao, Y., Tai, Y., Wu, Y., Zhao, C.: RVTensor: a light-weight neural network inference framework based on the RISC-V architecture. In: Gao, W., Zhan, J., Fox, G., Lu, X., Stanzione, D. (eds.) Bench 2019. LNCS, vol. 12093, pp. 85–90. Springer, Cham (2019)
14. Huang, G., Liu, Z., Van Der Maaten, L., Weinberger, K.Q.: Densely connected convolutional networks. In: Proceedings of the IEEE Conference on Computer Vision and Pattern Recognition (CVPR), pp. 4700–4708 (2017)

15. Jouppi, N.P., et al.: In-datacenter performance analysis of a tensor processing unit. In: Proceedings of the 44th Annual International Symposium on Computer Architecture (ISCA), pp. 1–12. IEEE (2017)
16. Krizhevsky, A.: Learning multiple layers of features from tiny images. University of Toronto, Technical report (2009)
17. Krizhevsky, A., Sutskever, I., Hinton, G.E.: Imagenet classification with deep convolutional neural networks. In: Advances in Neural Information Processing Systems (NeurIPS), pp. 1097–1105 (2012)
18. Liu, S., et al.: Cambricon: an instruction set architecture for neural networks. In: Proceedings of the 43rd International Symposium on Computer Architecture (ISCA), pp. 393–405. IEEE (2016)
19. Merolla, P.A., et al.: A million spiking-neuron integrated circuit with a scalable communication network and interface. Science **345**(6197), 668–673 (2014)
20. Russakovsky, O., et al.: Imagenet large scale visual recognition challenge. Int. J. Comput. Vis. **115**(3), 211–252 (2015). https://doi.org/10.1007/s11263-015-0816-y
21. Sandler, M., Howard, A., Zhu, M., Zhmoginov, A., Chen, L.C.: MobileNetV2: inverted residuals and linear bottlenecks. In: Proceedings of the IEEE Conference on Computer Vision and Pattern Recognition (CVPR), pp. 4510–4520 (2018)
22. Xie, S., Girshick, R., Dollár, P., Tu, Z., He, K.: Aggregated residual transformations for deep neural networks. In: Proceedings of the IEEE Conference on Computer Vision and Pattern Recognition (CVPR), pp. 1492–1500 (2017)
23. Xiong, X., Wen, X., Huang, C.: Improving RGB-D face recognition via transfer learning from a pretrained 2D network. In: Gao, W., Zhan, J., Fox, G., Lu, X., Stanzione, D. (eds.) Bench 2019. LNCS, vol. 12093, pp. 141–148. Springer, Cham (2019)
24. Zhao, Y., et al.: Cambricon-F: machine learning computers with fractal von Neumann architecture. In: Proceedings of the 46th International Symposium on Computer Architecture (ISCA), pp. 788–801. ACM (2019)

Improve Image Classification by Convolutional Network on Cambricon

Peng He[1,2], Ge Chen[1,2], Kai Deng[1,2], Ping Yao[1(✉)], and Li Fu[1]

[1] Institute of Computing Technology, Chinese Academy of Sciences,
HaiDian, Beijing 110108, China
{hepeng18s,chenge18s,dengkai19s,yaoping,fuli}@ict.ac.cn
[2] University of Chinese Academy of Sciences, Shijingshan, Beijing 14430, China

Abstract. Cambricon provides us with a complete intelligent application system, how to use this system for deep learning algorithms development is a challenging issue. In this paper, we exploit, evaluate and validate the performance of the ResNet101 image classification network on Cambricon with Cambricon Caffe framework, demonstrating the availability and ease of use of this system. Experiments with various operational modes and the processes of model inference show, the optimal running time of a common ResNet101 network that classifies the CIFAR-10 dataset on Cambricon is nearly three times faster than the baseline. We hope that this work will provide a simple baseline for further exploration of the performance of convolutional neural network on Cambricon.

Keywords: Cambricon · Convolutional neural network · ResNet101

1 Introduction

Image classification is a fundamental task in the field of computer vision that labels a picture to distinguish different categories visually and concisely. Classification task can also guide the development of other tasks: object detection [11], segmentation [15] and many more, such as instance segmentation, which performs per-pixel labeling of pictures at instance level. Therefore, since ResNet [18] was proposed as an effective image classification network at 2015, superior performance has enabled it to be applied as a backbone network to almost all other tasks [11,17,31]. Whether the ResNet network can run normally should be regarded as the basic standard to test whether an intelligent application system can run robustly.

As the calculation of neural network is a quite computationally intensive process, the computing capability of traditional CPU is far from meeting current computational complexity. Even the GPU is not designed originally specifically

---

P. He and G. Chen—Equal contribution.

W. Gao et al. (Eds.): Bench 2019, LNCS 12093, pp. 75–82, 2020.
https://doi.org/10.1007/978-3-030-49556-5_7

for artificial intelligence algorithms. The Cambricon chip is the first deep learning processor in the world as far as we know. It uses the hardware's digital logic structure, NFU (Neural Functional Units), to simulate the neural network connection structure to execute multiplication, addition, activation and other operations [7]. With ASIC (Application Specific Integrated Circuit) mode, which reduces a lot of unnecessary logic functions [22], Cambricon is extremely fast and consumes very low power, making it a superior alternative to GPU in video parsing, autonomous driving, and many more other real-world scenarios.

This work is implementing the ResNet101 classification network based on Cambricon with CIFAR-10 dataset [8]. By trying various operational modes, we find out the optimal operation strategy and running time to verify the performance and efficiency of Cambricon.

This year, joint with Cambricon, China RISC-V alliance, Sugon, and Intellifusion, BenchCouncil organizes four challenge tracks, including international AI system challenge based on RISC-V [19], international AI system challenge based on Cambricon chip [25,26,34], international AI system Challenge based on X86 platform [2,6,14] and international 3D face recognition algorithm callenge [12,35]. Notably, we won the third prize on the Cambricon Track of BenchCouncil Challenges.

2   Related Work

Image Classification. Image classification, a fundamental problem in computer vision, can be described as categorizing images into one of several predefined classes [1]. It forms the basis for other computer vision tasks such as localization [37], detection [11,16,27,28,31], and segmentation [15,17,32]. Traditionally, handcrafted features can be extracted from images using feature descriptors for the purpose of classification. The major disadvantage of this approach is that the accuracy of the classification result is profoundly dependent on the design of the feature extraction stage. In recent years, deep learning has developed to be a convenient, effective and robust tool to extract features from images, audio, etc, which does not require handcrafted features. Especially, DCNNs for image classification tasks achieved state-of-the-art results in the ImageNet Large Scale Visual Recognition Challenge since 2012 [1].

ResNet. In theory, the performance of the neural network should be positively related to the depth of the network, because the deeper the network, the more parameters it has, the more complicated it is. But the early experimenters observe that as the number of network layers increases, the model accuracy will rise first and then reach saturation, and continuing to increase layers will result in a decrease in accuracy sharply, which we called degradation [18]. ResNet's [17,18,24,33] proposal solves this problem very well. By introducing the residual network structure, it can make the network very deep, at the same time the final classification result is also very satisfactory. In this case, the depth of the network can be extended to tens, hundreds or even thousands of layers, providing the feasibility of extracting and classifying high-level semantic features. ResNet made a stunning appearance in the ILSVRC2015 competition, which raised the network depth to 152 layers, reducing the error rate to 3.57. In terms of image recognition error rate and network depth, it has greatly been improved compared with previous models. This also makes the network become the backbone network of the later convolutional neural network model, and many models with excellent performance subsequently are transformed on the basis of ResNet [11, 15–17, 27, 31].

Cambricon. CPU and GPU are designed to handle many different computing tasks originally. They have multiple functional logic units inside, which are widely applicable. But for a computationally intensive computing task, they are not so efficient [4, 5]. Current artificial intelligence algorithm mainly includes two aspects: convolutional neural network and recurrent neural network. From the point of view of decomposition, they are composed of a lot of matrix multiplication or tensor element-by-element multiplication, so the CPU will no longer be suitable for this algorithm, and the GPU will be better, but there is still a lot of room for improvement. Since the introduction of the Cambricon chip, it has sparked a wave of research and application of deep learning accelerators. It is designed for the local and computational characteristics of artificial intelligence algorithms and neural network models to achieve better performance acceleration ratio and computing capability consumption ratio. On this basis, the application scenarios targeted by the deep learning chip are further divided, so the high-performance computing architecture DaDianNao [7] for the server side, the ShiDianNao [3] for the edge-end device application scenario, the PuDianNao [29] for the more generalized machine learning algorithms, all appeared. And the Cambricon instruction set [36] for a wider range of machine learning accelerators and the Cambricon-X [20] for hardware acceleration using data sparsity have been proposed for better use of these architectures.

3 Experiments

3.1 Multiple Operating Modes of Cambricon

To support the Cambricon machine learning processor, Cambricon modifies the open source deep learning programming framework Caffe, and adds some functions like offline, multi-core forward inference and so on, to form Cambricon Caffe. It is compatible with native Caffe's python/C++ programming interface and the native Caffe network model [23]. Besides, it provides a convenient interface to run various types of deep learning applications and a series of APIs provided by the Cambricon Neuware Machine Learning Library (CNML) for efficient inference. CNML interacts with the Cambricon machine learning processor by calling the Cambricon Neuware Runtime Library (CNRT) and drivers. Applications can also call CNML or CNRT directly to use the Cambricon Machine Learning Processor [36].

In the Cambricon operating environment, a variety of different programming models are supported. Firstly, the Cambricon machine learning processor is a multi-core processor architecture with 32 cores and supports two parallel modes: model parallelism and data parallelism. The setting of two parallelism parameters is based on the specific model. Reasonable model parallelism and data parallelism can optimize the performance of MLU (Machine Learning Unit). The MLU also supports multi-card mode, such as multiple MLU cards installed on a single server, allowing the model to run on different cards or distributing the calculations to multiple MLU cards. MLU supports two different modes of operating mode: online and offline. Online mode refers to the mode that depends on the Cambricon Caffe framework to run, and offline mode refers to the mode that uses the runtime function interface directly from the framework.

3.2 Design Details

In this work, our main concern is the running time of the model, that is, selecting the most suitable model settings, and completing the inference process of the ResNet101 classification model on the CIFAR-10 dataset in the shortest time. As we mentioned above, in order to speed up the inference process of the model, we try to select multi-core, multi-card, offline operation mode.

First of all, for programming model, we can choose multi-core and multi-card. The multi-core is determined by model parallelism and data parallelism. MLU provides us with up to 32 cores. The degree of parallelism of model and data decides the number of cores used. We use grid computing to choose the best combination of model parallelism and data parallelism for this problem. On the other hand, the BenchCouncil [9,10,13,21,30] provides only one MLU in the runtime environment, we can't try the multi-card programming process. The source code of AIBench is publicly available from http://www.benchcouncil. org/benchhub/AIBench/ (Sign up to get access). In terms of the model's operating mode, the online process depends on the operation of the Cambricon Caffe framework, while the offline mode is independent of the framework, so we choose the offline mode. The final result of the operation is shown in the Fig. 1.

3.3 Results in Challenge

In the subsequent experiments, we test model inference on pre-trained ResNet101 with the CIFAR-10 dataset. The three parameters that need to be adjusted are: parallelism of the model, parallelism of the data, and number of threads. The degree of parallelism of model and data together determines the number of cores used by the model. Because BenchCouncil provides us with a total of 32 cores, single card MLU, in order to get the best inference time, we use the most number of cores. In addition, we did some experiments to find out the influence of threads on the speed of model inference. In order to fully use the 32 cores, our model parallel number and data parallel number will be set as 2/16, 4/8, 8/4, 16/2 and

32/1 in order. Meanwhile, we select 2, 4, 6, ..., 14, 16 to test the optimal number of threads. The experimental results are shown in Fig. 1. According to it, we can summarize as follow:

With the same degree of parallelism, the more threads, the longer the time of model inference: we believe that when the degree of parallelism of the model and the data both are 1, a total of 32 threads can be created, so the degree of parallelism and threads are mutually exclusive. Now, in order to maximize the number of cores, the degree of parallelism is also set to a maximum of 32, and then increase the number of threads, which will cause resource preemption among different threads, reducing the speed of reasoning.

Under the specific number of threads, when the model parallelism and data parallelism are 4 and 8, model inference time is the shortest, and it can be considered that the performance matching of the two factors is optimal.

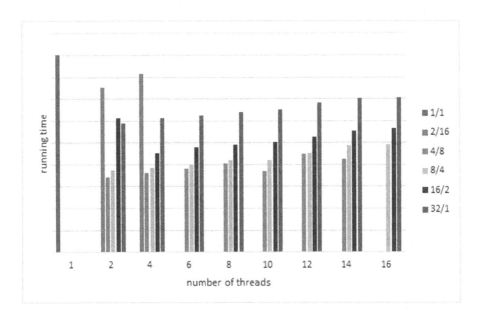

Fig. 1. Illustration of results of model inference under the influence of three factors. The abscissa represents the number of threads, and the ordinate represents the time of model inference. Different colors are different model and data parallelism matching. For example, 2/16 indicates that the model parallelism is 2 and the data parallelism is 16. Specifically, the first one is our baseline. Under certain thread numbers, the combination of different parallelism will cause MLU out of memory. For example, in 16 threads, if 2/16 is used, the memory will overflow, we don't display these results in this figure. (Color figure online)

4   Conclusion

In order to solve the problem of image classification on Cambricon, we find out a model setting that is most suitable for the execution of ResNet101 network, and adopt the multicore and multithreading method to transplant the network to the Cambricon operating environment for faster speed. Our transplantation is effective and efficient. We also record the differences among these combinations, and hope the implementation details publicly available can help the community adopt these useful strategies for object detection, scene parsing and semantic segmentation and advance related techniques.

Acknowledgements. The authors would like to thank BenchCouncil for BenchCouncil Testbed. The whole team is supported by Strategic Priority Research Program of the Chinese Academy of Sciences (Grant No. XDA19020400), Equipment Pre-Research Fund (Grant No. 61403120405, Grant No. 6141B07090131) and Spaceborne Equipment Pre-Research Project (Grant No. 305030704).

References

1. Bergstra, J., et al.: Theano: a CPU and GPU math compiler in python. In: Proceedings of the 9th Python in Science Conference, vol. 1, pp. 3–10 (2010)
2. Chen, M., Chen, T., Chen, Q.: An efficient implementation of the ALS-WR algorithm on x86 CPUs. In: Gao, W., et al. (eds.) Bench 2019. LNCS, vol. 12093, pp. 116–122. Springer, Cham (2020)
3. Chen, Y., Chen, T., Xu, Z., Sun, N., Temam, O.: DianNao family: energy-efficient hardware accelerators for machine learning. Commun. ACM **59**(11), 105–112 (2016)
4. Chen, Y., et al.: DaDianNao: a machine-learning supercomputer. In: Proceedings of the 47th Annual IEEE/ACM International Symposium on Microarchitecture, pp. 609–622. IEEE Computer Society (2014)
5. Coates, A., Huval, B., Wang, T., Wu, D., Catanzaro, B., Andrew, N.: Deep learning with cots HPC systems. In: International Conference on Machine Learning, pp. 1337–1345 (2013)
6. Deng, W., Wang, P., Wang, J., Li, C., Guo, M.: PSL: exploiting parallelism, sparsity and locality to accelerate matrix factorization on x86 platforms. In: Gao, W., et al. (eds.) Bench 2019. LNCS, vol. 12093, pp. 101–109. Springer, Cham (2020)
7. Fan, X., Li, H., Cao, W., Wang, L.: DT-CGRA: dual-track coarse-grained reconfigurable architecture for stream applications. In: 2016 26th International Conference on Field Programmable Logic and Applications (FPL), pp. 1–9. IEEE (2016)
8. Farabet, C., Martini, B., Corda, B., Akselrod, P., Culurciello, E., LeCun, Y.: NeuFlow: a runtime reconfigurable dataflow processor for vision. In: CVPR Workshops, pp. 109–116 (2011)
9. Gao, W., et al.: AIBench: towards scalable and comprehensive datacenter AI benchmarking. In: Zheng, C., Zhan, J. (eds.) Bench 2018. LNCS, vol. 11459, pp. 3–9. Springer, Cham (2019). https://doi.org/10.1007/978-3-030-32813-9_1
10. Gao, W., et al.: AIbench: an industry standard internet service AI benchmark suite. arXiv preprint arXiv:1908.08998 (2019)

11. Girshick, R., Donahue, J., Darrell, T., Malik, J.: Rich feature hierarchies for accurate object detection and semantic segmentation. In: Proceedings of the IEEE Conference on Computer Vision and Pattern Recognition, pp. 580–587 (2014)
12. Gong, T., Niu, H.: An implementation of ResNet on the classification of RGB-D images. In: Gao, W., et al. (eds.) Bench 2019. LNCS, vol. 12093, pp. 149–155. Springer, Cham (2020)
13. Hao, T., et al.: Edge AIBench: towards comprehensive end-to-end edge computing benchmarking. In: Zheng, C., Zhan, J. (eds.) Bench 2018. LNCS, vol. 11459, pp. 23–30. Springer, Cham (2019). https://doi.org/10.1007/978-3-030-32813-9_3
14. Hao, T., Zheng, Z.: The implementation and optimization of matrix decomposition based collaborative filtering task on x86 platform. In: Gao, W., et al. (eds.) Bench 2019. LNCS, vol. 12093, pp. 110–115. Springer, Cham (2020)
15. He, K., Gkioxari, G., Dollár, P., Girshick, R.: Mask R-CNN. In: Proceedings of the IEEE International Conference on Computer Vision, pp. 2961–2969 (2017)
16. He, K., Zhang, X., Ren, S., Sun, J.: Spatial pyramid pooling in deep convolutional networks for visual recognition. IEEE Trans. Pattern Anal. Mach. Intell. **37**(9), 1904–1916 (2015)
17. He, K., Zhang, X., Ren, S., Sun, J.: Deep residual learning for image recognition. In: Proceedings of the IEEE Conference on Computer Vision and Pattern Recognition, pp. 770–778 (2016)
18. He, K., Zhang, X., Ren, S., Sun, J.: Identity mappings in deep residual networks. In: Leibe, B., Matas, J., Sebe, N., Welling, M. (eds.) ECCV 2016. LNCS, vol. 9908, pp. 630–645. Springer, Cham (2016). https://doi.org/10.1007/978-3-319-46493-0_38
19. Hou, P., Yu, J., Miao, Y., Tai, Y., Wu, Y., Zhao, C.: RVTensor: a light-weight neural network inference framework based on the RISC-V architecture. In: Gao, W., et al. (eds.) Bench 2019. LNCS, vol. 12093, pp. 85–90. Springer, Cham (2020)
20. Jia, Y., et al.: Caffe: convolutional architecture for fast feature embedding. In: Proceedings of the 22nd ACM International Conference on Multimedia, pp. 675–678. ACM (2014)
21. Jiang, Z., et al.: HPC AI500: a benchmark suite for HPC AI systems. In: Zheng, C., Zhan, J. (eds.) Bench 2018. LNCS, vol. 11459, pp. 10–22. Springer, Cham (2019). https://doi.org/10.1007/978-3-030-32813-9_2
22. Kim, J.-Y., Kim, M., Lee, S., Jinwook, O., Kim, K., Yoo, H.-J.: A 201.4 GOPS 496 mW real-time multi-object recognition processor with bio-inspired neural perception engine. IEEE J. Solid-State Circ. **45**(1), 32–45 (2009)
23. Krizhevsky, A., Hinton, G., et al.: Learning multiple layers of features from tiny images. Technical report, Citeseer (2009)
24. Krizhevsky, A., Sutskever, I., Hinton, G.E.: ImageNet classification with deep convolutional neural networks. In: Advances in Neural Information Processing Systems, pp. 1097–1105 (2012)
25. Li, G., Wang, X., Ma, X., Liu, L., Feng, X.: XDN: towards efficient inference of residual neural networks on Cambricon chips. In: Gao, W., et al. (eds.) Bench 2019. LNCS, vol. 12093, pp. 51–56. Springer, Cham (2020)
26. Li, J., Jiang, Z.: Performance analysis of Cambricon MLU100. In: Gao, W., et al. (eds.) Bench 2019. LNCS, vol. 12093, pp. 57–66. Springer, Cham (2020)
27. Lin, T.-Y., Dollár, P., Girshick, R., He, K., Hariharan, B., Belongie, S.: Feature pyramid networks for object detection. In: Proceedings of the IEEE Conference on Computer Vision and Pattern Recognition, pp. 2117–2125 (2017)
28. Lin, T.-Y., Goyal, P., Girshick, R., He, K., Dollár, P.: Focal loss for dense object detection. In: Proceedings of the IEEE International Conference on Computer Vision, pp. 2980–2988 (2017)

29. Liu, S., et al.: Cambricon: an instruction set architecture for neural networks. In: ACM SIGARCH Computer Architecture News, vol. 44, pp. 393–405. IEEE Press (2016)
30. Luo, C., et al.: AIoT Bench: towards comprehensive benchmarking mobile and embedded device intelligence. In: Zheng, C., Zhan, J. (eds.) Bench 2018. LNCS, vol. 11459, pp. 31–35. Springer, Cham (2019). https://doi.org/10.1007/978-3-030-32813-9_4
31. Ren, S., He, K., Girshick, R., Sun, J.: Faster R-CNN: towards real-time object detection with region proposal networks. In: Advances in Neural Information Processing Systems, pp. 91–99 (2015)
32. Ronneberger, O., Fischer, P., Brox, T.: U-Net: convolutional networks for biomedical image segmentation. In: Navab, N., Hornegger, J., Wells, W.M., Frangi, A.F. (eds.) MICCAI 2015. LNCS, vol. 9351, pp. 234–241. Springer, Cham (2015). https://doi.org/10.1007/978-3-319-24574-4_28
33. Wang, F., et al.: Residual attention network for image classification. In: Proceedings of the IEEE Conference on Computer Vision and Pattern Recognition, pp. 3156–3164 (2017)
34. Wang, Y., Zeng, C., Li, C.: Exploring the performance bound of Cambricon accelerator in end-to-end inference scenario. In: Gao, W., et al. (eds.) Bench 2019. LNCS, vol. 12093, pp. 67–74. Springer, Cham (2020)
35. Xiong, X., Wen, X., Huang, C.: Improving RGB-D face recognition via transfer learning from a pretrained 2D network. In: Gao, W., et al. (eds.) Bench 2019. LNCS, vol. 12093, pp. 141–148. Springer, Cham (2020)
36. Zhang, S., et al.: Cambricon-X: an accelerator for sparse neural networks. In: The 49th Annual IEEE/ACM International Symposium on Microarchitecture, p. 20. IEEE Press (2016)
37. Zhou, B., Khosla, A., Lapedriza, A., Oliva, A., Torralba, A.: Learning deep features for discriminative localization. In: Proceedings of the IEEE Conference on Computer Vision and Pattern Recognition, pp. 2921–2929 (2016)

AI Challenges on RISC-V Using AIBench

RVTensor: A Light-Weight Neural Network Inference Framework Based on the RISC-V Architecture

Pengpeng Hou[1,2], Jiageng Yu[1(✉)], Yuxia Miao[1], Yang Tai[1], Yanjun Wu[1], and Chen Zhao[1]

[1] The Institute of Software, Chinese Academy of Sciences, Beijing, China
{pengpeng,jiageng08,yuxia,taiyang,yanjun,zhaochen}@iscas.ac.cn
[2] University of Chinese Academy of Sciences, Beijing, China

Abstract. The open-source instruction set architecture RISC-V has developed rapidly in recent years, and its combination mode of multiple sub-instruction sets has attracted the attention of IoT vendors. However, research on the IoT scenario inference framework based on the RISC-V architecture is rare. Popular frame-works such as MXNet, TensorFlow, and Caffe are based on the X86 and ARM architectures, and they are not optimized for the IoT scenarios. We propose RVTensor that a light-weight neural network inference framework based on the RISC-V architecture. RVTensor is based on the SERVE.r platform and is optimized for resource-poor scenarios. Our experiments demonstrate that the accuracy of RVTensor and the Keras is the same.

Keywords: RISC-V · Deep Learning · ResNet20 · SERVE.r

1 Introduction

This paper is for 2019 BenchCouncil International Artificial Intelligence System Challenges. The Challenges has four tracks: International AI System Challenge based on RISC-V (we participate in this), International AI System Challenge based on Cambricon Chip [1,2], International AI System Challenge based on X86 Plat-form [3–5], International 3D Face Recognition Algorithm Challenge [6,7].

The RISC-V instruction set architecture [8] consists of a basic instruction set and multiple extended instruction sets, which is more flexible than the X86 and ARM architectures. The flexible combination mode of the RISC-V architecture is suitable for the IoT domain with various requirements. The IoT vendors can personally combine and customize the instruction set according to the specific scenarios, so the RISC-V architecture has a good application prospect in the IoT field.

Few deep learning inference frameworks support the RISC-V architecture. TensorFlow [9], MXNet [10], Caffe [11], and PaddlePaddle [12] are based on the

W. Gao et al. (Eds.): Bench 2019, LNCS 12093, pp. 85–90, 2020.
https://doi.org/10.1007/978-3-030-49556-5_8

X86 and GPU architectures, lacking support for RISC-V architectures, and these frameworks often run on resource-rich servers and have few optimizations for the IoT domain.

We propose a deep learning inference framework RVTensor that is optimized for resource-poor application scenarios based on the RISC-V architecture. It has few third-party dependent libraries, small memory requirements, and small executable files. We have evaluated RVTensor by the ResNet20 model, and find that the accuracy of its results is the same as the Keras [13].

2   Overall Architecture

The overview of RVTensor architecture is shown in Fig. 1, it consists of four parts: model analysis, op operators, construction calculation graph, and execution calculation graph.

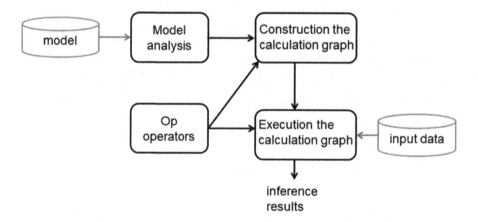

Fig. 1. Overview of RVTensor architecture.

Model Analysis. It mainly parses model files such as *.pb*, and extracts information such as operator operations and weight data.

Op Operators. It mainly includes the implementation of each operator, including *conv, add, active, pooling, fc* [14] and other operations. These operators are the basic computing unit of the neural network execution.

Construction the Calculation Graph. It builds a calculation graph based on the model analysis and the op operator modules. In the calculation graph, the order between the operators, the dependencies between the weights and the operators are clarified.

Execution the Calculation Graph. It obtains the inference results based on the input data (such as image data) and the calculation graph.

3 Optimization Skills

RVTensor is optimized for resource-poor scenarios by reducing dependencies on third-party libraries and increasing memory utilization. To reduce the dependence on third-party libraries, we propose many light-weight API interfaces, e.g., we re-implement thread function APIs. To improve memory utilization, we reuse the memory.

Re-implement thread API. Pthread [15] is a popular open-source thread library, which provides APIs such as thread creation, thread waiting, thread exit, thread lock. However, RVTensor mainly involves two thread functions: thread creation and thread waiting, most functions in the Pthread library are not involved. Therefore the Pthread is quite heavy for RVTensor, and we re-implemented the involved functions based on the RISC-V architecture instead of using the Pthread. The way we implement the functions is shown in Fig. 2. We propose the thread creation interface in thread.c. First, we allocate the stack memory for the new thread and then invoke the *clone* function to create the thread. The *clone* function is implemented in the clone.c file. In the clone.c, we first parse the parameters and then call the interface in the clone.s to create threads based on the parameters. The clone.s is an assembly file that wraps the *sys_clone* system call to really create the thread. Compared to the Pthread, the new thread API is more lightweight and more suitable for IoT scenarios.

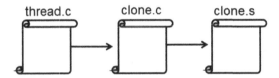

thread.c   clone.c   clone.s

Fig. 2. Thread function call procedure.

Memory Reuse. The hardware of the IoT scenario generally has a small memory capacity. If the memory optimization is lacking, the inference system is prone to have OOM errors [16]. We propose a memory reuse strategy to save the memory. The classic segment of the calculation graph is shown in Fig. 3(a), the memory space for the current op_i operator is necessary, and the space for the op_{i-1} and op_{i+1} do not need to be allocated immediately. So we create a global memory block for the current op operator to reuse.

The memory space M_{op} required for the op operator is calculated as follows:

$$M_{op} = \sum_{i=0}^{N} (M_{ii} + M_{ik} + M_{ib}) + M_o \qquad (1)$$

Where M_{ii} represents the size of the i-th input data, M_{ik} represents the kernel size of the i-th input data, M_{ib} represents the bias size of the i-th input data, and M_o represents the output size of the op operator.

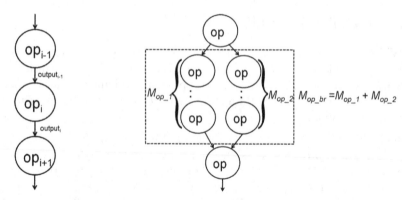

(a) segment of the calculation graph   (b) two sub-branches in the calculation graph

Fig. 3. Execution branch of calculation graph

The global memory block M_{pool} shared by each operator is calculated as follows:

$$M_{pool} = max(M_{op1}, M_{op2}, ..., M_{opn}) \qquad (2)$$

If the graph has multiple branches in a stage, as shown in Fig. 3(b), we treat the sub-branches as a atomic operation, take the sum of the M_{op_i} of each sub-branch as the M_{op_br} that represents the memory space needed in this stage, as shown in the following formula:

$$M_{op\_br} = \sum_{i=0}^{N} M_{op\_i} \qquad (3)$$

Where M_{op_i} represents the max M_{op} in the i-th sub-branch.

The memory reuse strategy saves memory space while reducing the number of memory allocations.

4   Evaluation

We evaluate RVTensor based on the SERVE.r platform [17], the test model is the ResNet20 [18], and the data set is the CIFAR-10 [19], involving 10,000 images. Our experiment refers to the benchmark for image classification in AIBench [20][21][22]. AIBench source code is publicly available from http:// www.benchcouncil.org/ben-chhub/AIBench/ (Sign up to get access) (Table 1).

Accuracy. We use the Keras as the baseline. After analyzing the test results, the accuracy of RVTensor on Top1 and Top5 is 77% and 98%, respectively, which is the same as the Keras. It should be noted that the Keras cannot be installed and run on the SERVE.r platform due to the memory limitation, so its accurate evaluation is based on the X86 platform.

Table 1. Accuracy based on the ResNet20 model.

	Top1	Top5
RVTensor	77%	98%
Keras	77%	98%

Performance. The average time to process each image is 13.51 s.

Execution File Size. The executable file size of RVTensor is 193 KB.

5   Future Work

The performance of RVTensor is still low, and we will improve it in the following ways:

- **Memory optimization.** Due to the limited memory of the SERVE.r, there will be memory swapping in and out, which will cause the time overhead of some op operators to increase significantly and reduce the performance. We will try to solve this issue.
- **Optimization for sparse convolution.** The relu activation will result in an ample number of zeros in the input data, these zeros occupy a large space and cause the convolution operation to be inefficient. We will optimize the sparse convolution operation.
- **The V instruction set adaptation.** We will try to re-implement the op operator based on the V instruction set, improving the operator execution efficiency.
- **Model pruning.** We will compress the model parameters through pruning techniques to make them more suitable for IoT scenes.

6   Summary

We propose a deep learning inference framework RVTensor for the IoT scenario based on the RISC-V architecture. We reduce the dependency on third-party libraries by implementing light-weight API interface, and save memory space during the op operator calculation process through the memory reuse strategy. Our experiments demonstrate that the accuracy of RVTensor and the Keras is the same, and RVTensors executable file is quite small.

References

1. Li, G., Wang, X., Ma, X., Liu, L., Feng, X.: XDN: towards efficient inference of residual neural networks on cambricon chips. In: Gao, W., et al. (eds.) Bench 2019, LNCS, vol. 12093, pp. 51–56. Springer, Cham (2019)

2. Li, J., Jiang, Z.: Performance analysis of cambricon mlu100. In: Gao, W., et al. (eds.) Bench 2019, LNCS, vol. 12093, pp. 57–66. Springer, Cham (2019)

3. Deng, W., Wang, P., Wang, J., Li, C., Guo, M.: PSL: exploiting parallelism, sparsity and locality to accelerate matrix factorization on x86 platforms. In: Gao, W., et al. (eds.) Bench 2019, LNCS, vol. 12093, pp. 101–109. Springer, Cham (2019)

4. Hao, T., Zheng, Z.: The implementation and optimization of matrix decomposition based collaborative filtering task on x86 platform. In: Gao, W., et al. (eds.) Bench 2019, LNCS, vol. 12093, pp. 110–115. Springer, Cham (2019)

5. Chen, M., Chen, T., Chen, Q.: An efficient implementation of the ALS-WR algorithm on x86 CPUs. In: Gao, W., et al. (eds.) Bench 2019, LNCS, vol. 12093, pp. 116–122. Springer, Cham (2019)

6. Xiong, X., Wen, X., Huang, C.: Improving RGB-D face recognition via transfer learning from a pretrained 2D network. In: Gao, W., et al. (eds.) Bench 2019, LNCS, vol. 12093, pp. 141–148. Springer, Cham (2019)

7. Gong, T., Huiqian, N.: An implementation of resnet on the classification of RGB-D images. In: Gao, W., et al. (eds.) Bench 2019, LNCS, vol. 12093, pp. 149–155. Springer, Cham (2019)

8. Risc-v. https://riscv.org/

9. Abadi, M., et al.: Tensorflow: a system for large-scale machine learning. In: 12th USENIX Symposium on Operating Systems Design and Implementation (OSDI 2016), Savannah, GA, November 2016, pp. 265–283. USENIX Association (2016)

10. Chen, T., et al.: MXNet: a flexible and efficient machine learning library for heterogeneous distributed systems, pp. 1–6 (2015)

11. Jia, Y., et al.: Caffe: convolutional architecture for fast feature embedding. In: Proceedings of the 22nd ACM International Conference on Multimedia, MM 2014, New York, NY, USA, 2014, pp. 675–678. Association for Computing Machinery (2014)

12. Paddlepaddle. https://www.paddlepaddle.org.cn/

13. Keras. https://keras.io/

14. Shelhamer, E., Long, J., Darrell, T.: Fully convolutional networks for semantic segmentation. IEEE Trans. Pattern Anal. Mach. Intell. **39**(4), 640–651 (2017)

15. Pthread. http://man7.org/linux/man-pages/man7/pthreads.7.html

16. Oom. https://en.wikipedia.org/wiki/Out_of_memory

17. Serve.r. https://github.com/ict-accel-team/SERVE.r

18. He, K., Zhang, X., Ren, S., Sun, J.: Deep residual learning for image recognition. In: 2016 IEEE Conference on Computer Vision and Pattern Recognition (CVPR), pp. 770–778, June 2016

19. Cifar-10. https://www.cs.toronto.edu/~kriz/cifar.html

20. Gao, W., et al.: Aibench: an industry standard internet service AI benchmark suite. arXiv preprint arXiv:1908.08998 (2019)

21. Gao, W., et al.: AIBench: towards scalable and comprehensive datacenter AI benchmarking. In: Zheng, C., Zhan, J. (eds.) Bench 2018. LNCS, vol. 11459, pp. 3–9. Springer, Cham (2019). https://doi.org/10.1007/978-3-030-32813-9_1

22. Aibench. http://www.benchcouncil.org/AIBench/index.html

AIRV: Enabling Deep Learning Inference on RISC-V

Yangyang Kong[✉]

State Key Laboratory of Information Security, Institute of Information Engineering,
Chinese Academy of Sciences, Beijing, China
kongyangyang@iie.ac.cn

Abstract. Recently the emerging RISC-V instruction set architecture (ISA) has been widely adopted by both academia and industry. Meanwhile, various artificial intelligence (AI) applications have been extensively deployed in cloud, edge, mobile and IoT devices due to latest breakthroughs in deep learning algorithms and techniques. Therefore, there is an increasing need for enabling deep learning inference on RISC-V. However, at present mainstream machine learning frameworks have not been ported to RISC-V, which poses challenges to deep learning application developers. In this paper, we explore approaches to enabling deep learning inference on RISC-V. Experimental results show that in our work, there is a great gap between the performance of deep learning inference on RISC-V and that on x86; thus compared with direct compilation on RISC-V, cross-compilation on x86 is a better option to significantly improve development efficiency.

Keywords: RISC-V · Deep learning · Machine learning framework · Cross-compile

1 Introduction

RISC-V [1] is a clean-slate, open and free instruction set architecture (ISA), which allows anyone to develop both open-source and proprietary implementations. Its modular design for extensibility and specialization makes itself suitable for computing systems ranging from microcontrollers to supercomputers. Hence RISC-V is attracting extensive attention from both academia and industry. Meanwhile, as deep learning has become state-of-the-art in domains such as computer vision, voice recognition, natural language processing, etc., artificial intelligence (AI) is experiencing a renaissance, and a large variety of AI applications are being deployed in a wide range of computing platforms, including cloud, edge, mobile and IoT devices. Therefore, deep learning is expected to be enabled on RISC-V for both research and commercial purposes. However, mainstream machine learning frameworks (e.g. TensorFlow [2]) do not have a full-fledged RISC-V port for now, posing challenges to the development of AI applications targeting RISC-V.

© Springer Nature Switzerland AG 2020
W. Gao et al. (Eds.): Bench 2019, LNCS 12093, pp. 91–98, 2020.
https://doi.org/10.1007/978-3-030-49556-5_9

On the other hand, since server and desktop markets are dominated by Intel x86, and mobile and IoT markets dominated by Arm, machine learning frameworks and applications have to be developed for different ISAs respectively, in order to cover various computing platforms. However, this may induce a large amount of development efforts. Fortunately, RISC-V would provide an unique opportunity for both machine learning frameworks and applications to be developed for only one ISA and to be deployed on a wide range of computing platforms. Therefore, machine learning frameworks and applications are especially worth porting to RISC-V.

In this paper, AIRV stands for "AI on RISC-V". Our vision is to enable a large variety of AI applications on a wide range of RISC-V platforms. At present, we focus on enabling deep learning inference on RISC-V, and evaluate the performance of deep learning inference on multiple platforms. Our contributions are summarized as follows:

- We explore approaches to enabling deep learning inference on RISC-V;
- We evaluate the performance of deep learning inference both on RISC-V and on x86;
- We show that in our work, compared with direct compilation on RISC-V, cross-compilation on x86 is a better option to reduce the development cycle of deep learning inference applications targeting RISC-V.

The paper is organized as follows. Section 2 summarizes related work. Section 3 briefly introduces the ResNet-20 deep neural network (DNN) and the CIFAR-10 dataset. Section 4 illustrates the architecture for deep learning inference applications in our work. Section 5 implements the architecture using TensorFlow Python, TensorFlow C and TensorFlow Lite for Microcontrollers, respectively. Section 6 compares two compilation methods: direct compilation and cross-compilation. Section 7 presents experimental results. Section 8 concludes the paper.

2   Related Work

Most prior work [3–5] focused on offloading deep learning inference tasks especially key kernels (e.g. convolution, activation, pooling) from RISC-V cores to a dedicated hardware accelerator to achieve high performance and/or energy efficiency for deep learning inference applications targeting mobile and/or IoT devices. They usually use a hardware/software co-design method which features an SoC incorporating RISC-V cores, a dedicated hardware accelerator for deep learning inference, and a specialized software toolchain comprised of customized libraries, compilers, etc.

In the aforementioned solutions, most deep learning inference tasks are actually executed on a deep learning accelerator, rather than a RISC-V core which is usually used as a microcontroller. Therefore, their solutions rely on dedicated hardwares and specialized softwares, which potentially incur additional programming efforts for application developers. Moreover, it may not be able to port the applications developed using their software tools to other RISC-V platforms especially those without a required hardware accelerator.

In this paper, we focus on directly running all deep learning inference tasks on a RISC-V based processor, instead of a dedicated hardware accelerator. One of our goals is to enable a large variety of deep learning inference applications on a wide range of RISC-V platforms using mainstream machine learning frameworks. Furthermore, we plan to accelerate deep learning inference on RISC-V using a pure hardware solution to improve performance and energy efficiency without incurring extra programming efforts for application developers, and we leave this optimization for future work.

3 Background

We briefly introduce the ResNet-20 deep neural network and the CIFAR-10 dataset, in preparation for illustration of the architecture for deep learning inference applications in our work.

3.1 ResNet-20

The ResNet [6] deep neural network originates from the ImageNet Large Scale Visual Recognition Challenge (ILSVRC) [7], which provides millions of labeled images for the contestants to train and evaluate their deep neural networks. On the ILSVRC 2015 classification task, ResNet achieved 96.4% accuracy on the ImageNet test set and won the first place, which outperformed human accuracy (94.9%) [7] on image classification.

The ResNet-20 deep neural network in this paper is a pre-trained model from the 2019 BenchCouncil International AI System and Algorithm Challenges [8], which consist of four tracks: International AI System Challenge based on RISC-V, International AI System Challenge based on Cambricon Chip, International AI System Challenge based on X86 Platform, and International 3D Face Recognition Algorithm Challenge. The topics of the tracks are derived from AIBench [9,10], the source code of which is publicly available from http://www. benchcouncil.org/benchhub/AIBench/ (sign up to get access). The ResNet-20 model is used to predict the most possible category of an image: airplane, automobile, bird, cat, deer, dog, frog, horse, ship, or truck. The input of the model is a color image with three channels (i.e. red, green and blue); each channel is comprised of 32×32 pixels and each pixel is an integer ranging from 0 to 255. The output of the model is a vector consisting of ten floating point numbers (with each number ranging from 0.0 to 1.0), indicating the possibilities of an image belonging to the aforementioned categories, respectively. Thus we can predict the most possible category of the image by finding the maximum element of the vector.

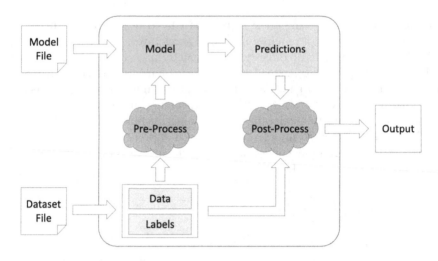

Fig. 1. Architecture for deep learning inference applications.

3.2   CIFAR-10

The CIFAR-10 [11] dataset consists of 60,000 color images and their labels; each image shares the same attributes with that described in Sect. 3.1. CIFAR-10 is divided into two parts: a training dataset containing 50,000 labeled images for training deep neural networks and a test dataset containing 10,000 labeled images for evaluating deep neural networks. The label is used to judge whether a deep neural network has made a right prediction on the corresponding image. In other words, a right prediction has been made if the category of the image predicted by the deep neural network is the same as the corresponding label; otherwise, it's a wrong prediction.

The ResNet-20 deep neural network model used in our work, is trained on the CIFAR-10 training dataset, and achieves 84.03% accuracy on the CIFAR-10 test dataset.

4   Architecture

In this section, we illustrate the architecture for deep learning inference applications developed in our work. As depicted in Fig. 1, the architecture involves loading a pre-trained deep neural network model and a labeled dataset from corresponding files, pre-processing the data before input into the model (e.g. reshaping, transforming, normalization), predicting on the data using the model, post-processing the predictions (e.g. checking the predictions using the labels, calculating prediction accuracy), and outputting useful information (e.g. logs, final results).

5   Implementations

We implement the architecture illustrated in Sect. 4 by using the ResNet-20 deep neural network model, the CIFAR-10 dataset and the TensorFlow machine learning framework. Three applications are developed using three TensorFlow libraries, i.e. TensorFlow Python, TensorFlow C and TensorFlow Lite for Microcontrollers, respectively.

The first application developed using the TensorFlow Python library can be successfully run on x86 and achieves 84.03% accuracy as expected. However, the application can not be successfully run on RISC-V because the TensorFlow Python library does not have a RISC-V version (for now). Although the library could be ported to RISC-V using Bazel, an open-source build tool, it may require a lot of developing efforts. For example, all machine-specific source code in the library must be properly modified. Thus we leave this port for future work.

Similarly, the second application developed using the TensorFlow C library can be successfully compiled and run on x86, and achieves 84.03% accuracy as well. However, the application suffers a similar problem as described above. Also, we leave the solution for future work.

The third application is developed using TensorFlow Lite for Microcontrollers, which is designed to have fewer dependencies. The application can be successfully compiled and run on RISC-V as well as on x86, and achieves 84.03% accuracy on both platforms.

6   Compilation Methods

In order to implement the architecture on RISC-V, as discussed in Sect. 5, the application developed using TensorFlow Lite for Microcontrollers needs to be compiled to produce a binary which can be executed on RISC-V. There are two compilation methods: direct compilation and cross-compilation. As illustrated in Fig. 2, direct compilation means compiling the application on RISC-V using the RISC-V toolchain to produce a RISC-V executable, while cross-compilation means compiling the application on x86 using the RISC-V toolchain to produce a RISC-V executable.

Direct compilation seems to be the simplest way to compile the application, since the required RISC-V toolchain has already been pre-installed on the host platform which is exactly the target platform as well. However, we show that direct compilation may not be a good option because there are resource and performance challenges when directly compiling the application on RISC-V in our work.

Resource Challenge. The application developed using TensorFlow Lite for Microcontrollers can not be successfully compiled on a RISC-V based FPGA board used in our work, due to limited memory on the board. Fortunately, this problem can be solved by augmenting the virtual memory.

Performance Challenge. Although the aforementioned problem can be solved, it takes more than three hours to complete the direct compilation process on the

Direct Compilation

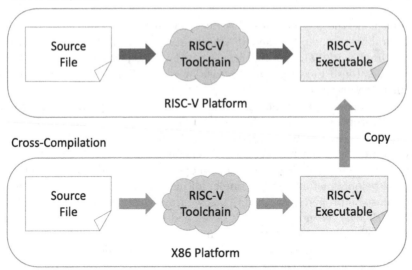

Fig. 2. Direct compilation vs. cross-compilation.

board, which is about 300× slower than the cross-compilation process on an x86 server used in our work. Therefore, we prefer to cross-compile the application on the server so that we can save a large amount of time, despite it also takes a little time to copy the produced RISC-V executable from the server to the board.

7   Experimental Results

We evaluate the performance of compiling and running the application illustrated in Sect. 5 on three different platforms: an Xilinx PYNQ Z2 FPGA board based on RISC-V, RISCV-QEMU [12] (a QEMU emulator for RISC-V), and an x86 server. The environment configurations of the platforms are listed in Table 1. The real time of compiling and running the application on the platforms is listed in Table 2 and illustrated in Fig. 3. Experimental results show that compiling the application on RISCV-QEMU and the RISC-V based FPGA board is about 16× and 293× slower than that on the x86 server, respectively; running the application on the two RISC-V platforms is about 28× and 620× slower than that on the x86 server, respectively. Therefore, high performance RISC-V based platforms are expected to be used to reduce the development cycle of applications targeting RISC-V.

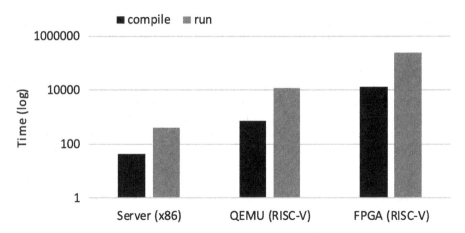

Fig. 3. Real time of compiling and running the application on the three platforms.

Table 1. Environment configurations of the three platforms.

	FPGA (RISC-V)	QEMU (RISC-V)	Server (x86)
OS	Linux 4.19.0	Linux 4.19.0	Linux 4.4.0
CPU	SiFive Rocket0, RV64GC, Sv39, 50 MHz, 1 core	RISC-V, RV64GCSU, Sv48, 8 cores	Intel Xeon E5-2697 v4 @ 2.30 GHz, 18 cores
Memory	180 MB	16 GB	64 GB
gcc	gcc 9.2.1	gcc 7.3.1	gcc 7.4.0
g++	g++ 9.2.1	g++ 7.3.1	g++ 7.4.0
Python	Python 2.7.16+	Python 2.7.14	Python 2.7.6
Python3	Python 3.7.4+	Python 3.6.4	Python 3.6.8
Make	GNU Make 4.2.1	GNU Make 4.2.1	GNU Make 4.2.1

Table 2. Real time of compiling and running the application on the three platforms.

	FPGA (RISC-V)	QEMU (RISC-V)	Server (x86)
Compile time (s)	12744.30	713.40	43.55
Run time (s)	250601.78	11429.58	404.21

8   Conclusions

In this paper, we explore approaches to enabling deep learning inference on RISC-V by implementing the architecture for deep learning inference applications using ResNet-20, CIFAR-10 and three TensorFlow libraries. At present, since TensorFlow does not have a full-fledged RISC-V port, only the application developed using TensorFlow Lite for Microcontrollers can be successfully compiled and run on RISC-V and achieves the expected accuracy. Still, we show that there are resource and performance challenges when directly compiling and running the application on two RISC-V platforms in our work, and cross-compiling the application on a high performance x86 platform is a better option for us to save a large amount of time. We evaluate the performance of compiling and running the application on three platforms: an Xilinx PYNQ Z2 FPGA board based on RISC-V, RISCV-QEMU, and an x86 server. Experimental results show that directly compiling the application on the two RISC-V platforms is about $16\times$ and $293\times$ slower than that on the x86 server, respectively; running the application on the two RISC-V platforms is about $28\times$ and $620\times$ slower than that on the x86 server, respectively. Therefore, high performance RISC-V based platforms are expected to be used to speed up the development of applications targeting RISC-V.

Future work involves implementing the architecture on RISC-V using TensorFlow Python, TensorFlow C, and other mainstream machine learning frameworks such as PyTorch. Furthermore, we plan to accelerate deep learning inference using a pure hardware solution to improve performance and energy efficiency without incurring extra programming efforts for application developers.

Acknowledgements. This work is supported by the Strategic Priority Research Program of Chinese Academy of Sciences, under Grant No. XDC02010200.

References

1. RISC-V. https://riscv.org
2. TensorFlow. https://www.tensorflow.org
3. Davidson, S., et al.: The celerity open-source 511-Core RISC-V tiered accelerator fabric: fast architectures and design methodologies for fast Chips. In: IEEE Micro, vol. 38, no. 2, pp. 30–41, March/April (2018)
4. Flamand, E., et al.: GAP-8: A RISC-V SoC for AI at the edge of the IoT. In: 2018 IEEE 29th International Conference on Application-specific Systems, Architectures and Processors (ASAP), Milan, pp. 1–4 (2018)
5. Louis, M.S., et al.: Towards deep learning using tensorflow lite on RISC-V. In: Third Workshop on Computer Architecture Research with RISC-V (CARRV) (2019)
6. He, K., Zhang, X., Ren, S., Sun, J.: Deep residual learning for image recognition. In: 2016 IEEE Conference on Computer Vision and Pattern Recognition (CVPR), Las Vegas, NV, pp. 770–778 (2016)
7. Russakovsky, O., et al.: ImageNet large scale visual recognition challenge. Int. J. Comput. Vis. **115**(3), 211–252 (2015). https://doi.org/10.1007/s11263-015-0816-y
8. BenchCouncil International AI System and Algorithm Challenges. http://www.benchcouncil.org/competitions.html
9. Gao, W., et al.: AIBench: An Industry Standard Internet Service AI Benchmark Suite. Technical report (2019)
10. Gao, W., et al.: AIBench: towards scalable and comprehensive datacenter AI benchmarking. In: Zheng, C., Zhan, J. (eds.) Bench 2018. LNCS, vol. 11459, pp. 3–9. Springer, Cham (2019). https://doi.org/10.1007/978-3-030-32813-9_1
11. CIFAR-10. https://www.cs.toronto.edu/~kriz/cifar.html
12. RISCV-QEMU. https://hub.docker.com/r/crva/riscv-qemu

AI Challenges on X86 Using AIBench

PSL: Exploiting Parallelism, Sparsity and Locality to Accelerate Matrix Factorization on x86 Platforms

Weixin Deng[(⊠)], Pengyu Wang[(⊠)], Jing Wang[(⊠)], Chao Li[(⊠)], and Minyi Guo[(⊠)]

Shanghai Jiao Tong University, Shanghai, China
{dengwxn,wpybtw,jing618}@sjtu.edu.cn, {lichao,guo-my}@cs.sjtu.edu.cn

Abstract. Matrix factorization is a basis for many recommendation systems. Although alternating least squares with weighted-λ-regularization (ALS-WR) is widely used in matrix factorization with collaborative filtering, this approach unfortunately incurs insufficient parallel execution and ineffective memory access. Thus, we propose a solution for accelerating the ALS-WR algorithm by exploiting parallelism, sparsity and locality on x86 platforms. Our PSL can process 20 million ratings and the speedup using multi-threading is up to 14.5× on a 20-core machine.

Keywords: Parallelism · Sparsity · Locality · Matrix factorization · ALS-WR · Acceleration

1 Introduction

There are lots of work on AI benchmarking [13,14,16,20,23][1]. Some important topics include neural network inference on RISC-V [19] and on Cambricon [21], matrix factorization on x86 [17], 3D face recognition [27] and etc. Matrix factorization is a popular solution to recommendation systems. Many recommendation systems recommend items to users by collaborative filtering based on historical records of items that the users have rated or bought. For example, online shopping websites recommend goods to buyers and movie rating websites recommend movies to users.

Recently, there are lots of research interest in improving the performance of many applications like matrix factorization [6,8,15] and graph processing [7,24]. One way is to accelerate through mathematical methods [6,15]. Another approach is to optimize on architecture features [7,8,24,26].

Alternating least squares with weighted-λ-regularization (ALS-WR) is proposed by Zhou et al. [28] to solve large-scale collaborative filtering. They use parallel Matlab on a Linux cluster as the experimental platform. Nowadays x86 has powerful vector instructions [1], Intel Math Kernel Library (Intel MKL) [3],

---

[1] The source code of AIBench is publicly available from http://www.benchcouncil.org/benchhub/AIBench/ (sign up to get access).

© Springer Nature Switzerland AG 2020
W. Gao et al. (Eds.): Bench 2019, LNCS 12093, pp. 101–109, 2020.
https://doi.org/10.1007/978-3-030-49556-5_10

and multi-core computing resources. As a result, x86 platforms have shown great potential in performance tuning. Equipped with flexible C++ and OpenMP [5], we implement ALS-WR on x86 platforms by exploiting parallelism, sparsity, and locality to achieve high performance.

The contributions of this paper are as follows:

- PSL, a multi-threaded ALS-WR implementation that scales well on x86.
- Achieving high parallelism by parallelizing loops.
- Reducing memory consumption by leveraging sparsity of input data.
- Improving spatial locality by adopting suitable layouts.

We organize the rest of paper as follows. Section 2 introduces background. Section 3 describes our design and implementation. Section 4 shows our evaluation. Finally, Sect. 5 concludes this paper.

2   Background

2.1   Alternating-Least-Squares with Weighted-λ-Regularization

ALS-WR is widely used in matrix factorization problems, in which Root Mean Square Error (RMSE) is used to evaluate the convergence. Let $R = \{r_{ij}\}_{n_u \times n_m}$ denotes the user-item matrix, in which r_{ij} represents the rating score of item j rated by user i and is either a real number or missing, n_u is the number of users and n_m is the number of items. Many recommendation systems try to predict the missing r_{ij} values from known ones.

This approach assigns each user and each item a feature vector. Each predicted rating of an item is calculated by the inner product of the corresponding user and item feature vectors. More specifically, let $U = [\boldsymbol{u}_i]$ be the user feature matrix, in which $\boldsymbol{u}_i \in \mathbb{R}^{n_f}$ for $1 \leqslant i \leqslant n_u$, and let $M = [\boldsymbol{m}_j]$ be the item feature matrix, in which $\boldsymbol{m}_j \in \mathbb{R}^{n_f}$ for $1 \leqslant j \leqslant n_i$. Here n_f is the dimension of the feature space.

By introducing a regularization factor $\lambda \in \mathbb{R}$, we define the objective function

$$f(U, M) = \sum_{ij}^{r_{ij} \text{ is known}} (r_{ij} - \boldsymbol{u}_i^{\mathrm{T}} \boldsymbol{m}_j)^2 \\ + \lambda \left(\sum_i n_{u_i} \|\boldsymbol{u}_i\| + \sum_j n_{m_j} \|\boldsymbol{m}_j\| \right). \tag{1}$$

The ALS-WR algorithm runs as follows:

Step 1. Initialize matrix M by setting the first row as the average ratings of every item, and assigning small random numbers for the rest.
Step 2. Fix M, solve U by minimizing the objective function.
Step 3. Fix U, solve M by minimizing the objective function similarly.
Step 4. Repeat Steps 2 and 3 until desired convergence of RMSE.

Let I_i^u denotes the set of items j that user i rated and n_{u_i} is the size of I_i^u, and let I_j^m denotes the set of users who rated item j and n_{m_j} is the size of I_j^m. We directly give the solution to minimizing the objective function here. When we fix M and update U, we have

$$A_i = M_{I_i^u} M_{I_i^u}^{\mathrm{T}} + \lambda n_{u_i} E,$$
$$V_i = M_{I_i^u} R(i, I_i^u)^{\mathrm{T}}, \tag{2}$$
$$\boldsymbol{u}_i = A_i^{-1} V_i, \ \forall i,$$

where E is the $n_f \times n_f$ identity matrix, $M_{I_i^u}$ denotes the sub-matrix of M where columns $j \in I_i^u$ are selected, and $R(i, I_i^u)$ is the row vector where columns $j \in I_i^u$ of the i-th row of R is taken.

Similarly when we fix U and update M, we have

$$A_j = U_{I_j^m} U_{I_j^m}^{\mathrm{T}} + \lambda n_{m_j} E,$$
$$V_j = U_{I_j^m} R(I_j^m, j), \tag{3}$$
$$\boldsymbol{m}_j = A_j^{-1} V_j, \ \forall j,$$

where $U_{I_j^m}$ denotes the sub-matrix of U where columns $i \in I_j^m$ are selected, and $R(I_j^m, j)$ is the column vector where rows $i \in I_j^m$ of the j-th column of R is taken.

After we have N predicted values $\hat{r}_i$ and N real values r_i, we use RMSE to evaluate convergence. RMSE is calculated as

$$\mathrm{RMSE}(\hat{r}, r) = \left(\frac{1}{N} \sum_{i=1}^{N} (\hat{r}_i - r_i)^2 \right)^{1/2}. \tag{4}$$

Optimization Opportunities. Analyzing main components of the ALS-WR algorithm gives us opportunities to have optimizations. There is numerous memory access, while some layouts are less efficient. Besides, there are loops that can be parallelized. Our PSL carefully solves these problems and therefore achieves high performance.

2.2   Supported Techniques

We introduce the following three relative techniques, which are adopted by PSL.

Vector Instructions. Advanced Vector Extensions (AVX) [1] contain a set of instructions for doing Single Instruction Multiple Data (SIMD) operations on x86 architecture. The vector operations use a set of special vector registers. For example, the maximum size of each vector register is 256 bits if the AVX instruction set is available, and 512 bits if the AVX512 instruction set is available. On large-scale data, vector operations are useful when the same operation is performed on multiple data elements and the dataflow allows parallel calculations.

Intel Math Kernel Library (Intel MKL). Intel MKL [3] is a library of optimized math functions. It equips with industry-standard C and Fortran APIs, which is convenient to programmers. For the ALS-WR algorithm, there are lots of performing linear algebra operations and solving linear equations. We use Intel MKL to do mathematical calculations in ALS-WR.

Non-Uniform Memory Access (NUMA). NUMA is a memory architecture for multi-core machines where processors are directly attached to their own local memory. It is fast to access local memory but relatively slower to access remote memory. In contrast, in uniform memory access (UMA) multi-core machines, generally only one processor can control the memory bus at a time. Since processors block the memory bus when accessing memory, it can lead to significant performance degradation as the number of cores increases. There are lots of research interest on NUMA-aware optimizations [9,10,22].

3 Design and Implementation

Benefiting from techniques mentioned in Sect. 2.2, we explore optimizations from parallelism, sparsity and locality on multi-core CPU architecture.

3.1 Optimization Opportunity of ALS-WR Algorithm

Our revised ALS-WR is described in Algorithm 1. It describes the process of updating U and M in one epoch. The function $\mathtt{linalg.solve}(A, B)$ returns matrix X such that $AX = B$. As suggested in Intel Guide [2], Intel MKL should run on a single thread when called from a threaded region of an application to avoid over-subscription of system resources. So we let Intel MKL run on a single thread, and make loops in lines 1 and 8 be multi-threaded.

Algorithm 1. Updating U and M in one epoch

1: **for** $i = 0$ **to** n_u **do in parallel**   8: **for** $j = 0$ **to** n_m **do in parallel**

2:   $M_i \leftarrow M[:, I_i^u]$ 9: $U_j \leftarrow U[:, I_j^m]$

3:   $R_i \leftarrow R[i, I_i^u]$ 10: $R_j \leftarrow R[I_j^m, j]$

4:   $V_i \leftarrow M_i R_i^{\mathrm{T}}$ 11: $V_j \leftarrow U_i R_j^{\mathrm{T}}$

5:   $A_i \leftarrow M_i M_i^{\mathrm{T}} + \lambda n_{u_i} E$ 12: $A_j \leftarrow U_j U_j^{\mathrm{T}} + \lambda n_{m_j} E$

6:   $U[:, i] \leftarrow \mathtt{linalg.solve}(A_i, V_i)$ 13: $M[:, j] \leftarrow \mathtt{linalg.solve}(A_j, V_j)$

7: **end for**   14: **end for**

3.2   Optimization Opportunity of RMSE Function

According to formula (4), the computation in ALS-WR only involves known ratings. So we should enumerate all known ratings r_{ij} and calculate the difference between r_{ij} and $\boldsymbol{u}_i^T \boldsymbol{m}_j$, rather than first calculate $U^T M$. In this way, we can save unnecessary overheads on unknown ratings. Similar to ALS-WR, we use multi-threading on the enumerating loop.

Our revised RMSE is presented in Algorithm 2. For the summation variable s in line 6, maintaining thread local copies of s and adding them up at last can avoid atomic operations.

Algorithm 2. Calculating RMSE

1: $s \leftarrow 0$
2: **for** r_{ij} **do in parallel**
3:     $U_i \leftarrow U[:, i]$
4:     $M_j \leftarrow M[:, j]$
5:     $\hat{r}_{ij} \leftarrow U_i^T M_j$
6:     $s \leftarrow s + (\hat{r}_{ij} - r_{ij})^2$
7: **end for**
8: **return** $(s/N)^{1/2}$

3.3   Sparsity and Locality Opportunity

First, since operations in lines 3 and 10 only access known ratings in rows and columns, R should be stored as a sparse matrix with compressed sparse row (CSR) and compressed sparse column (CSC) formats. By leveraging sparsity of input data, we reduce memory consumption. Second, U and M are feature matrixes and thus dense matrixes. As operations in lines 2, 6, 9 and 13 access columns of U and M, they should be stored in column-major order. These layouts of R, U and M improve spatial locality by increasing cache hits.

In all multi-threaded loops, the default first touch placement policy of NUMA allocates all new data in the memory closest to the loop thread [25], which is beneficial for memory access. For different threads, there are no race conditions on global data. Thus, no synchronization on global data is needed.

4   Evaluation

Experimental Setup. Our experiments are performed on a 20-core (2 sockets, each with 10 cores) machine with Intel Xeon Silver 4114 (hyper-threaded, 40 threads in total). The version of Intel Compiler and Libraries is 2019.4. The compiler options are `-mkl -O3 -qopenmp -std=c++17`. We also use Intel Vtune Amplifier 2019.4 to analyze core utilization and hotspots. The training parameters of ALS-WR are set as follows. The dimension of feature matrixes n_f is 100. The number of epochs is 30. The train-test data ratio is 4:1.

Data. MovieLens [4] is rating data collected from MovieLens website. We use ml-20m as our input data, which has 20 million ratings and 465,000 tag applications applied to 27,000 movies by 138,000 users.

4.1 Scalability

Figure 1 shows the speedup of execution time using different number of threads. As we can see, performance scales linearly as more threads are added (except the 40 threads hyper-threaded from 20 cores). The speedup is up to 14.5× when using 40 threads.

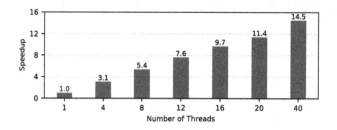

Fig. 1. Speedup of multi-threaded ALS-WR

Figure 2 shows the core utilization using different number of threads. It represents how efficiently the application utilized the available CPU cores and helps evaluate the parallel efficiency. As the number of threads rises from 1 to 20, the core utilization is increasing.

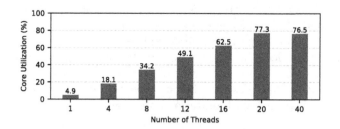

Fig. 2. Core utilization of multi-threaded ALS-WR

These show our implementation scales well. Besides, Intel hyper-threading is most effective when each thread performs different types of operations and there are under-utilized resources on the processor. However, Intel MKL uses most of the available resources and performs identical operations on each thread [2]. So we see the performance does not improve much when switching from 20 threads to 40 threads.

4.2 Hotspots

The top five hotspots of the 40-threaded ALS-WR are shown in Table 1. The first two functions are matrix multiplications and solving linear equations respectively. The overheads of the third function occur when accessing columns of dense matrixes. As for the fourth and the fifth, they relate to memory allocation. Therefore, further optimizing memory access and memory management might help gain better performance.

Table 1. Hotspots of the 40-threaded ALS-WR

Hotspots	Function	CPU time
1	cblas_sgemm	36.1%
2	LAPACKE_sgesv_work	23.7%
3	__intel_avx_rep_memcpy	10.8%
4	operator new	7.5%
5	[MKL SERVICE]@malloc	7.1%

4.3 Speedup of Different Optimization

Figure 3 shows the speedup of different optimization. The weakest baseline only implements sparse matrix function and is single threaded. Firstly, improving spatial locality brings 1.8× speedup. Secondly, using multi-threading with atomic operations offers 4.9× speedup. At last, when we replace atomic operations with thread local copies, we get a 2.9× speedup. Thus, it is vital to remove atomic operations. In total, using multi-threading provides up to 14.5× speedup.

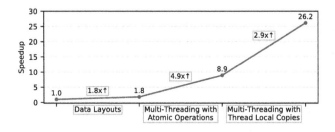

Fig. 3. Speedup of different optimization

5 Conclusion

This paper proposes a high performance multi-threaded implementation PSL for matrix factorization. We exploit parallelism, sparsity and locality for acceleration on x86 platforms. In particular, We analyze the speedup of different optimization. In the future, we will research on how to optimize memory access and memory management to gain better performance.

References

1. Advanced vector extensions. https://en.wikipedia.org/wiki/Advanced_Vector_Exte nsions

2. Intel guide for developing multithreaded applications. https://software.intel.com/ sites/default/files/m/d/4/1/d/8/GDMA_2.pdf

3. Intel math kernel library. https://software.intel.com/en-us/mkl

4. Movielens. https://grouplens.org/datasets/movielens/

5. Openmp. https://en.wikipedia.org/wiki/OpenMP

6. Ang, A.M.S., Gillis, N.: Accelerating nonnegative matrix factorization algorithms using extrapolation. Neural Comput. **31**(2), 417–439 (2019). https://doi.org/10. 1162/neco_a_01157

7. Balaji, V., Lucia, B.: Combining data duplication and graph reordering to acceler-ate parallel graph processing. In: Proceedings of the 28th International Symposium on High-Performance Parallel and Distributed Computing, HPDC 2019, pp. 133–144. ACM, New York (2019). https://doi.org/10.1145/3307681.3326609

8. Chen, J., Fang, J., Liu, W., Tang, T., Chen, X., Yang, C.: Efficient and portable als matrix factorization for recommender systems. In: 2017 IEEE International Parallel and Distributed Processing Symposium Workshops (IPDPSW), pp. 409–418, May 2017. https://doi.org/10.1109/IPDPSW.2017.91

9. Chen, S., Fang, J., Chen, D., Xu, C., Wang, Z.: Adaptive optimization of sparse matrix-vector multiplication on emerging many-core architectures. In: 2018 IEEE 20th International Conference on High Performance Computing and Communica-tions; IEEE 16th International Conference on Smart City; IEEE 4th International Conference on Data Science and Systems (HPCC/SmartCity/DSS), pp. 649–658, June 2018. https://doi.org/10.1109/HPCC/SmartCity/DSS.2018.00116

10. Elafrou, A., Karakasis, V., Gkountouvas, T., Kourtis, K., Goumas, G., Koziris, N.: Sparsex: a library for high-performance sparse matrix-vector multiplication on multicore platforms. ACM Trans. Math. Softw. **44**(3), 26:1–26:32 (2018). https:// doi.org/10.1145/3134442

11. Eyerman, S., Heirman, W., Bois, K.D., Fryman, J.B., Hur, I.: Many-core graph workload analysis. In: Proceedings of the International Conference for High Per-formance Computing, Networking, Storage, and Analysis, SC 2018 pp. 22:1–22:11. IEEE Press, Piscataway (2018). https://doi.org/10.1109/SC.2018.00025

12. Fog, A.: Optimizing software in C++. https://www.agner.org/optimize/ optimizing_cpp.pdf

13. Gao, W., et al.: AIBench: towards scalable and comprehensive datacenter AI bench-marking. In: Zheng, C., Zhan, J. (eds.) Bench 2018. LNCS, vol. 11459, pp. 3–9. Springer, Cham (2019). https://doi.org/10.1007/978-3-030-32813-9_1

14. Gao, W., et al.: Aibench: An industry standard internet service ai benchmark suite. arXiv preprint arXiv:1908.08998 (2019)

15. Gillis, N., Glineur, F.: Accelerated multiplicative updates and hierarchical ALS algorithms for nonnegative matrix factorization. Neural Comput. **24**(4), 1085–1105 (2012). https://doi.org/10.1162/NECO_a_00256

16. Hao, T., et al.: Edge AIBench: towards comprehensive end-to-end edge computing benchmarking. In: Zheng, C., Zhan, J. (eds.) Bench 2018. LNCS, vol. 11459, pp. 23–30. Springer, Cham (2019). https://doi.org/10.1007/978-3-030-32813-9_3

17. Hao, T., Zheng, Z.: The implementation and optimization of matrix decomposition based collaborative filtering task on x86 platform. In: Gao, W., Zhan, J., Fox, G., Lu, X., Stanzione, D. (eds.) Bench 2019. LNCS, vol. 12093, pp. 110–115. Springer, Cham (2019)

18. Hollowell, C., Caramarcu, C., Strecker-Kellogg, W., Wong, T., Zaytsev, A.: The effect of NUMA tunings on CPU performance. https://indico.cern.ch/event/304944/contributions/1672535/attachments/578723/796898/numa.pdf

19. Hou, P., Yu, J., Miao, Y., Tai, Y., Wu, Y., Zhao, C.: RVTensor: a light-weight neural network inference framework based on the RISC-V architecture. In: Gao, W., Zhan, J., Fox, G., Lu, X., Stanzione, D. (eds.) Bench 2019. LNCS, vol. 12093, pp. 85–90. Springer, Cham (2019)

20. Jiang, Z., et al.: HPC AI500: a benchmarksuite for HPC AI systems. In: 2018 Bench Council International Symposium on Benchmarking, Measuring and Optimizing, Bench 2018 (2018)

21. Li, G., Wang, X., Ma, X., Liu, L., Feng, X.: XDN: towards efficient inference of residual neural networks on Cambricon chips. In: Gao, W., Zhan, J., Fox, G., Lu, X., Stanzione, D. (eds.) Bench 2019. LNCS, vol. 12093, pp. 51–56. Springer, Cham (2019)

22. Li, S., Hoefler, T., Snir, M.: NUMA-aware shared-memory collective communication for MPI. In: Proceedings of the 22nd International Symposium on High-performance Parallel and Distributed Computing, HPDC 2013, pp. 85–96. ACM, New York (2013). https://doi.org/10.1145/2493123.2462903

23. Luo, C., et al.: AIoT bench: towards comprehensive benchmarking mobile and embedded device intelligence. In: Zheng, C., Zhan, J. (eds.) Bench 2018. LNCS, vol. 11459, pp. 31–35. Springer, Cham (2019). https://doi.org/10.1007/978-3-030-32813-9_4

24. Mukkara, A., Beckmann, N., Abeydeera, M., Ma, X., Sanchez, D.: Exploiting locality in graph analytics through hardware-accelerated traversal scheduling. In: Proceedings of the 51st Annual IEEE/ACM International Symposium on Microarchitecture, MICRO-51, pp. 1–14. IEEE Press, Piscataway (2018). https://doi.org/10.1109/MICRO.2018.00010

25. van der Pas, R.: How to befriend NUMA. https://www.openmp.org/wp-content/uploads/SC18-BoothTalks-vanderPas.pdf

26. Wang, P., Zhang, L., Li, C., Guo, M.: Excavating the potential of GPU for accelerating graph traversal. In: 2019 IEEE International Parallel and Distributed Processing Symposium (IPDPS), pp. 221–230, May 2019. https://doi.org/10.1109/IPDPS.2019.00032

27. Xiong, X., Wen, X., Huang, C.: Improving RGB-D face recognition via transfer learning from a pretrained 2D network. In: Gao, W., Zhan, J., Fox, G., Lu, X., Stanzione, D. (eds.) Bench 2019. LNCS, vol. 12093, pp. 141–148. Springer, Cham (2019)

28. Zhou, Y., Wilkinson, D., Schreiber, R., Pan, R.: Large-scale parallel collaborative filtering for the netflix prize. In: Fleischer, R., Xu, J. (eds.) AAIM 2008. LNCS, vol. 5034, pp. 337–348. Springer, Heidelberg (2008). https://doi.org/10.1007/978-3-540-68880-8_32

The Implementation and Optimization of Matrix Decomposition Based Collaborative Filtering Task on X86 Platform

Tianshu Hao[1] and Ziping Zheng[2(✉)]

[1] Institute of Computing Technology, Chinese Academy of Sciences, Beijing, China
haotianshu@ict.ac.cn
[2] Google, Inc., Mountain View, CA, USA
zipingz@google.com

Abstract. With the rapid development of the information age, the recommendation system becomes more and more significant to help people find hidden information from the big dataset in daily lives. Collaborative filtering is a popular technology often used in recommendation systems, which recommend items to users according to other users having the similar behaviors with the target user or according to the items having the alike properties with the target item. In this paper, we implement a parallel collaborative filtering algorithm called ALS-WR on the AMD x86 platform and use an adaptive granularity tuning method to obtain the best performance of 124.86 s in 30 training rounds.

Keywords: Recommendation systems · Collaborative filtering · Matrix decomposition

1 Introduction

With the arrival of the information age, users face a big challenge to extract useful information from a massive amount of data. In addition, it's also difficult for systems to recommend the items to the users who are interested in them. In that, the recommendation system, a kind of information filtering and pushing system, is usually utilized to find the connections between users and items [1]. Collaborative filtering, a key technique in recommendation systems, aims at filling the missing values of the user-item matrix with the help of similar users or items. Collaborative filtering has been widely used by a lot of commercial websites as well as social websites [2], such as Google News [3], Amazon [4], Netflix [5], Reddit [6] and YouTube [7]. The key part of collaborative filtering recommendation system is matrix factorization.

Movie recommendation is a representative application in various recommendation systems. As one of the most widely used movie dataset, MovieLens [8]

W. Gao et al. (Eds.): Bench 2019, LNCS 12093, pp. 110–115, 2020.
https://doi.org/10.1007/978-3-030-49556-5_11

collects movie rating data from MovieLens website over various periods, describing audiences' preferences for movies [9].

In this paper, we use python to implement the popular Alternating-Least-Square with Weighted-λ-Regularization (ALS-WR) algorithm on AMD x86 platform, and train 30 rounds using MovieLens dataset. Our method achieves a good result on the BenchCouncil International AI System and Algorithm Challenges. Benchcouncil provides four challenges tracks including RISC-V subject [28], Cambricon chip subject [26,27], X86 platform subject [22,23], and 3D face recognition algorithm challenge subject [24,25]. And these tracks use Benchcouncil AI benchmarks [17–21]. The source code of AIBench is publicly available from http://www.benchcouncil.org/benchhub/AIBench/ (Sign up to get access). Eventually, by optimizing and parallelizing the matrix decomposition process, the best training time of 30 rounds of our ALS-WR implementation is 124.86 s.

2 Related Work

2.1 ALS

ALS [10] is the abbreviation of alternating least squares, an algorithm always used in recommendation systems based on matrix decomposition. Traditional matrix decomposition Singular Value Decomposition (SVD) is very slow and cannot be used in sparse rating data because it is very common that the users can only rate few items, but ALS solves this problem well in a clever way which using an alternate strategy to update one matrix weight while fixing the another and then vice versa. ALS aims to find two low dimension matrices $X_{m \times k}$ and $Y_{n \times k}$ to approximate the given matrix $R_{m \times n}$.

$$R_{m \times n} \approx X_{m \times k} Y_{n \times k}^T \tag{1}$$

$X_{m \times k}$ calls the user matrix and $Y_{n \times k}$ calls the item matrix. In order to find the user and item matrices, the objective function is:

$$min_{x_u, y_i} L(X, Y) = \sum_{u,i} (r_{ui} - x_u^T y_i)^2 + \lambda(|x_u|^2 + |y_i|^2) \tag{2}$$

with λ being the regularization factor.

2.2 ALS-WR

The model mentioned above is suitable for the scenarios with a clear rating matrix. Nevertheless, users don't give explicit feedback in many cases, which means there is no direct rating. Therefore, we can only infer the preference of the users by their behavior. For example, in the TV recommendation scenario, the recommendation system can speculate the preference of users by analyzing the number of views and the view duration when users watch the TV program. However, there is no way to decide whether users love the TV program when users never watch it. ALS-WR solves above problem by confidence weight: we assign a larger weight to the item which has the explicit feedback and a smaller weight to the item which doesn't have the explicit feedback.

The objective function of ALS-WR [11] is:

$$min_{x_u, y_i} L(X, Y) = \sum_{u,i} c_{ui}(p_{ui} - x_u^T y_i)^2 + \lambda(|x_u|^2 + |y_i|^2) \tag{3}$$

$$p_{ui} = \begin{cases} 1 & if \ r_{ui} > 0 \\ 0 & if \ r_{ui} = 0 \end{cases} \tag{4}$$

$$c_{ui} = 1 + \alpha r_{ui} \tag{5}$$

with α being the confidence coefficient.

The solution method of above equation is least squares:

$$x_u = (Y^T C^u Y + \lambda I)^{-1} Y^T C^u r_u \tag{6}$$

$$y_i = (X^T C^i X + \lambda I)^{-1} X^T C^i r_i \tag{7}$$

2.3   OpenBLAS

Basic Linear Algebra Subprograms (BLAS) [12] is a library including a lot of linear algebra operations, such as vector addition, matrix decomposition and so on. Implementations of these operations can be optimized for speed on the upper application to pursue better performance. Considering AMD x86 processors are based on AMD Zen microarchitecture and OpenBLAS [13] has optimized its kernels for Zen-based processors using a template-based methodology [15,16], we adopt OpenBLAS as our low-level BLAS library to speedup our matrix and vector operations.

3   Implementation and Performance

3.1   Methodology

We present our methodology for implementing collaborative filtering on AMD x86 in Fig. 1.

3.2   Implementation

Firstly, we analyze the dataset. The dataset we used is MovieLens 20 M Dataset [8], which contains 20 million ratings and 465000 tag applications across 27000 movies by 13800 users. Table 1 shows the main data formats of this dataset.

Secondly, we implement a fast python collaborative filtering using ALS-WR for implicit feedback datasets [14]. Multi-threaded training routines are supported in our implementation, using Python and OpenMP to fit the AMD x86 CPU cores.

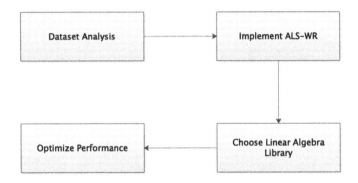

Fig. 1. Methodology

Table 1. Data format of movielens

File name	Attribute	Description
Movies	moviedID title geners	The attributes of movies
Rating	userID movieID rating timestamp	User ratings of the movie
Tags	userID movieID tag timestamp	User tags of the movie

Thirdly, we increase the speed of the program by fasting the matrix decomposition, compiling OpenBLAS library on AMD x86 machines.

Finally, we use a mix-grained (fine-grained and coarse-grained) parallel performance tuning framework. We tune both the threads of high-level ALS-WR algorithm and low-level matrix operations, getting the best performance with 256 threads.

3.3   Evaluation

Above all, we implement the ALS-WR algorithm based on OpenBLAS library on AMD x86 CPUs. Figure 2 shows the performance with the different total threads. The best performance reaches 124.86 s on 30 rounds using 256 threads.

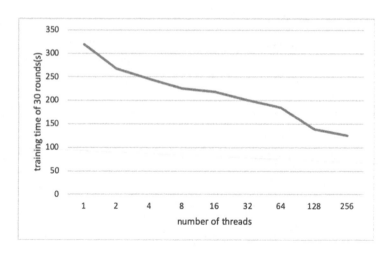

Fig. 2. Performance chart

4   Conclusion

This paper implements ALS-WR on AMD x86 CPUs. Moreover, we choose OpenBLAS as the underlying linear algebra library to optimize the matrix decomposition. Finally, we use an adaptive granularity tuning method to reach the best training performance (124.86 s for 30 rounds).

References

1. Recommender   system.   https://en.wikipedia.org/wiki/Recommender_system. Accessed 14 Oct 2019
2. Yang, B., Lei, Y., Liu, J., Li, W.: Social collaborative filtering by trust. IEEE Trans. Pattern Anal. Mach. Intell. **39**(8), 1633–1647 (2016)
3. Das, A.S., Datar. M., Garg, A., Rajaram, S.: Google news personalization: scalable online collaborative filtering. In: Proceedings of the 16th International Conference on World Wide Web, 8 May 2007, pp. 271–280. ACM (2017)
4. Linden, G., Smith, B., York, J.: Amazon. com recommendations: item-to-item collaborative filtering. IEEE Internet Comput. **1**(1), 76–80 (2003)
5. Netflix. http://www.netflix.com. Accessed 14 Oct 2019
6. Reddit. https://www.reddit.com. Accessed 14 Oct 2019
7. Youtube. https://www.youtube.com/. Accessed 14 Oct 2019
8. MovieLens. https://grouplens.org/datasets/movielens/
9. Harper, F.M., Konstan, J.A.: The movielens datasets: history and context. ACM Trans. Interact. Intell. Syst. (TIIS) **5**(4), 19 (2016)
10. ALS description in apache flink. https://ci.apache.org/projects/flink/flink-docs-release-1.2/dev/libs/ml/als.html. Accessed 25 Oct 2019
11. Zhou, Y., Wilkinson, D., Schreiber, R., Pan, R.: Large-scale parallel collaborative filtering for the netflix prize. In: Fleischer, R., Xu, J. (eds.) AAIM 2008. LNCS, vol. 5034, pp. 337–348. Springer, Heidelberg (2008). https://doi.org/10.1007/978-3-540-68880-8_32

12. BLAS. https://en.wikipedia.org/wiki/Basic_Linear_Algebra_Subprograms. Accessed 25 Oct 2019
13. Xianyi, Z., Qian, W., Saar, W.: OpenBLAS: An optimized BLAS library. Agosto, Accedido (2016)
14. Hu, Y., Koren, Y., Volinsky, C.: Collaborative filtering for implicit feedback datasets. In: 2008 Eighth IEEE International Conference on Data Mining, 15 December 2008, pp. 263–272. IEEE (2008)
15. Li, Z., et al.: AutoFFT: a template-based FFT codes auto-generation framework for ARM and X86 CPUs. In: Proceedings of the International Conference for High Performance Computing, Networking, Storage and Analysis, 17 November 2019, p. 25. ACM (2019)
16. Wang, Q., Zhang, X., Zhang, Y., Yi, Q.: AUGEM: automatically generate high performance dense linear algebra kernels on x86 CPUs. In: SC 2013: Proceedings of the International Conference on High Performance Computing, Networking, Storage and Analysis, 17 November 2013, pp. 1–12. IEEE (2013)
17. Gao, W., et al.: AIBench: an industry standard internet service AI benchmark suite. arXiv preprint arXiv:1908.08998, 13 August 2019
18. Gao, W., et al.: AIBench: towards scalable and comprehensive datacenter AI benchmarking. In: Zheng, C., Zhan, J. (eds.) Bench 2018. LNCS, vol. 11459, pp. 3–9. Springer, Cham (2019). https://doi.org/10.1007/978-3-030-32813-9_1
19. Hao, T., et al.: Edge AIBench: towards comprehensive end-to-end edge computing benchmarking. In: Zheng, C., Zhan, J. (eds.) Bench 2018. LNCS, vol. 11459, pp. 23–30. Springer, Cham (2019). https://doi.org/10.1007/978-3-030-32813-9_3
20. Jiang, Z., et al.: HPC AI500: a benchmark suite for HPC AI systems. In: Zheng, C., Zhan, J. (eds.) Bench 2018. LNCS, vol. 11459, pp. 10–22. Springer, Cham (2019). https://doi.org/10.1007/978-3-030-32813-9_2
21. Luo, C., et al.: AIoT bench: towards comprehensive benchmarking mobile and embedded device intelligence. In: Zheng, C., Zhan, J. (eds.) Bench 2018. LNCS, vol. 11459, pp. 31–35. Springer, Cham (2019). https://doi.org/10.1007/978-3-030-32813-9_4
22. Chen, M., Chen, T., Chen, Q.: An efficient implementation of the ALS-WR algorithm on x86 CPUs. In: Gao, W., et al. (eds.) Bench 2019, LNCS, vol. 12093, pp. 116–122. Springer, Cham (2019)
23. Deng, W., Wang, P., Wang, J., Li, C., Guo, M.: PSL: exploiting parallelism, sparsity and locality to accelerate matrix factorization on X86 platforms. In: Gao, W., et al. (eds.) Bench 2019, LNCS, vol. 12093, pp. 101–109. Springer, Cham (2019)
24. Xiong, X., Wen, X., Huang, C.: Improving RGB-D face recognition via transfer learning from a pretrained 2D network. In: Gao, W., et al. (eds.) Bench 2019, LNCS, vol. 12093, pp. 141–148. Springer, Cham (2019)
25. Gong, T., Niu, H.: An implementation of ResNet on the classification of RGB-D images. In: Gao, W., et al. (eds.) Bench 2019, LNCS, vol. 12093, pp. 149–155. Springer, Cham (2019)
26. Li, J., Jiang, Z.: Performance analysis of cambricon MLU100. In: Gao, W., et al. (eds.) Bench 2019, LNCS, vol. 12093, pp. 57–66. Springer, Cham (2019)
27. Li, G., Wang, X., Ma, X., Liu, L., Feng, X.: XDN: towards efficient inference of residual neural networks on cambricon chips. In: Gao, W., et al. (eds.) Bench 2019, LNCS, vol. 12093, pp. 51–56. Springer, Cham (2019)
28. Hou, P., Yu, J., Miao, Y., Tai, Y., Wu, Y., Zhao, C.: RVTensor: a light-weight neural network inference framework based on the RISC-V architecture. In: Gao, W., et al. (eds.) Bench 2019, LNCS, vol. 12093, pp. 85–90. Springer, Cham (2019)

An Efficient Implementation
of the ALS-WR Algorithm on x86 CPUs

Maosen Chen[1], Tun Chen[2(✉)], and Qianyun Chen[3]

[1] Qihoo 360 Technology Co. Ltd., Beijing, China
`chenmaosen@360.cn`
[2] SKL of Computer Architecture, Institute of Computing Technology,
Chinese Academy of Sciences, Beijing, China
`chentun@ict.ac.cn`
[3] College of Computing, Georgia Institute of Technology, Atlanta, Georgia
`qchen336@gatech.edu`

Abstract. With the continuous development of computers and big data
technology, more recommendation systems are applied in the fields of
online music, online movies, games, online shopping, and so on, to
solve information redundancy and effectively to recommend interesting products for users. In this paper, we implement and accelerate the
Alternating-Least-Squares with Weighted-λ-Regularization (ALS-WR)
by adopting a two-level parallel strategies on the x86-64 Zen-based CPUs.
As one of the most widely used recommendation algorithms, the ALS-
WR algorithm is based on matrix factorization. In the mathematical
discipline of linear algebra, a matrix decomposition or matrix factorization is a dimensionality reduction technique that factorizes a matrix
into a product of matrices. Therefore, vector and matrix operations are
the computational core of the ALS-WR algorithm, accelerating these
computational kernels can effectively improve the overall performance of
the ALS-WR algorithm. The experimental results show that our high-
performance ALS-WR implementation can achieve 185.09 s (with 100
features and 30 iterations) on the MovieLens 20 M dataset.

Keywords: ALS-WR · Matrix factorization · Matrix multiplcation ·
Recommendation algorithm

1 Introduction

Recommender systems are utilized in a variety of areas and are most commonly
recognized as multimedia recommenders like Netflix, YouTube, and Spotify,
product recommenders such as Amazon, Taobao in Alibaba, or content recommenders for social media platforms such as Facebook and Twitter [7]. These
systems aim to provide users with personalized online product or service recommendations by predicting the rating score or preference that a user would give to
an item based on users' buying or browsing behaviors. In this way, the user can
handle the increasing online information overload problem and improve customer

© Springer Nature Switzerland AG 2020
W. Gao et al. (Eds.): Bench 2019, LNCS 12093, pp. 116–122, 2020.
https://doi.org/10.1007/978-3-030-49556-5_12

relationship management. Given the predicted rating score, the business will then recommend preferable new items to the user for further purchases. There are three main kind of recommendation systems: content-based, collaborative filtering-based and deep learning based. Collaborative filtering method is simple and effective and widely used in lots of internet companies like Amazon [16], Google News [2], and other academic contests or related evaluations like AIBench [5,6], Edge AIBench [8], Netfix, HPC AI500 [13], AIoT Bench [17] and so on. AIBench is open source http://www.benchcouncil.org/benchhub/AIBench/. A major appeal of collaborative filtering is that it is domain free, yet it can address data aspects that are often elusive and difficult to profile using content filtering, while generally more accurate than content-based techniques. Collaborative filtering relies solely on the rating scores that a user gave to the item, where the features of the user (such as age and gender) or the item (such as perishable or not) itself do not play an important role in the algorithm.

BenchCouncil organizes a series of International AI challenges in 2019. It contains four challenges tracks: (1) International AI System Challenge based on RISC-V Subject [11]; (2) International AI System Challenge based on Cambricon Chip [14]; (3) International 3D Face Recognition Algorithm Challenge [23]; and (4) International AI System Challenge based on X86 Platform. Our work is based on the track 4. In this paper, we focus on the Alternating Least Squares with Weighted-λ-Regularization (ALS-WR) algorithm [24], one of the most commonly used approaches for performing matrix factorization on recommender systems on the MovieLens dataset [10] and update the two low-rank matrices' weight alternately which save a lot of time and operate in a clever way without hurting the performance. The ALS-WR algorithm was developed for the Netflix Prize competition, which also involved a sparse matrix of reviewers by items being reviewed. It has the advantage over the Stochastic Gradient Descent (SGD) [1] and Restricted Boltzmann Machines (RBM) [20] algorithms that require fewer features to be specified and has been previously been shown to have great efficiency potential on CPUs [18].

Assuming that we have a user-item rating matrix $R = \{r_{ij}\}_{u \times m}$. Each element r_{ij} represents a rating score of movie j rated by user i with its value neither being a real number or being missing, u indicates the number of users and m indicates the number of movies. A high-quality recommendation system can estimate some of the missing values based on the existing values.

In real-world problems, the user-item matrix R is normally large, so matrix factorization is introduced to decompose matrix R into products of smaller matrices. As presented in Fig. 1 [19], the user-item matrix R is decomposed by the product of two smaller matrices $U = [u_i]$ and $M = [m_j]$. In the factorization process, we assume each row of the user matrix U represents one user with d features. Similarly, each column of the item matrix M represents an analogous set of d features. In order to generate a low-rank approximation of the user-item matrix R, all we have to do is to perform a matrix multiplication of the user matrix U and the item matrix M.

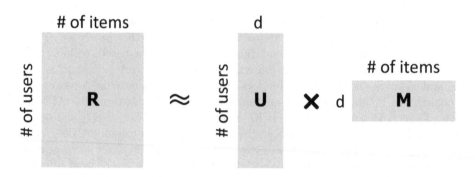

Fig. 1. Matrix factorization process.

First, we denote d features with each user by representing each user i has a d-dimensional vector x_i^T, which is normally referred to as the user latent vectors. Similarly, a movie j also has a d-dimensional vector y_j, and the rating score that we predict user i will give for movie j is the dot product of the two vectors, as presented in Eq. 1.

$$\hat{r_{ij}} = x_i y_j^T = \sum_d x_{id} y_{dj} \tag{1}$$

where $\hat{r_{ij}}$ represents the approximate pridction of the ground truth rating score r_{ij}.

Then we define the objective function to minimize the square of the difference between all rating scores in the dataset S and our predictions, as presented in Eq. 2.

$$L = \sum_{i,j \in S} (r_{ij} - x_i y_j^T)^2 + \lambda(\sum_i \|x_i\|^2 + \sum_j \|y_j\|^2) \tag{2}$$

where λ is a hyperparameter used for preventing overfitting of the user and item vectors.

2   Alternating Least Squares with Weighted-λ-Regularization

In order to solve this low-rank approximation problem, the iterative algorithm ALS-WR [24] is adopted. Many optimization [3,9] approaches are adopted for ALS-WR algorithm. ALS-WR starts by treating one set of latent vectors as constant. For this example, it picks the item vectors y_j, then takes the derivative of the loss function with respect to the user vectors x_i, and solve for the user vectors, as presented in Eq. 3.

$$\frac{\partial L}{\partial x_i} = -2 \sum_j (r_{ij} - x_i y_j^T) y_j + 2\lambda x_i = 0$$
$$= x_i = r_i Y (Y^T Y + \lambda I)^{-1} \tag{3}$$

where vector r_i represents the ith user from the rating score matrix with all scores for all movies; Y is a $m \times d$ representing all movies row vectors vertically stacked together; and I is the identity matrix with dimension $d \times d$.

Next, after updating the user vectors x_i, we take them as constant and alternatively update the item vectors y_j in a similar way, as presented in Eq. 4. Then we alternate back and forth and carry out these two steps until convergence.

$$\frac{\partial L}{\partial y_j} = y_j = r_j X (X^T X + \lambda I)^{-1} \tag{4}$$

2.1 The ALS-WR Process

In general, the ALS algorithm can be summarized as the following four steps:

1. Initialize matrix M by assigning the average rating for that movie as the first row, and small random numbers for the remaining entries.
2. Fix M, Solve U by minimizing the objective function (the sum of squared errors).
3. Fix U, solve M by minimizing the objective function similarly.
4. Repeat Steps 2 and 3 until a stopping criterion is satisfied.

Here we use the observed root-mean-square error (RMSE) as the stopping criterion on the MovieLens dataset. Each round we will update both matrices U and M, if the criterion is obtained, then we use the obtained matrices U and M to make final predictions on the test dataset.

2.2 Two-Level Parallelization

In each round of the ALS-WR algorithm, we need to update matrices U and M, respectively. In order to accelerate each iteration, we implement a two-level parallel method.

1. **High-level Parallelism.** In order to update each user's feature vector x_i, we need to take the rating score matrix R and the movie matrix M as inputs. This process contains native parallelism: we can parallel the computational operations of multiple users and update their feature vectors simultaneously. Similarly, while updating the movie matrix M, the same parallel strategy can be adopted.

Table 1. Experimental Environment

CPU	Arch	# of threads	L1d cache	OpenBLAS
AMD Zen	Zen	64	32 KB	0.3.7

2. **Low-level Parallelism.** The core operations of the ALS-WR algorithm are updating the user matrix U and the movie matrix M, as presented in Eq. 3 and Eq. 4, their operations can be simplified to some basic vector and matrix operations, such as matrix multiplication, matrix-vector multiplication, matrix transposition, and so on. These basic routines are provided by most of BLAS (Basic Linear Algebra Subprograms) libraries. Existing BLAS libraries, such as OpenBLAS [22] and Intel MKL [12], are highly optimized and tuned by researchers and vendors. These implementations have undergone extensive architecture-dependent tuning on specific microarchitecture features to pursue peak system performance. Most important of all, these BLAS libraries also provide high-performance multi-threaded implementations for users to make full use of their underlying computing resources. As for large matrix multiplication, we can replace it by the FFT algorithm. Efficient FFT librarlies [4, 12, 15] can accelerate this process. In our ALS-WR (Zen-ALSWR), we adopt OpenBLAS to carry out these vector and matrix operations.

3   Performance Evaluation

This section evaluates the performance of Zen-ALSWR on server-grade Zen x86-64 (AMD Zen microarchitecture [21]) CPUs. The experimental conditions are listed in Table 1. Considering OpenBLAS 0.3.7 version has been deeply optimized for its kernels for Zen Dhyana zen CPUs, we take this version as our underlying BLAS library to accelerate the performance of vector and matrix operations.

Table 2. MovieLens ml-20m dataset

Dataset	# Ratings	# Users	# Movies	Sparsity	RMSE Loss
All	20,000,263	138,493	25,809	0.540%	Null
Train	16,003,852	138,493	25,809	0.448%	2.882
Test	3,996,411	138,493	25,809	0.112%	2.473

Our experiments are based on the MovieLens ml-20m dataset. We randomly take 80% of the ml-20m dataset according to ratings as training data and take the remaining 20% of the data as the test dataset which is listed in Table 2. Moreover, we set the number of features as 100 and the number of iterations as 30, then the performance will be evaluated by recording the training time (wall clock time).

Figure 2 represents the performance of our Zen-ALSWR on AMD Zen CPUs. As the number of threads increases, the training time is greatly reduced. For the single-threaded Zen-ALSWR, it costs about 6237.28 s to complete the whole training process. When we adopt 64 threads within a node to parallel the training progress, the training time decreases into 185.09 s. Figure 2 shows that Zen-ALSWR seems to be a scalable and efficient implementation for large-scale collaborative filtering.

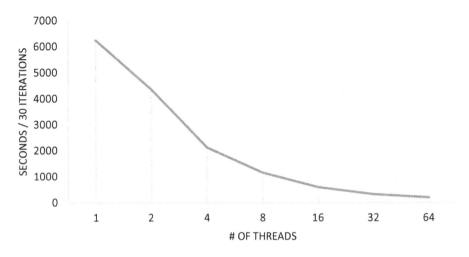

Fig. 2. The performance of the multithreaded Zen-ALSWR on MovieLens ml-20m dataset.

4   Conclusion

This paper introduces a high-performance ALS-WR implementation named Zen-ALSWR on AMD Zen CPUs. Because the parallel strategies are straightforward for the ALS-WR implementation, the Zen-ALSWR is designed to be scalable and efficient to very large datasets on server-grade CPUs.

References

1. Bottou, L., Bousquet, O.: The tradeoffs of large scale learning. In: Advances in Neural Information Processing Systems, pp. 161–168 (2008)
2. Das, A.S., Datar, M., Garg, A., Rajaram, S.: Google news personalization: scalable online collaborative filtering. In: Proceedings of the 16th International Conference on World Wide Web, pp. 271–280. ACM (2007)
3. Deng, W., Wang, P., Wang, J., Li, C., Guo, M.: PSL: exploiting parallelism, sparsity and locality to accelerate matrix factorization on x86 platforms. In: Gao, W., et al. (eds.) Bench 2019, LNCS, vol. 12093, pp. 101–109. Springer, Cham (2019)
4. Frigo, M., Johnson, S.G.: FFTW: an adaptive software architecture for the FFT. In: Proceedings of the 1998 IEEE International Conference on Acoustics, Speech and Signal Processing, ICASSP 1998 (Cat. No. 98CH36181), vol. 3, pp. 1381–1384. IEEE (1998)
5. Gao, W., et al.: AIBench: towards scalable and comprehensive datacenter AI benchmarking. In: Zheng, C., Zhan, J. (eds.) Bench 2018. LNCS, vol. 11459, pp. 3–9. Springer, Cham (2019). https://doi.org/10.1007/978-3-030-32813-9_1
6. Gao, W., et al.: AIBench: an industry standard internet service ai benchmark suite. arXiv preprint arXiv:1908.08998 (2019)
7. Gupta, P., Goel, A., Lin, J., Sharma, A., Wang, D., Zadeh, R.B.: WTF: the who-to-follow system at Twitter. In: Proceedings of the 22nd international conference on World Wide Web WWW (2013)

8. Hao, T., et al.: Edge AIBench: towards comprehensive end-to-end edge computing benchmarking. In: Zheng, C., Zhan, J. (eds.) Bench 2018. LNCS, vol. 11459, pp. 23–30. Springer, Cham (2019). https://doi.org/10.1007/978-3-030-32813-9_3

9. Hao, T., Zheng, Z.: The implementation and optimization of matrix decomposition based collaborative filtering task on x86 platform. In: Gao, W., et al. (eds.) Bench 2019, LNCS, vol. 12093, pp. 110–115. Springer, Cham (2019)

10. Harper, F.M., Konstan, J.A.: The movielens datasets: history and context. ACM Trans. Interact. Intell. Syst. (TIIS) 5(4), 19 (2016)

11. Hou, P., Yu, J., Miao, Y., Tai, Y., Wu, Y., Zhao, C.: RVTensor: a light-weight neural network inference framework based on the RISC-V architecture. In: Gao, W., et al. (eds.) Bench 2019, LNCS, vol. 12093, pp. 85–90. Springer, Cham (2019)

12. Intel: Intel math kernel library (intel mkl) 2019 update 4. https://software.intel.com/en-us/mkl (2019)

13. Jiang, Z., et al.: HPC AI500: a benchmark suite for HPC AI systems. In: Zheng, C., Zhan, J. (eds.) Bench 2018. LNCS, vol. 11459, pp. 10–22. Springer, Cham (2019). https://doi.org/10.1007/978-3-030-32813-9_2

14. Li, G., Wang, X., Ma, X., Liu, L., Feng, X.: XDN: towards efficient inference of residual neural networks on cambricon chips. In: Gao, W., et al. (eds.) Bench 2019, LNCS, vol. 12093, pp. 51–56. Springer, Cham (2019)

15. Li, Z., et al.: AutoFFT: a template-based FFT codes auto-generation framework for arm and x86 CPUs. In: Proceedings of the International Conference for High Performance Computing, Networking, Storage and Analysis, p. 25. ACM (2019)

16. Linden, G., Smith, B., York, J.: Amazon. com recommendations: item-to-item collaborative filtering. IEEE Internet Comput. 7(1), 76–80 (2003)

17. Luo, C., et al.: AIoT bench: towards comprehensive benchmarking mobile and embedded device intelligence. In: Zheng, C., Zhan, J. (eds.) Bench 2018. LNCS, vol. 11459, pp. 31–35. Springer, Cham (2019). https://doi.org/10.1007/978-3-030-32813-9_4

18. Makari Manshadi, F.: Scalable optimization algorithms for recommender systems (2014)

19. Ortega, F., Hernando, A., Bobadilla, J., Kang, J.H.: Recommending items to group of users using matrix factorization based collaborative filtering. Inf. Sci. 345, 313–324 (2016)

20. Salakhutdinov, R., Mnih, A., Hinton, G.: Restricted Boltzmann machines for collaborative filtering. In: Proceedings of the 24th International Conference on Machine Learning, pp. 791–798. ACM (2007)

21. Singh, T., et al.: Zen: a next-generation high-performance× 86 core. In: 2017 IEEE International Solid-State Circuits Conference (ISSCC), pp. 52–53. IEEE (2017)

22. Xianyi, Z., Qian, W., Chothia, Z.: OpenBLAS: an optimized BLAS library. https://github.com/xianyi/OpenBLAS (2019)

23. Xiong, X., Wen, X., Huang, C.: Improving RGB-D face recognition via transfer learning from a pretrained 2D network. In: Gao, W., et al. (eds.) Bench 2019, LNCS, vol. 12093, pp. 141–148. Springer, Cham (2019)

24. Zhou, Y., Wilkinson, D., Schreiber, R., Pan, R.: Large-scale parallel collaborative filtering for the Netflix prize. In: Fleischer, R., Xu, J. (eds.) AAIM 2008. LNCS, vol. 5034, pp. 337–348. Springer, Heidelberg (2008). https://doi.org/10.1007/978-3-540-68880-8_32

Accelerating Parallel ALS
for Collaborative Filtering on Hadoop

Yi Liang$^{(\boxtimes)}$, Shaokang Zeng, Yande Liang, and Kaizhong Chen

Faculty of Information Technology, Beijing University of Technology,
Beijing 100124, China
yliang@bjut.edu.cn

Abstract. Collaborative Filtering (CF) is an important building block
of recommendation systems. Alternating Least Squares (ALS) is the most
popular algorithm used in CF models to calculate the latent factor matrix
factorization. Parallel ALS on Hadoop is widely used in the era of big
data. However, existing work on the computational efficiency of parallel
ALS on Hadoop have two defects. One is the imbalance of data distribution, the other is lacking the fine-grained parallel processing on the
rating data. Aiming on these issues, we propose an integrated optimized
solution. The solution first optimizes the rating data partition with the
consideration of both the number of involved data records and the partitioned data size. Then, the multithread-based fine-grained parallelism
is introduced to process rating data records within a map task concurrently. Experimental results demonstrate that our solution can reduce
the overall runtime of Hadoop ALS by 82.17% by maximum.

Keywords: Collaborative Filtering · Alternating Least Squares ·
Hadoop

1 Introduction

Recommendation [1,3,5,14] systems are designed to analyze and find available
user data to recommend relevant and interesting items to consumers, which
have become increasingly indispensable for the online businesses. Collaborative
Filtering (CF) [2,4] is an important building block in recommendation systems,
which predicts the user preference based on the preferences of a group of users
who are considered to be similar to the active user. Alternating Least Squares
(ALS) [16,22] is the most popular algorithm used in CF models to calculate the
latent factor matrix factorization. ALS can easily be parallelized and efficiently
handle the CF models that incorporate implicit data, and hence, it has been
proved to be more general and efficient than traditional methods.

Map/Reduce is a parallel programming model as well as the corresponding framework that enables to process a massive volume of data with low-end

Supported by 2019 BenchCouncil AI System and Algorithm Challenge.

W. Gao et al. (Eds.): Bench 2019, LNCS 12093, pp. 123–137, 2020.
https://doi.org/10.1007/978-3-030-49556-5_13

computing nodes in a scalable and fault-tolerant manner. Hadoop is the most popular implementation of Map/Reduce. The parallel Hadoop implementations of ALS (for short, Hadoop ALS) are of great interest in the era of big data. In this paper, we mainly focus on the computational efficiency of parallel ALS on Hadoop. The user-item rating data are the major data to be processed in ALS. Existing works on Hadoop ALS have two limitations in the rating data processing. The first is the rating data distribution imbalance [13,15]. In Hadoop ALS, the rating data of a user or an item are represented as the $< key, value >$ record. The size of the records in the rating data are various. Existing works partition the rating data equally among the parallel map tasks in term of the data size and do not consider the different amounts of records involved in the partitioned data [23]. However, our observation demonstrates that the execution time of a parallel task is mainly determined by the amount of processed rating data records. Hence, existing rating data partition in Hadoop ALS leads the load among parallel tasks imbalance. The second limitation is lacking the fine-grained parallel processing on the rating data. In Hadoop ALS, the rating data are parallel processed by multiple map tasks. In each map task, a bunch of rating data records is processed in serial. However, these data records can be processed independently without any data dependency. Hence, more fine-grained parallelism should be exploited within a map task to accelerate Hadoop ALS.

Aiming to overcome the above limitations, an integrated optimized solution for Hadoop ALS is proposed. The solution first optimizes the rating data partition with the consideration of both the number of involved data records and the partitioned data size. Then, the multithread mechanism in each map task is introduced to process rating data records concurrently. With our solution, the load balance and fine-grained parallelism can be achieved to accelerate the rating data processing in Hadoop ALS. In generally, the main contributions of the paper can be summarized as follows.

1) Record-based rating data partition model. In this model, the rating data records are partitioned into HDFS files. Each data record is mapped into one HDFS file. To select the mapping file for a data record, the model partitions these HDFS files based on their size and the number of involved records. The model chooses the file with the minimum amount of records, when all files have the similar file size, so as to balance the amount of involved records in the rating data partitions and avoid the extreme situation that too many small-sized rating records are mapped into one partition.

2) Fine-grained parallelism within the map task. In our solution, the multithread mechanism is introduced into the map tasks. We adopt the producer-consumer model in rating data processing. That is, the main process of map task reads the rating data records and the forked threads parallel process these records. We also introduce the golden section search method to determine the map task number and the concurrent thread number, so as to balance the data parallel reading and processing capacity of Hadoop ALS.

3) Performance Evaluation. We evaluate our solution with the MovieLens 20M Dataset from GroupLens. Experimental results demonstrate that our

solution can reduce the overall runtime of Hadoop ALS by 82.17% by maximum, while not hurting RMSE of Hadoop ALS significantly.

Works in this paper are supported by 2019 BenchCouncil AI System and Algorithm Challenge. 2019 BenchCouncil AI System and Algorithm Challenge includes three system tracks and an algorithm track, i.e, Cambricon track [24,25], RISC-V track [26], X86 track [27,28], and 3D face recognition track [29]. The challenge uses BenchCouncil AIBench as baseline [17,18], which is publicly available from http://www.benchcouncil.org/benchhub/AIBench/(Sign up to get access). Also, BenchCouncil provides AI benchmarks for HPC [19], AIoT [21] and Edge [20].

The rest of the paper is organized as follows. Section 2 describes the principle of the ALS algorithm and implementation of Hadoop ALS. Section 3 proposes the record-based rating data partitioning model. Section 4 present the multithread-based fine-grained parallelism with the map task. In Sect. 5, the performance evaluation is present in detail. Section 6 describes the conclusion and future works.

2 Related Work

Many works optimize the ALS algorithm at the algorithm level. Based on Hadoop, [12] proposed the collaborative filtering algorithm KASR to reduce the load on the system by increasing parallelism at the thread level, so that it can reduce the energy consumption. Based on spark, [10] proposed a GPU-based NMF algorithm, which can achieve high-speed operation and effectively handle non-negative decomposition of high-order matrices and greatly improve computational efficiency. [8] enables the ALS algorithm to achieve high precision results with less iterations and time. [9] extends the HALS to a distributed version and compare with the existing ALS in Spark MLlib to proves its superiority. However, these works all optimize and accelerate the ALS algorithm at the algorithm level, but ignoring the load imbalance problem of the sparse dataset on the distributed computing platform, and lacking the work of optimizing the ALS algorithm from the system level.

There are also works for layered parameter optimization and system modeling for Hadoop. [6] and [7] construct a fine-grained what-if performance prediction model, which integrates MapReduce job summary information, Hadoop cluster configuration information in job runtime, program input data and cluster hardware resource configuration information. Based on this model, the authors simulate the running effect of the program by adjusting the dataset size and changing the core configurations, so as to further optimize the system.

[11] analyses various adjustment parameters on system level (number of map task running simultaneously for each microserver node, block size of HDFS), application level (application type and input data size), and architecture level (operating voltage and frequency). The authors also discuss the impact of the performance, power and energy efficiency of the Hadoop micro-benchmark. Their work enlightens us to adjust the parameters and optimize the system at different levels.

3   Background of Hadoop ALS

In this section, we first describe the principle of ALS algorithm, then analyze the problems existing in the parallel implementation of ALS on Hadoop.

3.1   Principle of ALS

Collaborative filtering is an important building block in recommendation systems, which generates recommendation based on the similarity of users or items. In the famous Netflix Prize algorithm competition, [16] proposed the collaborative filtering based on Alternating Least Squares (ALS), which has significant advantages over other algorithms on the computational efficiency because of the embarrassing parallel characteristic of ALS. ALS adopts the iterative way to solve a series of least squares regression problems. For the user-item rating matrix R, a low rank matrix X is found to approximate the original matrix R. Solving R can be expressed as follows.

$$R \approx X = UI^T, \tag{1}$$

where $U \in C^{m \times d}$, $I \in C^{n \times d}$ and C represent complex numbers, m and n represent the numbers of rows and columns of the matrix R and d represents the number of eigenvalues.

The specific process is to randomly generate U_0, and fix it to solve I_0, then fix I_0 to solve U_1, which is called alternating computing. ALS is convergent because each iteration reduces the reconstruction error which has a lower bound. However, the Matrix Factorization speed of ALS is slow with high computing cost, which reflects the characteristics of computing-intensive workload.

3.2   Hadoop Implementation of ALS

Hadoop is the most popular implementation of Map/Reduce program model. A typical Hadoop job consists at most one map phase and one reduce phase. Each phase is executed with parallel tasks. In Hadoop job, the input data are represent as the $< key, value >$ pairs, the map/reduce task consumes one pair each time. The user-item rating data are the major input data of ALS. In Hadoop ALS, the rating data are organized in term of UserID or ItemID. That is, all rating data associated with one user or item are represent by one $< key, value >$ pair, with UserID or ItemID as the key and all related rating data as the value. In Hadoop ALS, we call such $< key, value >$ pair as a rating data record.

Figure 1 shows the workflow of Hadoop ALS. In Hadoop ALS, the rating data are first preprocessed and partitioned.Then,for each data partition, an ALS map task is launched to process it. When all parallel map task finished, the new Matrix U and I are generated. The above operations are conducted iteratively until the number of iterations reaches the threshold.

In Hadoop ALS job, there isn't the reduce phase. ALS map task consumes one rating data record each time. There is no data dependency among record

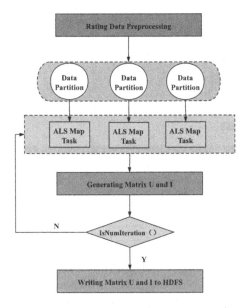

Fig. 1. Workflow of Hadoop ALS

processing. On the other hand, due to the uncertainty of user's rating behavior, the amount of rating data associated with users/items are various. Hence, the size of the data records are quite different in rating data.

4   User-Item Rating Data Partitioning

In this section, we first analyze the distribution and time consuming of the user-item rating data records, then propose the record-based partition model for the rating data.

4.1   Imbalance in Rating Data Processing

In Hadoop ALS, the user-item rating data are the major data to be processed iteratively. In each iteration, the user-item rating data need to be processed in term of user id and item id alternatively. Hence, in the Hadoop implementation of ALS, the user-item rating data are represented as $< key, value >$ list and stored in two copies. In one copy, a record has the key as the user id and the value as the collection of all rating data of a specific user and can be formatted as ⟨$userid, [itemid:rating, itemid:rating...]$⟩. The other copy has the key as the item id and the value as the collection of all rating data of a specific item, and can be formatted as ⟨$itemid, [userid:rating, userid:rating...]$⟩. On the data processing, the rating records are partitioned among the map tasks in the same data size. The map task reads one key-value record in each time and works out the statistics of the comprehensive rating data of one user or item.

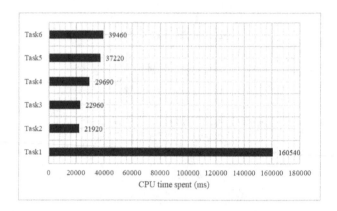

Fig. 2. Runtime of map tasks in Hadoop ALS

We evaluate the performance of ALS in Hadoop with the Movielen 20 M data on three computing nodes. The total size of user-item rating data is 724 MB. The number of map task is set to 6. In our evaluation, the jobs for the User and Item matrix training are dominant the execution time of parallel ALS in Hadoop. Among these, QR factorization is the core part, which takes up 86% of User and Item Matrix training time. Figure 2 demonstrates the load imbalance in the runtime of Item matrix training jobs. Among 6 map tasks, task 1 has the significantly longer execution time than the other five tasks, at least four times longer than others. We then analyze the data processed by each map task. Figure 3 shows the data size and the key-value records processed by the six tasks, respectively. Even though the rating data are partitioned equally in term of data size, the key-value records distribution among parallel map tasks are quite imbalanced. Particularly, the number of records processed by task #1 is 7 times larger than others at least. It is reasonable due to that with the amount of items growing up, the user has more possibility to give the explicit ratings to part of items randomly. This leads the various value numbers in key-value records, and thus, the various record numbers in rating data partitions. On the other hand, the computational complexity of QR factorization in Hadoop ALS is represent as km^3, where k is the record number and m is the feature number. Hence, in Hadoop ALS, tasks, which process the rating data partitions with larger record amount, will have longer runtime.

4.2 Record-Based Rating Data Partitioning

Based on our evaluation, We propose a record-based rating data partition model in this section. Be different from the data partition in Hadoop ALS, for the two rating data copies, the model partitions the data with the consideration of both the partition data size and the records involved in each partition.

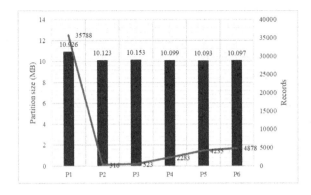

Fig. 3. Data size and record numbers of map tasks in Hadoop ALS

Figure 4 demonstrates the framework of our data partition model. In this model, the rating data are partitioned and stored into several HDFS files. Each data record is stored into only one file. The number of files is equal to that of map tasks in Hadoop ALS jobs. We implement the rating data partitioning in the rating data pre-processing job. The data partitioning algorithm is described in Algorithm 1.

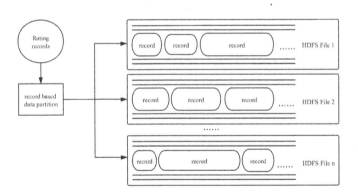

Fig. 4. Record-based rating data partitioning model

In this strategy, the inputs are the raw rating data record set and the number of map tasks, the output is the HDFS file set containing the partitioned rating data. The rating data are processed once a record. For each output file, a storing priority is assigned. The priority can be expressed as Eq. 2.

$$weight = (nv_i/N_v) \times w_v + (nr_i/N_r) \times w_r, \tag{2}$$

where, nv_i is the number of values in the output file, nr_i is the amount of records involved in output file i, N_v is the total number of values of all output files, N_r is

---

Algorithm 1: Rating data partitioning algorithm

Input: *the rating records list RecordsList,the number of output files OutputNum*
Output: *the output files set OutputfileSet*

1:   Initialize:OutputfileSet $\leftarrow \emptyset$;file $\leftarrow \emptyset$;
2:   **for** $i \leftarrow 1$ to OutputNum **do**
3:       $file_i \leftarrow createOutputfile(i)$;
4:       $file_i.nv \leftarrow 0$;
5:       $file_i.nr \leftarrow 0$;
6:       $AddFile(file_i, OutputfileSet)$;
7:   **for each** $record_i \in RecordsList$ **do**
8:       $CalculateFilesWeight(OutputfileSet)$;
9:       $file \leftarrow FindTheMinWeightFile(OutputfileSet)$;
10:      $WriteRecord(record_i, file)$;
11:      $UpdateWeight(record_i, file)$;
12:   **return** $OutputfileSet$;

---

the total amount of records stored in all output files, w_r and w_v are determined by empirical values, but they need to satisfy Eq. 3.

$$w_r + w_v = 1 \tag{3}$$

We initialize an OutputfileSet, each file of it has four attribute which are nv, nr, weight and there records list (Line 1). nv_i and nr_i of each output file are initialized to 0 (Lines 2 to 6). For each rating record, the following steps are conducted. First, the storing priority of each output file is calculated with Eq. 2 (Line 8). Second, the file with highest priority is selected as the record's target output. Once there are multiple files with the highest priority, the target output is selected randomly (Line 9). Finally, nv and nr of the selected output file are increased by the number of values in the rating record and by one, respectively (Line 10 to 11). Our partition strategy can balance the amount of records involved in output files and avoid the extreme situation that too many small-sized rating records are stored in one file. The priority weights w_r and w_v enable users to make trade-off between the balance of data size and the record amount among output files.

5   Multithread-Based Parallelism Within Map Task

As described in Sect. 2, the processing of each rating data record is independent. Existing Hadoop ALS processes the rating data records in serial within a map task. Hence, we introduce the multithread mechanism into the map task to achieve the fine-grained parallelism in Hadoop ALS. Based on the multithread mechanism, we adopt the Producer-Consumer model in the rating record processing. The model is shown in Fig. 5. The main process of map task acts as the producer to read the rating data records from HDFS files and put the records into the record queue. The multiple threads forked in a map task are taken as

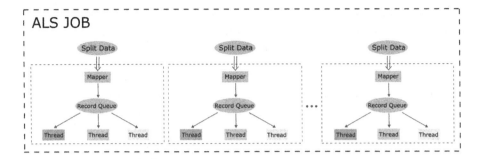

Fig. 5. Producer-Consumer model

consumers to fetch and compute the queued records concurrently. The proposed Producer-Consumer model not only pipelines the rating data reading and computing, but also enables the fine-grained parallelism of rating data computation within a map task.

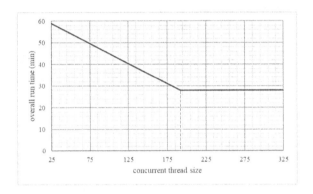

Fig. 6. Overall run time of different concurrent thread sizes

For a specific ALS job, the size of parallel map tasks determines its data reading capacity and the size of concurrent threads within the map task determines its data computing capacity. To achieve the capacity balance of data reading and computing, we need to make the trade-off between these two size settings. We first fix the map task size setting and examine Hadoop ALS performance under different concurrent thread size settings. As Fig. 6 shown, the execution time of Hadoop ALS job decreases with the concurrent thread size increase, and reaches to the minimum when the total size of concurrent threads across all map tasks is equal to the size of allocated computing resources. It is reasonable for that Hadoop ALS workload is computing-intensive and each thread needs to consume one computing core during its computation. Larger thread size setting leads to the less average workload dispatched to a thread. However, when the total size of threads exceeds that of allocated resources, the surplus threads will be suspended due to the computing resource contention and make no contributions to the Hadoop ALS performance improvement.

We further examine the relationship between Hadoop ALS performance and the map task size setting under the constraint of the fixed size of allocated computing resources. Denoting N as the size of allocated resources and m as the map task size, we set the concurrent thread size as $\frac{N}{m}$. As shown in Fig. 7, the relation function satisfies unimodal nonlinearity. Overall run time decreases with the map task size goes up, because the data reading capacity increases which matches the concurrent data computation capacity. Larger map task size leads to less inner concurrent threads, degrading rating data records processing throughput and in this situation, the capacity of data reading and computation is imbalance, which increases overall run time.

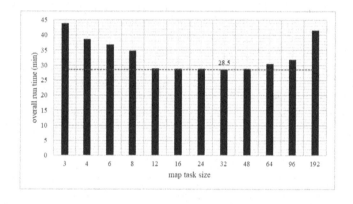

Fig. 7. Overall run time of different map task sizes

Hence, we adopt one-dimensional search strategy based on golden section heuristic method to find the optimal size settings. The search strategy can be described as Algorithm 2.

During the search, we attempt to find the optimal configuration for performance of ALS. In this algorithm, we record all attempted performance in the form of a tuple, (map task size, concurrent thread size), and all of tuples are stored in *Sampleset*. First, we initialize *Sampleset* and the search boundary as M_{min} and M_{max}(Line 1 to 2). Next, we iterated the following processing: we employ Golden Section Method to calculate candidate lower and upper boundaries(Line 4 to 5), and we find performance by these in *Sampleset*. If not find, set the map task size as b'_l or b'_u, the concurrent thread size as $\lceil \frac{M_{max}}{b'_l} \rceil$ or $\lceil \frac{M_{max}}{b'_u} \rceil$ to run ALS(Line 6 to 15). Then compare performance of two candidate boundaries, so as to determine how to update the search area(Line 16 to Line 19). The above operations are conducted iteratively until the lower and upper boundaries converge to small enough(Line 20). Finally, the optimal map task size is the one of the lower and upper boundaries that performs better(Line 21 to 22).

Algorithm 2: Optimized Map Task Size Searching Algorithm

Input: M_{min}: the minimum map task size, M_{max}: the maximum map task size, λ: the Golden Section coefficient, ϵ: the search threshold

Output: m: the optimal map task size

1:   $InitializeSampleset()$
2:   $b_l \leftarrow M_{min}; b_u \leftarrow M_{max}$
3:   **repeat**
4:     $b_l' \leftarrow b_l + (1 - \lambda)(b_u - b_l)$
5:     $b_u' \leftarrow b_l + \lambda(b_u - b_l)$
6:     if($FindByKey(Sampleset, b_l') ==$ False)
7:       $t_l \leftarrow runALS(b_l', UpRct(b_l', M_{max}))$
8:       $AddElement(Sampleset, (b_l', t_l))$
9:     else
10:      $t_l \leftarrow FindByKey(Sampleset, b_l')$
11:     if($FindByKey(Sampleset, b_u') ==$ False)
12:      $t_u \leftarrow runALS(b_u', UpRct(b_u', M_{max}))$
13:      $AddElement(Sampleset, (b_u', t_u))$
14:     else
15:      $t_u \leftarrow FindByKey(Sampleset, b_u')$
16:     if $(t_l \geq t_u)$
17:      $b_l \leftarrow b_l'$
18:     else
19:      $b_u \leftarrow b_u'$
20:   **until** $b_u - b_l \leq \epsilon$
21:   $m \leftarrow GetMinByValue(Sampleset, b_l, b_u)$
22:   return m

---

6   Performance Evaluation

We compare the performance of our optimized Hadoop ALS with the original Hadoop ALS from AIBench. Besides the record-based rating data partition model and the fine-grained parallelism within the map task, we optimize the JVM heap configurations of Hadoop ALS. In this section, we quantify the contributions of these optimization options to the performance enhancement of Hadoop ALS.

6.1   Experimental Design

The experiments are conducted on a cluster of 3 identical nodes supported by 2019 BenchCouncil AI System and Algorithm Challenge [17–21]. There is always one master node. Configurations of the cluster are described in Table 1. We execute Hadoop ALS on MovieLen dataset, which contains rating data of multiple users for movies and is often used as the dataset for recommendation system and machine learning algorithm evaluations. We use two metrics in our performance

Table 1. Experimental environment

Name	Configuration
CPU	X86 platform, 64 cores, 8 MB LLC
Memory	250 GB, 2667 MHz
OS	Kernel Linux 3.10.0
JVM	HotSpot JDK 8u221
Hadoop	Version 3.2.0
Mahout	Version 0.12.2

evaluations, Overall Run Time (ORT) for the computational efficiency and Root Mean Square Error (RMSE) for the training accuracy.

$$ORT = t_e - t_s \tag{4}$$

$$RMSE = \sqrt{\frac{\sum_i (v_i - v_i')^2}{n}} \tag{5}$$

where t_e and t_s represents the time stamp obtained at the end and the beginning of ALS algorithm, v_i' and v_i are the estimated value and the ground truth of instance i, respectively and n is the total number of observed values.

6.2   Performance Result Analysis

We first compare the overall performance of our optimized Hadoop ALS (OPHA) with the original Hadoop ALS (HA). The original Hadoop ALS are configured and executed in two ways, MP and MT. For MP, we disable the multithread mechanism in the map task and configure the size of map tasks as that of the allocated resources. For MT, we deploy one map task in each node and configure the thread size within a map task as the size of allocated resources in one node. The experimental results are shown in Fig. 8.

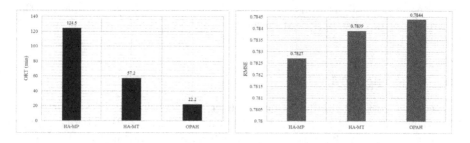

Fig. 8. ORT and RMSE of OPHA and original Hadoop ALS

The experimental results demonstrate that OPHA outperforms both HA-MP and HA-MT. The overall runtime is decreased by 82.17% and 61.19% respectively. However, RMSE is only increased by 0.22% by maximum. Even though all three Hadoop ALS implementations are executed with the same parallelism (that is, HA-MP with 180 parallel task processes, HA-MT and OPHA with 180 concurrent threads), HA-MP achieves the worst performance on overall runtime. This is for that, the process-level parallelism makes the rating data partitioned into more pieces and processed by map tasks separately, which leads to the higher possibility of load imbalance among these parallel tasks. On the other hand, the thread-level parallelism enables the data sharing among concurrent threads, and hence, increases the rating data records processing throughput within a map task and lower the possibility of load imbalance among map tasks. Compared to HA-MT, OPHA dispatches the rating data records among map tasks evenly and optimizes the map task size and concurrent thread size settings to balance the data reading and computation capacity, and hence, achieves better performance.

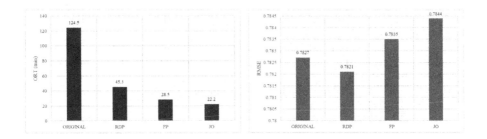

Fig. 9. Performance contributions of proposed optimization options

Figure 9 shows the performance enhancement contributions of all proposed optimization options, which include Record-based rating Data Partitioning (RDP), Fine-grained Parallelism (FP) and JVM heap size Optimization (JO). The overall runtime of Hadoop ALS can be reduced by 63.59% with RDP, further by 37.07% with FP, and finally by 22.18% with JO. The results prove that the rating data distribution imbalance and the serial data processing within the map task are the main sources of inefficiency of the original Hadoop ALS, and our integrated solution solve these two problems effectively.

7   Conclusion

In our work, we propose an integrated optimized solution for the parallel ALS on Hadoop, which incorporates the record-based rating data partition and multithread-based fine-grained parallelism within the map task. Experimental results demonstrate that our solution can reduce the overall runtime of Hadoop

ALS by 82.17% by maximum, while not hurting RMSE of Hadoop ALS significantly. In the future work, we will optimize the rating data partitioning strategy to accommodate the situation of larger-sized rating data and multi-waved map task execution.

References

1. Bokde, D., Girase, S., Mukhopadhyay, D.: Matrix factorization model in collaborative filtering algorithms: a survey. J. Procedia Comput. Sci. **49**(1), 136–146 (2015)
2. Hernando, A., Bobadilla, J., Ortega, F.: A non negative matrix factorization for collaborative filtering recommender systems based on a Bayesian probabilistic model. Knowl.-Based Syst. **97**(4), 188–202 (2016)
3. Deshpande, M., Karypis, G.: Item-based top-n recommendation algorithms. ACM Trans. Inf. Syst. (TOIS) **22**(1), 143–177 (2004)
4. Hanmin, Y., Zhang, Q., Bai, X.: A new collaborative filtering algorithm based on modified matrix factorization. In: Electronic and Automation Control Conference (IAEAC), pp. 147–151. IEEE (2017)
5. Yang, Z., Chen, W., Huang, J.: Enhancing recommendation on extremely sparse data with blocks-coupled non-negative matrix factorization. J. Neurocomput. **278**, 126–133 (2018)
6. Herodotou, H., Dong, F., Babu, S.: Mapreduce programming and cost-based optimization crossing this chasm with starfish. J. Proc. VLDB Endowment **4**(12), 1446–1449 (2011)
7. Herodotou, H.: Hadoop performance models. J. arXiv preprint arXiv, 1106.0940(2011)
8. Manda, W., Michael, B., Anthony, L., Hans, D.: Algorithmic acceleration of parallel ALS for collaborative filtering: speeding up distributed big data recommendation in Spark. In: 21st International Conference on Parallel and Distributed Systems(ICPADS), pp. 682–691. IEEE (2015)
9. Krzysztof, F., Rafal, Z.: Distributed nonnegative matrix factorization with HALS algorithm on Apache Spark. In: Artificial Intelligence and Soft Computing - 17th International Conference (ICAISC), pp. 333–342 (2018)
10. Bing, T., Linyao, K., Xia, Y., Zhang, L.: GPU-accelerated large-scale non-negative matrix factorization using spark. In: Collaborative Computing: Networking, Applications and Worksharing- 14th International Conference (EAI), pp. 189–201 (2018)
11. Maria, M., Katayoun, N., Setareh, R., Houman, H.: Hadoop workloads characterization for performance and energy efficiency optimizations on microservers. J. IEEE Trans. Multi-Scale Comput. Syst. **4**(3), 355–368 (2018)
12. Jyotindra, T., Mahesh, P., Anjana, P.: A Hadoop based collaborative filtering recommender system accelerated on GPU using OpenCL. J. Int. J. Eng. Sci. Res. Technol. **6**(9), 195–209 (2017)
13. Teflioudi, C., Makari, F., Gemulla, R.: Distributed matrix completion. In: 12th International Conference on Data Mining (ICDM), pp. 655–664. IEEE(2012)
14. Yu, H.-F., Hsieh, C.-J.,Dhillon, I., et al.: Scalable coordinate descent approaches to parallel matrix factorization for recommender systems. In: 12th International Conference on Data Mining (ICDM), pp. 765–774. IEEE(2012)
15. Zaharia, M., et al.: Resilient distributed datasets: a fault-tolerant abstraction for in-memory cluster computing. In: Proceedings of the 9th USENIX conference on Networked Systems Design and Implementation, pp. 15–28 (2012)

16. Zhou, Y., Wilkinson, D., Schreiber, R., Pan, R.: Large-scale parallel collaborative filtering for the Netflix prize. In: Proceedings of the 4th International Conference on Algorithmic Aspects in Information and Management, pp. 337–348 (2008)
17. Wanling, G., Fei, T., Wang, L., Zhan, J., Lan, C., et. al.: AIBench: an industry standard internet service AI benchmark suite. J. arXiv preprint arXiv:1908.08998 (2019)
18. Gao, W., et al.: AIBench: towards scalable and comprehensive datacenter AI benchmarking. In: Zheng, C., Zhan, J. (eds.) Bench 2018. LNCS, vol. 11459, pp. 3–9. Springer, Cham (2019). https://doi.org/10.1007/978-3-030-32813-9_1
19. Jiang, Z., et al.: HPC AI500: a benchmark suite for HPC AI systems. In: Zheng, C., Zhan, J. (eds.) Bench 2018. LNCS, vol. 11459, pp. 10–22. Springer, Cham (2019). https://doi.org/10.1007/978-3-030-32813-9_2
20. Hao, T., Huang, Y., Wen, X., Gao, W., Zhang, F., Zheng, C., Wang, L., Ye, H., Hwang, K., Ren, Z., Zhan, J.: Edge AIBench: towards comprehensive end-to-end edge computing benchmarking. In: Zheng, C., Zhan, J. (eds.) Bench 2018. LNCS, vol. 11459, pp. 23–30. Springer, Cham (2019). https://doi.org/10.1007/978-3-030-32813-9_3
21. Luo, C., et al.: AIoT bench: towards comprehensive benchmarking mobile and embedded device intelligence. In: Zheng, C., Zhan, J. (eds.) Bench 2018. LNCS, vol. 11459, pp. 31–35. Springer, Cham (2019). https://doi.org/10.1007/978-3-030-32813-9_4
22. Comon, P., Luciani, X., de Almeida, A.L.F.: Tensor decompositions, alternating least squares and other tales. J. Chemom. **23**, 393–405 (2009)
23. Liu, L.: Computing infrastructure for big data processing. Front. Comput. Sci. **7**, 165–170 (2013)
24. Li, G., Wang, X., Ma, X., Liu, L., Feng, X.: XDN: Towards efficient inference of residual neural networks on cambricon chips. In: Gao, W., et al. (eds.) Bench 2019, LNCS, vol. 12093, pp. 51–56. Springer, Cham (2019)
25. Li, J., Jiang, Z.: Performance analysis of cambricon mlu100. In: Gao, W., et al. (eds.) Bench 2019, LNCS, vol. 12093, pp. 57–66. Springer, Cham (2019)
26. Hou, P., Yu, J., Miao, Y., Tai, Y., Wu, Y., Zhao, C.: RVTensor: A light-weight neural network inference framework based on the RISC-V architecture. In: Gao, W., et al. (eds.) Bench 2019, LNCS, vol. 12093, pp. 85–90. Springer, Cham (2019)
27. Deng, W., Wang, P., Wang, J., Li, C., Guo, M.: PSL: exploiting parallelism, sparsity and locality to accelerate matrix factorization on x86 platforms. In: Gao, W., et al. (eds.) Bench 2019, LNCS, vol. 12093, pp. 101–109. Springer, Cham (2019)
28. Hao, T., Zheng, Z.: The implementation and optimization of matrix decomposition based collaborative filtering task on x86 platform. In: Gao, W., et al. (eds.) Bench 2019, LNCS, vol. 12093, pp. 110–115. Springer, Cham (2019)
29. Xiong, X., Wen, X., Huang, C.: Improving RGB-D face recognition via transfer learning from a pretrained 2D network. In: Gao, W., et al. (eds.) Bench 2019, LNCS, vol. 12093, pp. 141–148. Springer, Cham (2019)

AI Challenges on 3D Face Recognition Using AIBench

Improving RGB-D Face Recognition via Transfer Learning from a Pretrained 2D Network

Xingwang Xiong[✉], Xu Wen, and Cheng Huang

University of Chinese Academy of Sciences, Beijing, China
{xiongxingwang18,wenxu14,huangcheng14}@mails.ucas.edu.cn

Abstract. 2D Face recognition has been extensively studied for decades and has reached remarkable results in recent years. However, 2D Face recognition is sensitive to variations in poses, facial expressions and illuminations. Depth images provide valuable information to help model facial boundaries and understand the global facial layout and provide low frequency patterns. Intuitively, RGB-D images are more robust to external environments than RGB images. Unfortunately, RGB-D datasets are orders of magnitude smaller than 2D datasets and insufficient to train a deep CNN model as effective as RGB-based models. To tackle these challenges, we present an RGB-D ResNet50 model which can be transferred from a pretrained RGB model and takes RGB-D images as input. We achieved an accuracy of 94.64% and won the 1st place on *3D Face Recognition Algorithm Challenge, 2019 BenchCouncil International Artificial Intelligence System Challenges.*

Keywords: Face recognition · RGB-D images · Transfer learning

1 Introduction

Face recognition is one of the most significant topics in the field of Artificial Intelligence. In recent years, deep models (e.g. AlexNet [20], VGGNet [30], GoogLeNet [32] and ResNet [13]) based on convolutional neural network (CNN) have made great progress in face recognition. But neural network structure is just one side of the coin. To explore the potential of CNN, a dataset with abundant RGB face images is required. There are several such large scale RGB image datasets available online. After LFW (13,233 images) [15], dataset volume has grown all the way (e.g. IJB series [24], CASIA-WebFace [35] and MF2 [26]) to millions of images.

However, 2D face recognition under bad environmental illumination, large head pose or big expression variations still remains challenging. An RGB-D image contains one more channel of depth information compared with RGB images. Depth information provides clues about illumination, pose and scale,

---

The source code is available at https://github.com/xingwxiong/Face3D-Pytorch.

© Springer Nature Switzerland AG 2020
W. Gao et al. (Eds.): Bench 2019, LNCS 12093, pp. 141–148, 2020.
https://doi.org/10.1007/978-3-030-49556-5_14

and a stabler facial texture [40]. Intuitively, RGB-D image based face recognition models are more robust and could have a better performance [4], or a better upper bound at least.

Nowadays, depth sensors such as Microsoft Kinect [39] and Intel RealSense [18] are becoming easily available and popular, and even some mobile phones are equipped with depth cameras. RGB-D data volume is growing, but still far smaller than RGB ones. For example, Lock3DFace contains 5,711 images and video clips taken by Kinect V2 [37]. Datasets like ND 2006, Bosphorus and BU-3DFE also only have thousands of 3D face images [6,19,28,36]. Those datasets are insufficient to train an efficient CNN model.

To leverage conventional RGB-based works and depth features on limited RGB-D dataset, we present an RGB-D ResNet50 model which can be transferred from a pretrained RGB model and takes RGB-D images as input. We achieved a competitive accuracy of 94.64%, outperforming RGB models taking merely RGB images as input and RGB-D models training from scratch. And we won the 1st place on *3D Face Recognition Algorithm Challenge*, one track of *2019 BenchCouncil International Artificial Intelligence System Challenges*. To our knowledge, among all the winning teams, we are the only one who uses inter-modal transfer learning to improve RGB-D face recognition [9,34].

3D Face Recognition Algorithm Challenge's topic is derived from AIBench [7,8], one of benchmarking projects proposed by BenchCouncil. Besides AIBench, BenchCouncil also proposes several other active benchmarking projects, such as BigDataBench [33], HPC AI500 [17], AIoT Bench [23], Edge AIBench [11]. The source code of AIBench is publicly available from http://www.benchcouncil.org/benchhub/AIBench/ (Sign up to get access).

2019 BenchCouncil International Artificial Intelligence System Challenges contains a total of 4 challenge tracks, namely *International AI System Challenge based on RISC-V* [14], *International AI System Challenge based on Cambricon Chip* [21,22], *International AI System Challenge based on X86 Platform* [2,5,12] and *International 3D Face Recognition Algorithm Challenge* [9,34], respectively.

2   Related Work

Face recognition, one of the earliest tasks in computer vision, has been researched for decades. 2D face recognition has achieved remarkable results, while 3D face recognition gets less attention.

2.1   3D Face Datasets and 3D Face Recognition

Many organizations collect data or use simulation to create 3D face datasets. However, all of them are much smaller than that of 2D face. 3D face images are usually stored in three types: depth-image, point cloud and mesh. Among them, depth-image method is cheaper than the other ones, so it's widely used nowadays.

Traditional methods for cloud point images use distances to recognize faces, such as Iterative Closest Point (ICP) [3] and Hausdorff distance. However, these methods are quite limited. Extracting features is a more flexible method, which can deal with all types of images. In recent years, deep learning plays an important role in 3D face recognition and has a better performance [40] (Table 1).

Table 1. Some typical 3D face dataset

Name	Number of persons	Number of images	Data type
Bosphorus [28]	105	4,666	Point cloud
BU-3DFE [36]	100	2,500	Mesh
GavabDB [25]	61	540	Mesh
Lock3DFace [37]	509	5,671	Depth-image
ND 2006 [6]	888	13,450	Depth-image
FRGC Ver2.0 [27]	466	4,007	Depth-image
FaceWarehouse [1]	150	–	Depth-image
Intellifusion RGB-D dataset [7]	1,205	403,068	Depth-image

2.2 RGB-D Images and Datasets

RGB-D is one kind of depth-image. It combines an ordinary RGB image with depth map, which reflects the distance between the surface of items and a given viewpoint. Although containing more information, RGB-D images can only be collected by certain devices and acquisition of such RGB-D images might take a long time, which limits the scale of RGB-D datasets. RGB-D datasets are orders of magnitude smaller than 2D datasets due to the acquisition cost and insufficient to train a deep CNN model with considerable quality.

2.3 Transfer Learning on RGB-D Datasets

Now that RGB-D contains 2D images, transfer learning is a good method for RGB-D data. [16] uses transfer learning on RGB-D dataset to make action recognition. While [10] and [29] make saliency detection and object recognition respectively. Using transfer learning can solve the problems caused by limited datasets, because there are plenty of 2D datasets which can be used. Using a pre-trained model can save resources as well.

3 Transfer Learning from RGB to RGB-D

From the perspective of low-level patterns, depth images attend to have smooth variations, contrasts and borders, but lack texture information and high frequency patterns [31], which is exactly complementary to RGB images. RGB-D images can provide the model more diverse features, compared to merely

RGB images. This is the very motivation for us to use RGB-D model instead of RGB model for face recognition.

As shown in Fig. 1, in addition to changing the last fully connected layer, we also adjust the uppermost convolution layer of ResNet50 [13] in order to feed the model with 4-channel RGB-D images. We copy the parameters of the middle layers of the RGB model and then fine tune the entire RGB-D model on the target Intellifusion RGB-D dataset.

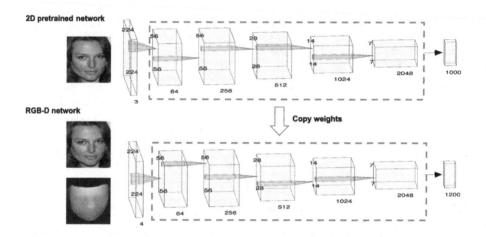

Fig. 1. Transfer learning from a pretrained RGB model.

4   Experiments

We conduct three experiments to compare the effects of depth images and inter-modal transfer learning on face recognition accuracy (see Table 2). The first experiment only uses RGB images and train the model on a pre-trained model. The second uses RGB-D images to train the RGB-D ResNet model from scratch. The third trains our RGB-D model on the target 3D dataset based on the 2D pretrained model.

Preprocessing. The faces and their landmarks in images are detected and aligned by MTCNN [38]. The images are horizontally flipped with a probability of 0.5 for data augmentation. Both RGB images and depth images are normalized to 0–1 range.

Train/test Split. The Intellifusion RGB-D face dataset contains 403,068 images of 1,205 people. We divide the dataset into a training set and a test set in a ratio of approximately 9:1. Categories with no more than 10 samples are removed. After discarding images in which no face is detected, there are 361,799 face images in the training set of 1,200 people and 40,809 images in the test set. Dataset is split under closed-set settings, which means identities in the testing set must appear in the training set.

Training Configuration. We train the models with batch size of 16 on 4 Nvidia Titan Xp GPUs. We use SGD as our optimizer with a momentum of 0.9. The learning rate is initialized to 0.001 and decayed by a factor of 0.1 every 7 epochs. Following the last fully connected layer is a softmax layer for classification and identification.

Evaluation Metric. We report the average recognition precision in test set of 1200 people.

Table 2. Comparisons on intellifusion RGB-D face dataset in accuracy (%).

Method	RGB images	Depth images	CNN models	Accuracy (%)
Pretrained on Imagenet	✓	✗	RGB ResNet50	94.47
Train from scratch	✓	✓	RGB-D ResNet50	88.36
Pretrained on Imagenet	✓	✓	RGB-D ResNet50	**94.64**

As shown in Table 2, the RGB-D model transfered from a 2D network has the best accuracy, compared to the RGB model taking merely RGB images as input and the RGB-D model traning from scratch. What's more, the inference speed of our RGB-D ResNet50 model is about 262.64 fps. And it shows that inter-modal transfer learning outperforms RGB models which take merely RGB images as input and RGB-D models training from scratch.

5 Conclusion

Compared to RGB images, RGB-D images contain more information about the global layout and enable the images to have stereoscopic effects. From a perspective of intuition, our RGB-D model is able to make more use of the information provided by depth images. But due to the limitation of the size of RGB-D datasets, it is difficult to develop a RGB-D model as efficient as RGB models. Using transfer learning from RGB to RGB-D can solve this problem. In this paper, we present an RGB-D ResNet50 model transferred from a pretrained RGB model and achieve an accuracy of 94.64%.

References

1. Cao, C., Weng, Y., Zhou, S., Tong, Y., Zhou, K.: Facewarehouse: a 3D facial expression database for visual computing. IEEE Trans. Vis. Comput. Graph. **20**(3), 413–425 (2013)

2. Chen, M., Chen, T., Chen, Q.: An efficient implementation of the ALS-WR algorithm on x86 CPUS. In: Gao, W., et al. (eds.) International Symposium on Benchmarking, Measuring and Optimization (Bench 2019). LNCS, vol. 12093, pp. 116–122. Springer, Heidelberg (2020)

3. Cheng, S., Marras, I., Zafeiriou, S., Pantic, M.: Statistical non-rigid ICP algorithm and its application to 3D face alignment. Image Vis. Comput. **58**, 3–12 (2017)

4. Cui, J., Zhang, H., Han, H., Shan, S., Chen, X.: Improving 2D face recognition via discriminative face depth estimation. In: 2018 International Conference on Biometrics (ICB), pp. 140–147. IEEE (2018)

5. Deng, W., Wang, P., Wang, J., Li, C., Guo, M.: PSL: exploiting parallelism, sparsity and locality to accelerate matrix factorization on x86 platforms. In: Gao, W., et al. (eds.) International Symposium on Benchmarking, Measuring and Optimization (Bench 2019). LNCS, vol. 12093, pp. 101–109. Springer, Heidelberg (2020)

6. Faltemier, T.C., Bowyer, K.W., Flynn, P.J.: Using a multi-instance enrollment representation to improve 3D face recognition. In: 2007 First IEEE International Conference on Biometrics: Theory, Applications, and Systems, pp. 1–6. IEEE (2007)

7. Gao, W., et al.: AIBench: towards scalable and comprehensive datacenter AI benchmarking. In: Zheng, C., Zhan, J. (eds.) Bench 2018. LNCS, vol. 11459, pp. 3–9. Springer, Cham (2019). https://doi.org/10.1007/978-3-030-32813-9_1

8. Gao, W., et al.: AIBench: an industry standard internet service AI benchmark suite. arXiv preprint arXiv:1908.08998 (2019)

9. Gong, T., Huiqian, N.: An implementation of resnet on the classification of RGB-D images. In: Gao, W., et al. (eds.) International Symposium on Benchmarking, Measuring and Optimization (Bench 2019). LNCS, vol. 12093, pp. 149–155. Springer, Heidelberg (2020)

10. Han, J., Chen, H., Liu, N., Yan, C., Li, X.: Cnns-based RGB-D saliency detection via cross-view transfer and multiview fusion. IEEE Trans. Cybern. **48**(11), 3171–3183 (2017)

11. Hao, T., et al.: Edge AIBench: towards comprehensive end-to-end edge computing benchmarking. In: Zheng, C., Zhan, J. (eds.) Bench 2018. LNCS, vol. 11459, pp. 23–30. Springer, Cham (2019). https://doi.org/10.1007/978-3-030-32813-9_3

12. Hao, T., Zheng, Z.: The implementation and optimization of matrix decomposition based collaborative filtering task on x86 platform. In: Gao, W., et al. (eds.) International Symposium on Benchmarking, Measuring and Optimization (Bench 2019). LNCS, vol. 12093, pp. 110–115. Springer, Heidelberg (2020)

13. He, K., Zhang, X., Ren, S., Sun, J.: Deep residual learning for image recognition. In: The IEEE Conference on Computer Vision and Pattern Recognition (CVPR), June 2016

14. Hou, P., Yu, J., Miao, Y., Tai, Y., Wu, Y., Zhao, C.: RVtensor: a light-weight neural network inference framework based on the RISC-V architecture. In: Gao, W., et al. (eds.) International Symposium on Benchmarking, Measuring and Optimization (Bench19). LNCS, vol. 12093, pp. 85–90. Springer, Heidelberg (2020)

15. Huang, G.B., Mattar, M., Berg, T., Learned-Miller, E.: Labeled faces in the wild: a database for studying face recognition in unconstrained environments (2008)

16. Jia, C., Kong, Y., Ding, Z., Fu, Y.R.: Latent tensor transfer learning for RGB-D action recognition. In: Proceedings of the 22nd ACM International Conference on Multimedia, pp. 87–96. ACM (2014)

17. Jiang, Z., et al.: HPC AI500: a benchmark suite for HPC AI systems. In: Zheng, C., Zhan, J. (eds.) Bench 2018. LNCS, vol. 11459, pp. 10–22. Springer, Cham (2019). https://doi.org/10.1007/978-3-030-32813-9_2

18. Keselman, L., Woodfill, J.I., Grunnet-Jepsen, A., Bhowmik, A.: Intel(R) realsense(TM) stereoscopic depth cameras. In: 2017 IEEE Conference on Computer Vision and Pattern Recognition Workshops (CVPRW), pp. 1267–1276. IEEE (2017)

19. Kim, D., Hernandez, M., Choi, J., Medioni, G.: Deep 3D face identification. In: 2017 IEEE International Joint Conference on Biometrics (IJCB), pp. 133–142. IEEE (2017)

20. Krizhevsky, A., Sutskever, I., Hinton, G.E.: ImageNet classification with deep convolutional neural networks. In: Advances in Neural Information Processing Systems, pp. 1097–1105 (2012)

21. Li, G., Wang, X., Ma, X., Liu, L., Feng, X.: XDN: towards efficient inference of residual neural networks on cambricon chips. In: Gao, W., et al. (eds.) International Symposium on Benchmarking, Measuring and Optimization (Bench 2019). LNCS, vol. 12093, pp. 51–56. Springer, Heidelberg (2020)

22. Li, J., Jiang, Z.: Performance analysis of cambricon MLU100. In: Gao, W., et al. (eds.) International Symposium on Benchmarking, Measuring and Optimization (Bench 2019). LNCS, vol. 12093, pp. 57–66. Springer, Heidelberg (2020)

23. Luo, C., et al.: AIoT bench: towards comprehensive benchmarking mobile and embedded device intelligence. In: Zheng, C., Zhan, J. (eds.) Bench 2018. LNCS, vol. 11459, pp. 31–35. Springer, Cham (2019). https://doi.org/10.1007/978-3-030-32813-9_4

24. Maze, B., et al.: IARPA janus benchmark-C: face dataset and protocol. In: 2018 International Conference on Biometrics (ICB), pp. 158–165. IEEE (2018)

25. Moreno, A.: GavabDB: a 3D face database. In: Proceedings of 2nd COST275 Workshop on Biometrics on the Internet 2004, pp. 75–80 (2004)

26. Nech, A., Kemelmacher-Shlizerman, I.: Level playing field for million scale face recognition. In: Proceedings of the IEEE Conference on Computer Vision and Pattern Recognition, pp. 7044–7053 (2017)

27. Phillips, P.J., et al.: Overview of the face recognition grand challenge. In: 2005 IEEE Computer Society Conference on Computer Vision and Pattern Recognition (CVPR 2005), vol. 1, pp. 947–954. IEEE (2005)

28. Savran, A., et al.: Bosphorus database for 3D face analysis. In: Schouten, B., Juul, N.C., Drygajlo, A., Tistarelli, M. (eds.) BioID 2008. LNCS, vol. 5372, pp. 47–56. Springer, Heidelberg (2008). https://doi.org/10.1007/978-3-540-89991-4_6

29. Schwarz, M., Schulz, H., Behnke, S.: RGB-D object recognition and pose estimation based on pre-trained convolutional neural network features. In: 2015 IEEE International Conference on Robotics and Automation (ICRA), pp. 1329–1335. IEEE (2015)

30. Simonyan, K., Zisserman, A.: Very deep convolutional networks for large-scale image recognition. arXiv preprint arXiv:1409.1556 (2014)

31. Song, X., Herranz, L., Jiang, S.: Depth CNNS for RGB-D scene recognition: learning from scratch better than transferring from RGB-CNNS. In: Thirty-First AAAI Conference on Artificial Intelligence (2017)

32. Szegedy, C., et al.: Going deeper with convolutions. In: Proceedings of the IEEE Conference on Computer Vision and Pattern Recognition, pp. 1–9 (2015)

33. Wang, L., et al.: BigDataBench: a big data benchmark suite from internet services. In: 2014 IEEE 20th International Symposium on High Performance Computer Architecture (HPCA), pp. 488–499. IEEE (2014)

34. Wang, Y., Zeng, C., Li, C.: Exploring the performance bound of cambricon accelerator in end-to-end inference scenario. In: Gao, W., et al. (eds.) International Symposium on Benchmarking, Measuring and Optimization (Bench 2019). LNCS, vol. 12093, pp. 67–74. Springer, Heidelberg (2020)
35. Yi, D., Lei, Z., Liao, S., Li, S.Z.: Learning face representation from scratch. arXiv preprint arXiv:1411.7923 (2014)
36. Yin, L., Wei, X., Sun, Y., Wang, J., Rosato, M.J.: A 3D facial expression database for facial behavior research. In: 7th International Conference on Automatic Face and Gesture Recognition (FGR06), pp. 211–216. IEEE (2006)
37. Zhang, J., Huang, D., Wang, Y., Sun, J.: Lock3Dface: a large-scale database of low-cost kinect 3D faces. In: 2016 International Conference on Biometrics (ICB), pp. 1–8. IEEE (2016)
38. Zhang, K., Zhang, Z., Li, Z., Qiao, Y.: Joint face detection and alignment using multitask cascaded convolutional networks. IEEE Signal Process. Lett. **23**(10), 1499–1503 (2016)
39. Zhang, Z.: Microsoft kinect sensor and its effect. IEEE Multimed. **19**(2), 4–10 (2012)
40. Zulqarnain Gilani, S., Mian, A.: Learning from millions of 3D scans for large-scale 3D face recognition. In: Proceedings of the IEEE Conference on Computer Vision and Pattern Recognition, pp. 1896–1905 (2018)

An Implementation of ResNet on the Classification of RGB-D Images

Tongyan Gong[1(✉)] and Huiqian Niu[2]

[1] Guizhou University of Finance and Economics, Guiyang, China
2278802241@qq.com
[2] Technology and Data Middle Platform, JD.com, Beijing, China
niuhuiqian@jd.com

Abstract. Facial recognition is to identify human faces from an image. It is becoming more and more important these days as it can be applied in multiple industries, such as bank, airport, e-business, etc. Because of the broad application prospects, face recognition is actively developed and researched by many people, companies and academic organizations. In this paper, we customize one of the facial recognition models developed in the recent years – ResNet on the Intellifusion 3D face dataset [1]. And then we evaluate the performance of the algorithm by adjusting the depth of the network, pre-processing steps of the pictures and also the learning rate.

Keywords: ResNet · Computer vision · RGB-D · Face recognition

1 Introduction

There has been a long research history in the area of computer vision and facial recoginition. In 1987, Sirovich and Kirby used Eigenface [2] in facial recognition for the first time. In 1998, Gary applied Continuously Adaptive Mean Shift (CAMSHIFT) algorithm for face tracking [5]. In recent years, the improvement of hardware resulted in a trend of using neural network for facial recognition. Krizhevsky has come up with convolution neural network to solve the image classification problem [6]. In 2015, Google published FaceNet [9], a new facial recognition model, which achieves record high accuracy on Labeled Faces in the Wild (LFW) dataset. Kaiming developed a new type of deep neural network with residual block in the same year, which provides a way to resolve some issues brought by the depth of the network [7]. Besides the development of new models, there are also researches focusing on bring the facial recognization to more hardware platforms and scenarios. CMU released OpenFace face recognition library in 2016 [4] providing a new benchmark for mobile platform. Anil discusses the state-of-art and challenges of facial recognition technology in the area of crime investigations [8]. In this paper, we implement a CNN network based on ResNet for face recognition. And then we employ the Intellifusion 3D dataset to evaluate the performance of our proposed network getting 82%. The influence of learning

© Springer Nature Switzerland AG 2020
W. Gao et al. (Eds.): Bench 2019, LNCS 12093, pp. 149–155, 2020.
https://doi.org/10.1007/978-3-030-49556-5_15

rate and inference time under different devices (CPU and GPU) are explored in experiments. Our code is implemented and optimized on the AIBench and its hardware platform [16–20] and this article takes part in the AI System and Algorithm Challenge organized by Benchcouncil. The source code of AIBench is publicly available from http:// www. benchcouncil. org/ benchhub/ AIBench/ (Sign up to get access). BenchCouncil AI Challenge includes four tracks: International AI System Challenge based on RISC-V Subject [27], International AI System Challenge based on Cambricon Chip Subject [25,26], International AI System Challenge based on X86 Platform Subject [21–23], and International 3D Face Recognition Algorithm Challenge Subject [24].

2   Related Work

2.1   Convolutional Neural Network

Convolutional neural network (CNN) is commonly used in extracting patterns from images as images can usually be represented in 2D matrix and convolutional neural network can easily applied on data in the form of 2D matrix. The basic layers used in forwarding the convolutional neural network are the convolution layer, down-sampling layer and non-linear activation layer. [12] also explained how one can implement convolutional layer using fast Fourier transform and it adopted the cuFFT library. As for other embedded systems, optimized FFT libraries [13–15] can be used for CPUs, especially for inference. Convolution layer basically convolves the input feature maps (assume it as a 2D matrix) with learnable kernels. For a full convolution, the output of the layer is given by:

$$z(u,v) = \sum_{i=-\infty}^{\infty} \sum_{-\infty}^{\infty} x_{i,j} k_{u-i,v-j} \tag{1}$$

Kernel can be considered as a feature pattern that we want to see to what extend each part of image matches. After convolution layer, feature mapping is created. However, the data amount is still large as the number of original images in the training set is usually large. Down-sampling provides a way to decrease the size of the data while still keeping the invariance extracted by the convolution layer as much as possible. More formally:

$$x_j^l = f(\beta_j^l down(x_j^{l-1}) + b_j^l) \tag{2}$$

Concretely, there are usually two ways of down sampling: max pooling and average pooling. For max pooling, the down function is picking the maximum value of the input matrix as the output; for average pooling, the down function is calculating the average value of the input matrix as the output. The down-sampling layer also helps improve the model performance by reducing the potential of over-fitting. And then there is non-linear activation layer. One of the most common non-linear activation function is the ReLu function:

$$f(x) = max(0, x) \tag{3}$$

Finally, the output of the layer will abandon the negative values in the input. The superiority of the convolutional neural network has been demonstrated to be effective in the computer vision task, thus we use it in this paper to do face recognition.

2.2 ResNet

With the three basic layers mentioned in the last section, scientists and engineers can use them multiple times in any combination to their own neural network fitting into the problem to solve. However, deeper network generates new issues, overfitting, taking more time to train and the degradation problem: accuracy of the network decreases rapidly in deeper network. To solve this problem, Kaiming added residual blocks into the deep neural network [7].

As a result, the stacked nonlinear layers are trained to fit into the mapping of $F(x) := H(x) - x$ in stead of $F(x) := H(x)$. In other words, the original mapping is changed to F(x)+x from $F(x)$. This change is based on the assumption that it is easier to optimize the residual mapping with the identity mapping, serving as a "shortcut" mechanism [7].

3   Work Description

3.1   Design

Since the ResNet has deeper network structure compared with early work and has better performance, we use a ResNet-like network in the paper to improve performance. Figure 1 shows the workflow of the system developed for this work.

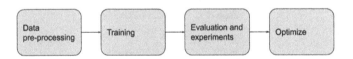

Fig. 1. Design of the workflow

3.2   Implementation

The dataset used is the Intellifusion 3D face data set. It contains around 400,000 faces from 1200 people, with the total size of around 36.8 GB. Each face contains one RGB image and one numpy array (.npy) representing the depth information of the image (Fig. 2).

(a) RGB Image

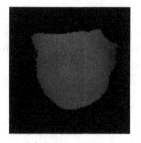

(b) Depth Image

Fig. 2. Example images in the data set [1]

The pre-processing of the dataset including: removing the noise data, resizing the images to 182*182, normalizing the pixels, randomly cropped and combining the RGB image and the depth image into a 4-channel RGB-D image. Then, we implement a Resnet model for training the data. The model structure is shown in Fig. 3.

| 7*7 conv, 64 |
| ReLu |
| maxpool /2 |
| 3*3 conv, 64 |
| ReLu |
| 3*3 conv, 64 |
| ReLu |
| 3*3 conv, 128 |
| ReLu |
| 3*3 conv, 128 |
| ReLu |
| 3*3 conv, 256 |
| ReLu |
| 3*3 conv, 256 |
| ReLu |
| 3*3 conv, 512 |
| ReLu |
| 3*3 conv, 512 |
| ReLu |
| 7*7, Avg pooling |
| Fully connected |

Fig. 3. Structure of the network

To improve the speed of the training, we used GPU to accelerate the training [10]. The GPU used is Nvidia GeForce RTX 2080. Table 1 shows the different average time for each iteraction for using GPU or without using GPU.

Table 1. Time spent comparison

	Using GPU	Using CPU
Time (min/iteration)	~7	~102

3.3 Evaluation

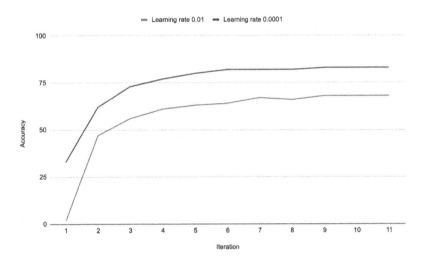

Fig. 4. Model accuracy with different settings

Based on the above implementation, we did some experiment on the performance/accuracy of the ResNet model by changing some variables. Figure 4 shows the improvement of the model in different settings.

4 Conclusion

This paper implements a variant of the CNN model with residual blocks and train the model on the Intellifusion 3D face data set. By experiment, we reach the best accuracy of 82% with learning rate as 0.001.

References

1. Intellifusion 3D face data set. http://125.39.136.212:8484/3dvggface2_1.tar.gz
2. Sirovich, L., Kirby, M.: Low-dimensional procedure for the characterization of human faces. JOSA A **4**(3), 519–24 (1987)

3. Turk, M., Pentland, A.: Eigenfaces for recognition. J. Cogn. Neurosci. **3**(1), 71–86 (1991)
4. Amos, B., Ludwiczuk, B., Satyanarayanan, M.: Openface: A general-purpose face recognition library with mobile applications. CMU School of Computer Science 6 June 2016
5. Bradski, G.R.: Computer vision face tracking for use in a perceptual user interface (1998)
6. Krizhevsky, A., Sutskever, I., Hinton, G.E.: ImageNet classification with deep convolutional neural networks. In: Advances in Neural Information Processing Systems, pp. 1097–1105 (2012)
7. He, K., Zhang, X., Ren, S., Sun, J.: Deep residual learning for image recognition. In: Proceedings of the IEEE Conference on Computer Vision and Pattern Recognition, pp. 770–778 (2016)
8. Jain, A.K., Klare, B., Park, U.: Face recognition: some challenges in forensics. In: Face and Gesture, 21 March 2011, pp. 726–733. IEEE (2011)
9. Schroff, F., Kalenichenko, D., Philbin, J.: FaceNet: a unified embedding for face recognition and clustering. In: Proceedings of the IEEE Conference on Computer Vision and Pattern Recognition, pp. 815–823 (2015)
10. Bouvrie, J.: Notes on convolutional neural networks (2016)
11. PyTorch CUDA semantics. https:// pytorch. org/ docs/ stable/ notes/ cuda. html. Accessed 27 Oct 2019
12. Vasilache, N., Johnson, J., Mathieu, M., Chintala, S., Piantino, S., LeCun, Y.: Fast convolutional nets with fbfft: a GPU performance evaluation. arXiv preprint arXiv:1412.7580, 24 December 2014
13. Li, Z., Jia, H., Zhang, Y., Chen, T., Yuan, L., Cao, L., Wang, X.: AutoFFT: a template-based FFT codes auto-generation framework for ARM and X86 CPUs. In: Proceedings of the International Conference for High Performance Computing, Networking, Storage and Analysis, 17 November 2019, p. 25. ACM (2019)
14. Frigo, M., Johnson, S.G.: FFTW: an adaptive software architecture for the FFT. In: Proceedings of the 1998 IEEE International Conference on Acoustics, Speech and Signal Processing, ICASSP 1998 (Cat. No. 98CH36181), 15 May 1998, vol. 3, pp. 1381–1384. IEEE (1998)
15. Takahashi, D.: FFTE: a fast fourier transform package (2005). http://www. ffte.jp/
16. Gao, W., et al.: AIBench: an industry standard internet service AI benchmark suite. arXiv preprint arXiv:1908.08998, 13 August 2019
17. Gao, W., et al.: AIBench: towards scalable and comprehensive datacenter AI benchmarking. In: Zheng, C., Zhan, J. (eds.) Bench 2018. LNCS, vol. 11459, pp. 3–9. Springer, Cham (2019). https:// doi. org/ 10. 1007/ 978- 3- 030- 32813- 9_1
18. Hao, T., et al.: Edge AIBench: towards comprehensive end-to-end edge computing benchmarking. In: Zheng, C., Zhan, J. (eds.) Bench 2018. LNCS, vol. 11459, pp. 23–30. Springer, Cham (2019). https:// doi. org/ 10. 1007/ 978- 3- 030- 32813- 9_3
19. Jiang, Z., et al.: HPC AI500: a benchmark suite for HPC AI systems. In: Zheng, C., Zhan, J. (eds.) Bench 2018. LNCS, vol. 11459, pp. 10–22. Springer, Cham (2019). https:// doi. org/ 10. 1007/ 978- 3- 030- 32813- 9_2
20. Luo, C., et al.: AIoT Bench: towards comprehensive benchmarking mobile and embedded device intelligence. In: Zheng, C., Zhan, J. (eds.) Bench 2018. LNCS, vol. 11459, pp. 31–35. Springer, Cham (2019). https:// doi. org/ 10. 1007/ 978- 3- 030- 32813- 9_4

21. Hao, T., Zheng, Z.: The Implementation and optimization of matrix decomposition based collaborative filtering task on x86 platform. In: Gao, W., et al. (eds.) International Symposium on Benchmarking, Measuring and Optimization (Bench 2019). LNCS, vol. 12093, pp. 110–115. Springer, Heidelberg (2020)

22. Chen, M., Chen, T., Chen, Q.: An efficient implementation of the ALS-WR algorithm on x86 CPUs. In: Gao, W., et al. (eds.) International Symposium on Benchmarking, Measuring and Optimization (Bench 2019). LNCS, vol. 12093, pp. 116–122. Springer, Heidelberg (2020)

23. Deng, W., Wang, P., Wang, J., Li, C., Guo, M.: PSL: exploiting parallelism, sparsity and locality to accelerate matrix factorization on x86 platforms. In: Gao, W., et al. (eds.) International Symposium on Benchmarking, Measuring and Optimization (Bench 2019). LNCS, vol. 12093, pp. 101–109. Springer, Heidelberg (2020)

24. Xiong, X., Wen, X., Huang, C.: Improving RGB-D face recognition via transfer learning from a pretrained 2D network. In: Gao, W., et al. (eds.) International Symposium on Benchmarking, Measuring and Optimization (Bench 2019). LNCS, vol. 12093, pp. 141–148. Springer, Heidelberg (2020)

25. Li, J., Jiang, Z.: Performance analysis of cambricon MLU100. In: Gao, W., et al. (eds.) International Symposium on Benchmarking, Measuring and Optimization (Bench 2019). LNCS, vol. 12093, pp. 57–66. Springer, Heidelberg (2020)

26. Li, G., Wang, X., Ma, X., Liu, L., Feng, X.: XDN: towards efficient inference of residual neural networks on cambricon chips. In: Gao, W., et al. (eds.) International Symposium on Benchmarking, Measuring and Optimization (Bench 2019). LNCS, vol. 12093, pp. 51–56. Springer, Heidelberg (2020)

27. Hou, P., Yu, J., Miao, Y., Tai, Y., Wu, Y., Zhao, C.: RVTensor: a light-weight neural network inference framework based on the RISC-V architecture. In: Gao, W., et al. (eds.) International Symposium on Benchmarking, Measuring and Optimization (Bench 2019). LNCS, vol. 12093, pp. 85–90. Springer, Heidelberg (2020)

Utilization of Resnet in RGB-D Facial Recognition Problems

Xi Xiong[✉]

The Ohio State University, Columbus, OH 43210, USA
`xiong.319@osu.edu`

Abstract. Resnet, from its emergence, has always been a state-of-the-art model for facial recognition problems. The 2019 Bench Council posted several challenges, including an International 3D Face Recognition Algorithm Challenge, which aims at soliciting new approaches to advance the state-of-the-art in face recognition. We focus on utilizing a 4-channeled Resnet on this new problem and achieve 90% validation set accuracy resulting in second prize on the Bench-19 International Artificial Intelligence System Challenges.

Keywords: Resnet · Facial recognition · RGB-D

1 Introduction

1.1 Motivation

International Open Benchmark Council (Bench Council) is a non-profit research institute, which aims to promote the standardization, benchmarking, evaluation, incubation, and promotion of Chip, AI, and Big Data techniques. In 2019 Bench Council posted several challenges, including the Cambircon track, RISC-V track, X86 track, and 3D face recognition track. The track we chose was 3D face recognition, which aims at soliciting new approaches to advance the state-of-the-art in face recognition. The source code of AIBench is publicly available from this website http://www.benchcouncil.org/benchhub/AIBench/ (Sign up to get access). An industry-leading internet service AI Benchmark Suite [1] is used in this competition. This paper depicts the effort made towards the utilization of Resnet of this RGB-D facial recognition problem. The problem is a classic face recognition task given traditional RGB face image plus depth information. The dataset consists of over 20000 faces of 1212 distinct personnel, many of them being celebrities, presented with jpeg images and Nd arrays representing depth information accordingly. The dataset includes faces from various races and also images from different ages of the same person. We try to approach the problem with different methods. Initially, we try to start with a 2D face recognition system which register 2d face landmarks and recognize faces by comparing face

© Springer Nature Switzerland AG 2020
W. Gao et al. (Eds.): Bench 2019, LNCS 12093, pp. 156–161, 2020.
https://doi.org/10.1007/978-3-030-49556-5_16

landmarks with registered face landmarks. This method achieves fairly good performance but lacks utilization of depth data, remaining a space of improvement. Further experiments show that the depth channel is extremely noisy for use in the face recognition system. Based on the fact that convolutional neural networks outperform other models in many image recognition tasks, we decided to approach the problem with deep convolutional neural networks.

1.2   Challenge

There are two main challenges that we face in this problem, being the inconsistency of data and difficulty in optimization. The first problem exists because the data provided are all of the different resolutions and sizes. To encounter this problem, we padded the images by 90 and used a center crop to format the images to 224*224 for training consistency. The padding was well-considered to compensate for different size of images. After cropping, the images are of the same size to feed into the network; this is a very conservative optimization to the dataset but judging from the results some minor additional noise is added to the dataset. The other challenge is the noise in data: when inspecting the image dataset, we find out that there are noise data that not belong to the personnel identity. Though we try to delete some of those data, the dataset is too large to be cleaned by hand, and this is very likely to affect the result of the training process. For efficiency and computing power limits, we only utilized an 18 layered version of Resnet, and might optimize the model to Resnet-50 for better performance.

1.3   Contribution

Traditional 2D face recognition method divide face recognition into face registration, face detection and face verification these three steps. In order to obtain good performance on such system, each part must function well at the same time. This is extremely hard since for each new situation encountered, we have to modify three parts to adapt the new case. Therefore, we merge all three parts into one deep Resnet and simplify the face recognition problem to a classification problem where our model predicts a label for input face image. We also take inspirations from a paper [2] that focused on transfer learning from a pretrained 2D network and [3] another paper that has a different implementation on a similar Resnet model.

2   Background and Related Work

As the universal approximation theorem implies, a feed-forward network with a few layers is enough to approximate any functions [5]. However, the network would become prone to over-fitting issues with the data, hence going for a deeper neural network is necessary for a better result in this problem. Since AlexNet, having only 5 layers, the state-of-the-art CNN has grown deeper, with the VGG network [6] and GoogleNet (also code-named Inception_v1) [7] had 19 and 22 layers respectively. Since the infamous vanishing gradient problem exists in the back-propagation process due to repeated multiplication making the gradient negligibly small, merely piling up layers does not work anymore. For the deeper it goes, the performances would be bottle-necked by this problem, and the results can even start degrading. Before Resnet came out, various methods are being carried out by different researchers in vain to solve the problem effectively. To mitigate this problem. As addressed in [6], they attempted to solve the problem by adding an auxiliary loss in a middle layer as extra supervision, but still in vain to solve the problem. Resnet [4] incorporates identity shortcut connections, which essentially skip the training of one or more layers creating a residual block. The residual block is a pre-activation variant of residual block [8] in which the gradients can pass through any shortcuts unimpededly. Because of its compelling results in various image recognition benchmarks, we chose Resnet as the building block of the model. As Resnet was implemented for RGB datasets, we optimized the network to have a fourth input depth information channel feeding into the network in addition to the 3 RGB channels, fitting the RGB-D problem.

3   Method

We deploy the dataset provided by Bench2019 for training and testing. Input images are either padded or cropped to 224×224 to feed into ResNet-18. There are 23,140 valid RGB-D images collected from 1212 identities. For the test set, we sample a subset uniformly over 1212 identities from original data.

Moreover, we employ accuracy as an evaluation metric for this classification problem setup. Trained by an Nvidia RTX 2080 for 40 epochs in less than an hour, our model achieves 90% accuracy on the validation set without parameter fine-tuning. However, the model received no further improvement if we increase training epochs. In further experiments we swap ResNet-18 for ResNet-50 while leaving hyper-parameters unchanged and the result is disappointing. The generalization for ResNet-50 in this problem setup is significantly worse than ResNet-18 that the validation accuracy drops to around 60%.

The network used to solve this problem is a modified version of Resnet-18, which follows the Resnet model from the 2015 Resnet academic publication, Deep Residual Learning for Image Recognition by He et al. [4]. The authors of this paper argue that stacking layers shouldn't degrade the network performance, because if we simply stack identity mappings upon the current network, and the resulting architecture would perform the same. This indicates that the deeper model should not produce a training error higher than its shallower counterparts.

Kaiming He's team hypothesize that letting the stacked layers fit a residual mapping is more straightforward than letting them directly fit the desired underlying mapping. We then modified the network to have 4 input channels as our model to fit the problem with an additional depth layer. The core idea of Resnet is introducing a so-called "identity shortcut connection" that skips one or more layers, as shown in Fig. 1:

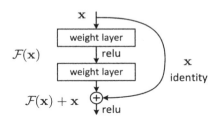

Fig. 1. Residual learning: a building block

Fig. 2 shows the whole model:

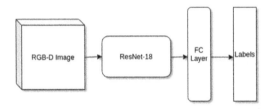

Fig. 2. General network architecture based on Resnet [1]

The abbreviated ResNet-18 block we implemented is shown in Fig. 3:

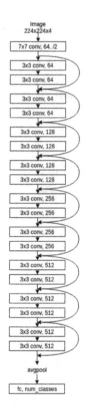

Fig. 3. General architecture of Resnet-18

4   Conclusion

In this paper, we apply the ResNet-18 network for large scale face recognition in a classification setup. Benefitting from the simplified problem setup, our solution combines face registration and face recognition module into a simple neural network that can be tuned by simply adjusting hyper-parameters and modifying the dataset. However, this simplified problem setup comes with severe drawbacks. First of all, we can improve performance by utilizing multi-node computing platforms and optimize the training process for more efficiency, as mentioned in this paper [8], which emphasizes methods of scalable and comprehensive data center AI benchmarking. Moreover, since the face registration step is merged into a neural network with the recognition part, it is hard for our model to generalize to new faces. Excessive training on new faces makes the model in favor of new faces, while insufficient fine-tune on new data reduces accuracy on new face class. Moreover, our solution lacks the capability to adjust behavior in the face registration step due to the big neural network setup. A potential solution to such problems of intractable face registration can be one-shot learning, which effectively computes a feature representation for new faces based on existing data.

References

1. Gao, W., Tang, F., Wang, L., Zhan, J., Lan, C., et al.: AI-bench: an industry standard Internet service AI benchmark suite (AIBench). arXiv:1908.08998 (2019)
2. Xiong, X., Wen, X., Huang, C.: Improving RGB-D face recognition via transfer learning from a pretrained 2D network. In: International Symposium on Benchmarking, Measuring and Optimization (Bench 2019) (2019)
3. He, K., Zhang, X., Ren, S., Sun, J.: Deep residual learning for image recognition. In: 2016 IEEE Conference on Computer Vision and Pattern Recognition (CVPR) (2016)
4. Anastasis Kratsios: Universal approximation theorems (stat.ML) (2019)
5. Simonyan, K., Zisserman, A.: Very deep convolutional networks for large-scale image recognition. arXiv preprint arXiv:1409.1556 (2014)
6. Szegedy, C., et al.: Going deeper with convolutions. In: Proceedings of the IEEE Conference on Computer Vision and Pattern Recognition, pp. 1–9 (2015)
7. He, K., Zhang, X., Ren, S., Sun, J.: Identity mappings in deep residual networks. arXiv preprint arXiv:1603.05027v3 (2016)
8. Gao, W., et al.: AIBench: towards scalable and comprehensive datacenter AI benchmarking. In: Zheng, C., Zhan, J. (eds.) Bench 2018. LNCS, vol. 11459, pp. 3–9. Springer, Cham (2019). https://doi.org/10.1007/978-3-030-32813-9_1

Benchmark

Building the DataBench Workflow
and Architecture

Todor Ivanov[1(⊠)], Timo Eichhorn[1], Arne Jørgen Berre[2],
Tomás Pariente Lobo[3], Ivan Martinez Rodriguez[3], Ricardo Ruiz Saiz[3],
Barbara Pernici[4], and Chiara Francalanci[4]

[1] Frankfurt Big Data Lab, Goethe University Frankfurt, Frankfurt, Hessen, Germany
{todor,timo}@dbis.cs.uni-frankfurt.de
[2] SINTEF AS, Trondheim, Norway
Arne.J.Berre@sintef.no
[3] ATOS SPAIN SA, Madrid, Spain
{tomas.parientelobo,ivan.martinez,ricardo.ruizsaiz}@atos.net
[4] Politecnico di Milano, Milan, Italy
{barbara.pernici,chiara.francalanci}@polimi.it

Abstract. In the era of Big Data and AI, it is challenging to know all technical and business advantages of the emerging technologies. The goal of DataBench is to design a benchmarking process helping organizations developing Big Data Technologies (BDT) to reach for excellence and constantly improve their performance, by measuring their technology development activity against parameters of high business relevance. This paper focuses on the internals of the DataBench framework and presents our methodological workflow and framework architecture.

Keywords: DataBench · Big Data · Benchmarking

1 Introduction

Organisations rely on evidence from the benchmarking domain to provide answers on how their processes are performing. There is extensive information on how and why to perform technical benchmarks for the specific management and analytics processes, but there is a lack of objective, evidence-based methods to measure the correlation between Big Data Technology (BDT) benchmarks and an organisation's business benchmarks and demonstrate return on investment (ROI). New benchmarking approaches are being developed in particular in the big data domain, which presents new technological challenges. To address these challenges new benchmark initiatives focusing on machine learning and artificial intelligence like MLPerf [9,10,13] and AIBench [4,5] are in development. Also, there are comprehensive studies [6,7] on the existing Big Data benchmarks that compare and discuss the different types of benchmarks and assessment metrics. However, to the best of our knowledge, these existing benchmarks focus on technological aspects and not on business indicators. The DataBench

© Springer Nature Switzerland AG 2020
W. Gao et al. (Eds.): Bench 2019, LNCS 12093, pp. 165–171, 2020.
https://doi.org/10.1007/978-3-030-49556-5_17

project addresses this significant gap in the current benchmarking community's activities, by providing verifiable benchmarks and evaluation schemes of BDT performance of high business impact and industrial significance.

The approach followed by DataBench starts with performing a comparative analysis of existing benchmarking initiatives and technologies. In fact, the goal of DataBench is not to create another benchmark, but to support an approach for efficient usage, evolution, extensions, and synergy of the available Big Data benchmarks from the international Big Data benchmarking community related to industrial requirements. Based on that, the project will proceed to develop a methodology and an economic and market analysis to assess the European and industrial significance of the BDT to be benchmarked. Industrial significance will be assessed through the investigation of the main Big Data use cases, that will allow the correlation of Big Data technical performance with business processes. Relying on all these inputs, the project will build the DataBench Toolbox, a tool which will connect and evaluate external benchmarking initiatives. Using the DataBench Toolbox and the methodology and metrics previously defined, evaluation and benchmarking will be carried out considering both business relevance and technical aspects. We foresee at least three different groups of potential users. The first group are people with a technical background that are interested in benchmarking a relevant BDT or application in their company. The second one are business people that would like to assess the usage of BDTs and applications from a business point of view. And the third one are providers of Big Data benchmarks that would like to offer their benchmarks to a broader audience of users. Currently, the Alpha version of the DataBench Toolbox has been released as a first attempt to showcase the main functions related to the Big Data technical benchmarking. More details about the project can be found in our vision paper [8] or on our DataBench website [2]. In another paper [11], we reported our initial findings on the relationship between business and technical performance indicators.

This paper focuses on describing the internal DataBench architecture. In particular, we divided it into three abstract layers: the methodological workflow, the framework architecture and the components implementation. In this paper, we look only at the first two. The Methodological Workflow (Sect. 2) describes the internal main processes and operations, while the Framework Architecture (Sect. 3) defines the logical components in which DataBench is implemented.

The paper is organized as follows: Sect. 2 presents the internal DataBench Methodological Workflow. Section 3 looks at the logical DataBench framework components. Finally, Sect. 4 summarizes our paper.

2   Methodological Workflow

This part describes in detail the internal processes and operations taking place in the DataBench framework and the logic behind this approach.

Figure 1 shows a schema of processes intended to illustrate different elements of the tooling support to be provided in DataBench to different set of users. A single user may have different roles, initially the following:

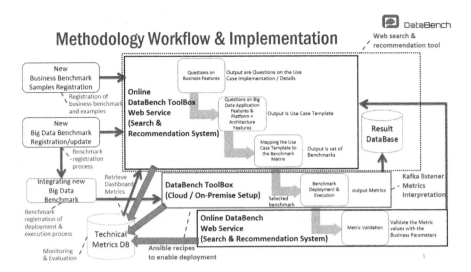

Fig. 1. DataBench methodological workflow (Color figure online)

– **Benchmarking Providers:** Organizations that own a particular benchmark. They can be the actual developers of the benchmark or the organizations that maintain them. These users can register and update their benchmarks.
– **Technical Users:** Users that would like to search and potentially execute a technical benchmark. This includes the possibility of searching, downloading, executing and giving the results of the execution back to the Toolbox.
– **Business Users:** Users that would like to search and understand the business value of specific big data solutions. These users would not need to run technical benchmarks, but rather search for similar cases, business indicators, etc.
– **DataBench Admin:** People in charge of the administration of the Toolbox.

There are several processes depicted in Fig. 1. On the left-hand side of the figure, the three boxes represent the registration process of two different kinds of benchmarks:

– The registration of data related to business-oriented big data benchmarks. The idea of the component located in the upper left corner of the figure ("New Business Benchmark Samples Registration") is to capture domain and industry specific best practices and blueprints associated to concrete business key performance indicators (KPIs).
– The registration of technical benchmarks. The two remaining components on the left represent the way the DataBench Toolbox will capture the necessary meta data and features about technical benchmarks to enable the search and recommendation processes ("New Big Data Benchmark Registration/Update" component), and to enable the automation of the deployment and the interpretation of the results of the execution of the benchmarks

("Integrating new Big Data Benchmark" component). Note that the registration of the automation provided by the second component is optional, in the sense that it requires the provision of deployment recipes and rules of interpretation of the results of the execution of the benchmarks which could prove a difficult task for some of the benchmarks analyzed so far. However, the aim in DataBench is to automate as many as possible technical benchmarks, so the documentation of the process to integrate the automation will be also a key part for future extensibility to other benchmarks.

The components in the center of the Fig. 1 show the full process from searching to executing and visualizing the results of benchmarks. This process is divided into the following steps:

– **Search and Recommendation System:** The upper central box shows the steps to define the search criteria a user could pose to the system with the aim to select a benchmark that suits their needs. Based on those criteria (technical, business, application or platform features), the system will offer a set of potential benchmarks that could fulfill the user needs, as well as associated material (blueprints, best practices in sectors, etc.) that might facilitate the decision of the selection of the right benchmark.
– **The DataBench Toolbox setup:** The middle central box (in green in Fig. 1) represents the process of deploying and enabling the execution either in cloud or in-premise of the selected benchmark. This could only happen if the registration of that benchmark provided the necessary recipes to allow the deployment. After the execution, the results of the benchmark will be sent back to the Toolbox for post-processing.
– **The validation of the metrics:** This process will allow in certain cases the matching of the technical metrics with business insights or key performance indicators (KPIs). The results of the benchmarks will be then visualized and compared to others, giving the user a clear added-value in comparison with the mere technical results that the execution of a technical benchmark may provide.
– **Monitoring and Evaluation:** This process gathers multiple metrics and internal component information with the goal to offer monitoring and evaluation capabilities to the different users of the DataBench framework. All the gathered information is stored in a central Technical Metrics Database. The data is prepared, integrated, processed and visualized into a dashboard web service that can be accessed by the different users. The key functionality of this process is to enable both DataBench administrators, technical and business users to monitor how the DataBench framework evolves in time as well as perform an evaluation of the current framework state.

At the point of writing this document, partners are in the process of defining and prototyping the look and feel of the different processes listed in this section. The initial alpha version of the DataBench Toolbox is currently implemented and will be described in detail in deliverable D3.2 [3].

3   Framework Architecture

To realize the processes described in the DataBench methodological workflow it was necessary to define and implement functional modules presented as part of the DataBench Framework Architecture in deliverable D3.1 [1]. The proposed modular framework is based on templates which are complemented with a web interface from where the user can decide and choose the metrics needed. The web interface will also act as a dashboard where the results of the executions will be gathered and shown to the user, as seen in Fig. 2.

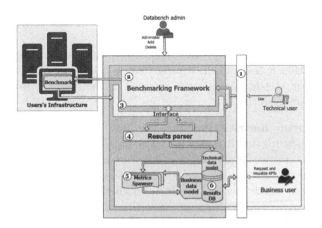

Fig. 2. DataBench framework architecture

The proposed modular DataBench Framework Architecture is composed of the following six interconnected modules described in detail in deliverable D3.1 [1]. The remaining two modules the Metrics DB and Metrics Dashboard are introduced in deliverable D5.3 [12] covering the functionality necessary for the DataBench monitoring and evaluation process.

1. **Web Interface** connects to the backend of the Toolbox and provides the different users with the functionality to choose which benchmarks they want to run. It is also in charge of providing a layer of configuration that the users can fill in to pre-configure the templates and the benchmarks to be run later on. The web module is also used to show in a dashboard the results of the executions and the derived metrics and business insights.
2. **Benchmark Framework Interface** module will be the main point of interaction for the administrator with the Benchmarking Framework, since he will be in charge of handling the integration, addition and deletion of the new, updated or modified benchmarks.
3. **Results Interface** enables the transfer of benchmark results to the framework either automatically by the benchmark run or manually by the user.

4. **Results Parser** converts the benchmark results into standardized data model to enable calculation of the business metrics in the next steps.
5. **Metrics Spawner** connects to the results DB module, so that it can parse the corresponding results from the technical data model and calculate the defined KPIs and at the end, write them back to the results DB.
6. **Results DB** is a place where the **Result Parsers** can store the data into and also have a place from where the web interface can read the results to show them in the dashboard.
7. **Metrics DB** is very similar to the **Results DB** module with the difference that it will store persistently the collected technical metrics. The goal is to reuse as much of the available functionality as possible, which means that the **Metric Spawner** and the **Results Parser** will be adapted to gather and prepare the metrics for the dashboards.
8. **Metrics Dashboards** offer the monitoring and evaluation functionality of the DataBench framework, represented as Platform, User (Profile) and Administrator Metrics Dashboards mapped to the different user functionality and privacy criteria.

The **Platform metrics** describe the key feature parameters of the DataBench framework that are used for static monitoring and evaluation. Examples for such metrics are total number of registered platform users, available registered benchmarks, number of use case scenarios, number of benchmark runs and others. These metrics will be available to all the different platform users to perform independent monitoring and evaluation of the platform environment.

The **User (Profile) metrics** are generated for each specific user and describe his/her activities when using the platform. Example metrics are the number of benchmark searchers, number of downloaded benchmarks, number of submitted benchmark results and history log of all operations performed by the user in the last 30 days. These metrics will be used by both business and technical users to monitor their usage of the platform as well as to have a convenient history of the latest operations.

The **Administrator metrics** are in a way combination of the above two categories. The goal of this type of metrics is to enable the full monitoring of the DataBench framework from the static platform metrics to the user actions and operations performed in the different profiles. The administrator view will enable the performance of end-to-end platform analysis on the utilization of the platform. It will help to discover patterns and trends in the user searches and most executed operations.

4   Conclusions and Future Work

This paper presents an initial overview of the internal DataBench Toolbox design. We introduce the DataBench Methodological Workflow followed by the Framework Architecture components as two abstract layers that describe in detail the functionalities in terms of internal processes, supported operations and user interfaces. By defining the technical functionality of each framework component, the next implementation step of picking the most suitable software technologies and frameworks becomes clear and easier to realize. The latest news about the DataBench development are available on the project webpage [2] together with extended documentation of the internal architecture and design presented in this paper.

Acknowledgements. This work has been partially funded by the European Commission H2020 project DataBench - Evidence Based Big Data Benchmarking to Improve Business Performance, under project No. 780966. This work expresses the opinions of the authors and not necessarily those of the European Commission. The European Commission is not liable for any use that may be made of the information contained in this work. The authors thank all the participants in the project for discussions and common work.

References

1. D3.1 DataBench Architecture, DataBench Toolbox (2018). https://www.databench.eu/wp-content/uploads/2018/10/databench-d3.1-ver.1.0.pdf
2. DataBench (2019). https://www.databench.eu
3. D3.2 DataBench toolbox alpha including support for reusing of existing benchmarks, DataBench toolbox (2019). https://www.databench.eu
4. Gao, W., et al.: AIBench: towards scalable and comprehensive datacenter AI benchmarking. In: Zheng, C., Zhan, J. (eds.) Bench 2018. LNCS, vol. 11459, pp. 3–9. Springer, Cham (2019). https://doi.org/10.1007/978-3-030-32813-9_1
5. Gao, W., et al.: Aibench: an industry standard internet service AI benchmark suite (2019). CoRR abs/1908.08998. http://arxiv.org/abs/1908.08998
6. Han, R., John, L.K., Zhan, J.: Benchmarking big data systems: a review. IEEE Trans. Serv. Comput. **11**(3), 580–597 (2018). https://doi.org/10.1109/TSC.2017.2730882
7. Ivanov, T., Rabl, T., Poess, M., Queralt, A., Poelman, J., Poggi, N., Buell, J.: Big data benchmark compendium. In: Nambiar, R., Poess, M. (eds.) TPCTC 2015. LNCS, vol. 9508, pp. 135–155. Springer, Cham (2016). https://doi.org/10.1007/978-3-319-31409-9_9
8. Ivanov, T., et al.: Databench: evidence based big data benchmarking to improve business performance. In: KDD 2018 Project Showcase Track (2018). https://www.kdd.org/kdd2018/files/project-showcase/KDD18_paper_1805.pdf
9. Kumar, S., et al.: Scale MLPerf-0.6 models on google TPU-v3 pods (2019). CoRR abs/1909.09756. http://arxiv.org/abs/1909.09756
10. Mattson, P., et al.: MLPerf training benchmark (2019). CoRR abs/1910.01500. http://arxiv.org/abs/1910.01500
11. Pernici, B., et al.: Relating big data business and technical performance indicators. In: Conference of the Italian Chapter of AIS, pp. 1–12 (2018)
12. D5.3 Assessment of technical usability, relevance, scale, complexity (2019). https://www.databench.eu
13. Verma, S., et al.: Demystifying the MLPerf benchmark suite (2019). CoRR abs/1908.09207. http://arxiv.org/abs/1908.09207

Benchmarking Solvers for the One Dimensional Cubic Nonlinear Klein Gordon Equation on a Single Core

B. K. Muite[1,2(✉)] and Samar Aseeri[3]

[1] Arvutiteaduse Instituut, Tartu Ülikool, 50409 Tartu, Estonia
benson.muite@ut.ee
[2] Kichakato Kizito, Nairobi, Kenya
[3] Extreme Computing Research Center, King Abdullah University of Science
and Technology, P.O. Box 1212, Thuwal 23955-6900, Saudi Arabia
samar.aseeri@kaust.edu.sa

Abstract. To determine the best method for solving a numerical problem modeled by a partial differential equation, one should consider the discretization of the problem, the computational hardware used and the implementation of the software solution. In solving a scientific computing problem, the level of accuracy can also be important, with some numerical methods being efficient for low accuracy simulations, but others more efficient for high accuracy simulations. Very few high performance benchmarking efforts allow the computational scientist to easily measure such tradeoffs in order to obtain an accurate enough numerical solution at a low computational cost. These tradeoffs are examined in the numerical solution of the one dimensional Klein Gordon equation on single cores of an ARM CPU, an AMD x86-64 CPU, two Intel x86-64 CPUs and a NEC SX-ACE vector processor. The work focuses on comparing the speed and accuracy of several high order finite difference spatial discretizations using a conjugate gradient linear solver and a fast Fourier transform based spatial discretization. In addition implementations using second and fourth order timestepping are also included in the comparison. The work uses accuracy-efficiency frontiers to compare the effectiveness of five hardware platforms

Keywords: Benchmarks · Numerical methods · Computer architecture

1 Introduction

One use case of high performance computing is for the rapid numerical simulation of partial differential equations. It can be a challenge to determine the best computer architecture to use for solving a particular type of partial differential

BKM was partially supported by HPC Europa 3 (INFRAIA-2016-1-730897). Compute time on Isamabard was partially supported by ESPRC grant EP/P020224/1.

W. Gao et al. (Eds.): Bench 2019, LNCS 12093, pp. 172–184, 2020.
https://doi.org/10.1007/978-3-030-49556-5_18

equation. The choice of numerical method may also depend on the computer architecture being chosen. Traditional numerical analysts often consider the efficiency of different computational methods on a single computational platform (see for example [22, 23, 28]), but there is less work comparing the effectiveness of different numerical methods on different computer architectures. In this work, several numerical methods for solving the one dimensional Klein Gordon equation,

$$u_{tt} = \Delta u - u + u^3, \tag{1}$$

on a single core are reviewed and their effectiveness evaluated on five hardware platforms.

2   Motivation

The solution of linear systems of equations is a time consuming process in numerical simulation of partial differential equations, and has motivated a number of benchmarks [2, 5, 8, 16]. The solution of many partial differential equations requires a choice of discretization methods, in space and typically also in time, each of which presents numerous choices, each of which may have different relative performance on different computer architectures [1, 7, 12–15, 20, 26, 27, 29, 35, 37]. Currently, there is great diversity in supercomputer architectures [39], it may therefore be a good idea to use different full solution algorithms and different implementations on different computer architectures. The Klein Gordon equation is chosen as a mini-application because it is relatively simple, can be used to evaluate different time stepping methods and spatial discretization methods, and is representative of seismic wave solvers, and weather codes, all of which use a large amount of high performance computing time [1, 15, 31, 43]. As a prelude to a three dimensional study of parallel solvers, a comparison of solvers for the one dimensional Klein Gordon equation on five architectures is presented showing the effects of discretization method on time to solution for a specified accuracy on a single core. Such a method of comparison can be informative in choosing where to run an application to get the most cost efficient numerical results.

3   Time Stepping Algorithms

The equations will be discretized first in time, and then in space. The Klein Gordon equation has a conserved energy. Numerical schemes which either conserve energy may still have phase errors, but have typically been found to be useful for preserving qualitative properties of the phenomena being simulated over long time periods [32].

3.1   Semi-implicit Second Order Leap Frog Method

The leap frog method is a common algorithm for wave equations, and can also be applied to the real cubic Klein Gordon equation

$$\frac{u_{n+1} - 2u_n + u_{n-1}}{\delta t^2} = (\Delta - 1)\frac{u_{n+1} + 2u_n + u_{n-1}}{4} + u_n^3 \tag{2}$$

The method is second order accurate and is semi implicit. It has the summation by parts formula:

$$\left\|\frac{u_{n+1} - u_n}{\delta t}\right\|^2 + \left\|\nabla\frac{u_{n+1} + u_n}{2}\right\|^2 - \int u_n^3 u_{n+1}$$

$$= \left\|\frac{u_n - u_{n-1}}{\delta t}\right\|^2 + \left\|\nabla\frac{u_n + u_{n-1}}{2}\right\|^2 - \int u_{n-1}u_n^3 \tag{3}$$

which gives a discrete conserved energy. This scheme requires the solution of a constant coefficient linear system of elliptic equations at each timestep.

3.2   A Semi-implicit Compact Fourth Order Leap Frog Method

To obtain a fourth order algorithm consider,

$$\frac{u_{n+1} - 2u_n + u_{n-1}}{\delta t^2} = (\Delta - 1)\, u_n + u_n^3 \tag{4}$$

for which time stepping error comes from approximating u_{tt}. As explained in among other places, [1], it is possible to approximate the leading order error term,

$$\frac{2(\delta t)^2}{4!}u_{n,tttt}$$

$$\approx \frac{2(\delta t)^2}{4!}\left((\Delta - 1)\, u_n + u_n^3\right)_{tt}$$

$$\approx \frac{2(\delta t)^2}{4!}\left((\Delta - 1)\, u_{n,tt} + 3u_n^2 u_{n,tt} + 6u_n u_{n,t}^2\right) \tag{5}$$

$$= \frac{2}{4!}\left((\Delta - 1 + 3u_n^2)\,(u_{n+1} - 2u_n + u_{n-1}) + 6u_n(u_{n+1} - u_n)(u_n - u_{n-1})\right)$$

One can subtract the leading error term to obtain a compact fourth order in time scheme

$$\frac{u_{n+1} - 2u_n + u_{n-1}}{\delta t^2}$$

$$= (\Delta - 1)\, u_n + u_n^3 \tag{6}$$

$$+ \frac{2}{4!}\left[(\Delta - 1 + 3u_n^2)\,(u_{n+1} - 2u_n + u_{n-1})\right.$$

$$\left. + 6u_n(u_{n+1} - u_n)(u_n - u_{n-1})\right].$$

This scheme requires the solution of a non-constant coefficient linear elliptic system of equations at each timestep.

4   Spatial Discretizations

In all cases, uniform grids are used. In schemes that use the Fast Fourier transform, time stepping is done in Fourier space, and the nonlinear term is calculated

Table 1. Stencils for high order finite difference schemes for the one dimensional Laplacian operator [19]

Order	Approximation for u_{xx}
2nd	$\frac{1}{(\delta x)^2}\left(u_{i-1} - 2u_i + u_{i+1}\right)$
4th	$\frac{1}{(\delta x)^2}\left(-\frac{u_{i-2}}{12} + \frac{4u_{i-1}}{3} - \frac{5u_i}{2} + \frac{4u_{i+1}}{3} - \frac{u_{i+2}}{12}\right)$
6th	$\frac{1}{(\delta x)^2}\left(\frac{u_{i-3}}{90} - \frac{3u_{i-2}}{20} + \frac{3u_{i-1}}{2} - \frac{49u_i}{20} + \frac{3u_{i+1}}{2} - \frac{3u_{i+2}}{20} \frac{u_{i+3}}{90}\right)$
8th	$\frac{1}{(\delta x)^2}\left(-\frac{u_{i-4}}{560} + \frac{8u_{i-3}}{315} - \frac{u_{i-2}}{5} + \frac{8u_{i-1}}{5} - \frac{205u_i}{72} + \frac{8u_{i+1}}{5} - \frac{u_{i+2}}{5} + \frac{8u_{i+3}}{315} - \frac{u_{i+4}}{560}\right)$

in real space, no de-aliasing is done. Derivatives in spectral space are calculated by multiplying by the wave number. Descriptions of implementations of spectral methods can be found in [9,11,18,38,40]. For the compact time stepping scheme, fixed point iteration is used to calculate the nonlinear term.

High order finite difference discretizations for the one dimensional laplacian operator are described in [19] and given in Table 1. A second iteration is not required to compute the nonlinear term, since the time discretization requires a variable coefficient elliptic equation to be solved at each timestep, for which the iterative conjugate gradient method is well suited, though multigrid methods can also be used.

5   Numerical Experiments

In cases where iterations are required, both for the conjugate gradient algorithm and for fixed point iterations using the FFT, the solution at the previous time step is used as an initial starting guess. For these programs, memory bandwidth is a limiting factor and to minimize the number of memory accesses, the coefficients are programmed using a matrix free approach [35]. The example programs are written in Fortran and can be found at [34]. In all cases, the programs are written in Fortran 90 with the compiler doing other optimizations – machine specific optimization such as use of intrinsics and vectorization directives is not done and is a useful further step. Accuracy of the computed numerical solution is evaluated by comparing to the exact travelling wave solution

$$u = \sqrt{2}\mathrm{sech}\left(\frac{x - ct}{\sqrt{1 - c^2}}\right) \qquad (7)$$

for $c = 0.5$, $t \in [0, 5]$ and $x \in [-9\pi, 9\pi)$ with periodic boundary conditions.

The finite difference programs were compiled and run, without much further tuning other than the choice of compilation flags. Each scheme is run several times, with the number of timesteps varied in powers of 2 from 2^6 upto 2^{15} and the number of grid points also taken in powers of 2 from 2^6 upto 2^{15}. Following the reproducibility criterea in [6], the programs are open source, with the exception of two of the fast Fourier transform libraries, but are run on closed source hardware. Error bounds indicating the reproducibility of the numerical experiments are not presented and will be considered in further work.

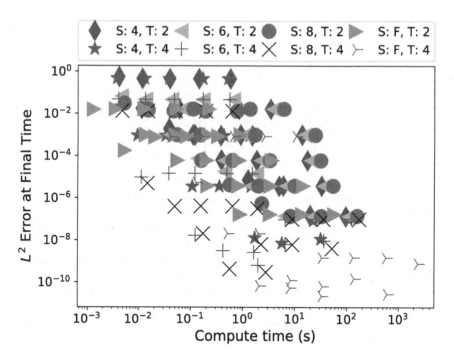

Fig. 1. Time to solution against accuracy for solution of the one dimensional Klein Gordon equation for a single Intel Haswell E5-2680v3 core. S gives the order of the spatial discretization for finite differences, while S: F indicates a Fourier spatial discretization. T gives the order of the temporal discretization.

5.1   Hazelhen

Hazelhen [24] is a Cray XC 40 supercomputer with Intel Haswell E5-2680v3 chips with a nominal speed of 2.5 GHz and 30 MB L3 Cache. Each node has 24 cores per node (2 chips with 12 cores each) with 136 GB/s bandwidth and 960 Gflops per node peak performance. FFTW 3 [17] is used to do the Fourier transforms. In this case, complex to complex Fourier transforms are used.

Results of accuracy against computation time are shown in Fig. 1. All computations have been done in double precision arithmetic. For low accuracy computations, a Fourier spectral discretization with second order time stepping is most efficient. For moderate accuracy computations, sixth or eighth order finite difference spatial discretizations with second order time stepping are most efficient. Finally for the highest accuracy, a fourth order time stepping scheme with Fourier spectral discretization is the most efficient. The computation time of the Fourier spectral methods can be reduced by almost half by using real to complex and complex to real Fourier transforms.

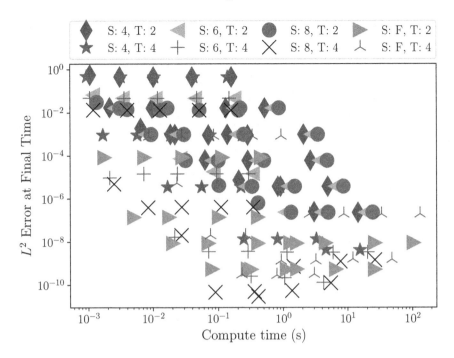

Fig. 2. Time to solution against accuracy for solution of the one dimensional Klein Gordon equation for a single NEC SX-ACE core. S gives the order of the spatial discretization for finite differences, while S: F indicates a Fourier spatial discretization. T gives the order of the temporal discretization.

5.2 Kabuki

Kabuki [25] is a NEC SX Ace supercomputer. Each node has 4 cores with 256 GB/s bandwidth and 256 Gflops peak performance. Each chip has a nominal speed of 1 GHz and each core has 1 MB vector cache. MathKeisan's FFT [36] is used to do the Fourier transform. In this case complex to complex Fourier transforms are used.

Results of accuracy against computation time are shown in Fig. 2. All calculations have been done in double precision arithmetic. For low levels of accuracy, finite difference spatial discretizations are the most efficient. For moderate levels of accuracy, a second order in time finite diffference method with a Fourier spatial discretization is most efficient. For the highest level of accuracy, a fourth order in time finite difference method and an eighth order in space finite difference method is most efficient. It is surprising that the error of the high order finite difference method is less than that of a Fourier spectral method and this requires further investigation. The computation time of the Fourier spectral methods can be reduced by almost half by using real to complex and complex to real Fourier transforms.

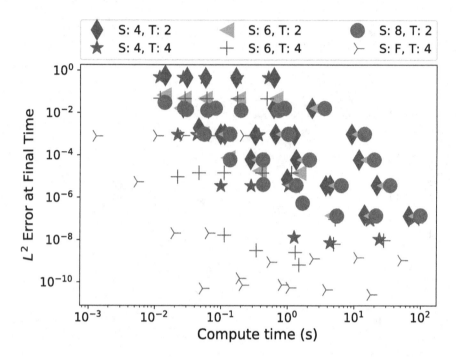

Fig. 3. Time to solution against accuracy for solution of the one dimensional Klein Gordon equation for a single AMD 6376 core. S gives the order of the spatial discretization for finite differences, while S: F indicates a Fourier spatial discretization. T gives the order of the temporal discretization.

5.3   Ibex: AMD Partition

Ibex [30] is a heterogeneous cluster and the AMD Abu Dhabi partition contains AMD 6376 chips with a nominal speed of 2.3 GHz and 16 MB L3 Cache. Each node has 64 cores per node (2 chips with 32 cores each) with 170 GB/s bandwidth and 590 Gflops per node peak performance. FFTW 3 [17] is used to do the Fourier transforms. In this case real to complex and complex to real Fourier transforms are used which reduce computation by a factor a little less than 2 compared to complex to complex Fourier transforms.

Results of accuracy against computation time are shown in Fig. 3. In this case, the Fourier spectral method with a fourth order time stepping is the most computationally efficient one to use.

5.4   Ibex: Intel Partition

Ibex [30] is a heterogeneous cluster and the Intel Skylake partition contains Intel Gold 6148 chips with a nominal speed of 2.6 GHz and 27.5 MB L3 cache. Each node has 40 cores with 256 GB/s bandwidth and 3760 Gflops per node peak performance. FFTW 3 [17] is used to do the Fourier transforms. In this case

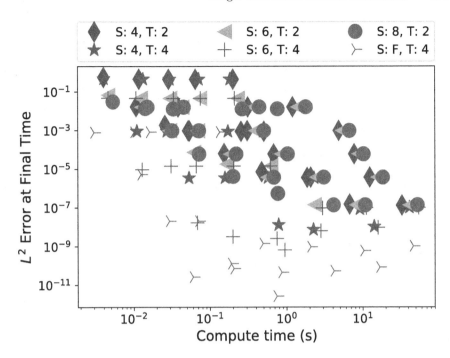

Fig. 4. Time to solution against accuracy for solution of the one dimensional Klein Gordon equation for a single Intel Gold 6148 core. S gives the order of the spatial discretization for finite differences, while S: F indicates a Fourier spatial discretization. T gives the order of the temporal discretization.

real to complex and complex to real Fourier transforms are used which reduce computation by a factor a little less than 2 compared to complex to complex Fourier transforms.

Results of accuracy against computation time are shown in Fig. 4. Except at the lowest accuracy levels, the Fourier spectral method with fourth order time stepping is the most computationally efficient one to use.

5.5   Isamabard

Isamabard [21,33] is a Cray XC 50 supercomputer with ARM Marvell Thunder X2 chips with a nominal speed of 2.1 GHz and 32 MB L3 cache. Each node has 64 cores (2 chips with 32 cores each) with 320 GB/s bandwidth and 1130 Gflops per node peak performance. The FFTW interface to the ARM performance library [4] is used to do the Fourier transforms. In this case real to complex and complex to real Fourier transforms are used which reduce computation by a factor a little less than 2 compared to complex to complex Fourier transforms.

Results of accuracy against computation time are shown in Fig. 5. Numerical experiments with finite difference methods were very sensitive to compiler

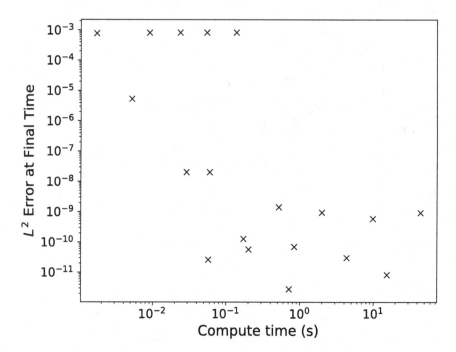

Fig. 5. Time to solution against accuracy for solution of the one dimensional Klein Gordon equation for a single ARM Thunder X2 core using a Fourier spatial discretization and a fourth order compact finite difference time stepping scheme.

optimization settings, and initial experiments with high optimization levels produced results with poor numerical accuracy and so are not shown. Reasons for this are under investigation. Only numerical experiments with the Fourier spectral method with fourth order time stepping gave reasonable results.

5.6   Efficiency Frontiers

A plot comparing the efficiency frontiers for all of the tested machines is shown in Fig. 6. These efficiency frontiers are obtained by calculating the convex hull of the data points for each tested platform.

Low order finite difference methods have a low computational intensity, thus high order finite difference methods which reuse data are able to produce much more accurate results without significant increases in computational time. The fast Fourier transform requires significant data movement, thus the eighth order finite difference method can sometimes be more efficient in getting high accuracy results within a specified time – though only second and fourth order time stepping schemes are tested here, results may differ for higher order time stepping schemes.

The NEC SX-ACE on Kabuki allows for all the bandwidth to be utilized by a single core, which is not possible on the Intel Haswell E5-2680v3 on Hazelhen.

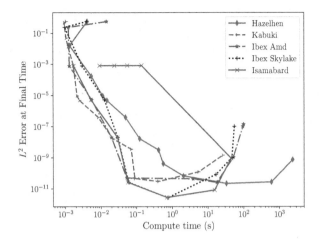

Fig. 6. A figure comparing efficiency frontiers for single Intel Haswell E5-2680v3 core on Hazelhen, a NEC SX-ACE core on Kabuki, a single AMD 6376 core on Ibex, a single Intel Gold 6148 core on Ibex and a single ARM Thunder X2 core on Isamabard for time to solution against accuracy for approximation of the one dimensional Klein Gordon equation.

This largely explains the greater single core performance on Kabuki compared to Hazelhen. On Ibex and Isamabard, real to complex and complex to real Fourier transforms are used, these reduce the number of computations that need to be done and the amount of data that needs to be moved by nearly a factor of two compared to the complex to complex transforms used on Kabuki and Hazelhen, giving Ibex and Isamabard significantly better performance compared to Hazelhen. Surprisingly, single core performance for the AMD 6376 chip on Ibex is similar to the single core performance of both the Intel Gold 6148 core on Ibex and the ARM Thunder X2 Core on Isamabard. This seems due to an innovative memory controller on the much older AMD 6376 chip and not much improvement in per core memory bandwidth on the newer ARM and Intel chips.

This initial study proposes a methodology for evaluating widely different computer architectures for their effectiveness in numerically solving partial differential equations to a specified accuracy. The current implementations are not optimal, and there is significant previous work in optimizing finite difference method implementations for minimizing compute time. In addition, many chips can use single, double and quadruple precision, with algorithms implemented in either a one precision, or in mixed precision, all of which can be used to increase computational efficiency [10]. The efficiency of the implementation can also be compared to hardware limits using the roofline [42] model and accurate measurements of bandwidth [41]. Further work will explore these issues.

Other studies have found that on a single multicore node, the performance advantage of the NEC SX-ACE is much reduced compared to a single core [3]. Performance evaluation for single nodes, and multiple nodes, in particular for three dimensional implementations would be good extensions of this work. In addition, comparisons of energy consumption to solution would also be helpful as this can be an important consideration for large scale simulation.

6   Conclusions

High order methods can take advantage of multiple floating point units and so, do not require much more computation time and give smaller error than low order methods. Their use should be encouraged in the numerical approximation of partial differential equations, this hold also for spectral element methods [26]. For benchmarks based on mini-applications, compute resources to solution at specified accuracy may be a good metric to use in evaluating performance rather than speed of performing a fixed set of operations. This would allow for architecture specific flexibility and can minimize cost to solution, though may require some programming effort.

Acknowledgements. We thank Holger Berger, José Gracia, John Linford and Simon McIntosh-Smith for helpful conversations. We thank Höchstleistungsrechenzentrum Stuttgart (HLRS), the KAUST Supercomputing Laboratory, the University of Tartu High Performance Computing Center and the GW4 Isamabard project for access to supercomputing resources used in development and testing.

References

1. Abdulkadir, Y.A.: Comparison of finite difference schemes for the wave equation based on dispersion. J. Appl. Math. Phys. **3**, 1544–1562 (2015). https://doi.org/10.4236/jamp.2015.311179
2. Adams, M.F., Brown, J., Shalf, J., Van Straalen, B., Strohmaier, E., Williams, S.: HPGMG 1.0: A Benchmark for Ranking High Performance Computing Systems, Lawrence Berkely National Laboratory Preprint (2014). https://escholarship.org/uc/item/00r9w79m. Accessed 16 July 2019
3. Afanasyev, I.V., et al.: Developing efficient implementations of Bellman-Ford and Forward-Backward Graph Algorithms for NEC SX-ACE. Supercomput. Front. Innov. **5**(3), 65–69 (2018). https://doi.org/10.14529/jsfi180311
4. Arm Performance Library. https://www.arm.com/products/development-tools/server-and-hpc/allinea-studio/performance-libraries. Accessed 16 Nov 2019
5. Aseeri, S., et al.: Solving the Klein-Gordon equation using Fourier spectral methods: a benchmark test for computer performance. In: HPC 2015 Proceedings of the Symposium on High Performance Computing, pp. 182–191. Society for Computer Simulation International (2015)
6. Aseeri, S., Muite, B.K., Takahashi, D.: Reproducibility in benchmarking parallel fast Fourier transform based applications. In: Companion of the 2019 ACM/SPEC International Conference on Performance Engineering - ICPE 2019, pp. 5–8 (2019). https://doi.org/10.1145/3302541.3313105
7. Auzinger, W., Březinová, I., Hofstätter, H., Koch, O., Quell, M.: Practical splitting methods for the adaptive integration of nonlinear evolution equations. Part II: comparisons of local error estimation and step-selection strategies for nonlinear Schrödinger and Wave equations. Comput. Phys. Commun. **234**, 55–71 (2018). https://doi.org/10.1016/j.cpc.2018.08.003

8. Bailey, D.H., et al.: The NAS parallel benchmarks. Int. J. High Perform. Comput. Appl. **5**(3), 63–73 (1991). https://doi.org/10.1177/109434209100500306
9. Balakrishnan, S., et al.: Parallel Spectral Numerical Methods. http://en.wikibooks. org/wiki/Parallel_Spectral_Numerical_Methods. Accessed 24 June 2019
10. Buttari, A., Dongarra, J., Kurzak, J., Luszczek, P., Tomov, S.: Using mixed precision for sparse matrix computations to enhance performance while achieving 64-bit accuracy. ACM Trans. Math. Softw. **34**(4), 17 (2008). https://doi.org/10.1145/1377596.1377597
11. Canuto, C., Hussaini, M.Y., Quarteroni, A., Zang, T.A.: Spectral Methods Fundamentals in Single Domains. Springer, Heidelberg (2010). https://doi.org/10.1007/978-3-540-30726-6
12. Cloutier, B., Muite, B.K., Parsani, M.: Fully implicit time stepping can be efficient on parallel computers. Supercomput. Front. Innov. **6**(2), 75–85 (2019). https://doi.org/10.14529/jsfi190206
13. Cloutier, B., Muite, B.K., Rigge, P.: A comparison of CPU and GPU performance for Fourier Pseudospectral Simulations of the Navier-Stokes, Cubic Nonlinear Schrödinger and Sine Gordon Equations. In: Proceedings of the 2012 Symposium on Application Accelerators in High Performance Computing, pp. 145–148 (2012). https://doi.org/10.1109/SAAHPC.2012.24
14. Chang, J., Nakshatrala, K.B., Knepley, M.G., Johnsson, L.: A performance spectrum for parallel computational frameworks that solve PDEs. Concurr. Comput. Pract. Exp. **30**, e4401 (2018). https://doi.org/10.1002/cpe.4401
15. Deconinck, W., et al.: Accelerating extreme-scale numerical weather prediction. In: Wyrzykowski, R., Deelman, E., Dongarra, J., Karczewski, K., Kitowski, J., Wiatr, K. (eds.) PPAM 2015. LNCS, vol. 9574, pp. 583–593. Springer, Cham (2016). https://doi.org/10.1007/978-3-319-32152-3_54
16. Dongarra, J., Heroux, M.A., Luszcek, P.: A new metric for ranking high-performance computing systems. Int. J. High Perform. Comput. Appl. **30**(1), 3–10 (2016). https://doi.org/10.1177/1094342015593158
17. Frigo, M., Johnson, S.G.: The design and implementation of FFTW. Proc. IEEE **93**(2), 216–231 (2005). https://doi.org/10.1109/JPROC.2004.840301
18. Fornberg, B.: A Practical Guide to Pseudospectral Methods. Cambridge University Press (1996). https://doi.org/10.1017/CBO9780511626357
19. Fornberg, B.: Generation of finite difference formulas on arbitrarily spaced grids. Math. Comput. **51**, 699–706 (1988). https://doi.org/10.1090/S0025-5718-1988-0935077-0
20. Gholami, A., Malhotra, D., Sundar, H., Biros, G.: FFT, FMM, or Multigrid? A comparative study of state-of-the-art poisson solvers for uniform and nonuniform grids in the unit cube. SIAM J. Sci. Comput. **38**(3), C280–C306 (2016). https://doi.org/10.1137/15M1010798
21. GW4: Isambard. https://gw4.ac.uk/isambard/. Accessed 9 Nov 2019
22. Hairer, E., Wanner, G.: Solving Ordinary Differential Equations I. Springer, Heidelberg (1993). https://doi.org/10.1007/978-3-540-78862-1
23. Hairer, E., Wanner, G.: Solving Ordinary Differential Equations II. Springer, Heidelberg (1996). https://doi.org/10.1007/978-3-642-05221-7
24. Höchstleistungsrechenzentrum Stuttgart (HLRS): Hazelhen. https://www.hlrs.de/systems/cray-xc40-hazel-hen/. Accessed 15 July 2019
25. Höchstleistungsrechenzentrum Stuttgart (HLRS): Kabuki. https://kb.hlrs.de/platforms/index.php/NEC_SX-ACE. Accessed 15 July 2019

26. Hutchinson, M., Heinecke, A., Pabst, H., Henry, G., Parsani, M., Keyes, D.: Efficiency of high order spectral element methods on petascale architectures. In: Kunkel, J.M., Balaji, P., Dongarra, J. (eds.) ISC High Performance 2016. LNCS, vol. 9697, pp. 449–466. Springer, Cham (2016). https://doi.org/10.1007/978-3-319-41321-1_23
27. Ibeid, H., Olson, L., Gropp, W.: FFT, FMM, and Multigrid on the Road to Exascale: Performance Challenges and Opportunities, arXiv:1810.11883v1 (2018)
28. Kassam, A.-K., Trefethen, L.N.: Fourth-order time-stepping for stiff PDEs. SIAM J. Sci. Comput. **26**(4), 1214–1233 (2005). https://doi.org/10.1137/S1064827502410633
29. Ketcheson, D.I., Mortensen, M., Parsani, M., Schilling, N.: More efficient time integration for Fourier pseudo-spectral DNS of incompressible turbulence. arXiv:1810.10197v1
30. King Abdullah University of Science and Technology Supercomputing Laboratory: Ibex. https://www.hpc.kaust.edu.sa/ibex. Accessed 9 Nov 2019
31. Komatitsch, D., et al.: SPECFEM3D Cartesian [software], GITHASH8 (1999). https://geodynamics.org/cig/software/specfem3d/. Accessed 16 July 2019
32. Leimkuhler, B., Reich, S.: Simulating Hamiltonian Dynamics. Cambridge University Press (2009). https://doi.org/10.1017/CBO9780511614118
33. McIntosh-Smith, S., Price, J., Poenaru, A., Deakin, T.: Scaling results from the first generation of ARM-based supercomputers. In: Proceedings of the Cray User Group 2019. http://uob-hpc.github.io/assets/cug-2019.pdf. Accessed 9 Nov 2019
34. Muite, B.K.: https://github.com/bkmgit/KleinGordon1D [software]. Accessed 16 July 2019
35. Müller, E.H., Scheichl, R., Vainikko, E.: Petascale solvers for anisotropic PDEs in atmospheric modelling on GPU clusters. Parallel Comput. **50**, 53–69 (2015). https://doi.org/10.1016/j.parco.2015.10.007
36. NEC. http://mathkeisan.com/ [software]. Accessed 16 July 2019
37. Pershin, I.S., Levchenko, V.D., Perepelkina, A.Y.: Performance limits study of stencil codes on modern GPGPUs. Supercomput. Front. Innov. **6**(2), 86–101 (2019). https://doi.org/10.14529/jsfi190207
38. Shen, J., Tang, T., Wang, L.-L.: Spectral Methods: Algorithms, Analysis and Applications. Springer, Heidelberg (2011). https://doi.org/10.1007/978-3-540-71041-7
39. Top500. https://www.top500.org/. Accessed 10 Nov 2019
40. Trefethen, L.: Spectral methods in MATLAB. SIAM **10**(1137/1) (2000). https://doi.org/10.1137/1.9780898719598
41. Treibig, J., Hager, G., Wellein, G.: LIKWID: a lightweight performance-oriented tool suite for x86 multicore environments. In: Proceedings of the First International Workshop on Parallel Software Tools and Tool Infrastructures. https://doi.org/10.1109/ICPPW.2010.38
42. Williams, S., Waterman, A., Patterson, D.: Roofline: an insightful visual performance model for multicore architectures. Commun. ACM **52**(4), 65–76 (2009). https://doi.org/10.1145/1498765.1498785
43. Yang, C., et al.: 10M-core scalable fully-implicit solver for nonhydrostatic atmospheric dynamics. In: SC 2016: Proceedings of the International Conference on High Performance Computing, Networking, Storage and Analysis, pp. 57–68 (2016). https://doi.org/10.1109/SC.2016.5

AI

Deep Reinforcement Learning
for Auto-optimization of I/O Accelerator
Parameters

Trong-Ton Pham[1(✉)] and Dennis Mintah Djan[2]

[1] HPC Software R&D Bull – Atos Technologies, Echirolles, France
`trong-ton.pham@atos.net`
[2] Artificial Intelligence and the Web Grenoble INP-Ensimag, Grenoble, France
`dennis-mintah.djan@grenoble-inp.org`

Abstract. Reinforcement Learning (RL) has made several advances in the machine learning domain especially Deep Reinforcement Learning. AlphaGo developed by DeepMind is a good example of how the deep neural network can train an agent to play and outperform professional Go players. Auto optimizing parameter is a relatively challenging research area. To automatically tune the parameters of the system, we formalize the problem into the setting of reinforcement learning model, where the aim is to train an agent whose goal is to find the optimum parameters by observing the state of the system and taking actions to maximize a cumulative reward. In this work, we solve this problem with the matrix version of Q-learning and the neural network version of Q-learning. We developed a new heuristic of Q-learning algorithm, called Dynamic Action Space (DAS), to further improve the robustness of the algorithm in finding the optimum state. The DAS approach significantly improved the convergence and stability of the algorithm. Then we tested the approach on three deep neural network variants, namely Deep Q-Networks (DQN), Double Deep Q-Networks (DDQN) and Dueling Networks. We show that the heuristic DAS model helps the Deep RL networks to converge better than the baseline Q-Learning model.

Keywords: Optimization · Q-learning · Deep reinforcement learning · I/O · HPC · Accelerator

1 Introduction

1.1 State of the Art

Auto optimizing parameter search is a relatively challenging research area. Recent advances in deep learning [3] have made remarkable progress and shown to be able to learn concepts directly through raw data such as pixels of images or other sensory data [11, 12]. Deep neural networks use multiple layers to learn the underlying representation between input and output and to obtain an approximate function that maps the input and output. These successes serve as a motivation for our approach of using reinforcement learning.

© Springer Nature Switzerland AG 2020
W. Gao et al. (Eds.): Bench 2019, LNCS 12093, pp. 187–203, 2020.
https://doi.org/10.1007/978-3-030-49556-5_19

The following works are closely related to our work, in using deep reinforcement learning to automatically tune parameters of systems. Yan Li et al. [6] used Double Deep Q-Networks [10] to design CAPES, which takes periodic measurements of a target computer system state and trains the network to suggest changes to the systems current parameter values. Techniques like Prioritized Experience Replay [24] was used to improve the convergence of the network.

S. Chenyang et al. [8] trained a deep reinforcement learning agent to automatically adjust parameters for image processing and demonstrated the network on problem of optimization base iterative CT reconstruction. H. Larson [20] used Deep Reinforcement learning for cavity filter tuning. Cavity filters are mechanical filters used in radio base stations, in production there are always physical deviations in the cavities and cross couplings of the filter which requires the filter to be tuned manually to make the magnitude responses fit some specifications. A deep deterministic policy gradient reinforcement agent was trained to tune filters with four poles and one transmission zero, or eight tuneable screws. The trained agent had an 87% success rate of tuning new filters.

R. Liessner et al. [21] shows how to use DQN to learn to control an optimization hyperparameter. The DQN was trained to adjust the learning rate of a gradient descent optimizer. Deep deterministic policy gradient algorithm was used to tune the hyperparameters of a Vehicle Energy Management system [22].

1.2   Optimization in HPC Context

Exascale supercomputers will require more and more automation [1] to overcome growing complexity in their administration and usage. Automated solutions are already in use to predict breakdown events [2] in HPC data centers. However, next generation solutions will be able to, not just predict events, but also automatically reconfigure the supercomputer to maintain operating performance in an optimal state. Such reconfigurations, that will affect all levels of the supercomputer, require an on-line monitoring of metrics and a dynamic adjustment of its operating state.

We have developed in our lab such software products concentrating on the optimization of the performance of I/O accesses on our HPC clusters. We provide 3 products that work together and make a continuously improving cycle as described in Fig. 1:

- **I/O Instrumentation:** an application I/O profiler for HPC applications.
- **I/O Pattern Analyzer:** a data analytics tool for classification of multiple jobs and accelerators automation.
- **Fast Accelerators:** Software and hardware accelerators targeting various I/O patterns such as pseudo random read and burst writes.

I/O Pattern Analyzer is a data analytics tool that serves two main tasks: classifying jobs into different application families and automatically setting up the fast accelerator with the optimal parameters for each job.

First, I/O Pattern Analyzer helps to classify automatically runs with similar behaviors into a same group, so we can apply the right accelerator and the optimized parameters for that job family. This task has been addressed in our previous work [4] on using Long Short-Term Memory (LSTM) model for classifying of HPC applications.

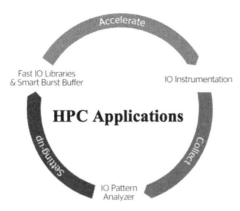

Fig. 1. Continuous improvement of I/O efficiency in HPC applications with three products: Instrumentation, Pattern Analyzer and Accelerators.

Second, I/O access can be optimized using accelerators such as data prefetchers or burst buffers depending on the application behavior. Each accelerator is provided with a set of configurable parameters that can be optimized for the best performance given the specific configuration of each cluster. The goal is to automate the setting up of the optimal I/O environment for an application, based on previous runs analysis. This work aims to solve this important point on the I/O Pattern Analyzer side.

For our specific case, we want to optimize the execution time or the required resources (CPU, memory, bandwidth, etc.) of the job run on the HPC cluster. Our solution is to find the optimal parameters iteratively. Each time a job is launched, it is launched with a combination of parameters. This run is monitored by the I/O Instrumentation and brings new information to find the best parameters. The next time this job is launched, new parameters are proposed and so on. After a certain number of runs, the proposed parameters must be the best parameters. This number of runs must be as small as possible to give the best acceleration performance as fast as possible.

In this work, we solve this problem using the Reinforcement Learning approach and more specifically with the matrix version of Q-learning and with the deep neural network versions. We develop a new heuristic of Q-learning for further improving the robustness of the algorithm in finding the optimum state. We also tested with 3 different variants of Deep Neural Network namely: Deep Q- Network (DQN), Double Deep Q- Network (DDQN) and Dueling Network.

2 Reinforcement Learning

2.1 Q-Learning Model

Reinforcement Learning is a branch of machine learning which deals with training of an agent to take actions within a defined environment to maximize a reward. More precisely RL consists of an agent, set of states, sets of actions which can perform in a state. The agent takes actions in environment allowing it to move from state to state and receive a reward. The function that indicates the action to take in a certain state is called the policy.

The goal of the agent is to learn a suitable policy that allows it to obtain the maximum reward.

Definitions of terms:

- **Agent:** Takes actions in the environment from a list of allowed actions in the state.
- **Actions:** List of possible moves the agent can do in that state. For example, in our context, vary the parameter values.
- **Future Rewards:** Maximizing the immediate reward is not enough for a good policy. It needs to consider the future actions to maximize also the future rewards of the episode. An action can give a very good reward, but if the next state is bad, then taking this action may be bad.

1) *Q-Learning Algorithm*

The Q learning was introduced by Christopher Watkings in 1989 [7]. The Q learning algorithm is based on Q-values that associates to each couple state/action one value of the goodness of the action (computed with the reward and discounted future reward). This value is not only composed of the reward, it also contains the discounted future reward. Choosing the best action is choosing the action that has the biggest Q-value in one state.

Q-learning algorithm creates a matrix M with one row per state and one column per action. Each entry Mi, j of this matrix contains the Q-value of action j in state i. The training part of the Q learning is to fill this matrix with values that give the optimal policy. To do it, the below algorithm iteratively tries actions, and depending of the outcome, updates the matrix.

Algorithm 1 Q learning training
---

procedure TRAIN(num_episode, env)
    $M \leftarrow$ matrix initialized with 0
    for $i \in [1, num\_episode]$ **do**
        state $\leftarrow$ start_episode(env)
        while not done(env) **do**
            $a \leftarrow$ decide_action(*state*)
            new_state, reward $\leftarrow$ do_action(env,a)
            $M \leftarrow$ update_rule(state, a, new_state, reward)
            state $\leftarrow$ *new_state*
    return M

The *start_episode* and *do_action* methods are defined in the environment and do NOT depend on the Q-learning algorithm. The action to take is decided in the **decide_action** method and the **update_rule** defines how to change the matrix of Q-values given a new observation.

2) *Update Rule*

After an observation, the matrix of Q-values needs to be updated. This update using the Bellman equation:

$$M[s, a] = (1 - \alpha)M[s, a] + \alpha\left(r + \gamma max_{a'} M[s', a']\right) \tag{1}$$

with:

M: Q-values matrix
s: current state
a: action taken
r: obtained reward after acting a in state s
s': new state
α (hyper-parameter): learning rate. It represents the importance of a new observation on the update of the Q-value ($0 < a < 1$).
γ (hyper-parameter): discount factor. If it is equal to 0, them the update will omit the next rewards. If it is equal or very close to 1, the Q-value can diverge.

3) *Exploration vs Exploitation*
The choice of an action during the training of the agent must be a compromise between exploration (choosing actions that are not the best-known actions) and exploitation (choosing the best). At the beginning of the training, the agent has no knowledge on the actions' outcomes. It needs to explore the environment to start learning. Because it has no way to select an action, this action is selected randomly and uniformly over the actions. This process is called exploration. It is also important for the agent to prioritize the action following the best policy it has learned so far. This part is called exploitation. It allows to focus the training more on the optimal policy and then to learn it faster.
To discover the environment, it is important to try new actions. But a too big exploration may take too much time. A limited exploration may not discover the environment enough to allow the agent to exploit. To handle this exploration/exploitation dilemma, the **decide_action** method of Algorithm 1 uses the ε-greedy algorithm. ε is the probability to take a random decision, with a probability $1 - ε$ the agent exploits the recommended action. This ε is called exploration rate and can change during the training. At the beginning, the priority is to explore the environment so ε can be equal to one or very close. But during the training, it can decrease. After a certain time of training, the priority is to exploit, ε can be set at a very small value.

2.2 DAS Q-Learning Model

1) DAS algorithm
This variant proposes to dynamically vary the step size of the action in the parameter space to allow the agent to explore faster. To achieve this, we specify a maximum skip (max_skip) or step size and dynamically generate an action space corresponding to this max_skip parameter. For example, in a 1D environment where the baseline agent has an action space of [0, −1, 1], if we specify a max_skip of 3, the action space is then as follows: [0, −1, +1, −2, +2, −3, +3]. This method increases the action space. The length of the action space can be calculated based on the formula:

$$length = 2 \times max\_skip \times dim + 1 \tag{2}$$

where dim is the dimension of the action space.

The noted change is the inclusion of the augmented action space. The agent can therefore explore with these actions to determine which action is better. This technique provides two benefits, it allows the agent to escape local minima and find the minimum point in smaller number of steps.

2) Evaluation on theoretical data

Evaluation of the models on 2D is done on two datasets: convex dataset and dataset with local minima and one global minimum. These data are generated with theoretical functions, so we can control the behaviors of each algorithm. Figure 2 shows the visualization of the generated data. Section 4.4 discusses the evaluation metrics. We discuss the results for the metric average steps to optimum. Section 4.3 also discusses into detail the environment model used in all the experiments.

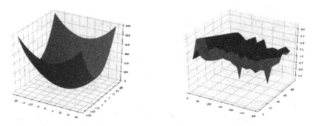

Fig. 2. Visualization of the data set: Convex (left) and Local Minima (right)

Convex

From Fig. 3 the first observation on the 2 models is that, all performed well on this dataset finding the minimum and remaining in that state. We notice that baseline takes 10 steps to get to the minimum after 100 episodes of training. While the DAS model as seen is other test, takes 3 steps to find the minimum. We also observe a better stability of the DAS model in staying at the minimum state.

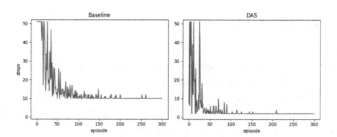

Fig. 3. Variation of the steps the agent takes to get to the optimum state in Convex dataset

Local Minima

The evaluation is performed using different starting points in the training to determine if these models can find the global minimum. The starting points were chosen to be as far as possible from the global minimum.

- Start close to the global minimum

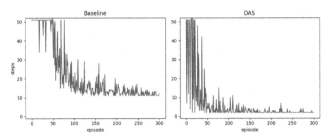

Fig. 4. Variation of the steps the agent takes to get to the optimum state in Local Minima dataset

From Fig. 4, the two models do find the optimum state and converge. As observed from the other evaluation, the DAS Model takes fewer steps averagely 3 steps to reach the minimum from episode 200.

- Start close to the local minimum

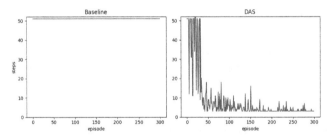

Fig. 5. Variation of the steps the agent takes to get to the optimum state in Local Minima dataset (more than 50 steps represent inability to find the optimum)

Figure 5 shows that the baseline model to be stuck at one of the local minima as it could not find the optimum after 300 episodes. We note that the DAS model has no difficulty in finding and staying at the optimum point.

These results confirm our intuition that the applied heuristic helped the Q-learning algorithm converge faster and more stable than the baseline implementation. In the next section, we will concentrate on applying the 2 method in training our deep neural networks.

3 Deep Reinforcement Learning

This section describes the three algorithms that combine deep neural networks and reinforcement learning to solve our optimization problem. Our goal is to train deep reinforcement agent to obtain directly the optimum parameters of I/O accelerators for a specific job by observing and processing training data.

3.1 Deep Q-Networks (DQN)

The Deep Q-Network is a deep neural network proposed by [15]. It is a multi-layered neural network that accepts as input state s and outputs a vector of action values to be chosen at the state **Q (s, a; θ)**, where the weights of this network are referred to as θ. However, deep Q-network is known to be unstable or sometimes diverge when a nonlinear function approximator is being used [6]. We discuss the two techniques presented by [15] to solve these challenges.

1. Experience Relay: The transitions states, actions, rewards, next states received from each step in the training is kept in a memory or database and later sampled uniformly from this memory to tune and update the network parameters. This is done to break the temporal correlation introduced by traditional training process that sequentially samples data, preventing overfitting of the network and hence termed as experience replay [15].
2. Target Network: This technique also helps the DQN converge, a target network which is the same as the model being trained with parameters θ', except that its parameters are updated differently. Two ways can be envisaged:

    - Getting weights from a previous iteration
    - Using a slowly updated Q-Network.

We consider the second way in updating our values for the target Q-network:

$$\theta' = \theta' \times (1 - tau) + \theta \times tau \tag{3}$$

where tau is the update rate of the target network.
The target used by DQN is

$$Target_{DQN} = (r + \gamma Q(s', argmax_{a'} Q(s', a'; \boldsymbol{\theta}'), \boldsymbol{\theta}') \tag{4}$$

where **r** is immediate reward from the environment and γ is discount factor. Hence target network (with parameters θ') is used to select the best action in the next state by the argmax operator and estimate the Q-value with the target network.

3.2 Double Deep Q-Networks (DDQN)

The main idea behind this model is to decouple action selection and action evaluation. We observed from (4) that the same target network is used for to select the best action in the next state and used to evaluate the Q-value at the same time. This makes the network more likely to overestimate values.

To solve this, we utilize the online model to determine the best action in the next state and use the target network to evaluate the action. The following equation shows how the loss function is updated [10]

$$Target_{DDQN} = (r + \gamma Q(s', argmax_{a'} Q(s', a'; \theta), \theta')) \tag{5}$$

We note the difference between **Target$_{DQN}$** and **Target$_{DDQN}$** is that the later using the model with parameters θ to get the best action using the argmax and calculate the Q-value using the target network parameters θ'.

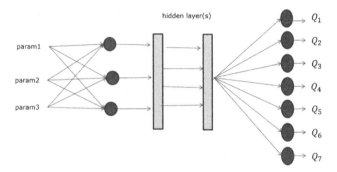

Fig. 6. Architecture of DQN and DDQN model

Figure 6 shows the general architecture of the DQN and DDQN networks. The input is the set of parameters that need to optimize, and the output is the vector containing the predicted Q values by the neural networks.

3.3 Dueling Networks

The main behind this dueling architecture is that for many states, it is unnecessary to estimate the value of each action. This network features two streams of computation, the value and advantage streams, sharing a convolutional encoder, and merged by a special aggregator [19].

The value **V(s)** stream in effect gives an estimate how good a state is, and the advantage stream **A(s)** gives an estimate of how good an action is in a state

$$Q(s, a) = V(s) + A(s, a) - \frac{1}{|A|} \sum_{a=1}^{|A|} A(s, a) \tag{6}$$

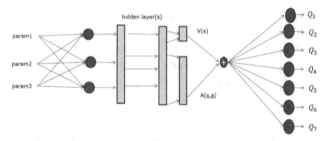

Fig. 7. Architecture of the Dueling network

As we can see in the Fig. 7 above, the final layer of the Dueling network is decoupled into two separate streams to estimate the state value and the advantage of each action.

4 Experiments and Results

4.1 Datasets

The evaluation of the 3 different models is done in two folds: theoretically generated data and real data from applications run on the cluster. The aim is to test the robustness of the algorithms on theoretically difficult patterns and finally test the performance of real data. We perform test on the theoretical data in 2 dimensions, followed by the test on 2 different real datasets generated by Job Synthetizer tool.

Job Synthesizer is a tool developed by our lab that allows to generate applications which make I/O following several predefined patterns such as (i.e. sequential, random or stride). After an application is generated, we run it with different parameters of I/O accelerator on our cluster and measure the execution time of each run. We store all the different parameters and the time of execution in our database for the experiment.

The I/O accelerator chosen for our experiment is the Small Read Optimizer (SRO) which run on compute nodes to improve the performance of the HPC applications. This accelerator targets multiple and concentrated small I/O (typically < 4 kB). Based on real-time analysis of the I/O distribution in files space, this module prefetches automatically blocks of file being frequently accessed, leading to an acceleration of the following I/O in those areas.

Table 1 describes the various dataset used in the evaluation in detail. Three parameters of IO accelerator considered in this experiment are CLUSTER_THRESHOLD, BIN_SIZE and PREFETCH_SIZE. As observed in Table 2, CLUSTER_THRESHOLD takes integer values from 2 to 8, with increment steps of 2 and BINSIZE, PREFETCH_SIZE value range are in bytes.

Table 1. Description of dataset

Name	Size	Description of parameters
Dataset1	168	CLUSTER_THRESHOLD: min = 2 max = 8 step = 2 BIN_SIZE: min = 1048576 max = 11534336 step = 2097152 PREFETCH_SIZE: min = 1048576 max = 32505856 step = 5242880
Dataset2	264	CLUSTER_THRESHOLD: min = 2 max = 8 step = 2 BIN_SIZE: min = 1048576 max = 11534336 step = 2097152 PREFETCH_SIZE: min = 1048576 max = 32505856 step = 3145728

4.2 Network Model

The network consist of the input layer which size is equivalent to the dimension of the state. The hidden layer of the network consists of 2 hidden layers of the same size. The output layer is a fully connected layer of size equal to the action size. We chose 2 hidden layers as [6], as shown that adding more layers becomes a problem of diminishing returns, with each additionally layer adding significantly more computation while returning lower gains in training success.

The network is trained for several episodes equal to the number of episodes specified. In each step the model parameters are updated, and the target model parameters are updated in (3) at the rate **tau** = 0.01. The optimizer used for the training is the Adam Optimizer due to its high convergence speed and good at escaping from certain local minima.

During the training phase, in each step of an episode, we generate the transition (state, reward, action, next state, done), where done is a boolean which represents the end of an episode. The transition is stored in a memory of capacity 10,000. At the end of each step in an episode, a batch of the memory (batch size) is selected and used to update the model parameters.

4.3 Environment Model

To be able to apply a reinforcement learning to any problem there must be an environment with states, actions and episodes (start and end of the environment). A reward function must also be defined. For now, we assume that there is one environment per job. The environment's states are the possible combinations of parameters. A transition (action) between two states is a change of parameters. To reduce the number of actions, an action is one update of a given step of one parameter. The more actions, the longer the training. This step can be different for every parameter (step p1 for P1, …). There is also one action to not perform any modifications, this allows to stay in the optimal state when it is found. This makes in total 7 actions for 3 parameters. Table 2 shows the action space of an agent with three parameters.

One episode starts in one state, one combination of parameters. During the episode, the agent moves inside the space of parameters thanks to actions. Its goal is to find the optimal combination of parameters and stay on it. Because an episode needs to end, it is a succession of 50 actions. This number is an arbitrary value. It allows to start from any start state, find the optimal state and loop on it few times in one episode.

Table 2. Action space of the agent

Action	P1	P2	P3
0	0	0	0
1	$-step_{p1}$	0	0
2	$+step_{p1}$	0	0
3	0	$-step_{p2}$	0
4	0	$+step_{p2}$	0
5	0	0	$-step_{p3}$
6	0	0	$+step_{p3}$

As there exists impossible values for parameters, some actions are not possible to take. For instance, it is impossible to have a cluster threshold smaller than 1. It may also be useful to give a maximum value for parameters to avoid unrealistic values. The agent must learn to not use impossible actions. If it does, the episode ends, and the agent receives a very low reward.

4.4 Rewards

The agent's goal is to maximize the sum of rewards in an episode. In our case, the goal is to minimize the duration of a run. Then, the reward given to the agent depends on the duration. To transform a minimization problem into a maximization, we use the inverse function. The duration of the jobs is normalized using the min-max method between 0 and 1. Without this normalization, the reward would have different scale depending on the job's duration (i.e. a job longer than another one would always give smaller reward). As the inverse of 0 is undefined and the limit when the normalized duration tends to 0 is infinity, it cannot be used directly to avoid too huge rewards. A parameter is used to avoid this:

$$reward = \frac{1}{duration_{normalized} + \phi}$$

$$\frac{1}{1+\phi} \leq reward \leq \frac{1}{\phi}$$

(7)

$= 0.2$ for all experiments. The maximum reward an agent should get is 50 if it stays at the optimum.

4.5 Model Validation

During the training, it is mandatory to evaluate the learning phase. The evaluation must give an overview on the quality of the learning. For this purpose, some indicators are provided:

- **Sum of reward:** As the goal of a reinforcement learning agent is to maximize the sum of reward obtained per episode, we can monitor it during the training.
- **Number of steps to the optimum:** The episode starts in one state. By performing actions, the agent must move to the optimum state. Based on this we have the metric *average steps to optimum*. A value greater than 50 represents that the agent couldn't converge to the optimum
- **Number of stays in the optimum:** In the optimum parameter search, once the optimum state is reached, the agent needs to learn that it has to stay in this state. Based on this we have the metric *average steps to optimum*. A value greater than 50 represents that the agent could not converge to the optimum
- **Success:** represents the percentage of episodes the agent converged at the optimum

4.6   Results and Discussion

1) *Dataset1*

   Table 3 compares the results of the 3 models DQN, DDQN and the Dueling Network without the heuristic (baseline) and with the DAS heuristic. Considering the baseline charts, we observe that only the dueling network stabilizes and converges at the optimum state from episode 400, as DQN and DDQN take all 50 steps without converging at the optimum. With the DAS heuristic, all models converge at the optimum from episode 600. The DAS heuristic has a great impact on especially the DQN and DDQN models, as we move from a non-convergent model to a convergent one. This is a huge gain from this approach. We observe from Table 5 the summary of the evaluation in numerical metrics to observe the gain of the DAS approach on the three models. Any interesting observation is that for each model there is an average of 10 steps decrease to the optimum in the second metric. For the Dueling network, the baseline model converges to the optimum and performs better than the DQN-DAS and DDQN-DAS. The DAS heuristic does bring significant improvement, especially on the 2 metrics: average steps to the optimum and average steps in the optimum. On this dataset, we note that the Dueling Network with DAS outperform all the other models.

2) *Dataset2*

   Table 4 compares the results of the 3 models on dataset2 with and without the DAS heuristic. For the DQN model, we observe that both the baseline model and the DAS heuristic version are unable to converge at the optimum state. The DDQN model shows a similar result as DQN, the DAS and baseline model cannot converge at the optimum. Irrespective of this, DAS version of DQN and DDQN show improvement performance in Table 5 in all three metrics.

   Considering the Dueling Network, the baseline model converges to the optimum from 800 episodes. The DAS version performs better converging to the optimum state from 600 episodes.

3) *Overall results*

   Table 5 summaries the overall results on the experiments on the three deep Q-network models. Generally, we note that DAS heuristic improves the convergence of the models. In our two datasets we tried our models on, we start each agent from one fixed state and observe the trajectory to the optimum. It will be interesting to observe the agents using different start points and note the improvement of the DAS heuristics on this case.

We consider the validation metrics: success, average steps to optimum and average steps in optimum. In parenthesis in the DAS row we note the percentage gain obtained. As explained earlier for the average steps to optimum, the lower the value the better and for the average steps in optimum, the higher the value the better.

Table 3. Variation on the number of steps with 3 networks to the optimum on Dataset1

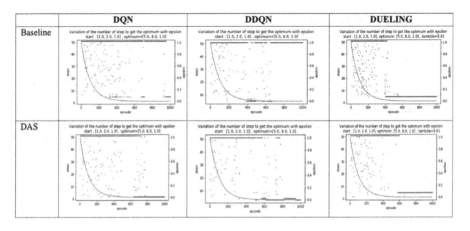

Table 4. Variation on the number of steps 3 networks to the optimum on Dataset2

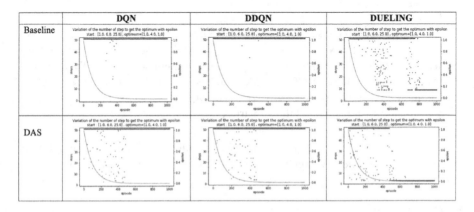

Table 5. Summary of results with the respective improvement of DAS heuristic over the baseline method

Dataset	Model	Success (improvement %)	Average steps to optimum	Average steps in optimum
Dataset1	DQN	22.6	43.45	5.978
	DQN-DAS	**43.5 (+92.5%)**	**32.2 (+35%)**	**16.8 (+181%)**
	DDQN	23.8	42.13	7.474
	DDQN-DAS	**47 (+97.5%)**	**30.2 (+28.3%)**	**20.12 (+169.2%)**
	Dueling	71.6	29.28	28.296
	Dueling-DAS	**74.3 (+3.8%)**	**16.57 (+43.4%)**	**31.87 (+11.2%)**
Dataset2	DON	1.1	50.9	0.036
	DQN-DAS	**6.5 (+490%)**	**49.33 (+1.4%)**	**0.31 (+761%)**
	DDQN	0.3	50.9	0.01
	DDQN-DAS	**6.6 (+2100%)**	**49.2 (+3.3%)**	**0.39 (+3800%)**
	Dueling	40.3	36.6	12.84
	Dueling-DAS	**59.6 (+47.9)**	**23.89 (+34.7%)**	**25.45 (+98.2%)**

Overall the DAS model gives a maximum improvement of 23% in Dataset1 and gives a maximum improvement of 19% in Dataset2 in terms of the success metric. In Table 5 section of dataset2, we note the significant improvement of DAS heuristics, decreasing the average number of steps to the optimum from 36 to 23 and staying on average twice as longer in the optimum state.

5 Conclusion and Perspective

In this paper, we presented our Reinforcement Learning approach for optimization of the I/O accelerator parameters to improve the performance of HPC applications. We introduced a new Dynamic Action Space (DAS) heuristic to the Q-Leaning algorithm and applied it to the deep reinforcement learning models: DQN, DDQN and Dueling network.

Our study demonstrated that the DAS heuristic applied on the Q-Learning algorithm helps to find the optimum faster and with lesser interactions. The implementation of this methods with three deep neural networks also showed the improvement in most of the case comparing to the baseline method. We believe that the tuning of the hyper-parameters for theses network, which sometime is not straightforward, can further improve the performance of the Deep Q-Networks.

Our objective in this study is to enhance the performance of the application running on real HPC clusters. One promising direction is to deploy this model on a real data center to benefit from the massive data collected to train our deep reinforcement models and test the scalability of the proposed method.

Future work also includes the combination with the classification model proposed in our previous work [4] to close the loop from collecting data, classifying jobs into similar groups and automatically applying the right I/O accelerator parameters for the job. This will create an autonomous system for monitoring and administrating HPC cluster in the next decade.

References

1. Abraham, E., et al.: Preparing HPC applications for exascale: challenges and recommendations. In: 18th International Conference on Network-Based Information Systems (NBiS) (2015)
2. Gainaru, A., Cappello, F., Snir, M., Krammer, W.: Failure prediction for HPC systems and applications: current situation and open issues. Int. J. High Perform. Comput. Appl. **27**, 273–282 (2013)
3. Goodfellow, I., Bengio, Y., Courville, A.: Deep Learning. MIT Press, Cambridge (2016)
4. Pham, T.T., Pister, M., Couvee, P.: Recurrent neural network for classifying of HPC applications. In: Proceedings of HPC - Spring Simulation Conference (2019)
5. Sutton, R.S., Barto, A.G.: Reinforcement Learning: An Introduction. MIT Press, Cambridge (2018)
6. Li, Y., Chang, K., Bel, O., Miller, E.L., Long, D.: CAPES: unsupervised storage performance tuning using neural network-based deep reinforcement learning (2017)
7. Watkins, C., Dayan, P.: Q-learning. Mach. Learn. **8**(3–4), 279–292 (1989)
8. Chenyang, S., Liyuan, C., Steve, J., Xun, J.: Intelligent parameter tuning in optimization-based iterative CT reconstruction via deep reinforcement learning. IEEE Trans. Med. Imaging **37**(6), 1430–1439 (2018)
9. Mnih, V., et al.: Playing atari with deep reinforcement learning (2013)
10. Hasselt, V., Guez, H., Silver, D.: Deep reinforcement learning with double Q-learning (2016)
11. Schaul, T., Quan, J., Antonoglou, I., Silver, D.: Prioritized experience replay. In: Proceedings of ICLR (2015)
12. Krizhevsky, A., Sutskever, I., Hinton, G.: Imagenet classification with deep convolutional neural networks. Adv. Neural. Inf. Process. Syst. **25**, 1106–1114 (2012)
13. Sermanet, P., Kavukcuoglu, K., Chintala, S., LeCun, Y.: Pedestrian detection with unsupervised multi-stage feature learning. In: Proceedings of the International Conference on Computer Vision and Pattern Recognition (CVPR 2013). IEEE (2013)
14. Sutton, S., Barto, A.G.: Introduction to Reinforcement Learning. MIT Press, Cambridge (1998)
15. Mnih, V., et al.: Humanlevel control through deep reinforcement learning. Nature **518**(7540), 529 (2015)
16. Abadi, M., et al.: TensorFlow: a system for large-scale machine learning. In: Proceedings of the 12th Symposium on Operating Systems Design and Implementation (OSDI 2016). USENIX Association, Savannah (2016)
17. Bengio, Y.: Practical recommendations for gradient-based training of deep architectures. In: Montavon, G., Orr, G.B., Müller, K.-R. (eds.) Neural Networks: Tricks of the Trade. LNCS, vol. 7700, pp. 437–478. Springer, Heidelberg (2012). https://doi.org/10.1007/978-3-642-35289-8_26
18. Bengio, Y.H., Louradour, Y., Lamblin, P.: Exploring strategies for training deep neural networks. Mach. Learn. Res. **10**, 1–40 (2009)
19. Wang, Z., de Freitas, N., Lanctot, M.: Dueling network architectures for deep reinforcement learning. In: ICLR (2016)

20. Larsson, H.: Deep reinforcement using deep Q-learning to control optimization hyperparameters learning for cavity filter tuning (2018)
21. Liessner, R., Schmitt, J., Dietermann, A., Baker, B.: Hyperparameter optimization for deep reinforcement learning in vehicle energy management (2019)
22. Schaul, T., Quan, J., Antonoglou, I., Silver, D.: Prioritized experience replay. In Proceedings of ICLR (2015)

Causal Learning in Question Quality Improvement

Yichuan Li[✉], Ruocheng Guo, Weiying Wang, and Huan Liu

Arizona State University, Tempe, AZ 85281, USA
{yichuan1,rguo12,wwang239,huanliu}@asu.edu

Abstract. To improve the quality of questions asked in Community-based questions answering forums, we create a new dataset from the website, Stack Overflow, which contains three components: (1) context: the text features of questions, (2) treatment: categories of revision suggestions and (3) outcome: the measure of question quality (e.g., the number of questions, upvotes or clicks). This dataset helps researchers develop causal inference models towards solving two problems: (i) estimating the causal effects of aforementioned treatments on the outcome and (ii) finding the optimal treatment for the questions. Empirically, we performed experiments with three state-of-the-art causal effect estimation methods on the contributed dataset. In particular, we evaluated the optimal treatments recommended by the these approaches by comparing them with the ground truth labels – treatments (suggestions) provided by experts.

1 Introduction

In recent years, community-based question answering (CQA) forums (Stack Overflow[1], Quora[2] and Zhihu[3]) have attracted millions of users all over the world monthly[4]. These websites can provide useful answers to askers who post questions, and provide a platform for more experienced users (e.g., experts) to share knowledge with askers as well as other users looking for such answers through search engines [1].

However, the submitted questions can be unclear, lack of background information, and the chaos question format. For such questions, the members and moderators of Stack Overflow community will delete the poor quality questions[2]. From Fig. 1, the ratio of unanswered questions has been increased in recent years indicating that more and more low-quality questions have been posted in the communities. Examples of low-quality questions[5] are listed in Table 1. Although websites like Stack Overflow have explicit, detailed guidance

---

[1] https://stackoverflow.com/.
[2] https://www.quora.com/.
[3] https://www.zhihu.com.
[4] https://stackexchange.com/sites?view=list#questionsperday.
[5] https://meta.stackexchange.com/questions/180692/why-do-i-receive-downvotes-when-i-am-genuinely-trying-to-learn/.

© Springer Nature Switzerland AG 2020
W. Gao et al. (Eds.): Bench 2019, LNCS 12093, pp. 204–214, 2020.
https://doi.org/10.1007/978-3-030-49556-5_20

on how to ask good questions[6], the fact is that the experts still have to spend considerable time on understanding the real need of askers (e.g., via comments).

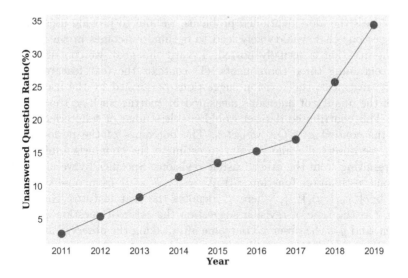

Fig. 1. The ratio of unanswered questions increased in recent years

Table 1. Example of raw questions and improved questions

Raw Question	Revised Question
C# Math Confusion	Why does using float instead of int give me different results when all of my inputs are integers?
[php] session doubt	How can I redirect users to different pages based on session data in PHP?
Android if else problems	Why does str == "value" evaluate to false when str is set to "value"?

To help users improve the quality of questions, many existing methods[3–5] build binary classification models for question quality detection, but these approaches do not give revision suggestions to improve the quality of questions. The drawback of these approaches is that beginners still cannot learn the tips of asking good questions from their failures. To overcome this limitation, in [6] a method is proposed to map low-quality questions to a category of revision suggestions. However, this method does not evaluate the outcome after taking this revision suggestion. In other words, beginners does not whether this suggestion is the best or not. In [7] improvements are made by the hand-crafted features.

---

[6] https://stackoverflow.com/help/how-to-ask.

In [8], it further improved the approach with the latent space generated by neural encoder. These improvements are black-box in the sense that they might not be fully understandable by real-world CQA users. Even with the recommended improvements, users may not know why they need to take these revisions.

To address the aforementioned problems, we aim to provide users the revision suggestions that would likely lead to optimal outcomes in the draft page before the question is actually posted. Toward this goal, we contribute a new dataset containing three components: (1) context: the text features of questions, (2) treatment: the revision suggestions performed by the users and (3) outcome: the quality of questions measured by metrics such as the number of answers. This contributed dataset would enable studies of counterfactual inference in the context of CQA websites. The outcomes of the performed revisions can be observed while we aim to estimate the counterfactual outcomes – those resulting from the other feasible revisions. Specifically, we aim to learn an outcome estimation function $E[Y|X = x_q, T = t]$ from observation data denoted by $\{(x_q, t, y)_i\}_{i=1}^n$, where x_q denotes the text features from the raw question, t is the type of revision suggestion the asker of question q has actually taken, and y is the observed outcome after taking the observed suggestions. In evaluation, we evaluate the improvement of treatment t_i over t_j, denoted by $E[Y|X = x_q, T = t_i] - E[Y|X = x_q, T = t_j], i \neq j$, where t_i is recommended by the proposed model. In addition, we also compare the aforementioned improvement with the improvement observed in the data, denoted by $\hat{E}[Y|X = x_q, T = t_i] - \hat{E}[Y|X = x_q, T = t_j], i \neq j$. In the inference stage, this model evaluates each suggestion through inferring their potential outcomes, and choose the one with the optimal inferred outcome. The best out of the models considered in this work can only reach a 0.16 accuracy score, which leaves a great space for future improvement.

Our main contributions of this work can be summarized as follows:

- We created the dataset which allows researchers to study the problem of question improvement in the CQA settings. The dataset contains three main components: (1) context: text features of questions, (2) treatment: revision suggestions and (3) outcome: indicators of the quality of the revised question.
- We demonstrate the utility of our dataset in three SOTA counterfactual inference models. This dataset contains rich information in the revision treatment and various kinds of outcomes. Researchers can discover the treatment from the revision text and estimate the causal effect simultaneously.

2   Related Work

Predicting Question Quality via Classification: [3–5] proposed to classify questions into two classes: high-quality and low-quality. In particular, authors of [3] leveraged logistic regression for the detection of unclarified questions with several input features from the askers, the questions, and the answers. [5] employs features from similar labeled questions which are retrieved by Elasticsearch, general search engine, and users' comment on clarification to train a logistic regression model. [4] uses a feed-forward neural network with n-gram text features to identify the questions that are not well-formed. Only notified questions need to be improved to attract high-quality answers, these methods cannot give the revision suggestions for the users. Towards giving the category of revision suggestion, [6] maps the question to a possible revision suggestion. [9] identifies the revision intentions of revisions in Wikipedia. However, these datasets do not afford the outcome after revision. So it is hard to evaluate whether the result of taking such revision.

Direct Improvement Approach: [7] makes improvement on the handcrafted features like *add more n-grams* and *decrease average token length* to improve the score generated through Gaussian random process. These discrete feature revisions are hard for users to follow in the real world. [10] and [8] make improvement on the text directly. [10] use a Metropolis-Hastings sampling method to sample the words until the transition function converges. [8] uses a variational recurrent autoencoder (VRAE) to encoder the text into hidden space, make improvements on hidden vectors then decoder the revised vector into a new text. However, these methods cannot keep the meaning consistency during the revision. For example, when an input sequence is *you are both the same size.*, output sequence would be *you are both wretched men.*

Data for Learning Causal Effects: The standard dataset format for learning causal effects can be denoted by (X, T, Y), where X is the feature matrix, T is the vector of assigned treatment and Y is the vector of observed outcome [11]. For example, with the Infant Health and Development Program (IHDP) [12] dataset, we aim to estimate the causal effects of home visits of specialists on children's cognitive test scores. Another widely adopted dataset for causal effect estimation is News [13]. This dataset comes with the bag-of-word representation randomly sampled news as the features, the type of devices used to read the news (e.g., mobile or desktop) as the treatment and the readers' opinions as the outcome. However, the treatment and outcome of this dataset are not directly related to natural language. In contrast, the features and treatments of the contributed dataset by this work are both textual. This makes it more flexible for researchers to create new causal inference tasks by extracting different types of treatments based on their need. Recently, massive observational datasets with rich auxiliary information (e.g., social networks [14–16], product networks [17] and language models [18,19]) have also been adopted for the causal effect estimation. A summary of the related datasets can be found in [20].

Our work is based on [6]. We add real outcomes for each improvement type and expand the size from 3,631 to 34,303, about 10 times larger than before. Table 2 shows the difference between our dataset and others.

Table 2. Comparison of related resources in terms of improvement suggestion and future outcome

Dataset Name	Treatments	Outcome	Size
Our dataset	Available	Available	34,303
WIS_HT_2014[6]	Available	Unavailable	3,631
Identify Unclear[5]	Unavailable	Available	6 million
Wikipedia Revisions[9]	Available	Unavailable	7,170

3   Problem Statement

In this work, we are interested in answering two questions:

– What is the answer count difference when the question takes a specific revision suggestion?
– Is a certain revision suggestion the optimal suggestion for their questions?

For the first question, we use serval causal inference models to estimate the causal effects of each revision suggestion on the outcome motioned in the Introduction part. The model will predict the outcome $P(Y|X = x_q, T = t_k)$ after taking specific revision suggestion t_k. We consider the text feature of question x_q as the confounders which affect both treatment and outcome, the categories of revision suggestions, $t_k \in \{t_1, t_2, \cdots, t_K\}$, as the treatment, and the number of answers question gets Y as the outcome. The causal directed acyclic graphics (DAG) is shown in Fig. 2. Our goal is to estimate of outcome under each revision suggestion $E(Y|X = x_q, T = t_k)$.

To answer the second question, we aim to choose the treatment which causes the greatest improvement in the outcome. This problem can be formulated as

$$\arg\max_{t_k} E(Y|X = x_q, T = t_k) - Y_0, \tag{1}$$

where Y_0 is the outcome without taking any revision.

4   Dataset

This section describes how the contributed dataset is created in details. First, we present descriptions of the types of suggestions and the outcome in our dataset. Then, we discuss the process of data crawling.

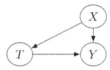

Fig. 2. Causal diagram (DAGs) for the problem of finding optimal intervention. X denotes the features describing the question before revision(s), T denotes the category of revision suggestion applied to the text, and Y signifies the outcome which is measured by the number of answers to the question.

4.1 Dataset Description

- Based on [6], and the categories of suggestions from the Stack Overflow instruction[7], we assign revision suggestions into the following seven categories:
  - **Clarification**: the askers provide additional context and clarify what they want to achieve.
  - **Example**: the askers added an output or input format or included the expected results for their problems.
  - **Attempt**: the possible attempts askers have tried in the process of solving their problems.
  - **Solution**: the askers add content to or comment on the solution found for the questions. The Stack Overflow community explicitly encourages contributions where the user asks the question also provides the final answers. Some askers append their solutions and other users create an answer in the discussion.
  - **Code**: modification of the source code, only considering code additions;
  - **Version**: inclusion of additional details about the hardware or software used (program version, processor specification, etc.);
  - **Error Information**: warning message and stack trace information of the problem;
- We use the **answer count** within a month as the outcome. We only consider the answer count between the two neighboring revisions in terms of time. In other words, for control effects (answer count before the revision), we only calculate the answer between the current revision and the revision right before the current one. The time interval can vary from years to days. To remove the influence of the length of the time intervals, we define the answer count per month as the outcome. Samples of the dataset can be found in Table 3.

4.2 Dataset collection

All data of Stack Overflow are available[8]. Stack Overflow also offers a data explorer website[9] where users can use SQL queries to select interesting subsets.

---

[7] https://stackoverflow.com/help/how-to-ask.
[8] https://archive.org/details/stackexchange.
[9] https://stackexchange.com/.

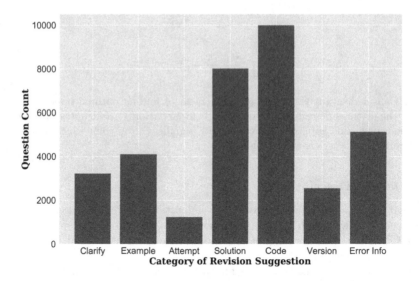

Fig. 3. The number of revision suggestions in each category.

For convenience, we use the data explorer to select question revision histories from the *PostHistory* data table, and the answer count from *Post* data table. The revision records contain all pairs of the text of revision comments and questions. The editors will leave a short comment to summarize the change, like *add introduction about problem* and *add input template* etc. So we can use keywords in the comments to determine the label (type) of each question revision. For example, we label *add introduction about problem* with the type of *Clarification* and *add input template* as *Example*. Detail information about data collection. To avoid the data duplication problem, we assume that each question revision only has one revision label. Therefore, we remove the comments with multiple keywords. There are many different topics in Stack Overflow, for example, *Ask Ubuntu*, *English Language Usage*, *Code Golf* and *Bitcoin* etc. For the domain consistency, we only extract the text from the main site of Stack Overflow.

5   Experiment

5.1   Methods

To exhibit that this dataset can be used to study causal inference problems including causal effect estimation, treatment assignment mechanism (policy) evaluation and optimization, we perform an evaluation of the three SOTA causal inference models on it. Here, we introduce the three SOTA causal inference models as below:

Table 3. Example instances of the contributed dataset: PO stands for previous outcome, LO stands for later outcome (the outcome after treatment).

Raw Question	Revised Question	Suggestion	PO	LO
I have a simple table in SQL Server 2005, I wish to convert this to XML (using the "FOR XML" clause). ...	**Solved**: I was hoping for something elegant and tidy...	Solution	2	0
I have one directory of files in a folder that I want to optimize and then output to a different folder.). ...	**I have tried** the following Makefile. This does the build, but it will rebuild all the files every time.	Attempt	1	0
I am trying to send a custom token to an existing API via WSO2.). ...	Here's a wire **log** dump from the request (without the actual tokens).	Error Info	1	1
I am calling it in my view like this ...	The problem seems to be the **data** that 'Pygment.rb' is **acting on**.	Example	1	0
My first question here, but stackoverflow has been a highly valued resource for me the past year.	... **Thread.Abort()** bypasses all the logic and kills the thread without cleaning up...	Clarification	0	0

- **Bayesian Additive Regression Trees** [21] (BART) is an additive error mean regression model. It is a *sum-of-trees* model, and each tree's complexity is constrained by a regularization prior to be a weak learner.
- **Counterfactual Regression Networks** [22] (CFRnet): This model learns a balanced representation of the control and treatment groups.
- **Causal Effect Variational Autoencoder** [23] (CEVAE): This model estimates the unknown confounders from observation data through Variantional Autoencoders.

All these models take the input of features and treatment (X, T) to predict the outcome $E[Y|X, T]$. The input features are listed in Table 4.

5.2 Model Evaluation

We evaluate the SOTA models with this dataset on two tasks and use two groups of metrics to evaluate the treatment estimation and optimal suggestion accuracy.

Causal Effect Estimation: Given the dataset denoted by $\{(x_q, t, y)_i\}_{i=1}^n$, these metrics quantifies the how the outcome y changed if we select different treatment t. In our experiment, these metric help us understand how the answer count changed if we had tried different revision suggestions that are unobserved in the dataset. We estimate the conditional average treatment effect (CATE) for each revision suggestion separately. CATE explicitly considers the causal effect

Table 4. Features used in treat effect estimation models

Feature Groups	Description
Num. of words	Number of word in the question
Num. of unique words	Number of unique tokens in the question
Num. of herfs	Number of herf links in the question
Num. of keywords	Number of keywords in the question
Avg. len. of words	Average length of each word in the question
Avg. of word embedding	Average of word embedding vector

conditioned on the features X. This is because CATE aims to consider the heterogeneity of causal effects among instances with different features.

$$\tau(x_q) := \mathbb{E}(Y|X = x_q, T = t_k) - \mathbb{E}(Y|X = x_q, T = t_0)$$

Our target is to learn the function $\hat{\tau}$ which enables us to approximate the CATE such that the error metrics: (1) the mean squared error of CATE estimation and (2) Precision in Estimation of Heterogeneous Effect (PEHE) [21] are minimized:

$$\epsilon_{ATE_k} = \mathbb{E}_k \left[(\hat{\tau}_k(X) - \tau_k(X))^2 \right]$$

$$PEHE_k = \frac{1}{|U|} \sum_{u \in U} \left(Y_u^{k1} - Y_u^{k0} - \hat{\tau}(X_u) \right)^2,$$

where k denotes the k-th treatment (revision category) and U is the set of all instances in the test set. Small values of $PEHE_k$ and ϵ_{ATE_k} indicate accurate estimation of both observed and counterfactual example.

Exact Match: In this task, we measure the accuracy of the causal inference models. Here, accuracy is defined as the probability to recognize the optimal category of revision suggestions from the category of users' revision.

5.3   Result

Table 5 shows the performance of the state-of-the-art (SOTA) models for causal effect estimation on the two aforementioned tasks: (1) treatment effects evaluation and (2) optimal revision suggestion prediction on our dataset. We found that BART achieves the best performance in counterfactual inference. We found that CFRnet achieves the best prediction accuracy.

Table 5. Performance for various methods

	ϵ_{ATE}	PEHE	Accuracy
BART	0.041	0.661	0.086
CFRnet	0.508	1.030	0.161
CEVAE	0.169	1.522	0.126

6 Conclusion

In this work, we propose a new dataset to provide the revision suggestion for low-quality question in Stack Overflow. This dataset contains three components: (1) context: the text features of questions, (2) treatment: categories of revision suggestions and (3) outcome: the measure of question quality . Based on this dataset, we test three SOTA causal inference models to estimate the counterfactual effects of each revision suggestion. BART [21] achieves the best result in counterfactual inference models, with 0.661 PEHE. CFRnet [22] achieves 0.161 accuracy in the task of detecting the optimal revision suggestions compared to the experts annotation.

The contributed dataset can facilitate research on evaluating the causal effect of deploying different categories of text revisions on questions and find the optimal revision in the context of CQA.

Acknowledgement. This material is based upon work supported by ARO/ARL and the National Science Foundation (NSF) Grant #1610282, NSF #1909555.

References

1. Anderson, A., Huttenlocher, D., Kleinberg, J., Leskovec, J.: Discovering value from community activity on focused question answering sites: a case study of stack overflow. In: Proceedings of the ACM SIGKDD International Conference on Knowledge Discovery and Data Mining, pp. 850–858, August 2012
2. Correa, D., Sureka, A.: Chaff from the wheat: characterization and modeling of deleted questions on stack overflow. In: Proceedings of the 23rd International Conference on World Wide Web, pp. 631–642. ACM (2014)
3. Kato, M., White, R.W., Teevan, J., Dumais, S.: Clarifications and question specificity in synchronous social Q&A. ACM, April 2013
4. Faruqui, M., Das, D.: Identifying well-formed natural language questions. arXiv e-prints, page arXiv:1808.09419, August 2018
5. Trienes, J., Balog, K.: Identifying unclear questions in community question answering websites. In: Azzopardi, L., Stein, B., Fuhr, N., Mayr, P., Hauff, C., Hiemstra, D. (eds.) ECIR 2019. LNCS, vol. 11437, pp. 276–289. Springer, Cham (2019). https://doi.org/10.1007/978-3-030-15712-8_18
6. Yang, J., Hauff, C., Bozzon, A., Houben, G.-J.: Asking the right question in collaborative q&a systems. In: Proceedings of the 25th ACM Conference on Hypertext and Social Media, HT 2014, pp. 179–189. ACM , New York (2014)

7. Mueller, J., Reshef, D.N., Du, G., Jaakkola, T.: Learning optimal interventions. arXiv preprint arXiv:1606.05027 (2016)
8. Mueller, J., Gifford, D., Jaakkola, T.: Sequence to better sequence: continuous revision of combinatorial structures. In: Precup, D., Teh, Y.W., (eds.) Proceedings of the 34th International Conference on Machine Learning, volume 70 of Proceedings of Machine Learning Research, pp. 2536–2544. International Convention Centre, Sydney, 06–11 August 2017. PMLR
9. Yang, D., Halfaker, A., Kraut, R., Hovy, E.: Identifying semantic edit intentions from revisions in Wikipedia. In: Proceedings of the 2017 Conference on Empirical Methods in Natural Language Processing, Copenhagen, Denmark, September 2017, pp. 2000–2010. Association for Computational Linguistics (2017)
10. Miao, N., Zhou, H., Mou, L., Yan, R., Li, L.: CGMH: constrained sentence generation by metropolis-hastings sampling. CoRR, abs/1811.10996 (2018)
11. Guo, R., Cheng, L., Li, J., Richard Hahn, P., Liu, H.: A survey of learning causality with data: problems and methods (2018)
12. Hill, J.L.: Bayesian nonparametric modeling for causal inference. J. Comput. Graph. Stat. **20**(1), 217–240 (2011)
13. Johansson, F.D., Shalit, U., Sontag, D.: Learning representations for counterfactual inference (2016)
14. Guo, R., Li, J., Liu, H.: Learning individual treatment effects from networked observational data. arXiv preprint arXiv:1906.03485 (2019)
15. Li, J., Guo, R., Liu, C., Liu, H.: Adaptive unsupervised feature selection on attributed networks. In: Proceedings of the 25th ACM SIGKDD International Conference on Knowledge Discovery & Data Mining, KDD 2019, Anchorage, AK, USA, 4–8 August 2019, pp. 92–100 (2019)
16. Shakarian, P., Bhatnagar, A., Aleali, A., Shaabani, E., Guo, R.: Diffusion in Social Networks. SCS. Springer, Cham (2015). https://doi.org/10.1007/978-3-319-23105-1
17. Rakesh, V., Guo, R., Moraffah, R., Agarwal, N., Liu, H.: Linked causal variational autoencoder for inferring paired spillover effects. In: Proceedings of the 27th ACM International Conference on Information and Knowledge Management, pp. 1679–1682. ACM (2018)
18. Veitch, V., Sridhar, D., Blei, D.M.: Using text embeddings for causal inference. arXiv preprint arXiv:1905.12741 (2019)
19. Cheng, L., Guo, R., Liu, H.: Robust cyberbullying detection with causal interpretation. In: Companion Proceedings of The 2019 World Wide Web Conference, pp. 169–175. ACM (2019)
20. Cheng, L., Moraffah, R., Guo, R., Candan, K.S., Raglin, A., Huan, L.: A practical data repository for causal learning with big data. In: 2019 BenchCouncil International Symposium on Benchmarking, Measuring and Optimizing (Bench 2019) (2019)
21. Chipman, H.A., George, E.I., McCulloch, R.E., et al.: Bart: bayesian additive regression trees. Ann. Appl. Stat. **4**(1), 266–298 (2010)
22. Shalit, U., Johansson, F.D., Sontag, D.: Estimating individual treatment effect: generalization bounds and algorithms. In: Proceedings of the 34th International Conference on Machine Learning, vol. 70, pp. 3076–3085. JMLR. org (2017)
23. Louizos, C., Shalit, U., Mooij, J.M., Sontag, D., Zemel, R., Welling, M.: Causal effect inference with deep latent-variable models. In: Advances in Neural Information Processing Systems, pp. 6446–6456 (2017)

SparkAIBench: A Benchmark to Generate AI Workloads on Spark

Zifeng Liu, Xiaojiang Zuo, Zeqing Li, and Rui Han[✉]

Department of Computer Science, Beijing Institute of Technology, No. 5 Zhongguancun South Street, Haidian District, Beijing 100081, China
hanrui@bit.edu.cn

Abstract. With the rapid development of artificial intelligence and cloud computing technologies, more and more workloads embed AI algorithms are deploying on cloud systems. For lack of sufficient achievements on generating AI workloads in recent years, designing and developing an efficient benchmark for AI workloads will be significant helpful for optimization of job execution time and cluster resource utilization. SparkAIBench proposed in this paper is a user customized benchmark and is able to automatically generate a variety of AI workloads by transforming user requirements into JSON objects. Besides, cooperated with a DRL-based job scheduling optimizer, a real scenario is introduced in this paper to demonstrate how SparkAIBench works.

Keywords: AI workloads · Benchmark · Cloud computing

1 Introduction

Recent years, distributed machine (deep) learning workloads, referred to as AI workloads, are rapidly becoming prevalent and potential applications in cloud computing. Amount of frameworks have been proposed to support executions of such workloads in a parallel manner, e.g. Spark MLlib [1], BigDL [2], and Tensorflow [3]. Meanwhile, both increasing scale of training data and rapid development of training models bring a higher learning accuracy, but sharply extend the training time as well, which is primarily determined by the provision of cluster resource (a.k.a. the decision of job scheduling). Such resource-intensive and time-consuming characteristics of AI workloads increase the interest of benchmarking and understanding them to help system operators make decisions, resource provisioning and job scheduling optimization.

Existing typical schedulers, for example YARN-like schedulers [4], are commonly allocating a fix amount of resources to each workload at beginning, thus unable to take advantage of the extra resources when they turn to available, so recent years has witnessed a kind of dynamic and self-adaptive job scheduler according to cluster state and resource availability. The state-of-the-art technology for implementation is leveraging Deep Reinforcement Leaning (DRL) technology that trains a self-learning agent in a trial-and-error manner to obtain optimal scheduling decisions. DRL-based scheduler, today, mostly trains agent through the cluster traces generated by running workloads

© Springer Nature Switzerland AG 2020
W. Gao et al. (Eds.): Bench 2019, LNCS 12093, pp. 215–221, 2020.
https://doi.org/10.1007/978-3-030-49556-5_21

whose characteristics (e.g. the number of executor) are configured manually [5, 6], due to the lack of frameworks that enable generating diverse and customized user workloads automatically. As talked in literature [7], which presents a survey of today's prevalent techniques for big data system benchmarking, workloads generation is one of the most important aspect in benchmarking, generating in a manual manner is quite complicated and may cause to an inaccurate result for agent training. At the same time, the major efforts on generating workloads today do not focus on AI domain, for instance, some frameworks provide workloads to represent *specific application scenarios* [8, 9], and some other benchmarks support I/O operations when generating workloads [10, 11]. But in one word, those studies are unable to automatically generate user customized AI workloads.

To bridge the gap, this paper we present a benchmark to generate AI workloads, which supports a variety of AI algorithms, changeable input data size, as well as parametric method for submission. The contributions we make are as follows:

1. A user customized and automatic AI workloads generator, SparkAIBench, is designed in this paper. It firstly transforms the user requirement into a JSON object, where user is able to specify which AI algorithms are going to use, at the same time other characteristics of workloads such as data size setting, submission interval setting of each algorithm and job queue selection are also available to users.
2. We demonstrate a use case to illustrate how SparkAIBench works in a real job scheduling optimization scenario. In that scenario, we introduce a DRL-based scheduling optimizer that leverages running traces of AI workloads to make optimal decisions according to cluster states.

2 SparkAIBench

2.1 Process of Workload Generation

Figure 1 shows the process of generating AI workloads by combing specific AI algorithms and training data sets.

At *step 1*, reading a requirement of AI workloads generation from a JSON file, SparkAIBench is able to know how many workloads should be generated, as well as the size of training data set for each workload. The next step, as depicted at *Step 2*, is to select specific machine learning algorithms within Spark MLlib or BigDL according to value of "*algorithms*", note that, even though *Step 2* and *Step 3* are depicted in a parallel manner, *Step 2* is always executed before *Step 3*, this is because only when the algorithm is selected can its data size setting be effective. Hence at *Step 3*, according to selected algorithms and the value of "*data_size*", SparkAIBench chooses corresponding data generation methods to obtain the training data sets and send them into HDFS. After that, the final step shown at *Step 4* is to package the above algorithms into a assembly jar and put it into YARN-based Spark platform as an application according to extra parameters of JSON object. Eventually, the application and generated training data compose the required AI workloads.

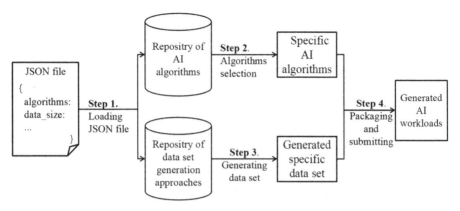

Fig. 1. The overall generation process in SparkAIBench.

2.2 Available AI Algorithms

In general, AI workloads consist of specific AI algorithms, training data sets and other workload characteristics such as the number of CPU and size of memory. For the sake of generating user customized AI workloads, available algorithms supported by SparkAIBench are respectively listed in the following Table 1. Here the traditional machine learning algorithms come from Spark MLlib while BigDL is responsible for deep leaning algorithms.

Table 1. Available algorithms in SparkAIBench.

Framework	Algorithm	Domain	Data generator
Spark MLlib	Linear regression	Regression analysis	SELF
	LDA	Text mining	SELF
	Bayes	Classification	LibSVM
	SVM	Classification	LibSVM
	FP-growth	Frequent itemset mining	BDGS
	k-means	Clustering	BDGS
	ALS	Recommendation	BDGS
BigDL	LeNet	Image classification	MINST
	Inception	Image classification	ImageNet
	VGG	Image classification	CIFAR-10
	ResNet	Image classification	CIFAR-10
	RNN	Natural language processing	Tiny Shakespeare texts corpus
	Auto-encoder	Image classification	MINST

On the other hand, to prepare the training data sets for above algorithms, we adopt several data generation methods and divide them into three categories: (1 BDGS (Big Data Generate Suit) [12], which is a tool for generating text/graph/table data, is suit for FP-Growth, k-means and ALS algorithms; (2 PUBLIC is composed of some public shared training data sets, such as MINST for LeNet, CIFA-10 for VGG, and LibSVM [13] for SVM; (3 SELF, an application developed by ourselves, is to bridge the gap of unsupported algorithms in above data generation methods. As different algorithms utilize different methods to generate their training data, we present the corresponding method name in the column of *"Data Generator"* in Table 1.

2.3 Expression of Workload Generation Requirement

In order to flexibly and controllably represent a user requirement of AI workloads generation, we transform it into a JSON object with several configurable parameters shown in Table 2 (i.e. keys of such JSON object), and insert the object into a JSON file.

Table 2. Configurable parameters in generating AI workloads.

Name	Description
interval	Submission interval among different algorithms
algorithms	An integer array with a size of 13 represents which algorithms are selected
data_size	An integer array with a size of 13 represents the data scale of each selected algorithm
queue	The job queue where the algorithms are submitted to
priority	The job priority of each algorithm

Within each JSON object, an integer array, as the value of key *"algorithms"*, composed of 0 and 1 represents whether algorithms are selected or not. Take the array [0, 1, 0, 1, 1, 0, 0, ...] as an example, it means that the first, third and fourth algorithms are selected. Similarly, the value of key *"data_size"* is also represented by a numerical sequence, but with a detailed data set size to express the expected scale of training data set. For instance, [0, 1500, 1000, 0, ...] is saying that 1500 records would be prepared for the second algorithm and 1000 records for the third algorithm. Note that there are also some data generation methods unable to customize data size, for example the method of LibSVM, which can only specify data size into "small", "middle" and "large" by setting the value as 0, 1 or 2.

After setting workloads' algorithms and their data size, one should configure the job submission information to deeply vary the types of workloads. In our design, AI workloads, generated in the same batch, can be separately submitted with various time slot by specifying the *"interval"* parameter. Moreover, different workloads can be assigned into different job queues and with different scheduling priorities, by adapting the parameters of *"queue"* and *"priority"* to implement this.

3 Use Case

This section we will demonstrate how SparkAIBench works in cloud job scheduling optimization. As shown in Fig. 2, a DRL-based job scheduling optimizer, as the role of agent in DRL mechanism, is introduced, hence the aim of SparkAIBench in this scenario is to generate various AI workloads for training the *job scheduling optimizer* (agent). Considering the reality and targeting a faster convergence for DRL agent, we design a *Reward Estimator* to evaluate the effect of scheduling policy. We have implemented and evaluated the above components on YARN-based Spark.

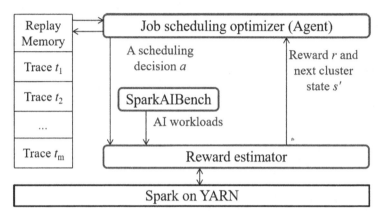

Fig. 2. Applying SparkAIBench in job scheduling optimization on YARN.

3.1 Reward Estimator

The estimator is regarded as a reward function used in DRL mechanism. If carrying out a scheduling decision makes a lower average job latency (i.e. average job complement time), it means the scheduling decision improves cluster's performance, and vice versa. Hence, in order to quantify the feedback from cluster to DRL agent, we take scheduling decision a, AI workloads and current cluster resource state s as inputs, and calculate the difference of job latency between before and after executing the decision. Each time the estimator would return a reward value r and the next cluster state s' after conducting a decision, these components make up a trace t, in which $t = <s, a, r, s'>$, for training agent and store t into *Replay Memory* module, which is so called *Experience Replay* in DRL to get a faster convergence of the loss function.

3.2 Job Scheduling Optimizer (Agent)

Reward Estimator focus on timely rewards from Spark cluster to detailed scheduling decisions, while the accumulated reward is the actual criterion to measure the performance of optimizer. In DRL-based optimizer (agent), two neural networks (NN) are introduced, which both take expected accumulated reward as output and with the same model structure. One called MainNet always updates its parameters when receives a trace t and is in charge of making a job scheduling decision, the other, namely TargetNet, directly copies parameters from the former after a period of time. With the increasing generation of AI workloads from SparkAIBench, rewards, as well as traces, become various and sufficient, leading to a more credible and accurate training result. Furthermore, each trace t is stored into *Replay Memory*, hence agent can obtain a better training effect by sampling a certain number of historical traces randomly from this module.

3.3 Proposing Requirements of AI Workloads Generation

The following Fig. 3 presents a web page which is responsible for setting a user requirement of AI workloads generation. In this case, compared with algorithms in Table 1, we can find that algorithms including Linear Regression with a data set of 1000 records, SVM with a level of "large" data set and k-means with a data set of 1500 records are selected by a user. Meanwhile, observing the left part of Fig. 3, all the selected algorithms are assigned into the same queue named "queueA" and with the same job priority of 5. Besides, in this batch of AI workloads, their submission times will be 15 s apart. Through this way, the we implement transforming a user requirement into a JSON object with changeable parameters we have talked in Sect. 2.3.

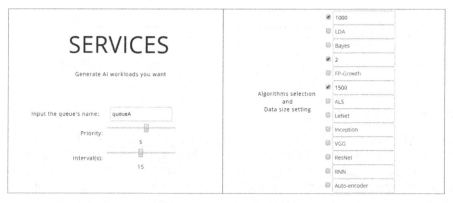

Fig. 3. UI of requirement setting for AI workloads generation.

4   Conclusion

To day, deploying AI workloads on cloud platform to offer intelligent services has been a promising trend among cloud service providers. Due to the complexity and long training period of AI workloads, there is an urgent need to design a benchmark to help system operators optimize cluster's performance. For this target we introduced a user customized benchmark, SparkAIBench, with the ability of generating various AI workloads through a configurable user requirement file. In addition, to present its manner of working, we introduced a DRL-based job scheduling optimizer that possesses the ability of making optimal scheduling decisions by training traces of AI workloads generated from SparkAIBench.

References

1. Meng, X., Bradley, J., Yavuz, B., et al.: MLlib: machine learning in apache spark. J. Mach. Learn. Res. **17**(1), 1235–1241 (2016)
2. Dai, J., Wang, Y., Qiu, X., et al.: BigDL: a distributed deep learning framework for big data. arXiv preprint arXiv:1804.05839 (2018)
3. Abadi, M., Barham, P., Chen, J., et al.: Tensorflow: a system for large-scale machine learning. In: 12th {USENIX} Symposium on Operating Systems Design and Implementation ({OSDI} 16), pp. 265–283 (2016)
4. Vavilapalli, V.K., Murthy, A.C., Douglas, C., et al.: Apache hadoop yarn: yet another resource negotiator. In: Proceedings of the 4th annual Symposium on Cloud Computing, vol. 5. ACM (2013)
5. Zhang, H., Stafman, L., Or, A., et al.: Slaq: quality-driven scheduling for distributed machine learning. In: Proceedings of the 2017 Symposium on Cloud Computing, pp. 390–404. ACM (2017)
6. Bao, Y., Peng, Y., Wu, C.: Deep learning-based job placement in distributed machine learning clusters. In: IEEE INFOCOM 2019-IEEE Conference on Computer Communications, pp. 505–513. IEEE (2019)
7. Han, R., John, L.K., Zhan, J., et al.: Benchmarking big data systems: a review. IEEE Trans. Serv. Comput. **11**(3), 580–597 (2018)
8. Baset, S., Silva, M., Wakou, N.: Spec cloud™ IaaS 2016 benchmark. In: Proceedings of the 8th ACM/SPEC on International Conference on Performance Engineering, pp. 423–423. ACM (2017)
9. Zhan, J.F., Gao, W.L., Lei, W.: Big data bench: an open-source big data benchmark suite. Chin. J. Comput. **39**(1), 196–211 (2016)
10. Chen, Y., Ganapathi, A., Griffith, R., et al.: The case for evaluating mapreduce performance using workload suites. In: 2011 IEEE 19th Annual International Symposium on Modelling, Analysis, and Simulation of Computer and Telecommunication Systems, pp. 390–399. IEEE (2011)
11. Gridmix. https://hadoop.apache.org/docs/r1.2.1/gridmix.html
12. Ming, Z., et al.: BDGS: a scalable big data generator suite in big data benchmarking. In: Rabl, T., Jacobsen, H.-A., Raghunath, N., Poess, M., Bhandarkar, M., Baru, C. (eds.) WBDB 2013. LNCS, vol. 8585, pp. 138–154. Springer, Cham (2014). https://doi.org/10.1007/978-3-319-10596-3_11
13. Hsu, C.W., Chang, C.C., Lin, C.J.: A practical guide to support vector classification (2003)

Big Data

Benchmarking Database Ingestion Ability with Real-Time Big Astronomical Data

Qing Tang[1(✉)], Chen Yang[1], Xiaofeng Meng[1], and Zhihui Du[2]

[1] School of Information, Renmin University of China,
Beijing, People's Republic of China
`tangqing@ruc.edu.cn`
[2] Department of Computer Science and Technology, Tsinghua University,
Beijing, People's Republic of China
`http://idke.ruc.edu.cn/index.htm`

Abstract. Time domain astronomical observation is developing towards a super large field of view and a very high cadence sampling and this requires that TB of star tables should be handled in realtime and PB offline data should be explored efficiently. A large class of typical scientific applications represented by time domain astronomy poses new challenges for the management and analysis of large scientific data. A set of widely representative benchmarks including the corresponding application background, data generation, test indicators and test process is developed based on the practical application of large scientific data and the application characteristics of large data management system. Finally, experimental results and analysis based on the current mainstream databases, which include relational database, non-relational databases and memory database are given. A variety of database selection schemes are employed to verify the results. Our analyzing results show that the two-tier architecture can meet the basic needs of the astronomical system, and also shows the feasibility and validity of the proposed benchmark.

Keywords: Benchmarking · Real-time · Astronomical data · Ingestion

1 Introduction

1.1 Motivation

With the development of astronomical observation and data processing technology, time domain astronomical observation is developing towards a large field of view and a higher time sampling rate. Different from the previous management of astronomical data based on file system, the management of time domain astronomical data needs to integrate short-term online data and long-term offline data to form a new mode of deep integration and complete data management and analysis, which requires novel design under the guidance of new concepts and knowledge. Existing single database read-write performance can not meet the

W. Gao et al. (Eds.): Bench 2019, LNCS 12093, pp. 225–233, 2020.
https://doi.org/10.1007/978-3-030-49556-5_22

requirements. It needs to design a database behind STLF (Short-Timescale and Large Field-of-view) [1] sky survey to support continuous analysis on streaming data, real-time analysis on short-term data and complexity analysis on long-term historical data.

The primary task of designing a database is to build a good benchmark. Through the analysis of several benchmark hot papers [2–5], we can see that the core of a good benchmark needs to build a reasonable data set, a reasonable benchmark methodology, and a clear and definite set of workload. On the basis of the points above, we need to ensure the fairness of benchmark, the rationality of data generation and the practicability of measurement.

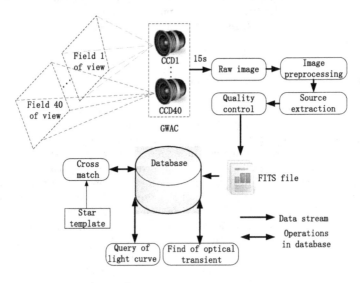

Fig. 1. Data processing workflow in GWAC [7].

1.2   Background

The application background of this paper is the GWAC (Ground Wide Angle Camera) astronomical data project [6]. GWAC is built in China, which consists of 40 wide angle telescopes with 18 cm aperture. Each telescope equips 4k × 4k charge coupled device CCD(Charge Coupled Device) detector. Cameras cover 5000 degree^2. Temporal sampling is 15 s. Cameras detect objects of fixed sky area lasts for 10 h each observation night. GWAC camera array divides the whole 5000 degree^2 observation sky into 40 blocks [7]. As shown in Fig. 1, all CCDs generate data synchronously every 15 s. The original data collected from astronomical observations are images, which are transformed into catalogue data recorded in one row per star through pre-processing. The GWAC catalog data indicators are:

(I) The catalog data has about 1.7×10^5 records per image, and the whole camera array generates 6.8×10^6 records in 15 s. There are about $2400 \times 40 = 96000$ images per night, which requires about 2 TB of storage overhead.

(II) If a design cycle is 10 years, GWAC will generate super-large catalogues in the order of 3PB~6PB.

At the same time, in such a massive level of data, we also need to achieve real-time query of short-term scales. Similar application scenarios such as Taobao, Qunar and other large e-commerce websites. In order to meet such challenges, the current mainstream solution is to build multilevel cache architecture to form a new database. Due to the different types of databases at different levels, traditional benchmarking can not meet such multi-level requirements. Therefore, for such special scenarios, we need to build new benchmarking to deal with such problems. In terms of performance requirements and application characteristics, these applications have the following commonalities:

- **Quick response:** The system needs to query the current information quickly and feedback the corresponding results. At the same time, the current information needs to be saved quickly and can not be lost.
- **Massive storage of data:** When the amount of data storage reaches the PB level or above, the cost of other data storage systems currently used is too high, or they can not meet the business requirements at all.
- **Timeliness of data analysis:** Queries need to be completed in a very short time and data analysis, while the analysis results are fed back to users.
- **High cost performance:** Users need to reduce the cost as much as possible when the system meets the above performance indicators, so they need to minimize the use of memory and the requirements of CPU, network and other parts.

In terms of data structure, GWAC's data model is relatively simple. It uses the Key-Value model of most cloud data management systems to store data, in which Key is the star ID, that is, the index, and Value is the attribute value of a specific star. Over time, new attribute values are added to Value. The existing properties values are as follows Table 1.

For the GWAC Astronomical Big Data Project, its data characteristics are very distinct, which is different from the traditional data sets such as Wikipedia [8], the National Center for Biotechnology Information (NCBI) [9] and other data sets. The characteristics of data are structured, massive and high frequency. The most typical feature is that the data simulator generates data every 15 s with a data volume of 170,000 rows, and a total of 20 nodes together to generate data.

2   Benchmark Methodology

After defining the data characteristics, the benchmark of GWAC astronomical project is constructed according to the data characteristics. The specific methods are as follows: (I) According to the characteristics of data sets and the corresponding astronomical phenomena, the corresponding workloads are analyzed in depth, and the frequent basic operating units are extracted; (II) The benchmark test specifications are determined; (III) The loads based on various software

Table 1. GWAC catalog data properties.

Num	Attribute	Type	Num	Attribute	Type
1	redis_key	string	21	magcalibe	double
2	jd_str	string	22	sigma_base	double
3	ccdNum	string	23	sigma_ext	double
4	zone	string	24	tag_valid	int
5	starId	long	25	magdiff	double
6	alpha	float	26	lastCMtempname	string
7	delta	float	27	starBelong	string
8	pixx	double	28	abSignal	string
9	pixy	double	29	abVal	double
10	mag	string	30	abQuality	double
11	mage	double	31	abRank	double
12	thetaimage	long	32	sigma_ext_median	double
13	flags	float	33	mag_interval_num	int
14	ellipticity	float	34	sigmedthreshold	double
15	classstar	float	35	data11	double
16	background	float	36	data12	double
17	fwhm	float	37	data13	double
18	vignet	float	38	data14	double
19	magnorm	double	39	data15	double
20	magcalib	double			

stacks are provided; (IV) The multi-tenant mixed load versions are provided according to different evaluation requirements.

After defining the characteristics of the data and the construction method, it is very important to establish a clear and definite workload. Because the benchmark is mainly aimed at GWAC astronomical phenomena, through communication with astronomers, we have identified the existing main workloads, including seven query statements, Data Real-time storage and Data persistence. The test benchmark is sufficient for the manufacturing process as shown in Fig. 2.

3 Test Indicator

Because of the particularity of designing database, we need to use many kinds of databases. Therefore, the selected test indicators should cover the characteristics of many databases. For in-memory databases, we need to consider the database response time, CPU utilization, cache missing rate, data compression rate and minimum memory space. At the same time, according to the characteristics of the system, the following indicators need to be considered:

- **Storage efficiency:** The most important measure of astronomical project, in order to meet the second scientific goal, which needs 15 s to complete

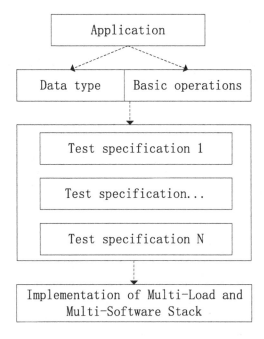

Fig. 2. Test benchmark construction method.

the storage. The content of storage completed in 15 s is the amount of data produced by each GWAC camera taking a picture at a time. One camera produces about 440 M data at a time. Therefore, the basic storage requirement is not less than 44 M/s. If the storage speed is lower than this, it will not be considered.

- **Persistence efficiency:** The system needs to be persisted in 14 h, that is, the work of the day in the real scene. The last night's data must be persisted during the next day or it will affect the next night's data entry. Therefore, the persistence threshold is 14 h.
- **Input anomaly rate:** Because of the change of cluster environment, the stability of each database system in the same network environment can be reflected intuitively by obtaining the inbound anomaly rate.

4   Experiments and Results Analysis

4.1   Experimental Data

In order to simulate the pressure test of GWAC data on the system more truly, the gwac_dbgen simulator is rewritten as gwac_dbgen_cluster, which can be used to simulate the synchronous generation of catalogue data streams by multiple CCDs. Each simulated CCD generates data at the rate of generating about 170,000 planetary data every 15 s (in order to restore the real scene as much as possible, each time). The number of rows generated in the catalog data is not necessarily equal, with 39 columns per row.

4.2   Database Selection

Most of the existing cloud data management systems are open source and widely used in mass data management systems. For massive data management, the current mainstream databases include relational databases, non-relational databases and memory databases. For these types of databases, we use a variety of database selection schemes to verify the feasibility and validity of the benchmark through the analysis of the test results. The test database we selected is as follows:

- **Oracle:** Oracle is the first open commercial relational database management system launched in 1983. It uses standard SQL structured query language, supports multiple data types, and provides object-oriented data storage support.
- **MYSQL:** MySQL is an open source relational database management system, using the most commonly used database management language - Structured Query Language (SQL) for database management.
- **Redis:** Redis is an open source (BSD licensed), in-memory data structure store, used as a database, cache and message broker. It supports data structures such as strings, hashes, lists, sets, sorted sets with range queries, bitmaps, hyperloglogs, geospatial indexes with radius queries and streams.
- **Hbase:** HBase is a distributed column-oriented database based on Hadoop file system. It's an open source project, and it extends horizontally. HBase is a data model, similar to Google's large table design, which can provide fast random access to massive structured data. It takes advantage of the fault tolerance provided by Hadoop's file system (HDFS).
- **Kafka:** Kafka, originally developed by Linkedin, is a distributed, partition-supported, replica-based, zookeeper coordinated distributed messaging system. Its greatest feature is that it can process large amounts of data in real time to meet a variety of demand scenarios: batch processing system based on hadoop, etc. Low latency real-time systems, storm/Spark streaming engine, web/nginx logs, access logs, message services, etc.

4.3   Experimental Environment

In the test, the cloud computing cluster platform composed of 20 servers is used. The cluster consists of one master node and 19 slave nodes. The slave nodes physical cluster is a homogeneous environment, the nodes are interconnected by 10 Gigabit Ethernet.The configuration of cluster environment is shown in the Table 2.We design a distributed data generator to simulate the GWAC working process test data set. The existing properties values are as follows Table 1.

4.4   Experimental Results and Analysis

According to the test design, several tests were carried out, each running time was 8 h. The size of each file tested is about 1.5 GB, and a total of 1920 files are generated by the data generator. The total amount of data tested is 2.8 TB.

Table 2. Experimental server configuration.

Configuration	Performance test environment	
	Hardware	Software
Master	Memory: 96 GB Hard disk: 3.5 TB CPU:E5-2603 v3 @ 1.60 GHz	Ubuntu 14.04.5 Redis_3.2.5 HBase_1.2.4 MySQL_5.6.33 Kafka
Slave	Memory: 96 GB Hard disk: 30 TB CPU:E5-2603 v3 @ 1.60 GHz	Ubuntu 14.04.5 Redis_3.2.5 HBase_1.2.4 MySQL_5.6.33 Kafka

Table 3. Test results for different databases (Part 1).

DataBase	Average storage time
HBase	340 s
MySQLcluster	1700 s
Oracle	50.7 s
Rediscluster	6.4 s
Kafka	20.5 s

Table 4. Test results for different databases (Part 2).

DataBase	Persistence time	Compression rate	Input anomaly rate
Redis+HBase	4.8 h	40%	2.50%
Redis/HBase	6 h	40%	4.60%
Redis+MySQL	201 h	100%	1.00%
Redis/MySQL	202 h	100%	1.00%
Kafka+HBase	10.9 h	100%	2.50%

Table 3 lists the average insertion time of individual file data, where the Oracle database is deployed on a single machine and the rest are deployed in cluster mode. The results in Table 4 are the total storage time for each test data.

The test includes data transmission program, data cross authentication program, data warehousing script and data persistence script. The CPU usage rate was maintained between 65% and 85% in many different database storage experiments, and the abnormal rate in different database storage experiments was as follows: Redis+HBase-2.5%, Redis/HBase-4.6%, Redis+MySQL-1.0%,

Redis/MySQL-1.0%, Kafka+HBase-2.5%. The test results show that the basic requirements of astronomical system can be met only when two-tier architecture is used, while the storage time and persistence time can be relatively optimal when Redis and HBase are running simultaneously. For Redis and MySQL, Redis runs faster because the data in Redis is not compressed. At the same time, the scheme has the following characteristics: (I) Allowing astronomers to compare the latest data and offline data in real time; (II) Data compression can greatly reduce the requirement for memory; (III) Data can be saved to hard disk at the same time of observation, which improves the security of data.

5   Summary

The development of modern astronomical observation and data processing technology make it possible for time domain astronomical observation to develop towards a larger field of view and a higher time sampling rate. It also injects new vitality into modern time domain astronomical observation, including supernovae, gamma bursts, and microgravity lenses [10]. The discovery and follow-up observation of microgravitational lens events have benefited from the development of modern time-domain astronomical observation and data processing technology. With the continuous development of database management system, the benchmark of database system evaluation also develops. Based on the analysis and summary of several benchmark papers, this paper compares their own benchmarks, and obtains a set of benchmarks suitable for scenes with data characteristics in large astronomical data projects. However, the existing evaluation benchmarks still can not cover all aspects completely. Future work will further improve the evaluation system to enable it to more effectively evaluate the data management system of similar scenarios.

Acknowledgement. This research was partially supported by the grants from the National Key Research and Development Program of China (No. 2016YFB1000602, 2016YFB1000603); the Natural Science Foundation of China (No. 61532016, 61532010, 91846204, 91646203, 61762082); the Fundamental Research Funds for the Central Universities, the Research Funds of Renmin University (No. 11XNL010); and the Science and Technology Opening up Cooperation project of Henan Province (172106000077).

References

1. Yang, C., et al.: AstroServ: a distributed database for serving large-scale full life-cycle astronomical data. In: Li, J., Meng, X., Zhang, Y., Cui, W., Du, Z. (eds.) BigSDM 2018. LNCS, vol. 11473, pp. 44–55. Springer, Cham (2019). https://doi.org/10.1007/978-3-030-28061-1_6
2. Amp lab big data benchmark. https://amplab.cs.berkeley.edu/benchmark/
3. Ghazal, A., et al.: Bigbench: towards an industry standard benchmark for big data analytics. In SIGMOD 2013 (2013)

4. Huang, S., Huang, J., Dai, J., Xie, T., Huang, B.: The HiBench benchmark suite: characterization of the MapReduce-based data analysis. In: 2010 IEEE 26th International Conference on Data Engineering Workshops (ICDEW), pp. 41–51. IEEE (2010)

5. Wang, L., Zhan, J., Luo, C., Zhu, Y., Yang, Q., He, Y., et al.: Bigdatabench: a big data benchmark suite from internet services (2014)

6. Wan, M., et al.: Column store for GWAC: a high-cadence, high-density, large-scale astronomical light curve pipeline and distributed shared-nothing database. Publ. Astron. Soc. Pac. **128**(969), 114501114532 (2016)

7. Chen, Y., Zujian, W., Xiaofeng, M., Wei, R., Rihui, X., Chunkai, W., et al.: Data management challenges and real-time processing technologies in astronomy. J. Comput. Res. Dev. **54**(02), 248–257 (2017)

8. Wikipedia. https://www.wikipedia.org/

9. National Center for Biotechnology Information. https://www.ncbi.nlm.nih.gov/

10. Chao, W., Ma, D., Hai-Jun, T., Xiang-Ru, L., Jian-Yan, W.: Study and development of a fast and automatic astronomical-transient-identification system. Acta Automatica Sinica **43**(12), 2170–2177 (2017)

A Practical Data Repository for Causal Learning with Big Data

Lu Cheng[1(✉)], Ruocheng Guo[1], Raha Moraffah[1], K. Selçuk Candan[1],
Adrienne Raglin[2], and Huan Liu[1]

[1] Arizona State University, Tempe, AZ, USA
{lcheng35,rguo12,rmoraffa,candan,huanliu}@asu.edu
[2] Army Research Laboratory, Adelphi, MD, USA
adrienne.raglin2.civ@mail.mil

Abstract. The recent success in machine learning (ML) has led to a massive emergence of AI applications and the increases in expectations for AI systems to achieve human-level intelligence. Nevertheless, these expectations have met with multi-faceted obstacles. One major obstacle is ML aims to predict future observations given real-world data dependencies while human-level intelligence AI is often beyond prediction and seeks the underlying causal mechanism. Another major obstacle is that the availability of large-scale datasets has significantly influenced causal study in various disciplines. It is crucial to leverage effective ML techniques to advance causal learning with *big data*. Existing benchmark datasets for causal inference have limited use as they are too "ideal", i.e., small, clean, homogeneous, low-dimensional, to describe real-world scenarios where data is often large, noisy, heterogeneous and high-dimensional. It, therefore, severely hinders the successful marriage of causal inference and ML. In this paper, we formally address this issue by systematically investigating existing datasets for two fundamental tasks in causal inference: *causal discovery* and *causal effect estimation*. We also review the datasets for two ML tasks naturally connected to causal inference. We then provide hindsight regarding the *advantages*, *disadvantages* and the *limitations* of these datasets. Please refer to our github repository (https://github.com/rguo12/awesome-causality-data) for all the discussed datasets in this work.

Keywords: Causal learning · Treatment effect estimation · Causal discovery · Datasets · Big data · Benchmarking

1 Introduction

The goal of a myriad of scientific research is to understand the *causal mechanisms* that reveal outcomes of interventions and counterfactuals [10]. Compared to the extensive literature on causal inference in statistics, econometrics, biostatistics

---

R. Guo and R. Moraffah—Equal contribution.

© Springer Nature Switzerland AG 2020
W. Gao et al. (Eds.): Bench 2019, LNCS 12093, pp. 234–248, 2020.
https://doi.org/10.1007/978-3-030-49556-5_23

and epidemiology, the interest in discovering causal relations and estimating causal effects within computer science (data science especially) has been rapidly growing recently. On one hand, as big data has significantly influenced causal study in various disciplines, it is important to leverage machine learning (ML) techniques to enhance our capability of modeling complex and large-scale data; On the other hand, ML seeks correlations among data to predict future observations. The discovered patterns have limited use when the goal is, instead, to understand the underlying causal mechanisms. One needs to go beyond *correlations* to assay causal structures underlying statistical dependencies.

A major challenge of studying causal inference with big data is the lack of benchmark datasets. Although growing computer power enables us to easily collect massive amount of data, it is extremely challenging to obtain the *groundtruth* from *observational data*. This is due to the fundamental question in causal inference that we can not observe the *counterfactuals*. Most existing benchmark datasets for learning causality are therefore, synthetic or semi-synthetic. They are often clean, small-scale, homogeneous and low-dimensional while real-world data is noisy, large-scale, heterogeneous and high-dimensional. Additionally, as there is no unified principle to regulate the data simulation processes, it is hard to evaluate the models and interpret the empirical results. To address these issues, we first summarize existing datasets for the two fundamental tasks in causal inference: *causal discovery*, problem of discovering the underlying causal structure of data; and *causal effect estimation*, problem of estimating causal effect of a certain set of variable on others. We seek to answer two research questions: i) What are the *advantages* and *disadvantages* of these datasets? ii) What are the *limitations* in existing datasets? In addition, we investigate datasets for two ML problems that are naturally connected to causal inference, i.e., off policy evaluation and debiasing recommender system. The main contributions are:

- We formally address an urgent but almost untouched problem that hinders the marriage of causal inference and ML. That is, the lack of benchmark datasets for causal learning with big data.
- We investigate existing datasets for two fundamental causal inference tasks, i.e., *causal discovery* and *causal effect estimation*, as well as two ML tasks that have been recently studied from the causal inference perspective.
- We answer important research questions regarding the advantages, disadvantages and limitations of these datasets. We aim to offer some crude remarks that can draw attentions from researchers to together create and share new benchmark datasets for causal learning with big data.

2   Causal Discovery

Causal discovery from empirical data is a fundamental problem in many scientific domains. Causal discovery addresses the problem of learning the underlying causal mechanisms and the causal relationships amongst variables in the data. Datasets for this task are collected from either pure observational data or with both observational data and experimental data in hand. Papers in this area can be divided into three major categories:

- Learning causal direction (causal or anti causal relations) between two variables. Specifically, given the observations $\{(x_i, y_i)\}_{i=1}^n$ of random variables, the goal is to infer the causal direction, i.e. whether $x \rightarrow y$ or $y \rightarrow x$.
- Learning the trio-relationships (V-structures) and directions among three variables.
- Learning the underlying Causal Bayesian Network (CBN) of the data which is used to show the relationships between all the variables in the data.

2.1 Datasets

Common datasets for learning causal direction between two variables are:

- *Tübingen Cause-Effect Pairs (TCEP)* [27]: This dataset consists of real-world cause-effect samples which are collected across various subject areas. The groundtruths are true causal direction provided by human experts. This dataset is expected to contain diverse functional dependencies due to the fact that pairs are collected from diverse origins.
- *AntiCD3/CD28* [31]: A dataset with 853 observational data points corresponding to general perturbations without specific interventions. This dataset is used in protein network problem.
- *Note* [26]: One innovative way of testing causal/anti-causal learning algorithms is to test the model on causal time series datasets to infer the direction of the arrow. To achieve this, [26] used a dataset containing quarterly growth rates of the real gross domestic product (GDP) of the UK, Canada and USA from 1980 to 2011.
- *Pittsburgh Bridges* [2]: There are 108 bridges in this dataset. The following 4 cause-effect pairs are known as groundtruth in this dataset. They are 1) Erected (Crafts, Emerging, Mature, Modern) $\rightarrow$ Span (Long, Medium, Short), 2) Material (Steel, Iron, Wood) $\rightarrow$ Span (Long, Medium, Short); 3) Material (Steel, Iron, Wood) $\rightarrow$ Lanes (1, 2, 4, 6); 4) Purpose (Walk, Aqueduct, RR, Highway) $\rightarrow$ type (Wood, Suspen, Simple-T, Arch, Cantilev, CONT-T).
- *Abalone* [2]: This dataset contains 4,177 samples and each sample has 4 different properties. Sex, Length, Diameter and Height. The property sex has three values, male, female and infant. The length, diameter, and height are measured in mm and treated as discrete values. The groundtruth contains three cause-effect pairs.

In order to evaluate the performance of a model for distinguishing cause from effect on the above-mentioned benchmark datasets, the accuracy of the model on the datasets is calculated and reported. Next we introduce the datasets used in learning the CBN. As real-world datasets are often not available, we describe the benchmark synthetic datasets below:

- *Lung Cancer Simple Set (LUCAS)* is a synthetic dataset which was made publicly available through the causality workbench [12]. The true causal DAG consists of 12 binary variables: 1) Smoking, 2) Yellow Fingers, 3) Anxiety, 4) Peer Pressure, 5) Genetics, 6) Attention Disorder, 7) Born on Even Day, 8) Car Accident, 9) Fatigue, 10) Allergy, 11) Coughing and 12) Lung Cancer. The true causal graph consists of causal edges between variables.
- A common approach to generate synthetic data in learning CBN is to use a random generation of chordal graphs approach [18,36].

Moreover, there is a line of research which focuses on causal discovery problems from both observational and interventional data. In this task, we can assume that an intervention on every node of the underlying Bayesian Network is allowed. Below is the dataset designed and used in this task:

Gene Perturbation Data: Usually some yeast genes are selected from the data. Some observations from this data are as follows: the gene YFL044C reaches 2 genes directly and has an indirect influence on all 11 remaining genes; finally, the genes YML081W and YNR063W are reached by almost all other genes. One common way of evaluating Causal Bayesian Networks and in general structural learning problems on the above-mentioned datasets is to measure structural Hamming distance (SHD). The SHD is defined as the minimum number of edge insertions, deletions, and changes required to transform one model into another [40].

2.2   Advantages, Disadvantages, and Limitations

Advantages. There exists a number of real-world datasets for the task of learning the causal direction between two variables that can be used in future research. These datasets are collected for real world scenarios and are annotated by the experts in corresponding fields, which make these desirable and useful for research in this field.

Disadvantages. There exists no large-scale data for the task of finding the underlying Bayesian Network of the data, which is one of the most important tasks in causal inference. Moreover, no real-world data is available for the task of learning V-structure (i.e. trio-relationships among variables), which makes it difficult to verify the proposed methods, and therefore, researchers often evaluate their proposed methods on only the datasets available for causal direction discovery and fail to show the effectiveness of them on finding the relationships between three variables.

Limitations. Many machine learning algorithms require huge number of samples to be trained on. However, for the task of causal discovery, the only real-world dataset available is LUCAS data which contains only 12 variables. Therefore, it is hard for the researchers to leverage the available dataset in big data scenarios and train a machine learning model on it. Moreover, collecting datasets with groundtruth for underlying CBN of all variables available in the data is a tremendously difficult task due to the lack of availability of human experts and resources to annotate the data and come up with the groundtruth.

Another limitation is that there exists no real-world dataset for the problem of detecting V-Structure from the data, which also requires human resources and can be costly and time consuming.

3   Causal Effect Estimation

The task of causal effect estimation is to investigate to what extent manipulating the value of a potential cause would change the value of the outcome variable. Following the literature [17,24,33,35], the variable that we seek to manipulate is the *treatment* and the corresponding variable that we observe from measuring the effect of that manipulation is *outcome*. In this task, the treatment can be a single variable taking binary values, discrete values or continuous values, or multiple treatment variables that take various values. *Potential Outcomes* framework is widely used in the literature of causal effect estimation [28,30]. Potential outcomes are defined as:

Potential Outcome. Given an instance i and the treatment t, the potential outcome of i under treatment t, denoted by y_i^t, is the value that y would have taken if the treatment of instance i had been set to t. With this definition, the individual treatment effect (ITE) is:

$$\tau_i = \mathbb{E}[y_i^t] - \mathbb{E}[y_i^c], \tag{1}$$

where y_i^c (y_i^t) denotes the potential outcome of the i-th instance under control (treatment). Intuitively, ITE is referred to as the expected difference between the two potential outcomes. Average treatment effect, or ATE, is then the average of ITE over the whole population. It is defined as: $\bar{\tau} = \mathbb{E}_i[\tau_i]$. Based on these definitions, we introduce two widely used evaluation metrics. Given the ground truth of ATE ($\bar{\tau}$) and the inferred ATE $\hat{\bar{\tau}}$, the mean absolute error (MAE) on ATE is widely adopted. It is defined as:

$$\epsilon_{MAE\_ATE} = |\bar{\tau} - \hat{\bar{\tau}}|. \tag{2}$$

In addition, the inferred ITEs can be evaluated by the precision in estimation of heterogeneous effect (PEHE). Formally, PEHE is defined as:

$$\epsilon_{PEHE} = \frac{1}{n} \sum_{i=1}^{n} (\tau_i - \hat{\tau}(\mathbf{x}_i))^2, \tag{3}$$

where τ_i denotes the ground truth ITE of the instance i and $\hat{\tau}(\mathbf{x}_i)$ signifies the corresponding estimate.

3.1   Datasets with Binary Treatment

- *Jobs.* The dataset consists of two parts. The first part is from the randomized trial study by LaLonde [19] (297 treated and 425 control). The second part is the PSID comparison group (2,490 control) [37]. The features are the same as those used in [6]. In addition, this dataset has groundtruth of ATT. One common metric used for evaluation on this dataset is policy risk (PR) [35].

- *IHDP.* This is a dataset with simulated treatments and outcomes, which is initially complied by [14]. The most widely used simulation setting is the setting "A" in the NPCI package[1]. This dataset comprises 747 instances (139 treated and 608 control). There are 25 features describing the children and their mothers from the original IHDP data [8]. We can study the problem of estimating ITE and ATE from observational data using this dataset.
- *ACIC Benchmark.* ACIC benchmark is from ACIC data analysis challenge 2017 [13]. The features of ACIC benchmark are also from the original IHDP data [8]. Various settings have been adopted to synthesize treatments and outcomes. The ACIC dataset contains 58 features and 4,302 instances.
- *Twins.* The Twins dataset in [1] is used to study the individual treatment effect of twins' weights on their mortality in the first year of lives. In [24], the authors focused on the twins with weights less than 2 kg to get a more balanced dataset in terms of the outcome. This results in a dataset consisting of 11,984 such twins. Each twin-pair is represented by 46 features relating to the parents, the pregnancy and birth. As both potential outcomes are considered as available in the dataset, to simulate an observational study, one of the two treatments need to be sampled for each twin-pair. To generate confounding bias, Louizos et al. [24] sampled treatments from the inferred propensity scores.
- *News.* The News dataset is introduced in [17]. In this dataset, each instance is a news item. The features are originally word counts. The treatment is defined as whether the news is consumed on a mobile device or on desktop. The outcome is the readers' experience. In addition, we need to assume that users prefer to read some news items on mobile devices. To model this, a topic model is trained on a large set of documents and two centroids are defined in topic space. Then, the treatment is simulated as a function of the similarity between the topic distribution of the news item and the two centroids. Finally, the potential outcomes of a news item are defined as a function of (1) the similarity between the topic distribution of the news item and the two centroids (2) and the treatment. The dataset consists of 5,000 new items and the topic model is a LDA model with 50 topics trained from the NY Times corpus[2].

3.2   Datasets with Binary Treatment and Network Information

- *BlogCatalog* is an online social network service where users can post blogs. Each instance is a blogger. Each edge signifies the friendship between two bloggers. This dataset comes with 5,196 instances, 173,468 edges and 8,189 observed features. Guo et al. [11] extended the original BlogCatalog dataset [21] for the task of causal effect estimation. In particular, treatments and outcomes are synthesized based on the observed features, the social network structure and the Homophily phenomenon [34].

---

[1] https://github.com/vdorie/npci.
[2] Downloaded from the UCI repository [7].

- *Amazon* [29] is an extension of the original dataset [25]. The goal is to estimate the causal effect of positive (or negative) reviews on the sales of products. Each instance is a product. Each edge represents the co-purchase relationship. The observed features are bag-of-word representation of the product description. Two datasets are created, one for positive and one for negative reviews. For the positive (negative) case, we say a product is under treatment iff (1) receives more than three reviews and (2) is rated higher (lower) than three stars. The counterfactual outcome is set as the observed sales of the most similar product with an opposite treatment status. The positive (negative) dataset contains 50,000 positive (20,000 negative) instances, 10,000 (5,000) controlled instances and 96,132 (28,136) edges.

3.3   Datasets with Multiple Treatments

- *Twins-Mult.* Yoon et al. [42] extended the Twins dataset to 4 treatments by considering the combination of the original treatment and the sex of the infant. The method to sample treatments are adapted accordingly.
- *News-Mult.* Schwab et al. [33] adapted the News dataset to multiple treatments. Instead of using two centroids, $k + 1$ centroids are randomly picked in the topic space where k is the number of treatments and the rest represents the control group. Then the treatment is sampled from a Bernoulli distribution $t|x \sim Bern(softmax(\kappa \bar{y}_j))$ where $\kappa \in \{10, 7\}$ and the unscaled outcome is calculated as $\bar{y}_j = \tilde{y}_j * [D(z(X), z_j) + D(z(X), z_c)]$. $z(X)$ denotes the topic distribution of the news item with bag-of-word features X, z_j signifies the centroid of the instances receiving treatment j, z_c represents the centroid for the control, and $\tilde{y}_j \sim \mathcal{N}(\mu_j, \sigma_j) + \epsilon$ where $\mu_j \sim \mathcal{N}(0.45, 0.15)$, $\sigma_j \sim \mathcal{N}(0.1, 0.05)$ and $\epsilon \sim \mathcal{N}(0, 0.15)$. D is the Euclidean distance function. Then the true outcome of the j-th treatment is $y_j = C\bar{y}_j$, where $C = 50$.
- *TCGA.* In [33], the authors introduced the TCGA dataset which is a collection of gene expression data from types of cancers in 9,659 individuals [41]. There are four possible clinical treatments: medication, chemotherapy, surgery or both surgery and chemotherapy. The outcome is the risk of recurrence of cancer. Similar to the News dataset, $k + 1$ points in the original feature space (gene expression features) are selected as centroids. Treatments and outcomes are simulated accordingly.

3.4   Datasets with Continuous Treatment

The treatment can also take continuous values. Here, we introduce a dataset for the study of causal effect estimation with continuous variable.

NMES. The National Medical Expenditures Survey (NMES) dataset is complied by [9]. We study the problem of estimating the treatment effect of the amount of smoking on the medical expenditure. Both the treatment and the outcome variables are continuous. The dataset consists of 10 features describing each of the 9,708 individuals.

3.5   Advantages, Disadvantages, and Limitations

Advantages. Most of the existing datasets are collected to solve treatment effect estimation problems. For example, the Jobs dataset is collected to answer the causal question: Does job training help people to get employed? Moreover, studying these datasets can provide insights for decision making in real-world scenarios. For example, an employer can decide whether it is necessary to participate the job training program based on the individual treatment effect.

Disadvantages. It is often impossible to collect data with ground truth for counterfactual outcomes – outcomes could have been observed iff another treatment had been assigned. Instead, researchers mainly rely on semi-synthetic datasets, where treatments and outcomes are synthesized based on certain data-generating process. Therefore, developing high-quality data simulation models can be a time-consuming and labor-intensive task.

Limitations. Existing benchmark datasets are not suitable in estimating causal effects in many real-world applications due to the unavailability of counterfactual outcomes. For example, it is convenient to collect climate data from Google earth engine and user behavior data from Twitter in order to develop ML models to predict user behavior from climate statistics. Nevertheless, to understand how climate changes influence user behavior, we need to collect data from the same user under exactly the same conditions with different climate. This is often impossible in real-world scenarios.

In terms of estimating average treatment effects, the challenges arise from how to design cheap, easy-to-implement, reliable and ethical experiments. In addition, the importance of reducing the sample size and time in need for a statistically significant randomized trial is still underestimated in the data mining and machine learning community. Another limitation of current datasets for causal effect estimation is the missing of the underlying structure between instances. The potential types of structure include (but are not limited to) networks and temporal dependencies.

4   Causal Inference in ML

4.1   Off-Policy Evaluation

Given that an existing policy h_0 selects actions based on item features and observes corresponding rewards (e.g., online Q&A communities [22], recommender systems [32]). This process generates log data with the form (x, y, δ, p) where $x \in \mathcal{X}$ is the context (feature vector), $y \in \mathcal{Y}$ is the selected action. $\mathcal{X}$ and $\mathcal{Y}$ are the input space and the output space respectively. p is the probability of y being selected given x and $\delta(x, y) : \mathcal{X} \times \mathcal{Y} \rightarrow \mathbb{R}$ denotes the feedback/reward received. The goal of off-policy evaluation is to exam the performance of a new policy h on future observations using the log data generated from h_0.

First, we give a formal problem definition. Given the input features $x \in \mathcal{X}$, the output prediction of selected action $y \in \mathcal{Y}$ and a hypothesis space $\mathcal{H}$ of *stochastic policies* [38], which is calculated from the observed data. Additionally, the inputs are assumed drawn from a fixed but unknown distribution $Pr(\mathcal{X}), x \overset{i.i.d}{\sim} Pr(\mathcal{X})$. A hypothesis $h(\mathcal{Y}|x) \in \mathcal{H}$ makes predictions by sampling $y \sim h(\mathcal{Y}|x)$. In an interactive learning system, we can only observe the feedback $\delta(x, y)$ for y sampled from $h(\mathcal{Y}|x)$. For instance, in a recommender system, $\mathcal{X}$ are the attributes of the items, $\mathcal{Y}$ is set of items recommended by the system, and δ denotes the user feedback, e.g., whether a user clicks on the item or not. In precision medicine, $\mathcal{X}$ denotes the patients' attributes, $\mathcal{Y}$ is the set of received treatments. We then collect the outcomes δ from patients. A large δ indicates high user's satisfaction with y for x. The expected rewards of a hypothesis $R(h)$ is defined as [38]

$$R(h) = \mathrm{E}_{x \sim Pr(\mathcal{X})} \mathrm{E}_{y \sim h(\mathcal{Y}|x)} [\delta(x, y)]. \tag{4}$$

Then, the goal is to maximize the reward with policy $h(\mathcal{Y}|x)$ given data $\mathcal{D} = \{(x_1, y_1, \delta_1), (x_2, y_2, \delta_2), ..., (x_n, y_n, \delta_n)\}$ collected from the system using policy $h_0(\mathcal{Y}|x)$, i.e., $y_i \sim h_0(\mathcal{Y}|x), \delta_i = \delta(x_i, y_i)$. Evaluation of the proposed policy is extremely hard due to sample selection bias and partial information.

Dataset from Real World

Music Streaming Sessions Dataset (MSSD). This dataset from Spotify[3] consists of over 160 million listening sessions with user interaction information. It has metadata for approximately 3.7 million unique tracks referred to in the logs, making it the largest collection of such track data currently available to the public [5]. In particular, it consists of music streaming sessions with corresponding user interactions, audio features and metadata describing the tracks streamed during the sessions, and snapshots of the playlists listened to during the sessions [5]. The log data contains rich information such as session id, timestamp, contextual information about the stream, and the timing and type of user interactions within the stream. A subset of MSSD is crawled and labelled by a uniformly random shuffle to satisfy the conditions of RCT.

Semi-simulated Datasets

Bandit Data Generation. Despite log data is ubiquitous in the real world, it is often hard to gather for researchers in academia. In search of alternatives, synthetic or semi-synthetic data is often used for off-policy evaluation. Here, we present a widely used bandit data generating approach proposed in [3]. This approach converts the training partition of a full-information multi-class classification dataset $D^* = \{[x_i, y_i^*]\}_{i=1,...,n}$ with $y_i^* \in \{0, 1\}^k$ into a partial-information bandit dataset for training off-policy learning methods while the test dataset remains intact to evaluate the new policy. To this end, the optimal policy is known because $\delta(x_i, y_i^*) > \delta(x_i, \rightharpoondown y_i)$ where $\rightharpoondown y_i$ is any of the items/treatments other than y_i^*. Therefore, given x_i, the optimal policy selects action y_i^*. Then we simulate a bandit feedback dataset from a logging policy h_0 by sampling $y_i \sim h_0(\mathcal{Y}|x_i)$ and collecting feedback $\triangle(y_i^*, y_i)$, which is the loss between groundtruth and the recommended item. h_0 can be logistic regression

---

[3] https://www.spotify.com/.

and is often trained with a small portion (e.g. 5%) of the training set. $\triangle(y^*, y)$ is then the Hamming loss or Jaccard index between the label y^* and the sampled label y for input x. This completes the procedure of generating a bandit dataset $\mathcal{D} = \{[x_i, y_i, \triangle(y_i^*, y_i), h_0(y_i|x_i)]\}_{i \in \{1,...,n\}}$. One thing to note is that the propensity score function $h_0(y_i|x_i)$ is usually estimated from data directly, which may introduce undesired biases. A large-scale real-world dataset[4] containing accurately logged propensities is introduced in [20].

Limitations. While this data generating method has been adopted wildly in off-policy evaluation in contextual bandits [16,38,39], it has several limitations:

- It might not be clear how it can be used in other applications of off-line evaluations. Take the medical study for an example, mapping the concept of binary multi-label $\in \{0, 1\}$ to treatments indicates that several drugs may be assigned to the same patient simultaneously. This might be detrimental to the patients' health due to the interactions between drugs. In addition, estimation of propensity score function using a small portion of the supervised training set is not appropriate in medical study as the underlying mechanism of treatment selection is often not fully understood.
- The predefined hypothesis h_0 can largely affect the performance of the new policy. By using the above mentioned method, we can obtain h_0 with nearly 100% accuracy, i.e., $y = y^*$ for all x in the training set. Nevertheless, it is often impossible for a real-world system to have an optimal policy. Consequently, how many training data should be used to estimate h_0? What is the desirable accuracy that h_0 should achieve? Answering these questions is critical for the evaluation.
- The mismatch of synthetic data and the observed data from true environment is often unavoidable in practice, resulting in policies that do not generalize to the real environment [15].

4.2 Causal Inference for Recommendation

Causal inference is also particularly useful in learning de-biased recommender policies. Consider a recommender system that takes as input a user $u_i \in \mathcal{U}$ from the user population $\mathcal{U}$ and outputs the prediction of possible products $p_j \in \mathcal{P}$. The recommendation policy decides what products the recommender system shows to its users. Most existing "de-biased" recommendation systems aim to find the optimal treatment recommendation policy that maximizes the reward with respect to the control recommendation policy for each user, i.e., individual treatment effect. Traditional recommender systems are biased as they use the click data (or ratings data) to infer the user preferences. These data encode users' selection bias, i.e., users do not consider each product independently.

The input data of learning a recommendation policy consists of products each user decided to look at and those each user liked/clicked. The treatment is the recommended products and the outcome is whether this user clicks this product.

---

[4] http://www.cs.cornell.edu/~adith/Criteo/.

Standard datasets for recommender systems are not applicable in the evaluation of the deconfounded recommender systems due to the lack of outcomes for counterfactuals. Consequently, simulated or semi-simulated datasets are often the preferred alternatives. The core idea of generating an eligible dataset to evaluate a recommendation policy is to ensure the distributions of the training and test set are different, that is, to exam if the deconfounded recommendation policy is generalizable. A more generalizable policy indicates a less-biased recommender system. Next, we introduce several datasets that have been used in recent publications [4,23,32]. Based on the different data collection/generation mechanisms, we divide the data into three categories: data collected from RCT, semi-simulated datasets and simulated datasets.

Randomized Control Trial (RCT)

Yahoo-R3. Music ratings collected from Yahoo! Music services. This dataset contains ratings for 1,000 songs collected from 15,400 users with two different sources. One of the sources consist of ratings for randomly selected songs collected using an online survey conducted by Yahoo! Research. The other source consists of ratings supplied by users during normal interaction with Yahoo! Music services. The rating data includes at least ten ratings collected for each user during the normal use of Yahoo! Music services and exactly ten ratings for randomly selected songs for each of the first 5,400 users in the dataset. The dataset includes approximately 300,000 user-supplied ratings, and exactly 54,000 ratings for randomly selected songs[5].

Semi-synthetic Datasets

- *MovieLens10M.* User-movie ratings collected from a movie recommendation service. It has 71,567 unique users and 10,677 unique products. The ratings are on a 1–5 scale [4]. The treatment is binary indicating if a user has rated an item, the outcome is if rating is greater or equal to 3.
- *Netflix.* This dataset includes 480,189 unique users and 17,770 unique products. The treatment is if a user has rated an item, the outcome is if rating is greater or equal to 3.
- *ArXiv.* User-paper clicks from the 2012 log-data of the arXiv pre-print server. The data are binarized: multiple clicks by the same user on the same paper are considered to be a single click. The treatment in this dataset is if a user has viewed the abstract of a paper, outcome is if she downloaded the paper.

Now the question is how to generate new datasets from existing datasets to evaluate de-biased recommender systems. One common approach is to ensure the different distributions between the training/validation sets and the test set. Previous work [4,23] has tried to create two test splits from the standard datasets – regular and skewed. The regular split is generated by randomly selecting the exposed items for each user into training/validation/test sets with proportions 70/20/10, i.e., the standard method that researchers use to evaluate recommendation models. The skewed split re-balances the splits to better approximate an

---

[5] https://webscope.sandbox.yahoo.com/catalog.php?datatype=r.

intervention. In particular, it first samples a test set with roughly 20% of the total exposures such that each item has uniform probability. Training and validation sets are then sampled from the remaining data (as in a regular split) with 70/10 proportions. The test set then has a different exposure distribution from the training and validation sets. Experimental results have shown that causality-embedded recommender systems can largely improve the performance on the skewed split while present similar performance compared to baseline models on the regular split.

Simulated Datasets
Coat Shopping Dataset [32]. This is a synthetic dataset that simulates customers shopping for a coat in an online store. The training data was generated by giving Amazon Mechanical Turkers a simple web-shop interface with facets and paging. Users were asked to find the coat in the store that they wanted to buy the most. Afterwards, they had to rate 24 of the coats they explored (self-selected) and 16 randomly picked ones on a five-point scale. The dataset contains ratings from 290 Turkers on an inventory of 300 items. The self-selected ratings are the training set and the uniformly selected ratings are the test set.

Limitations. RCT for a recommender system is often not an option in real-world applications. For example, a recommender system that randomly recommends songs to its users can largely degrade user experience. Leveraging simulated/semi-simulated datasets to show the generalizability of a de-biased recommender system is technically sound, but the mismatch of synthetic data and the observed data from the true environment is often unavoidable.

Humans are biased in nature. A desired recommender systems should be able to capture idiosyncratic user preferences in order to make personalized recommendations. Therefore, debiasing recommender system may not necessarily make better recommendations than a biased one. A more intriguing question to ask may be what causes a recommendation system to make certain suggestions and how to quantify their causal effects. Such systems are causally interpretable and can help identify the underlying causal relations between users and items. As a result, another limitation of current datasets is the lack of formal definitions of elements for causal studies such as treatments that indicate user's characteristics, features of recommendable items, and the corresponding potential outcomes.

5   Conclusions and Future Work

In this paper, we discuss the **advantages, disadvantages** and **limitations** of existing benchmark datasets for the two fundamental tasks in causal inference. We then present applications of causal inference in two standard ML tasks and investigate how to leverage existing datasets to evaluate the causality-embedded ML models. Our goal is to provide easier access to researchers who share similar research interests in causal learning and more importantly, to draw attentions and seek contributions from research communities to together create and share new benchmark datasets for causal learning with big data.

Acknowledgement. This material is based upon work supported by ARO/ARL and the National Science Foundation (NSF) Grant #1610282, NSF #1909555.

References

1. Almond, D., Chay, K.Y., Lee, D.S.: The costs of low birth weight. Q. J. Econ. **120**(3), 1031–1083 (2005)
2. Bache, K., Lichman, M.: UCI machine learning repository (2013). http://archive. ics.uci.edu/ml
3. Beygelzimer, A., Langford, J.: The offset tree for learning with partial labels. In: Proceedings of the 15th ACM SIGKDD International Conference on Knowledge Discovery and Data Mining, pp. 129–138. ACM (2009)
4. Bonner, S., Vasile, F.: Causal embeddings for recommendation. In: Proceedings of the 12th ACM Conference on Recommender Systems, pp. 104–112. ACM (2018)
5. Brost, B., Mehrotra, R., Jehan, T.: The music streaming sessions dataset. In: The World Wide Web Conference, pp. 2594–2600. ACM (2019)
6. Dehejia, R.H., Wahba, S.: Propensity score-matching methods for nonexperimental causal studies. Rev. Econ. Stat. **84**(1), 151–161 (2002)
7. Dua, D., Graff, C.: UCI machine learning repository (2017). http://archive.ics.uci. edu/ml
8. Duncan, G.J., Brooks-Gunn, J., Klebanov, P.K.: Economic deprivation and early childhood development. Child Dev. **65**(2), 296–318 (1994)
9. Galagate, D., Schafer, J., Galagate, M.D.: Package 'causaldrf' (2015)
10. Guo, R., Cheng, L., Li, J., Hahn, P.R., Liu, H.: A survey of learning causality with data: problems and methods. arXiv preprint arXiv:1809.09337 (2018)
11. Guo, R., Li, J., Liu, H.: Learning individual treatment effects from networked observational data. arXiv preprint arXiv:1906.03485 (2019)
12. Guyon, I., et al: Design and analysis of the causation and prediction challenge. In: Guyon, I.,et al. (eds.) Proceedings of the Workshop on the Causation and Prediction Challenge at WCCI 2008. Proceedings of Machine Learning Research PMLR, Hong Kong, 03–04 June 2008, vol. 3, pp. 1–33. http://proceedings.mlr. press/v3/guyon08a.html
13. Hahn, P.R., Dorie, V., Murray, J.S.: Atlantic Causal Inference Conference (ACIC) data analysis challenge 2017. Technical report (2018)
14. Hill, J.L.: Bayesian nonparametric modeling for causal inference. J. Comput. Graph. Stat. **20**(1), 217–240 (2011)
15. Jiang, N., Li, L.: Doubly robust off-policy value evaluation for reinforcement learning. arXiv preprint arXiv:1511.03722 (2015)
16. Joachims, T., Swaminathan, A., de Rijke, M.: Deep learning with logged bandit feedback (2018)
17. Johansson, F., Shalit, U., Sontag, D.: Learning representations for counterfactual inference. In: International Conference on Machine Learning, pp. 3020–3029 (2016)
18. Kocaoglu, M., Dimakis, A., Vishwanath, S.: Cost-optimal learning of causal graphs. In: Proceedings of the 34th International Conference on Machine Learning, vol. 70, pp. 1875–1884. JMLR. org (2017)
19. LaLonde, R.J.: Evaluating the econometric evaluations of training programs with experimental data. Am. Econ. Rev. **76**, 604–620 (1986)
20. Lefortier, D., Swaminathan, A., Gu, X., Joachims, T., de Rijke, M.: Large-scale validation of counterfactual learning methods: a test-bed. arXiv preprint arXiv:1612.00367 (2016)

21. Li, J., Guo, R., Liu, C., Liu, H.: Adaptive unsupervised feature selection on attributed networks. In: Proceedings of the 25th ACM SIGKDD International Conference on Knowledge Discovery and Data Mining, pp. 92–100. ACM (2019)
22. Li, Y., Guo, R., Wang, W., Huan, L.: Causal learning in question quality improvement. In: 2019 BenchCouncil International Symposium on Benchmarking, Measuring and Optimizing (Bench 2019) (2019)
23. Liang, D., Charlin, L., Blei, D.: Causal inference for recommdendation (2016)
24. Louizos, C., Shalit, U., Mooij, J.M., Sontag, D., Zemel, R., Welling, M.: Causal effect inference with deep latent-variable models. In: Advances in Neural Information Processing Systems, pp. 6446–6456 (2017)
25. McAuley, J., Pandey, R., Leskovec, J.: Inferring networks of substitutable and complementary products. In: Proceedings of the 21th ACM SIGKDD International Conference on Knowledge Discovery and Data Mining, pp. 785–794. ACM (2015)
26. Mitrovic, J., Sejdinovic, D., Teh, Y.W.: Causal inference via kernel deviance measures (2018). CoRR abs/1804.04622. http://arxiv.org/abs/1804.04622
27. Mooij, J.M., Peters, J., Janzing, D., Zscheischler, J., Schölkopf, B.: Distinguishing cause from effect using observational data: methods and benchmarks (2014). CoRR abs/1412.3773. http://arxiv.org/abs/1412.3773
28. Neyman, J.S., Dabrowska, D.M., Speed, T.P.: On the application of probability theory to agricultural experiments. Essay on principles. Stat. Sci. **5**, 465–480 (1990). Ann. Agric. Sci. **10**, 1–51 (1923). Section 9. Translated and Edited by Dabrowska, D.M., Speed, T.P
29. Rakesh, V., Guo, R., Moraffah, R., Agarwal, N., Liu, H.: Linked causal variational autoencoder for inferring paired spillover effects. In: Proceedings of the 27th ACM International Conference on Information and Knowledge Management, pp. 1679–1682. ACM (2018)
30. Rubin, D.B.: Bayesian inference for causal effects: the role of randomization. Ann. Stat. **6**, 34–58 (1978)
31. Sachs, K., Perez, O., Pe'er, D., Lauffenburger, D.A., Nolan, G.P.: Causal protein-signaling networks derived from multiparameter single-cell data. Science **308**(5721), 523–529 (2005). https://doi.org/10.1126/science.1105809. https://science.sciencemag.org/content/308/5721/523
32. Schnabel, T., Swaminathan, A., Singh, A., Chandak, N., Joachims, T.: Recommendations as treatments: debiasing learning and evaluation. arXiv preprint arXiv:1602.05352 (2016)
33. Schwab, P., Linhardt, L., Karlen, W.: Perfect match: a simple method for learning representations for counterfactual inference with neural networks. arXiv preprint arXiv:1810.00656 (2018)
34. Shakarian, P., Bhatnagar, A., Aleali, A., Shaabani, E., Guo, R.: Diffusion in Social Networks. SCS. Springer, Cham (2015). https://doi.org/10.1007/978-3-319-23105-1
35. Shalit, U., Johansson, F.D., Sontag, D.: Estimating individual treatment effect: generalization bounds and algorithms. In: Proceedings of the 34th International Conference on Machine Learning, vol. 70, pp. 3076–3085. JMLR. org (2017)
36. Shanmugam, K., Kocaoglu, M., Dimakis, A.G., Vishwanath, S.: Learning causal graphs with small interventions. In: Advances in Neural Information Processing Systems. pp. 3195–3203 (2015)
37. Smith, J.A., Todd, P.E.: Does matching overcome Lalonde's critique of nonexperimental estimators? J. Econ. **125**(1–2), 305–353 (2005)

38. Swaminathan, A., Joachims, T.: Counterfactual risk minimization: learning from logged bandit feedback. In: International Conference on Machine Learning, pp. 814–823 (2015)
39. Swaminathan, A., Joachims, T.: The self-normalized estimator for counterfactual learning. In: Advances in Neural Information Processing Systems, pp. 3231–3239 (2015)
40. Tsamardinos, I., Brown, L.E., Aliferis, C.F.: The max-min hill-climbing bayesian network structure learning algorithm. Mach. Learn. **65**(1), 31–78 (2006). https://doi.org/10.1007/s10994-006-6889-7
41. Weinstein, J.N., et al.: The cancer genome atlas pan-cancer analysis project. Nat. Genet. **45**(10), 1113 (2013)
42. Yoon, J., Jordon, J., van der Schaar, M.: GANITE: estimation of individualized treatment effects using generative adversarial nets (2018)

Datacenter

LCIO: Large Scale Filesystem Aging

Matthew Bachstein[1](✉), Feiyi Wang[2], and Sarp Oral[2]

[1] University of Tennessee, Knoxville, USA
mbachste@vols.utk.edu
[2] Oak Ridge National Laboratory, Oak Ridge, USA
{fwang2,oralhs}@ornl.gov

Abstract. Performance of file systems shift during their life cycles. Evaluating this performance change over time is not trivial. Complexity arises in the interplay between external (i.e. application I/O workloads) and internal (i.e. the filesystem state) factors. Many benchmarks can test how a filesystem performs at the current snapshot state, but to observe the change over time necessitates that the filesystem state mutate (age) between benchmark runs. For a large-scale HPC parallel filesystem, the sheer scale and amount of interacting components during I/O operations magnify these challenges.

There have been several approaches that address different aspects of filesystem aging, from creating statistically realistic filesystem images to file age distributions. The common drawbacks are the scale to be evaluated and the time needed to converge; none of the methods in literature targeted network or parallel file systems. Also, none were evaluated with a filesystem image over 300 GiB, most under 50 GiB, yet almost all took between a half hour to 7 h to converge. For a large-scale parallel file system, these methods are impractical as far as time and resources needed (a typical large PFS is in the PB range). Additionally, HPC filesystem I/O workloads are drastically different from local system workloads used in earlier studies.

This paper presents the design, implementation and evaluation of LCIO synthetic filesystem aging benchmark, which aims to address the question of "how will the filesystem perform at different stages of its life cycle?". As such, being able to answer that question as realistically as feasible in a reasonable time is where LCIO contributes.

1 Introduction

Benchmarking a filesystem is a theoretically simple concept that is exacerbated by the complex interactions of many multifaceted variables: media type, storage environment, disk caching behavior, etc. In an HPC environment with a parallel filesystem, additional variables such as the interconnect and filesystem client and server configurations will also come into play. The various benchmarks created over time generally fall into three broad categories, Macrobenchmarks, Trace Replays, and Microbenchmarks [5,11]. In particular, Traeger et al. [11] provides a thorough survey on filesystem benchmarking.

© Springer Nature Switzerland AG 2020
W. Gao et al. (Eds.): Bench 2019, LNCS 12093, pp. 251–261, 2020.
https://doi.org/10.1007/978-3-030-49556-5_24

Previous studies [1,3,5,10] have shown the importance of accounting for aging in evaluating filesystem performance. These studies focus on testing how various filesystems (ext4, btrfs, xfs, zfs) deal with aging. Conway et al. [3] shows how simple action like a 'git pull' can, over time, cause decreases in performance. This is incredibly useful data but unfortunately these studies were not run on parallel filesystems, instead focusing on local filesystems.

Additionally, parallel filesystems are quite architecturally different from standard workstation filesystems, for instance the split of metadata and data I/O path, as well as the necessity of a storage area network, which now means that network latencies between clients and filesystem servers must be accounted for alongside other factors e.g. transfer sizes and filesystem native block size.

Two existing well known parallel filesystem benchmarks are MDtest and IOR [6,7]. These provide good tests of specific aspects of the filesystem. MDtest stresses the metadata subsystem of the filesystem, using a create - stat - delete pattern across multiple clients in parallel. IOR stresses read/write performance in both an N-1 (multiple client processes doing I/O to a single shared file) pattern and a N-M (multiple client processes doing I/O to multiple individual or shared files) pattern. However, MDtest and IOR results are highly dependent on the underlying filesystem state. In effect, these two tests give performance characteristics of the current snapshot when the benchmarks were ran.

To increase the amount of context these benchmarks can give, we identified a need to be able to mutate the underlying filesystem image to allow IOR and MDtest to provide a performance curve for the filesystem as it ages. Without a synthetic aging system, the only way to obtain such data would be to routinely benchmark the filesystem while in production over the system's lifetime. However, these benchmarks often find use in the acquisitions process for new systems. Without this synthetic aging process, all that MDtest and IOR will report is the performance of a freshly formatted, empty, clean system (which will not reflect the aged filesystem performance). In this paper we present the LCIO synthetic aging benchmark, which provides this aging process to increase the amount of information that these existing benchmarks yield, as well as provide additional points of data that will be useful to system architects and engineers.

2   Problem Definition and Implementation

The aforementioned approaches in filesystem aging start by defining some statistical parameters, then computing an appropriate distribution(s) to fit those parameters. This is also the general approach taken by LCIO, but with different considerations. Both Impressions [1] and Geriatrix [5] need global state management. Impressions creates a single filesystem image, adequate for benchmarking from a single client process, but not suitable for handling split and synchronous access across several thousand client processes. Geriatrix is also not suitable for parallel access, since it tries to converge to a time distribution as well. This would involve a state synchronization at every time step so that each rank has a constant view of the time distribution for the convergence to succeed.

To efficiently age a large-scale filesystem, the aging process must not only respect common HPC practices for preventing bottlenecks and serializations (such as using POSIX or MPIIO interfaces and using MPI coordinated parallel execution and access), but also create a realistic filesystem state at the end. To this end, LCIO makes each process as independent as possible, accepting trade-offs in realism for efficiently creating many (possibly large) files. Most network based filesystems store a large amount of files, but HPC parallel filesystems are somewhat unique in the variance of file sizes being stored [12,13]. Compared to most workstation filesystems, HPC systems have a 'fat tail'; multi-terabyte files are not that uncommon. Additionally, most HPC large-scale filesystems have periodic purge policies (for capacity management) in place that prevent very many long lived files. With these considerations in mind, it was decided that LCIO should focus primarily on the file size distribution, and converge to that as efficiently as possible. The benefit to this approach is the removal of global state synchronization, as each process does not need any non-local information beyond the target size distribution.

By design, each LCIO client process stores a copy of the target distribution, and can generate file sizes from that distribution without needing to communicate with any other processes. This also gives an easy convergence to the wanted distribution; having N processes generating file sizes with the same distribution implies that the global distribution of file sizes is the same as the local one.

Other design considerations include modular support of non-POSIX I/O interfaces (i.e., MPIIO), which is not uncommon in HPC. As such, LCIO supports running its aging and I/O testing using the MPIIO interface. The modular plugin design of LCIO was inspired by the FIO workload generator [2], which allows for easily swapping the I/O method to accommodate different architectures and systems.

Respecting the minimal synchronization rule, the aging process for LCIO operates as much as possible on a per-process level. Each process is responsible for its own working file set. LCIO borrows from Impressions and Geriatrix in that an initial state is written to the system prior to aging.

To age the system, there are two parameters that control the overall traffic passed to the filesystem, 'ops' and 'epochs'. An 'op' is a combined delete and create operation. An 'epoch' is a collection of ops. Epochs are synchronized, ops are not.

In the configuration file, the field for 'ops' is interpreted as 'ops per epoch'. As such, the total number of operations is calculated as ops × epochs. This approach was chosen to provide the most versatility, and to allow the aging to work even if the underlying filesystem cannot handle a multitude of outstanding requests. Increasing the epochs and decreasing the ops would still allow for the same total amount of operations, while decreasing the simultaneous load on the filesystem. Setting ops = 0 will effectively render a static image to be written to the system without aging.

Since the aging process consists of writing many files of various sizes and for large sizes, it is often impractical to allocate a write buffer of that size for a single write and then free it, the 'buffer_size' option is provided to streamline this process. The user can set the buffer size to the size that they wish and that same buffer will be reused multiple times to create the required file. This can act as a tuning parameter or a stress parameter, since all but one write call will be the buffer size, with the last call being remainder of the file size. Setting the buffer size to the filesystem's native (or configured) block size can speed up the process and give an optimal performance number. In the same manner, changing the buffer size to smaller or larger values can induce different behaviors in the underlying filesystem, possibly showing how well the system responds to non-optimal write sizes.

Various other options are provided to allow for some versatility. As an example, the user can specify that `fallocate` should be used instead of batching up write calls. Other standard options include the option to `fsync` after writes, and the process overlap amount which dictates how many processes can share one directory.

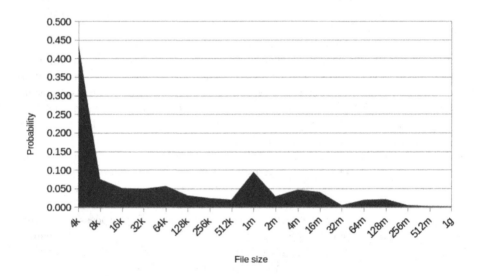

Fig. 1. File size distribution used

3   Evaluation

LCIO was evaluated on a test and development system using the IBM's Spectrum Scale filesystem technology [4] with a capacity of 2.9 PiB (3.2 PB). This test and development system is a building block for the production parallel file system at Oak Ridge Leadership Computing Facility (OLCF). For further details on the hardware and software configuration of OLCF's HPC environment please refer to [12].

Given the potential parameter space to explore, it was determined that presenting results for all possible combinations of parameters was not feasible. Therefore, our evaluation and testing focused on LCIO's primary contribution, i.e., generating a large amount of files on a parallel filesystem. As such, LCIO is used to generate increasing numbers of files to test the behavior of the filesystem as it ages and its internal fragmentation and utilization increases.

The distribution of file sizes that LCIO used for generating the synthetic image is detailed in Fig. 1. This file size distribution was obtained using a parallel filesystem profiler (fprof [13]) on a large-scale HPC production filesystem, formatted with 1.1 billion inodes of which 1 billion of those consumed at peak in production [8,9]. To determine the performance impacts of aging upon the filesystem, after each LCIO run, both MDtest and IOR were executed to obtain performance numbers. Due to time constraints, LCIO runs were only executed with the POSIX interface; similarly with the IOR benchmark (MDtest doesn't have an MPIIO option).

The LCIO runs were done in an exponential type manner from ten thousand (10k) files, up to one billion files. Unfortunately, both the one hundred million (100m) and one billion (1b) file runs were not able to complete within the maximum job length time that was allowed, which was eight hours. Both of those runs were interrupted in the 'write image' portion, with the 100m run at about 40% completion, and the 1b at about 10% completion. Even though those runs did not finish completely, IOR and MDtest were still ran afterwards for completeness, as those runs still generated a substantial amount of traffic. Of the two benchmarks, IOR gave the most interesting results, and consequently is the focus of the impact section.

3.1 Performance and Scalability of LCIO

Each run was given 128 MPI ranks that spread evenly over 8 physical client nodes, with the sole exception of the 1b run, which was given 256 ranks over 8 nodes. The runs were set such that each process would write a minimum of 400 GiB worth of data over the course of a run; this number was chosen as a middle ground between execution time and traffic load. The smaller the number of files, more epochs were needed to get the needed amount of data traffic, with a minimum of 5 epochs. As the number of files increased, the amount of files per process increased, and with it the probability of writing a larger file. This can be seen in Table 1, where the size delta went from 10 GiB to 500 GiB. The only run that exceeded 5 epochs was the 10k run, which needed 50 epochs to generate the minimum number of write calls.

The time taken to the write the initial file image is trivially parallel, and as can be seen in Table 2 a perfect scaling is observed as expected. Since the 100m and 1b runs did not complete and thus do not have a time stamp, the time to completion can be estimated by taking the amount of data written and comparing it to the probabilistic expected value of the file distribution with the given number of files; once done, backing out the amount that was written from the expected size gives the percentage completed in 8 h. This can then

Table 1. Bytes written per run size

Number of files	Average data written per rank	Total execution time (s)
10k	442 GiB	3,712.0
100k	453 GiB	3,678.6
500k	480 GiB	4,247.0
1m	530 GiB	4,710.3
10m	1.14 TiB	12,515.9

be extrapolated to yield the estimated time to completion. Table 3 shows this comparison. Since the smaller runs generated data less than 0.1% of the total filesystem size (the size resolution for the IOR benchmark), the size at finish values could not be directly calculated.

Table 2. Time for initial write

Number of files	Time for initial image(s)	Number of ranks
10k	7.03	128
100k	80.4	128
500k	386.5	128
1m	706.9	128
10m	7,573.2	128
100m	[72, 040]	128
1b	[288, 160]	256

Table 3. Actual/expected size of image

Number of files	Approx. final image size	Expected initial image size
10k	<1 TiB	82.6 GiB
100k	<1 TiB	826.1 GiB
500k	2.9 TiB	4.03 TiB
1m	11.9 TiB	8.06 TiB
10m	95.2 TiB	80.6 TiB
100m	315.4 TiB	806.6 TiB
1b	845.1 TiB	8.06 PiB

Another interesting observation from LCIO was the time taken per epoch. Figure 2 plots the time to finish of the first 5 epochs for the LCIO runs that were able to run to completion. This shows a few interesting results. First, the warm-up/caching behavior is really only apparent on the 10m file run, the rest seem to be constant over the epochs. Secondly, we see the large delta between the 10k and 100k runs, roughly an order of magnitude. Thirdly, and perhaps most interesting, is the clustering of the 100k, 500k, and 1m runs around the 800 s mark. This suggests an area to where the filesystem's load balancer has been calibrated.

This evaluation shows that LCIO is only constrained by the available I/O resources per node; LCIO scales directly with the problem size.

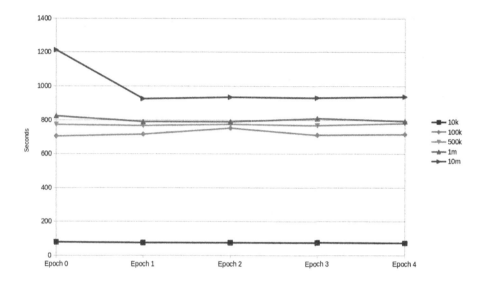

Fig. 2. Time per epoch

3.2   Filesystem Aging Performance Impact

To observe the performance of a LCIO-aged filesystem, both MDtest and IOR were ran after each LCIO execution. Between aging executions, but after the MDtest and IOR runs, the files from the previous LCIO run were deleted to prevent file size pollution. A checkpoint run of IOR and MDtest, where the two benchmarks were ran without the LCIO generated files, was conducted about the halfway mark (between the 100k and 500k runs) to check for changes in the 'base' state.

For the purpose of comparison, both MDtest and IOR benchmarks ran three times with a different topology each time: M processes with N files and unique directories per process (M-N Unique), M processes with N files in the same directory (M-N), and M processes accessing one file in the same directory (M-1). Both benchmarks were given the same resource set, 64 MPI tasks split evenly across 8 nodes (8 tasks/node).

IOR was configured to transfer an aggregate of 256 GiB. MDtest used 2^{20} files in total. Of the two benchmarks, IOR gave the most interesting results (Table 4).

Table 4. Filesystem utilization after aging runs

Run size	Used filesystem capacity (%)	Used inodes (%)
Base	53.3	68.0
10k	53.3	68.0
100k	53.3	68.0
500k	53.4	68.1
1m	53.7	68.3
10m	56.5	70.0
100m	63.9	75.2
1b	81.7	87.3

Plotting the mean throughput IOR values shows what one would expect to see with a mature parallel filesystem, consistent performance with a slight downward trend as the system gets more and more laden with files. Both M-N runs show higher performance than the M-1 run, as expected (Fig. 3).

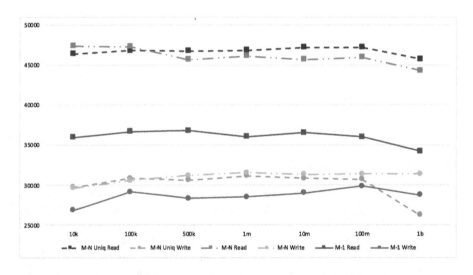

Fig. 3. Mean read/write throughput (MiB)

What is more interesting is the behavior of the standard deviation of each test. Figure 4 shows a large outlier on the write test at the 1b (83.7% utilization) mark. This comes from the first write test only achieving 12,713 MiB/s, whereas the last 3 averaged 31,000 MiB/s. This was mimicked in the two previous runs to a lesser extent. The M-N unique test consistently had the first write test slower than the rest. This seems to be the warm up behavior of the system; once the filesystem has the requested files in its working cache, the throughput returns to the previous average value (Fig. 5).

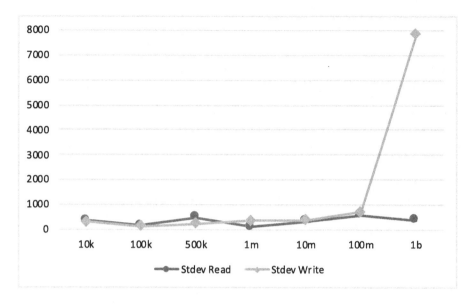

Fig. 4. M-N unique read/write throughput std. dev.

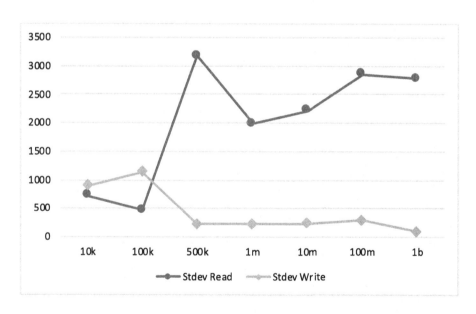

Fig. 5. M-N read/write throughput std. dev.

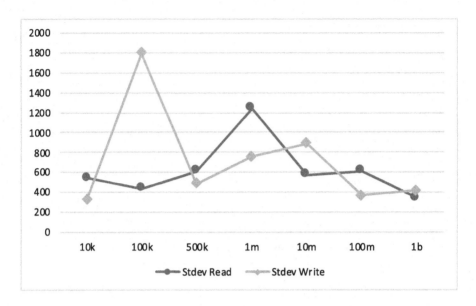

Fig. 6. M-1 read/write throughput std. dev.

The M-N runs show a different set of behaviour. The mean read throughput has a has a slight downward trend, as would be expected, and the mean write speed seems to be constant. The standard deviation however shows that the variance in the write speeds decreases, whereas the read variance increases quickly as the filesystem ages. The placement of the flagging runs was not consistent; the first, second, and third read tests were all found to have the most variance contribution at different capacities.

The M-1 runs, Fig. 6, show a interesting convergence in the deviations as age increases. This might be since the M-1 topology does not allow for easy distribution of work among the filesystem targets, but investigating why is beyond the scope of this paper. However, all these tests show that the behavior of a filesystem changes as it is ages.

4   Conclusion

Benchmarking a parallel filesystem is a complicated task. There are a large number of variables that can be modified, and each combination thereof yields a different piece of information. LCIO adds the ability to test the response of the filesystem as it ages. In particular, LCIO enhances the information generated by other benchmarks by allowing the tester to modify the underlying filesystem state to their needs in a scalable, straightforward manner.

References

1. Agrawal, N., Arpaci-Dusseau, A.C., Arpaci-Dusseau, R.H.: Generating realistic impressions for file-system benchmarking. Trans. Storage **5**(4), 16:1–16:30 (2009). https://doi.org/10.1145/1629080.1629086
2. Axboe, J.: FIO: flexible I/O tester. https://github.com/axboe/fio
3. Conway, A., et al.: File systems fated for senescence? Nonsense, says science!. In: 15th USENIX Conference on File and Storage Technologies (FAST 2017), pp. 45–58. USENIX Association, Santa Clara (2017). https://www.usenix.org/conference/fast17/technical-sessions/presentation/conway
4. IBM: IBM spectrum scale (2018). https://en.wikipedia.org/wiki/IBM_Spectrum_Scale
5. Kadekodi, S., Nagarajan, V., Ganger, G.R.: Geriatrix: aging what you see and what you don't see. A file system aging approach for modern storage systems. In: 2018 USENIX Annual Technical Conference (USENIX ATC 2018), pp. 691–704. USENIX Association, Boston (2018). https://www.usenix.org/conference/atc18/presentation/kadekodi
6. LLNL: IOR HPC benchmark (2017). https://www.nersc.gov/users/computatio nal-systems/cori/nersc-8-procurement/trinity-nersc-8-rfp/nersc-8-trinity-benchm arks/ior/
7. (NERSC), N.E.R.S.C.C.: MDtest (2013). https://www.nersc.gov/users/computati onal-systems/cori/nersc-8-procurement/trinity-nersc-8-rfp/nersc-8-trinity-bench marks/mdtest
8. OLCF, O.R.L.C.F.: SPIDER storage system (2018). https://www.olcf.ornl.gov/ol cf-resources/data-visualization-resources/spider/
9. OpenSFS: Lustre (2018). http://lustre.org/documentation/
10. Smith, K.A., Seltzer, M.I.: File system aging - increasing the relevance of file system benchmarks. SIGMETRICS Perform. Eval. Rev. **25**(1), 203–213 (1997). https://doi.org/10.1145/258623.258689
11. Traeger, A., Zadok, E., Joukov, N., Wright, C.P.: A nine year study of file system and storage benchmarking. Trans. Storage **4**(2), 5:1–5:56 (2008). https://doi.org/10.1145/1367829.1367831
12. Vazhkudai, S.S., et al.: The design, deployment, and evaluation of the coral pre-exascale systems. In: Proceedings of the International Conference for High Performance Computing, Networking, Storage, and Analysis, SC 2018, pp. 52:1–52:12. IEEE Press, Piscataway (2018). http://dl.acm.org/citation.cfm?id=3291656.3291726
13. Wang, F., Sim, H., Harr, C., Oral, S.: Diving into petascale production file systems through large scale profiling and analysis. In: Proceedings of the 2nd Joint International Workshop on Parallel Data Storage & Data Intensive Scalable Computing Systems, PDSW-DISCS 2017, pp. 37–42. ACM, New York (2017). https://doi.org/10.1145/3149393.3149399

BOPS, A New Computation-Centric Metric for Datacenter Computing

Lei Wang[(✉)], Wanling Gao, Kaiyong Yang, and Zihan Jiang

Institute of Computing Technology, Chinese Academy of Sciences, Beijing, China
{wanglei_2011,gaowanling,yangkaiyong,jiangzihan}@ict.ac.cn

Abstract. For emerging datacenter (in short, DC) workloads, such as online Internet services or offline data analytics, how to evaluate the upper bound performance and provide apple-to-apple comparisons are fundamental problems. To this end, an unified computation-centric metric is an essential requirement. FLOPS (FLoating-point Operations Per Second) as the most important computation-centric performance metric, has guided computing systems evolutions for many years. However, our observations demonstrate that the average FLOPS efficiency of the DC workloads is only 0.1%, which implies that FLOPS is inappropriate for DC computing. To address the above issue, inspired by FLOPS, we propose BOPS (Basic Operations Per Second), which is the average number of BOPs (Basic OPerations) completed per second, as a new computation-centered metric. We conduct the comprehensive analysis on the characteristics of seventeen typical DC workloads and extract the minimum representative computation operations set, which is composed of integer and floating point computation operations of arithmetic, comparing and array addressing. Then, we propose the formalized BOPS definition and the BOPS based upper bound performance model. Finally, the BOPS measuring tool is also implemented. To validate the BOPS metric, we perform experiments with seventeen DC workloads on three typical Intel processors platforms. First, BOPS can reflect the performance gap of different computing systems, the bias between the peak BOPS performance (obtaining from micro-architecture) gap and the average DC workloads' wall clock time gap is no more than 10%. Second, BOPS can not only perform the apple-to-apple comparison, but also reflect the upper bound performance of the system. For examples, we analyze the BOPS efficiency of the Redis (the online service) workload and the Sort (the offline analytics) workload. And using the BOPS measuring tool–Sort can achieve 32% BOPS efficiency on the experimental platform.

Keywords: Datacenter · Metric · Computation

1 Introduction

To perform data analysis or provide Internet services, more and more organizations are building internal datacenters, or renting hosted datacenters.

© Springer Nature Switzerland AG 2020
W. Gao et al. (Eds.): Bench 2019, LNCS 12093, pp. 262–277, 2020.
https://doi.org/10.1007/978-3-030-49556-5_25

As a result, DC (datacenter) computing has become a new paradigm of computing. The proportion of DC has outweighed HPC (High Performance Computing) in terms of market share (HPC only takes 20% of total) [2]. How to evaluate the performance efficiency and provide apple-to-apple comparisons are fundamental problems. There is an urgent need for a unified metric. For HPC, FLOPS is a powerful metric and has promoted its rapid evolution and optimization over a period of decades [13]. However, for DC, there is still no such metric.

Generally, the wall clock time is used as a ground truth metric for the computer system. Based on it, the performance metrics are classified into two categories. One is the user-perceived metric, which can be intuitively perceived by the user, such as requests per second [12], sorting number per second [4]. The other is the computation-centered metrics, which are related to specific computation operations, such as FLOPS (FLoating-point Operations Per Second).

User-perceived metrics can be intuitively perceived by the user. But, user-perceived metrics have two limitations. First, user-perceived metrics are hard to measure the upper bound performance of computer systems, which is the foundation of the quantitative evaluation. For example, for the matrix multiply workload, the deep optimized version gains 62,000X out performance of the original Python version on the same Intel multi-core processor platform [16]. So, we wonder the performance efficiency and the upper bound performance of the matrix multiply workload on this platform. Second, different user-perceived metrics cannot be used to perform the apple-to-apple comparison. For example, requests per second and sorting number per second cannot be used for comparison. We cannot obtain the performance efficiency for different type of workloads on the target system.

Computation-centric metrics solve the above limitations. Different workloads can perform the apple-to-apple comparisons. Furthermore, the performance numbers of the metric can be measured by the micro-architecture of the system, the specific micro benchmark and the real-world workload. By using these different numbers, we can build the upper bound model, which allows us to understand the upper bound performance of the computer system. For example, FLOPS motivates continuously exploring to achieve upper bound performance. Also, the winner of Gordon Bell prize and TOP500 ranking represents the best FLOPS performance currently [1]. However, FLOPS is insufficient for DC anymore. Our experiments show that the average FLOPS efficiency is only 0.1% for DC workloads, so that it cannot represent the actual execution performance for DC. OPS (operations per second) is another computation-centric metric. OPS [23] is initially proposed for digital processing systems. The definitions of OPS are extended to the artificial intelligence processor [8,11,19,22]. All of them are defined in terms of one or more fixed operations, such as the specific matrix addition operation. However, these operations are only a fraction of diverse operations in DC workloads.

In this paper, inspired by FLOPS [13] and OPS [23], Basic OPerations per Second (BOPS for short) is proposed to evaluate DC computing systems. The contributions of the paper are described as follows.

First, Based on workload characterizations of seventeen typical DC workloads, we find that DC workloads are data movement dominated workloads, which have more integer and branch operations. Then, following the rule of choosing a representative minimum operation subset, we define BOPs as the integer and floating point computation operations of arithmetic, comparing and array addressing (related with data movement). For the quantitative evaluation, the formalized BOPS definition and the BOPS based upper bound performance model are also given, Finally, we implement the Sort workload as the first BOPS measuring tool.

Second, we validate the BOPS metric on three typical Intel processors systems with seventeen typical DC workloads. Results show that BOPS can reflect the performance gap of different systems, and the bias between the peak BOPS performance (obtaining from micro-architecture) gap and the average DC workloads' wall clock time gap is no more than 10%. Furthermore, BOPS can not only perform the apple-to-apple comparison, but also reflect the upper bound performance of the system. The Redis (the online service workload) and the Sort (the offline analytics workload) can perform the BOPS performance comparison. The BOPS efficiency of the Sort workload achieves 32% of the peak performance of the Intel Xeon E5645 platform, and the attained upper bound performance efficiency (calculating by the BOPS based upper bound model) of Sort achieves 68%.

The remainder of the paper is organized as follows. Section 2 states background and motivations. Section 3 defines BOPS, and reports how to use it. Section 4 is the evaluations of BOPS. Section 5 summarizes the related work. Section 6 draws a conclusion.

2   Background and Motivations

2.1   Background

The Computation-Centric Metric. The computation-centric metric is effective for the co-design across different layers. Generally, a computation-centric metric has performance upper bound on the specific architecture according to the micro-architecture design. For example, the peak FLOPS is computed as follows.

$$FLOPS_{Peak} = Num_{CPU} * Num_{Core} * Frequency * Num_{FloatingpointOperationsPerCycle}$$
$$(1)$$

The measurement tool is used to measure the performance of systems and architectures in terms of metric values, and report the gap between the real value and the theoretical peak one. For example, HPL [13] is a widely used measurement tool in terms of FLOPS. The FLOPS efficiency of a specific system is the ratio of the HPL's FLOPS to the peak FLOPS.

$$FLOPS_{Efficiency} = FLOPS_{Real}/FLOPS_{Peak} \qquad (2)$$

In our experiments, the real FLOPS obtaining from the HPL benchmark is 38.9 GFLOPS, and the FLOPS efficiency of the E5645 platform is 68%.

The Upper Bound Performance Model. The bound and bottleneck analysis can be built under the computation-centric metric. For example, the Roofline model [27] is a famous upper bound model based on FLOPS. There are many system optimization works [20, 26], which are performed based on the Roofline model in the HPC domain.

$$FLOPS_{AttainedPeak} = min(OI * MemBand_{Peak}, FLOPS_{Peak}) \qquad (3)$$

The above equation of the Roofline model indicates that the attained workload performance bound of a specific platform is limited by the computing capacity of the processor and the bandwidth of the memory.

DCMIX. We Choose the DCMIX [28] as benchmarks for DC computer systems. DCMIX is designed for modern datacenter computing systems, which has 17 typical datacenter workloads (including online service and data analysis workloads). Latencies of DCMIX workloads are ranged from microseconds to minutes. The applications of DCMIX involve Big Data, artificial intelligence (AI), OLAP, and OLTP. As shown in Table 1, there are two categories of benchmarks in the DCMIX, which are Micro-Benchmarks (kernel workloads) and Component benchmarks (real DC workloads).

Table 1. Workloads of the DCMIX

Name	Type	Domain	Category
Sort	Offline analytics	Big Data	MicroBench
Count	Offline analytics	Big Data	MicroBench
MD5	Offline analytics	Big Data	MicroBench
MatrixMultiply	Offline analytics	AI	MicroBench
FFT	Offline analytics	AI	MicroBench
Union	Offline analytics	OLAP	MicroBench
Redis	Online service	OLTP	Component
Xapian	Online service	Big Data	Component
Masstree	Online service	Big Data	Component
Bayes	Offline analytics	Big Data	Component
Img-dnn	Online service	AI	Component
Moses	Online service	AI	Component
Sphinx	Online service	AI	Component
Alexnet	Offline analytics	AI	Component
Convolution	Offline analytics	AI	Component
Silo	Online service	OLTP	Component
Shore	Online service	OLAP	Component

2.2 Motivations

Requirements of the DC Computing Metric. We define the requirements from the following perspectives. First, **the metric should reflect the performance gaps of different DC systems**. The wall clock time metric always reflect the performance gaps of different systems. Also, the computation-centric metric should preserve this characteristic. We can use the bias between the computing metric gap and the wall clock time gap to evaluate this requirement. Second, **the metric should reflect the upper bound performance of the DC system and facilitate measurements**. Focusing on different system design, the metric should be sensitive to design decisions and reflect theoretical performance upper bound. Then, the gap between real and theoretical values is useful to understand the performance bottlenecks and guide the optimizations.

Experimental Platforms and Workloads. We choose DCMIX as DC workloads. Three systems equipped with three different Intel processors are chosen as the experimental platforms, which are Intel Xeon E5310, Intel Xeon E5645 and Intel Atom D510. The two former processors are typical brawny-core processors (OoO execution, four-wide instruction issue), while Intel Atom D510 is a typical wimpy-core processor (in-order execution, two-wide instruction issue). Each experimental platform is equipped with one node. The detailed settings of platforms are shown in Table 2.

Table 2. Configurations of hardware platforms.

CPU type		CPU Core	
Intel ®Xeon E5645		6 cores@2.4 GHZ	
L1 DCache	L1 ICache	L2 Cache	L3 Cache
6×32 KB	6×32 KB	6×256 KB	12 MB
CPU type		CPU Core	
Intel ®Xeon E5310		4 cores@1.6 GHZ	
L1 DCache	L1 ICache	L2 Cache	L3 Cache
4×32 KB	4×32 KB	2×4 MB	None
CPU type		CPU Core	
Intel ®Atom D510		2 cores@1.6 GHZ	
L1 DCache	L1 ICache	L2 Cache	L3 Cache
2×24 KB	2×32 KB	2×512 KB	None

The Limitation of FLOPS for DC. Corresponding with requirements of the DC computing metric, we evaluate the FLOPS from two aspects. One is reflecting the performance gaps of different DC systems, another is reflecting the upper bound performance.

The performance gaps are from three folds. First, the performance gaps between E5310 and E5645, the peak FLOPS performance gap is 2.3X (25.6 GFLOPS v.s. 57.6 GFLOPS), and the gap of the average wall clock time is 2.1X. The bias is 9%. Second, the performance gaps between D510 and E5645, the peak FLOPS gap is 12X (4.8 GFLOPS v.s. 57.6 GFLOPS), and the gap of the average wall clock time is 7.4X. The bias is 62%. Third, for the performance gaps between D510 and E5310, the peak FLOPS gap is 5.3X, the gap of the average user-perceived performance metrics is 3.4X. The bias is 60%. **The bias of the peak FLOPS performance gap and the average wall clock time gap between the two systems equipped with Intel Xeon or Intel Atom processors is more than 60%.** This is because that E5645 & E5310 and D510 are totally different micro-architecture platforms, E5645 & E5310 are designed for high performance floating point computing, while D510 is a low power microprocessor for mobile computing. But, DC workloads are data movement intensive workloads, so the performance gaps between Xeon and Atom become narrowed.

For reflecting the upper bound performance, we use six microbenchmarks of DCMIX to reveal the limitations of FLOPS for DC. The FLOPS of DC workloads is only 0.08 GFLOPS on average (only 0.1% of the peak).

The Characteristics of DC Workloads. In order to define the new metric for the DC computing, we perform a careful workload characterization of DC workloads firstly. We choose the DCMIX as the DC workloads. For traditional benchmarks, we choose HPCC, PARSEC, and SPECPU. We have used HPCC 1.4, which is a representative HPC benchmark suite, for the experiment. We run all of the seven benchmarks in HPCC. PARSEC is a benchmark suite composed of multi-threaded programs, and we deploy PARSEC 3.0. For SPEC CPU2006, we run the official floating-point benchmark (SPECFP) applications with the first reference inputs. The experimental platform is the Intel Xeon E5645.

We choose GIPS (Giga-Instructions per Second) and GFLOPS (Giga-Floating point Operations Per Second) as the performance metrics. Corresponding to performance metrics, we choose IPC and CPU utilization as the efficiency metrics. As shown in the Fig. 1 (please note that the Y axis in the figure is in

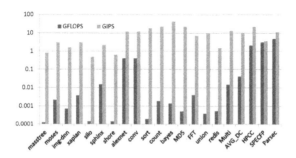

Fig. 1. GIPS and FLOPS of workloads.

logarithmic coordinates), the average GFLOPS of DC workloads is two magnitude orders lower than that of traditional benchmarks, while the GIPS of DC workloads is in the same magnitude order as the traditional benchmarks. And **the average FLOPS efficiency is only 0.1% for DC workloads**. Furthermore, the average IPC of DC workloads is 1.1 and that of traditional benchmarks is 1.4, the average CPU utilization of DC workloads is 70% and that of traditional benchmarks is 80%. These metrics imply that DC workloads can utilize the system resource as efficiently as traditional benchmarks. The poor FLOPS efficiency does not lie in the lower execution efficiency. In fact, the floating point operation intensity of DC workloads (0.05 on average) is much lower, which leads to the low FLOPS efficiency.

In order to analyze the execution characteristics of DC workloads, we choose the instruction mixture to perform the further analysis. From the retired instructions breakdown, we have three observations as follows. First, the load/store instructions of DC workloads take 42% of total instructions. Furthermore, **the ratio of data movement related instructions is 60%**, which include the load, store, array addressing instructions (we obtaining the array addressing instructions through analyzing the integer and floating point instructions). **So, DC workloads are data movement dominated workloads**. Second, the integer/FP instructions of DC workloads take 39% of total instructions. Furthermore, **for DC workloads, the ratio of integer to floating point instructions is 38**, while the ratios for HPCC, Parsec and SPECFP are 0.3, 0.4, and 0.02, respectively. That is the main reason why FLOPS does not work in DC computing. Third, **DC workloads have more branch (comparing) instructions**, with the ratio of 19%, while the ratios of HPCC, Parsec and SPECFP are 16%, 11%, and 9%, respectively. So, **DC workloads are data movement dominated workloads, which have more integer and branch operations**.

3 BOPS

BOPS (Basic OPerations per Second) is the average number of BOPs (Basic OPerations) for a specific workload completed per second. In this section, we present the definition of BOPs and how to measure BOPS with or without the available source code.

3.1 BOPs Definition

We summarize basic operations of DC from three classes, which are Data Movement, Arithmetic Computation and Comparing.

Data Movement. For the FLOPS metric, it is designed for numerical calculation, especially for high floating point operation intensity algorithm, such as the floating point operation intensity (OI) of HPL is O(N), and the data movement can be ignored (one orders of magnitude lower than the floating point operations). On the other hand, in order to process the massive data in time, the complexity of DC workloads are always low, and the operation intensity (the total number of floating point and integer operations divided by the total byte number of memory access) of DC workloads is $O(1)$. So, the data movement can not be ignored. We choose the array addressing computation operations corresponding to data movement-related operations. So, the first class in BOPs is **array addressing operations**, such as loading or storing array values $P[i]$.

Arithmetic Computation. The arithmetic operations is the key operations for the workload's algorithm implementations. We take the basic arithmetic computation operations into BOPs. So, the second class is **the arithmetic operations**, such as $X + Y$.

Comparing. DC workloads have more comparing operations. So we take conditional comparing related computation operations into the BOPs, the third class is **the comparing operations**, such as $X < Y$.

The detailed operations of BOPs are shown in Table 3. Each operation in Table 3 is counted as 1 except for N-dimensional array addressing. Note that all operations are normalized to 64-bit operation. For arithmetic operations, the number of BOPs is counted as the number of corresponding arithmetic operations. For array addressing operations, we take the one-dimensional array $P[i]$ as the example. Loading the value of $P[i]$ indicates the addition of an i offset to the address location of P, so the number of BOPs increases by one. And, it can also be applied to the calculation of the multi-dimensional array. For comparing operations, we transform them to subtraction operations. We take $X < Y$ as an example and transform it to $X - Y < 0$, so the number of BOPs increases by one.

Table 3. Normalization operations of BOPs.

Operations	Normalized value
Add	1
Subtract	1
Multiply	1
Divide	1
Bitwise operation	1
Logic operation	1
Compare operation	1
One-dimensional array addressing	1
N-dimensional array addressing	1 * N

Through the definition of BOPs, we can see that in the comparison with FLOPS, BOPS concerns not only the floating-point operations, but also the

integer operations. On the other hand, like FLOPs, BOPs normalize all operations into 64-bit operations, and each operation is counted as 1. The delays of
different operations are not considered in the normalized calculation of BOPs,
because the delays can be extremely different in different micro-architecture platforms. For example, the delay of the division in Intel Xeon E5645 processor is
about 7–12 cycles, while in Intel Atom D510 processor, the delay can reach up to
38 cycles [6]. Hence, the consideration of delays in the normalization calculations
will lead to architecture-related issue.

3.2   How to Measure BOPs

Source-Code Level Measurement. We can calculate BOPs from the source
code of a workload, and this method needs some manual work (inserting the
counting code). However, it is independent with the underlying system implementation, so it is fair to evaluate and compare different system and architecture
implementations. To measure BOPs in the source code level, we need to insert
the counting code and the debug flag. To count BOPs, we will turn on the debug
flag, and for the performance evaluation, we will turn off the debug flag.

Another thing we need to take into account is the system built-in library
functions. For the calculation of the system-level functions, such as Strcmp()
function, we implement user-level functions manually, and then count the number
of BOPs through inserting the counting code.

Instruction Level Measurement Under X86_64 Architecture. The
source-code measurement need to analyze the source code, which costs a lot
especially for complex system stacks (e.g., Hadoop system stacks). Instruction level measurement can avoid this high analysis cost and the restriction
of needing the source code, but it is architecture-dependent. We propose an
instruction-level approach to measure BOPs, which uses the hardware performance counter to obtain BOPs. Since different types of processors have different
performance counter events, for convenience, we introduce an approximate but
simple instruction level measurement method under X86_64 architecture. That
is, we can obtain the number of related instructions through the hardware performance counters. And BOPs can be calculated according to the following equation
(please note that this equation is for Intel E5645, which equipped with 128-bit
SSE FPUs and ALUs).

$$BOPs = Integer\_All + FP\_All \qquad (4)$$

$$Integer\_All = Integer\_Ins + 2 * SSE\_Integer \qquad (5)$$

$$FP\_All = FP\_Ins + SSE\_Scalar + 2 * SSE\_Packed \qquad (6)$$

Please note that our instruction level measurement method includes all of floating point and integer instructions under X86_64 architecture, which does not
exactly conform to the BOPS definition. So, it is a approximate measurement method, and does not suit for the performance evaluation among different

micro-architectures (such as CISC Vs. RISC). However, on the same Intel X86_64 platforms, the deviation between the instructions level measurement and the source code level measurement is no more than 0.08, through our experiments on Intel Xeon E5645.

3.3   How to Measure the System with BOPS

The Peak BOPS of the System. BOPS is the average number of BOPs for a specific workload completed per second. The peak BOPS can be calculated by the micro-architecture with the following equation.

$$BOPS_{Peak} = Num_{CPU} * Num_{Core} * Frequency * Num_{BOPsPerCycle} \quad (7)$$

For our Intel Xeon E5645 experimental platform, the CPU number is 1, the core number is 6, the frequency of core is 2.4 GHZ, BOPs per cycle is 6 (The E5645 equips two 128-bit SSE FPUs and three 128-bit SSE ALUs, and according to the execution port design, it can execute three 128-bit operations per cycle). So $BOPS_{Peak} = 1 * 6 * 2.4G * 6 = 86.4\,GBOPS$.

The BOPS Measuring Tool. We provide a BOPS measuring tool to measure the performance of DC systems. At present we choose Sort in the DCMIX as the first BOPS measuring tool. To deal with the diversity of DC workloads, we will develop a series of representative workloads as the BOPS measuring tools. We choose Sort as the first BOPS measuring tool for it is the most widely used workload in the DC [3]. And the Sort workload realizes the sorting of an integer array of a specific scale, the sorting algorithm uses quick sort algorithm and the merge algorithm. The program is implemented by C++ and MPI. The scale of the Sort workload is 10E8 records, and BOPs of that is 529E9. The details of BOPs can be found in the Table 4, Please note that BOPs value will change as the data scale changes.

Table 4. BOPs of the sort measuring tool

Operations	Counters
Arithmetic operations	106E9
Comparing operations	36E9
Array addressing operations	387E9
Total	529E9

Measuring the System with BOPS. The measuring tool can be used to measure the real performance of the workload on the specific system. Furthermore, the BOPS efficiency can be calculated by the following equation.

$$BOPS_{Efficiency} = BOPS_{Real}/BOPS_{Peak} \quad (8)$$

For example, Sort has 529E9 BOPs. We run Sort on the Xeon E5645 platform and the execution time is 18.7 s. $BOPS_{Real} = 529E9/18.7 = 28\,GBOPS$. For the Xeon E5645 platform, the peak BOPS is 86.4 GBOPS, the real performance of Sort is 28 GBOPS, so the efficiency is 32%.

The Upper Bound Performance Model. We modify the Roofline model through changing the metric from FLOPS to BOPS, we call it as BOPS based upper bound model.

$$BOPS_{AttainedPeak} = min(OI_{BOPS} * MemBand_{Peak}, BOPS_{Peak}) \qquad (9)$$

$BOPS_{Peak}$ and $MemBand_{Peak}$ are the peak performance of the platform, and the operation intensity (OI_{BOPS}) is the total number of BOPs divided by the total byte number of memory access. For example, the OI of the sort benchmark is 3.0, the peak memory bandwidth is 13.8 GB/s, the peak BOPS is 86.4 GBOPS. So, the attained peak BOPS of the Sort is 41.4 GBOPS and the attained BOPS efficiency is 68%.

$$BOPS_{AttainedEfficiency} = BOPS_{Real}/BOPS_{AttainedPeak} \qquad (10)$$

4   Evaluations

4.1   Experimental Platforms and Workloads

We choose DCMIX as DC workloads, and choose three typical HPC microbenchmarks (HPL, Graph500, and Stream) as the experimental workloads too. Three systems equipped with three typical Intel processors are chosen as the experimental platforms, which are Intel Xeon E5310, Intel Xeon E5645 and Intel Atom D510. The detailed settings of platforms are shown in Table 2.

4.2   The BOPS Metrics for DC Systems Evaluations

Figure 2 is the visualized BOPS based upper bound performance model (Eq. 9). There are six DCMIX microbenchmarks, one typical component benchmarks (the Redis workload) and three typical HPC microbenchmarks in the Figure. And three experimental platforms are also in the figure. We see that all of performance metrics are unified to BOPS metric, which include the peak performance of the system (such as the 'Peak of E5645' is the peak performance of the E5645 platform), and the performance of the workload (such as performances of the Sort workload under different platforms). So, we can do the following evaluations. First, analyzing the performance gaps of different systems. Second, performing the apple-to-apple comparison for DC systems. Third, analyzing the upper bound performance of DC systems.

The Performance Gaps Across Different DC Platforms. Reflecting the performance gaps of different DC systems is the first requirements for BOPS. From Fig. 2, we see that:

First, for the performance gaps between E5310 and E5645, the peak BOPS performance gap is 2.3X (38.4 GBOPS v.s. 86.4 GBOPS), the gap of the average wall clock time is 2.1X. The bias is only 10%.

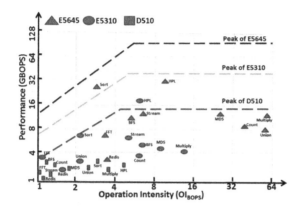

Fig. 2. Evaluation of three intel processors platforms with BOPS.

Second, for the performance gaps between D510 and E5645, the peak BOPS performance gap is 6.7X (12.8 GBOPS v.s. 86.4 GBOPS), the gap of the average wall clock time is 7.4X. The bias is only 9%.

Third, for the performance gaps between D510 and E5310, the peak BOPS performance gap is 3X, the gap of the average wall clock time is 3.4X. The bias is only 10%.

So, the bias between the peak BOPS performance gap and the average wall clock time gap is no more than 10%.

The Apple-to-Apple Comparison of DC Systems. We take the Redis workload (the typical online service workload) and the Sort workload (the typical data analytic workload) as the example to illustrate the apple-to-apple comparison. On the E5645 platform, the Redis workload is 2.9 GBOPS, the performance efficiency of theory peak is 20% and that of the theory upper bound is 34% (Redis is a single-threaded server and we deploy it on the single specific CPU core). The Sort workload is 28 GBOPS, the efficiency of the theory peak is 32% and that of the theory upper bound is 68% (Sort is a multi-threaded workloads). We see that the Sort workload is more efficiency on the E5645 platform, and we can also do the optimizations base on the upper bound performance model (more details are in the next section). On the other hand, the user-perceived metric of Redis is 122,000 Requests/S and that of Sort is 8.3E6/S (sorting 8.3E6 number elements per seconds), we can not get any insight from these user-perceived metrics. So, we can do the apple-to-apple comparisons with BOPS, whatever they are different type workloads (online services v.s. offline data analytics) or different implements (single-threaded Vs. multi-threaded) (Table 5).

Table 5. The apple-to-apple comparison for DC workloads.

	Redis	Sort
BOPS	2.9 G	28 G
BOPS efficiency	20%	32%
BOPS attained efficiency	34%	68%

The Upper Bound Performance of DC Systems. We use the Sort measuring tool to evaluate the upper bound performance of DC systems. The peak BOPS is obtained by Eq. 7. The real BOPs values are obtained by the source-code level measurement, and BOPS efficiency is obtained by Eq. 8. As shown on the Table 6, BOPS efficiencies of E5645, E5310 and D510 are 32%, 20% and 21%, respectively. Furthermore, using the BOPS based upper bound performance model (Eq. 9 and Eq. 10), we get the BOPS attained efficiency of E5645, E5310 and D510 are 68%, 49% and 51%. So we see that the BOPS value is more reasonable to reflect the peak performance and the upper bound performance of real DC systems.

Table 6. The BOPS efficiency of DC platforms.

	E5645	D510	E5310
Peak BOPS	86.4 G	12.8 G	38.4 G
Real BOPS	28 G	2.7 G	7.7 G
BOPS efficiency	32%	21%	20%
BOPS attained efficiency	68%	49%	51%

5   Related Work

The performance metrics can be classified into two categories. One is the user-perceived metric, another is the computation-centric metric.

User-perceived metrics can be further classified into two categories: one is the metric for the whole system, and the other is the metric for components of the system. The examples of the former include data sorted in one minute (MinuteSort), which measures the sorting capability of a system [3], and transactions per minute (TPM) for the online transaction system [7]. The examples of the latter include the SPECspeed/SPECrate for the CPU component [5], the input/output operations per second (IOPS) for the storage component [18], and the data transfer latency for the network component [9].

There are many computation-centric metrics. FLOPS (FLoating-point Operations Per Second) is a computation-centric metric to measure the computer system, especially in field of the scientific computing that makes heavy use of floating-point calculations [13]. The wide recognition of FLOPS indicates the maturation of high performance computing. MIPS (Million Instructions Per Second) [17] is another famous computation-centric metric, which is defined as the million number of instructions the processor can process in a second. The main limitation of MIPS is that it is architecture-dependent. There are many derivatives of the MIPS, including MWIPS and DMIPS [24], which use synthetic workloads to evaluate the floating point operations and integer operations, respectively. The WSMeter metric [21], which is defined as the quota-weighted sum of MIPS of a job, is also a derivative of MIPS, and hence it is also architecture-dependent. Unfortunately, modern DCs are heterogeneous, which consist of different types of hardware. OPS (Operations Per Second) is another computation-centric metric. OPS [23] is initially proposed for digital processing systems, which is defined as the 16-bit addition operations per second. The definitions of OPS are then extended to Intel Ubiquitous High Performance Computing [10] and artificial intelligence processors, such as Tensor Processing Unit [8,19] and Cambricon processor [11,22]. All of these definitions are in terms of one or more fixed operations. For example, Operations are 8-bit matrix multiplication operations in TPU and 16-bit integer operations in Cambricon processor, respectively. However, the workloads of modern DCs are comprehensive and complex, and the bias to one or more fixed operations can not ensure the evaluation fairness.

For each kind of metrics, the corresponding tools or benchmarks [15] are proposed to calculate the values. For user-perceived metrics—SPECspeed/SPECrate, SPECCPU is the benchmark suite [5] to measure the CPU component. For computation-centric metrics, Whetstone [14] and Dhrystone [25] are the measurement tools for MWIPS and DMIPS, respectively. HPL [13] is a widely used measurement tool for FLOPS.

For computation-centric metrics, the Roofline model [27] is the famous performance model. The Roofline model can depict the upper bound performance of given workloads, when different optimization strategies are adopted to the target system. The original Roofline model [27] adopts FLOPS as the performance metric.

6 Conclusion

For the system and architecture community, performing the apple-to-apple comparison and obtaining the upper bound performance of the specific system are very important for the system evolution, design and optimization. This paper proposes a new computation-centric metric-BOPS that measures the DC computing system. The metric is independent with the underlying systems and hardware implementations, and can be calculated through analyzing the source code. As an effective metric for DC, BOPS can truly reflect not only the performance gaps of different systems, but also the efficiency of DC systems and can be used to perform the apple-to-apple comparison. All of these characteristics are foundations of quantitative analysis for DC systems.

Acknowledgment. This work is supported by the National Key Research and Development Plan of China Grant No. 2016YFB1000201.

References

1. https://www.hpcwire.com/2015/11/20/top500/
2. Date center growth. https://www.enterprisetech.com
3. Sort benchmark. http://sortbenchmark.org/
4. Sort program. Available in hadoop source distribution, src/examples/org/a-pache/hadoop/examples/sort
5. SPEC CPU. http://www.spec.org/cpu
6. Technical report. http://www.agner.org/optimize/microarchitecture.pdf
7. TPCC. http://www.tpc.org/tpcc
8. Abadi, M., et al.: Tensorflow: a system for large-scale machine learning. In: Operating Systems Design and Implementation, pp. 265–283 (2016)
9. Cardwell, N., Savage, S., Anderson, T.E.: Modeling TCP latency, vol. 3, pp. 1742–1751 (2000)
10. Carter, N.P., et al.: Runnemede: an architecture for ubiquitous high-performance computing, pp. 198–209 (2013)
11. Chen, Y., et al.: DaDianNao: a machine-learning supercomputer. In: International Symposium on Microarchitecture, pp. 609–622 (2014)
12. Cooper, B.F., Silberstein, A., Tam, E., Ramakrishnan, R., Sears, R.: Benchmarking cloud serving systems with YCSB. In: Proceedings of the 1st ACM symposium on Cloud computing, SoCC 2010, pp. 143–154. ACM, New York (2010). https://doi.org/10.1145/1807128.1807152
13. Dongarra, J., Luszczek, P., Petitet, A.: The linpack benchmark: past, present and future. Concurr. Comput.: Pract. Exp. **15**(9), 803–820 (2003)
14. Harbaugh, S., Forakis, J.A.: Timing studies using a synthetic whetstone benchmark. ACM Sigada Ada Lett. **2**, 23–34 (1984)
15. Hennessy, J.L., Patterson, D.A.: Computer Architecture: A Quantitative Approach. Elsevier, Amsterdam (2012)
16. Hennessy, J.L., Patterson, D.A.: A new golden age for computer architecture. Commun. ACM **62**(2), 48–60 (2019)
17. Jain, R.: The Art of Computer Systems Performance Analysis, vol. 182. Wiley, Chichester (1991)
18. Josephson, W., Bongo, L.A., Li, K., Flynn, D.: DFS: a file system for virtualized flash storage. ACM Trans. Storage **6**(3), 14 (2010)
19. Jouppi, N.P., et al.: In-datacenter performance analysis of a tensor processing unit, pp. 1–12 (2017)
20. Kamil, S., Chan, C.P., Oliker, L., Shalf, J., Williams, S.: An auto-tuning framework for parallel multicore stencil computations, pp. 1–12 (2010)
21. Lee, J., Kim, C., Lin, K., Cheng, L., Govindaraju, R., Kim, J.: WSmeter: a performance evaluation methodology for Google's production warehouse-scale computers. In: Proceedings of the Twenty-Third International Conference on Architectural Support for Programming Languages and Operating Systems, pp. 549–563. ACM (2018)

22. Liu, S., et al.: Cambricon: an instruction set architecture for neural networks. In: International Symposium on Computer Architecture, pp. 393–405 (2016)
23. Nakajima, M., et al.: A 40GOPS 250mw massively parallel processor based on matrix architecture. In: IEEE International on Solid-State Circuits Conference, 2006. ISSCC 2006. Digest of Technical Papers, pp. 1616–1625. IEEE (2006)
24. Pesovic, U., Jovanovic, Z., Randjic, S., Markovic, D.: Benchmarking performance and energy efficiency of microprocessors for wireless sensor network applications. In: MIPRO, 2012 Proceedings of the 35th International Convention, pp. 743–747. IEEE (2012)
25. Weicker, R.: Dhrystone: a synthetic systems programming benchmark. Commun. ACM **27**(10), 1013–1030 (1984)
26. Williams, S., et al.: Optimization of geometric multigrid for emerging multi- and manycore processors, p. 96 (2012)
27. Williams, S., Waterman, A., Patterson, D.: Roofline: an insightful visual performance model for multicore architectures. Commun. ACM **52**(4), 65–76 (2009)
28. Xiong, X., et al.: DCMIX: generating mixed workloads for the cloud data center. In: Zheng, C., Zhan, J. (eds.) Bench 2018. LNCS, vol. 11459, pp. 105–117. Springer, Cham (2019). https://doi.org/10.1007/978-3-030-32813-9_10

Anomaly Analysis and Diagnosis for Co-located Datacenter Workloads in the Alibaba Cluster

Rui Ren[1,2(✉)], Jinheng Li[3], Lei Wang[1], Yan Yin[1], and Zheng Cao[4]

[1] Institute of Computing Technology, Chinese Academy of Sciences, Beijing, China
{renrui,wanglei_2011,yinyan}@ict.ac.cn
[2] China Electronics Technology Research Institute of Cyberspace Security CO., LTD., Beijing, China
[3] City University of Hong Kong, Hong Kong, China
leeebucks@gmail.com
[4] Alibaba, Hangzhou, China
cao@uni-heidelberg.de

Abstract. In warehouse-scale cloud datacenters, co-locating online services and offline batch jobs is an efficient approach to improving datacenter utilization. In this paper, we perform a deep analysis on the released Alibaba workload dataset, from the perspective of anomaly analysis and diagnosis. we first performed raw data preprocessing, including data supplementing, filtering, correlation and aggregation, and generating the container-level, batch-level and server-level resource usage data finally. Then based on the summary data, we illustrate the overall cluster usage distribution of online container services and batch jobs. Obviously, there are several abnormal nodes in the co-located cluster, and we explore the causes of anomalies from three aspects: (1) unbalanced co-located workloads distribution; (2) skew co-located workload resource utilization; (3) system failures or job instance failures. In addition, we also give some cases of abnormal nodes, which show that frequent system failures and unbalanced workload distribution have a great impact on abnormal nodes, the skew co-located workload resource utilization and frequent instance failures are the causes of abnormalities, too.

Keywords: Alibaba trace · Co-located workloads · Anomaly analysis · Causes diagnosis

1 Introduction

With the popularity of internet services, cloud datacenter has become the infrastructure, which contains thousands of machines. Aiming at improving the overall

This work is supported by National Key Research and Development Plan of China No. 2017YFB1001602.

resource utilization, co-locating online services and offline batch jobs is an efficient approach. However, it also results in exponentially increased complexity for datacenter resource management. Alibaba tried to deploy batch jobs and latency-critical online services on the same machines. They use Sigma [1] to schedule online service containers for the production jobs, and Fuxi [2] scheduler to manage the batch workloads. To better understand the interactions among the co-located workloads and their real-world operational demands, Alibaba first released a co-located trace dataset (https://github.com/alibaba/clusterdata) in Aug 2017.

For Alibaba's production cluster traces, recent studies [3–5] have analyzed the characteristics from the perspective of imbalance phenomenon, co-located workloads (how the co-located workloads interact and impact each other), the elasticity and plasticity of semi-containerized cloud. However, these works do not further analyze the abnormal node in the cluster. Actually, discovering the cluster anomalies quickly is very important, for it helps to locate bottlenecks, troubleshoot problems, avoid failures and improve utilization.

In this paper, we perform a deep analysis on the released Alibaba co-located trace dataset [6], from the perspective of anomaly analysis and diagnosis. This dataset describes the machine information and job scheduling information of a co-located workload cluster, which contains 1.3k machines that run both online container services and batch jobs. Based on these data, we first perform raw data preprocessing, including data supplementing, filtering, correlation and aggregation, and generating the container-level, batch-level and server-level resource usage data finally. Then we illustrate the overall cluster usage, heatmaps of the online container services and batch jobs. Obviously, there are several abnormal nodes in the co-located workload cluster, and we explore the causes of anomalies from three aspects: (1) unbalanced co-located workloads distribution; (2) skew co-located workload resource utilization; (3) system or job instance failures. At last, we also give some cases of abnormal nodes, which show that frequent system failures and unbalanced workload distribution have a great impact on abnormal nodes, the skew co-located workload resource utilization and frequent instance failures are the causes of anomalies, too.

2 Usage Characteristics of Alibaba Trace

The Alibaba trace data contains cluster information of a production cluster in 12 hours period, and contains about 1.3k machines that run both online services and offline batch jobs. And the dataset includes six files: *server_event.csv*, *server_usage.csv*, *batch_instance.csv*, *batch_task.csv*, *container_event.csv* and *container_usage.csv*, which can be classified into two categories: resource data and workload data.

Raw Data Preprocessing. In order to understand the resource utilization of online container services, batch job workloads and servers, we first supplement the missing data and filter abnormal data. Such as, for the missing machine

149, 602 and *930* in file *server_usage.csv*, all resource data is completed with 0. We also find that there are several missing resource usage records on 335 machines, and there missing data are filled up by linear interpolation method. In addition, we find that some online container instances are duplicated and have two memory allocation values in file *container_event.csv*, and we remove these anomalous records that requested memory is greater than 0.9[1].

Then we aggregate all the container-level, batch-level and server-level resource usage statistics by the machine id and recording interval, respectively.

(1) *Generating container-level resource usage data.* Because the file *container_usage.csv* samples the resource usage of each container every 300s. So at every time interval, we aggregate all the container-level resource usage statistics by machine id based on *container* → *machine_Id* mapping recorded in the *container_event.csv* [3]. Here, we calculate $Cpu(ci)_{m,I_x}$ and $Mem(ci)_{m,I_x}$, which indicate the total CPU usage and memory usage of all container instances that running on machine m at every time interval I_x.

(2) *Generating batch-level resource usage data.* Cheng et al. [4] have calculated the batch job workload resource usage by subtracting the usage of containers from the overall usage of the cluster. However, we think their calculation method is not accurate enough, for there are resources that occupied by the OS operations on machines, except for the resources used by containers and batch tasks. So we generate the batch-level resource usage data based on actual occupation time of batch task instances.

The file *batch_instance.csv* records the start time, end time and location (machine) of all batch task instances. For each time interval, according to the positions of batch tasks' start time and end time, there are four situations that shown in Fig. 1.

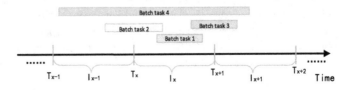

Fig. 1. Four situations for the positions of batch tasks' start and end time.

So we can calculate the actual occupation time of batch task instances during every time interval, according to formula (1).

$$\begin{cases} RT(bi)_{m,I_x} = t(bi)_{end} - t(bi)_{start} & (t(bi)_{start} \ge t_x \ \& \ t(bi)_{end} \le t_{x+1}) \\ RT(bi)_{m,I_x} = t(bi)_{end} - t_x & (t(bi)_{start} \le t_x \ \& \ t(bi)_{end} \le t_{x+1}) \\ RT(bi)_{m,I_x} = t_{x+1} - t(bi)_{start} & (t(bi)_{start} \ge t_x \ \& \ t(bi)_{end} \ge t_{x+1}) \\ RT(bi)_{m,I_x} = t_{x+1} - t_x & (t(bi)_{start} \le t_x \ \& \ t(bi)_{end} \ge t_{x+1}) \end{cases} \quad (1)$$

---

[1] If the requested memory of one container is greater than 0.9, all the requested memory of containers may be exceed the machine memory, which is obviously unreasonable.

Here, $RT(bi)_{m,I_x}$ represents the real occupation runtime of batch task instance bi that running on machine m and during the time interval I_x ($I_x = [t_x, t_{x+1}]$); $t(bi)_{start}$ and $t(bi)_{end}$ are the start time and end time of batch task instance bi. And then, the CPU usage and memory usage that occupied by all batch tasks during every interval can be derived based on the actual occupation time. That is, we calculate $Cpu(bi)_{m,I_x}$ and $Mem(bi)_{m,I_x}$, which indicate the total CPU usage and memory usage of all batch tasks that running on machine m at every time interval I_x.

(3) *Generating server-level resource usage data.* Similarly, based on the file *server_usage.csv*, we calculate the average resource utilization for each time interval and each machine, which includes the Cpu usage Cpu_{m,I_x}, memory usage Mem_{m,I_x} and disk usage $Disk_{m,I_x}$.

Distributions of Resource Utilization. Based on the aggregated resource utilization data of batch tasks and online container services, Fig. 2 gives the box-and-whisker plot that showing CPU usage and memory usage distributions. We observe that on the same machine, the aggregated CPU usage of online containers is lower than that of batch tasks, while the aggregated memory usage of online containers is higher than that of batch tasks. It implies that most batch jobs are computational tasks, and the online container services (long-running jobs) are more memory-demanding.

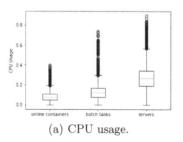
(a) CPU usage.

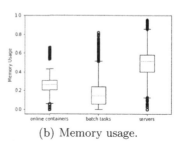
(b) Memory usage.

Fig. 2. The box-and-whisker plot that showing CPU and memory usage distribution.

In addition, we also respectively plot the resource usage heatmap of online containers and batch tasks in Fig. 3 and Fig. 4. Figure 3 shows that, there are no running online containers from the range of machine *132* to *151*, machine *418* to *553*. During the tracing interval, the resource utilization (CPU usage and memory usage) of online containers is relatively stable. Figure 4 shows that, there are no running batch tasks from 52800 s (14.7 h) in several machine regions, such as the region of machine *95* to *127*, machine *275* to *296*, machine *753* to *760*, and machine *830* to *906*. Since most batch tasks are short jobs, the resource utilization is not as stable as that of long-running jobs, especially the memory usage is fluctuating. We can conclude that, the resource utilization of online services and batch jobs vary on different nodes. We still draw the conclusions that, the online containers are the long-running jobs with more memory-demanding, so the memory usage is relatively stable; while the memory usage of batch jobs is fluctuating, for most batch tasks are short jobs.

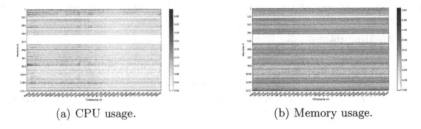

(a) CPU usage.   (b) Memory usage.

Fig. 3. The resource usage heatmap of online containers.

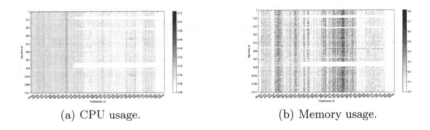

(a) CPU usage.   (b) Memory usage.

Fig. 4. The resource usage heatmap of batch tasks.

3   Anomaly Analysis

Intuitively, by observing the overall cluster usage, we see that there are some abnormal nodes[2] in the cluster. Therefore, we try to find out which nodes are the abnormal nodes through Isolation Forest (iForest) [7]. In the experiments, we choose 3 dimensions Cpu_{m,I_x}, Mem_{m,I_x} and $Disk_{m,I_x}$ to build the machine-resources matrix. Then we apply the Isolation Forest (iForest) [7] algorithm to this machine-resources matrix, and output the anomaly scores. If one machine's anomaly score is smaller, the probability that it is an abnormal node is higher. The distribution of machines' anomaly scores is shown in Fig. 5. In this figure, there are 81 machines have anomaly scores that are less than 0, which can be considered as abnormal nodes.

In addition, we analyze the possible causes of anomalies from three aspects: (1) unbalanced co-located workload distribution[3]; (2) skew co-located workload resource utilization; and (3) failures.

---

[2] abnormal nodes are the nodes which are few and different in the cluster.

[3] Here, the workload distribution means the number of workloads on nodes.

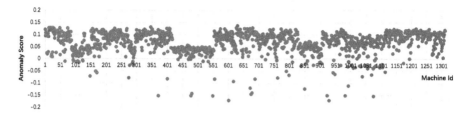

Fig. 5. The anomaly score.

3.1   Unbalanced Co-located Workload Distribution

In this section, we analyze the number distribution of the online services and batch workloads on nodes, and try to discover the association of workload distribution and the abnormal nodes.

First, we have statistics on the numbers of batch tasks and online container at each node, and we observe that, most of the batch task numbers are in the range of 35 to 71, and most of the online container numbers are in the range of 7 to 10.

Based on the number of batch tasks and online containers on machines, we classify the distribution of the co-located workloads. First, we define $Num(bi)_{m,I_x}$ and $Num(ci)_{m,I_x}$ as the number of batch task instance bi and container instance ci that running on machine m. And the non-zero values of $Num(bi)_{m,I_x}$ and $Num(ci)_{m,I_x}$ are mapped to 1, the zero values remains unchanged. Second, for each machine, we combine all the mapped batch task numbers and container numbers to form a (143+143)-dimensional[4] vector. That is, it generates a matrix of 1313 × 286. At last, the Kmeans [8] algorithm is applied to the generated number matrix and is used for classification.

In our experiments, all machines in the Alibaba cluster can be classified into 8 *workload distribution categories*, which include:

- **Type 1**: The online containers and batch tasks are always co-located running on machines, which is shown in Fig. 6 (a). There are 72.8% of nodes have the co-located workloads, which belong to **Type 1**.
- **Type 2**: No running workloads on machines, which is shown in Fig. 6 (b). The machine *372, 478, 481, 550, 602, 924, 930, 983, 1075* belong to **Type 2**, and have low CPU usage (about 1%).
- **Type 3**: Batch tasks are running only, which is shown in Fig. 6 (c). There are 170 nodes that belonging to **Type 3**, which including: *66, 132–151, 237, 265, 390, 418–549, 551–553, 973, 982, 987, 1004, 1008, 1028, 1029, 1043, 1055, 1057, 1058, 1081, 1083*.
- **Type 4**: Online container instances are running only, which is shown in Fig. 6 (d). There are 11 nodes that only have online containers (belonging to **Type 4**), which including: *161, 171, 556, 763, 791, 800, 851, 943, 949, 1069, 1113*.

---

[4] The number of recording interval is 143.

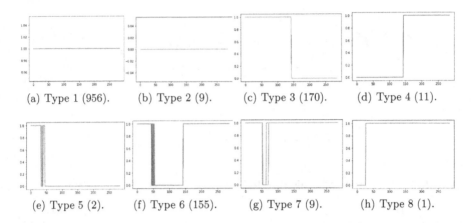

(a) Type 1 (956).   (b) Type 2 (9).   (c) Type 3 (170).   (d) Type 4 (11).

(e) Type 5 (2).   (f) Type 6 (155).   (g) Type 7 (9).   (h) Type 8 (1).

Fig. 6. Categories of co-located workload distribution. The first 143 abscissas indicate whether the online containers run on nodes, and the last 143 abscissas indicate whether the batch tasks run on nodes.

- **Type 5**: Batch tasks are running only during the first few hours of tracing, which is shown in Fig. 6 (e). There are just 2 nodes that belonging to **Type 5**, which including: *401, 689*.
- **Type 6**: The online containers and batch tasks are co-located on machines, but no batch tasks run during the latter few hours of tracing, which is shown in Fig. 6 (f). There are 150 nodes that belonging to **Type 6**, which including: *88–127, 275–296, 683, 723, 753–760, 830–850, 852–906, 965, 986, 993, 1079, 1096*.
- **Type 7**: The online containers and batch tasks are co-located on machines, but no batch tasks run during a short time of tracing, which is shown in Fig. 6 (g). There are 9 nodes that belonging to **Type 7**, which including: *619–626, 794*.
- **Type 8**: The online containers and batch tasks are co-located on machines, but no batch tasks run during the first few hours of tracing, which is shown in Fig. 6 (h). There is only one machine *618* that belonging to **Type 8**.

From the 8 *workload distribution categories*, we see that the co-located workload distribution is unbalance. And the co-located workload distribution is different, which leads to the difference in resource utilization on nodes.

On the other hand, we calculate the average cosine similarity of all nodes for each type. In the experiment, we also choose the 3 dimensions Cpu_{m,I_x}, Mem_{m,I_x} and $Disk_{m,I_x}$ to build the machine-resources matrix, which is used to calculate cosine similarity. Table 1 lists the average cosine similarities of all nodes for each workload distribution category, which shows that the resource utilization in the same workload distribution category is very similar.

Table 1. Average cosine similarity of all nodes for each workload distribution category.

m	Type 1	Type 2	Type 3	Type 4	Type 5	Type 6	Type 7
similarity	99.17%	99.19%	98.05%	98.23%	99.64%	98.98%	99.17%

3.2 Skew of Co-located Workload Resource Utilization

In the Alibaba cluster, online container services and batch jobs are deployed on most nodes. During different time periods, the resource requirement and utilization of online services and batch jobs vary. On these co-location nodes, we explore the impact of resource utilization distribution on abnormal nodes.

In order to describe the skew condition for the resource utilization of both workloads, we define resource utilization ratio according to Formula (2): Cpu_ratio is the ratio between the CPU usage of batch jobs and online containers, and Mem_ratio is ratio between the memory usage of batch jobs and online containers. That means, the larger the ratio is, the higher the resource utilization of batch jobs is; the lower the ratio is, the higher the resource utilization of the online containers is.

$$Cpu\_ratio_{m,I_x} = \frac{Cpu(bi)_{m,I_x}}{Cpu(ci)_{m,I_x}}$$

$$Mem\_ratio_{m,I_x} = \frac{Mem(bi)_{m,I_x}}{Mem(ci)_{m,I_x}} \tag{2}$$

We perform a statistical analysis of the Cpu_ratio and Mem_ratio ranges, and then plot the Fig. 7 that illustrates the histogram and cumulative distribution function (CDF) curve of different ratio ranges. In Fig. 7(a), 74.4% of Cpu_ratio is greater than 1, which means the batch tasks are CPU-intensive workloads with higher cpu utilization. And the Cpu_ratio in the range of (1, 2.8) accounts for 60.85%. In Fig. 7(b), 76.59% of Mem_ratio is less than 1, which means the memory occupied by the batch tasks is not high, and the online containers have higher memory requirements and utilization. And the Mem_ratio in the range of (0.1, 1.4] accounts for 89.88%. In addition, there are spikes on the range of (0,0.1] and (10,20], whose percentage is 10.38% and 0.64%.

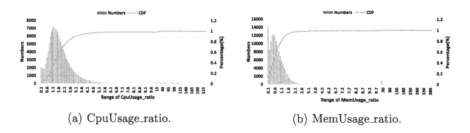

(a) CpuUsage_ratio.   (b) MemUsage_ratio.

Fig. 7. The histogram and cumulative distribution function (CDF) curve of different ratio ranges.

Furthermore, we define a skew threshold of resource utilization ratio, which is used to find the nodes with skew utilization. For instance, supposing we set the skew thresholds of resource utilization ratio as 0.3 and 3. Then for each machine, we count the number of resource utilization ratios Num_skew that are less than 0.3 and lager than 3. If a machine has more skew resource utilization ratios, the machine can be considered as an utilization-slanted node, which can be further concerned.

3.3   Failures

System Failures. Obviously, the system errors or failures is an obvious cause of an abnormal node. In the Alibaba trace, there are 7 machines have recorded 'softerror', which are shown in Table 2.

Table 2. The number of softerrors in machines.

m	372	401	618	689	731	930	1075
$Num(softerror)^a$	5	4	2	3	1	12	12

^{a} $Num(softerror)$ indicates the number of softerrors in machines.

And the timeline of softerrors on different machines is illustrated in Fig. 8. In computing systems, a softerror is a type of error where a signal or datum is wrong. The errors may be caused by a defect, usually understood either to be a mistake in design or construction, or a broken component. After observing a soft error, there is no implication that the system is any less reliable than before. However, frequent softerrors generally indicate some faults in systems. For instance, there are frequent softerrors on the machine *930, 1075* and *372*, which have no running workloads. And a few machines has occurred the softerrors at a certain time, such as the machine *689* has softerror at the timestamp of 50623 s, 52005 s and 52219 s, and so on.

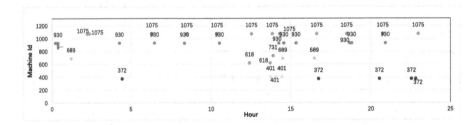

Fig. 8. The softerror machine.

Failed Instances. The file *batch_instance.csv* record the status of each batch instance, which includes *Failed, Interrupted, Ready, Running, Terminated*, and *Waiting*. And the status of *Failed* indicates an instance does not run successfully. We illustrate the failed instances number of nodes in Fig. 9, and we see that there are several spikes on the curve, which means several nodes have more failed instances.

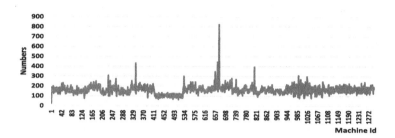

Fig. 9. The failed instance number of machines.

We also give the top 10 nodes that have the most failed instances in Table 3. In the co-located cluster, we find that the machine 679 has the most failed batch instances, and the average value of failed instances number is about 161. That is, the batch instance failed on a node is common, and the Fuxi JobMaster can process these failures based on its fault tolerance mechanism [2]. However, if there are a lot of failed batch instances on a node, which means some states of this node may be not suitable for batch tasks. Meanwhile, these nodes with large number of failed instances are likely to be abnormal nodes, which needs to be concerned. Actually, in the job level, JobMaster will estimate the machine health based on the worker statuses as well as the failure information collected by FuxiAgent. In particular, if one instance is reported failed on a machine, the machine will be added into the instance's blacklist. If a machine is marked as bad machine by a certain number of instances, this machine will be added into task's blacklist and no longer be used by this tasks.

Table 3. The top 10 machines that have the most failed instances.

m	679	680	673	341	823	664	232	1006	536	1040
$Num(FIns)^a$	823	471	444	433	392	347	307	306	299	297

[a] $Num(FIns)$ indicates the number of failed batch instances in machines.

3.4 Abnormal Cases Study

We have calculate the anomaly scores of all machines by utilizing iForest algorithm. By sorting all anomaly scores in descending order, we selected the top 25 abnormal nodes in Table 4, and analyze the possible anomalies causes of these nodes. And we can conclude that:

(1) Unbalanced co-located workload distribution has a great impact on the resource utilization of cluster nodes, which leads to abnormal nodes. Among the top 25 abnormal nodes, except for three nodes that belonging to **Type 1**, other nodes have imbalance in co-located workload distribution. And the top 8 nodes and the 10th node belong to **Type 2**, which have no running workloads. So in order to maintain the stability and balance of cluster

Table 4. The top 25 abnormal nodes.

Top	m	Anomaly score	Categories	Unbalanced workload distribution	Skew co-workload utilization	Softerrors	Failed instances
1	930	−0.1709	Type 2	No workloads		Frequent softerrors	0
2	602	−0.1709	Type 2	No workloads			0
3	1075	−0.1527	Type 2	No workloads		Frequent softerrors	0
4	550	−0.1525	Type 2	No workloads			0
5	372	−0.1524	Type 2	No workloads		Frequent softerrors	0
6	478	−0.1522	Type 2	No workloads			0
7	983	−0.1508	Type 2	No workloads			0
8	924	−0.1506	Type 2	No workloads			0
9	676	−0.1451	Type 1		Heavier online services		289
10	481	−0.1428	Type 2	No workload			0
11	679	−0.1395	Type 1		Heavier online services		823
12	851	−0.1223	Type 4	No batch jobs			0
13	673	−0.1198	Type 1		Heavier online services		444
14	993	−0.1105	Type 6	Unbalanced batch tasks			101
15	618	−0.0928	Type 8	Unbalanced batch tasks		Softerrors	166
16	556	−0.0833	Type 4	No batch jobs			0
17	689	−0.0827	Type 5	Unbalanced workloads		Softerrors	155
18	401	−0.0826	Type 5	Unbalanced workloads		Softerrors	140
19	275	−0.07879	Type 6	Unbalanced batch tasks			115
20	763	−0.0774	Type 4	No batch jobs			0
21	149	−0.0724	Type 3	No online services			177
22	1039	−0.0720	Type 1		Lighter online services		117
23	800	−0.0662	Type 4	No batch jobs			0
24	1069	−0.0646	Type 4	No batch jobs			0
25	949	−0.0629	Type 4	No batch jobs			0

resource utilization, different workloads should be distributed more evenly to each node.

(2) Skew co-located workload resource utilization also results in several abnormal nodes. For instance, there are four nodes that are belonging to **Type 1**. And the machine *673*, *676* and *679* have heavier online services (high memory usage), for the number of online container instances are 17, 19 and 18, respectively; the machine *1039* has a skew on the batch tasks and online container number, for the average number of batch tasks is 71, while the number of online container is 1.

(3) Frequent system failures have a large impact on system status. By checking the top 25 anomaly nodes, there are 6 nodes have occurred softerrors. Frequent softerrors result in machines becoming unavailable, such as the machine *930*, *1075* and *372*, with no running jobs. Due to the softerror at a certain time, the machines may have exceptions, which can affect the scheduling and execution of jobs. For example, there are no online services running on the machine *689* and *401*, and the batch tasks are running only during the first few hours of tracing. By checking the machine status, the machine *689* has softerror at the timestamp of 50623 s, 52005 s and 52219 s, and there is no running batch tasks from 50400 s; the machine *401* has softerror at the timestamp of 49854 s, 50018 s, 51325 s and 51515 s, and there is no running batch tasks from 49800 s, too. The reason may be that, cluster management system is unable to continue scheduling and executing new jobs on these machines due to system failures.

Summary. In Alibaba's co-located workload cluster, unreasonable scheduling and workload imbalance are the main causes of anomalies, which should be focused on.

4   Related Work

In 2011, Google open-sourced the publicly available cluster trace data [9], which is a 29-day trace of over 25 million tasks across 12,500 heterogeneous machines. And there are several works on analyzing Google trace from different perspectives [10–13]. Different from the Google trace, the Alibaba trace that was released in 2017, which contains information about the co-located container and batch workloads. Lu et al. [3] performed characterization of the Alibaba trace to reveal the imbalance phenomena in clouds, such as spatial imbalance, temporal imbalance, imbalanced resource demands and utilization. Cheng et al. [4] focused on providing a unique and microscopic view about how the co-located workloads interact and impact each other. Liu et al. [5] revealed that the resource allocation of the Alibaba semi-containerized co-location cluster achieves high elasticity and plasticity. Our study focuses on a unique view about anomalies and causes in co-located workloads cluster.

5 Conclusion

Based on the preprocessed Alibaba co-located workloads dataset, we conducted in-depth analysis from the aspects of workload characteristics and anomalies. Our analysis reveals several insights that the performance discrepancy of machines in Alibaba's production cluster is relatively large, for the distribution and resource utilization of co-located workloads are not balanced. For example, the resource utilization (especially memory utilization) of batch jobs is fluctuating and not as stable as that of online containers, and the reason is that the online containers are long-running jobs with more memory-demanding and most batch jobs are short jobs. Meanwhile, based on the distribution of co-located workload instance numbers, the machines can be classified into 8 workload distribution categories. And most patterns of machine resource utilization curves are similar in the same workload distribution category. We also use the iForest algorithm to detect abnormal nodes, and find that the there are three causes that lead to anomalies: (1) unbalanced co-located workload distribution4; (2) skew co-located workload resource utilization; (3) failures. And in the Alibaba's co-located workload clusters, the collaboration between online service scheduler (Sigma) and batch jobs scheduler (Fuxi) should be focused on.

References

1. Maximizing CPU resource utilization on alibaba's servers (2018). https://102.alibaba.com/detail/?id=61
2. Zhang, Z., Li, C., Tao, Y., Yang, R., Tang, H., Xu, J.: Fuxi: a fault-tolerant resource management and job scheduling system at internet scale. In: Proceedings of the VLDB Endowment (2014)
3. Lu, C., Ye, K., Xu, G., Xu, C., Bai, T.: Imbalance in the cloud: an analysis on alibaba cluster trace. In: IEEE International Conference on Big Data (Big Data) (2017)
4. Cheng, Y., Chai, Z., Anwar, A.: Characterizing co-located datacenter workloads: an alibaba case study. https://arxiv.org/abs/1808.02919 (2018)
5. Liu, Q., Yu, Z.: The elasticity and plasticity in semi-containerized co-locating cloud workload: a view from alibaba trace. In: Proceedings of ACM Symposium on Cloud Computing (SOCC) (2018)
6. Alibaba trace (2017). https://github.com/alibaba/clusterdata
7. Liu, F.T., Ting, K.M., Zhou, Z.H.: Isolation forests. In: Proceedings of International Conference on Data Mining (2008)
8. Wikipedia. k-means clustering (2018). https://en.wikipedia.org/wiki/K-means_clustering
9. Google cluster workload traces. https://github.com/google/cluster-data
10. Reiss, C., Tumanov, A., Ganger, G.R., Katz, R.H., Kozuch, M.A.: Heterogeneity and dynamicity of clouds at scale: Google trace analysis. In: The Third ACM Symposium on Cloud Computing(SoCC) (2012)
11. Zhang, Q., Hellerstein, J.L., Boutaba, R.: Characterizing task usage shapes in google compute clusters. In: Large Scale Distributed Systems and Middleware Workshop(LADIS) (2011)

12. Liu, Z., Cho, S.: Characterizing machines and workloads on a google cluster. In: 41st International Conference on Parallel Processing Workshops (2012)
13. Di, S., Kondo, D., Cirne, W.: Characterization and comparison of cloud versus grid workloads. In: IEEE International Conference on Cluster Computing(CLUSTER) (2012)

Performance Analysis and Workload Generator

SSH-Backed API Performance Case Study

Anagha Jamthe[1(✉)], Mike Packard[1], Joe Stubbs[1], Gilbert Curbelo III[2], Roseline Shapi[3], and Elias Chalhoub[1]

[1] Texas Advanced Computing Center, Austin, TX, USA
{ajamthe,mpackard,jstubbs,echalhoub}@tacc.utexas.edu
[2] California State University of Monterey Bay, Marina, CA, USA
gcurbelo@csumb.edu
[3] Mississippi Valley State University, Itta Bena, MS, USA
rshapi@usapglobal.org

Abstract. We establish that SSH is a viable transport mechanism for API access to HPC resources. In this paper, we study the performance and scalability properties of SSH using various SSH libraries (Python, Java, Linux command line client). We consider SSH daemon configuration changes that improve the API scalability significantly. We observe that, for the memory and CPU resources available on the test machines, our SSH-based API performs sufficiently well until a certain threshold of requests per second (RPS). At 90 RPS, 99% of the requests finish in less than two seconds. At 50 RPS, almost 90% of the requests finish in one second, which shows that the API is responsive enough under these loads. However, as the number of concurrent requests increases past 100, we see a gradual increase in time to complete requests. We perform load tests for the SSH API by sending bursts of concurrent connections and continued sustained connections over time and observe an acceptable responsiveness from the remote systems in both cases. With this study we conclude that SSH performance is sufficient for API access to computational HPC resources.

Keywords: Application Programming Interface (API) · High Performance Computing (HPC) · High Throughput Computing (HTC) · J2SSH Maverick · Paramiko · ssh2-python · Locust · Jetstream

1 Introduction

HPC computing and storage resources are increasingly being accessed via web interfaces and HTTP APIs as opposed to direct command-line interface. All cloud providers, including: Amazon AWS [1], Google Cloud Platform [2], and Microsoft Azure [3], provide such services. At the Texas Advanced Computing Center (TACC), Tapis Cloud APIs [4,5] currently enable 14 different official

W. Gao et al. (Eds.): Bench 2019, LNCS 12093, pp. 295–305, 2020.
https://doi.org/10.1007/978-3-030-49556-5_27

projects (a total of nearly 20,000 total registered client applications) to manage data, run jobs on the HPC and HTC systems, and track provenance and metadata for computational experiments. When jobs are run on HPC machines, hundreds of files are needed to be transferred between storage and execution systems for staging input data and archiving output data. The underlying APIs that perform these asynchronous file transfers through SFTP are expected to securely transfer files without significant delays. In order to understand and potentially improve performance and scalability of the Tapis Files management APIs, we study performance of SSH as a protocol.

SSH (also referred to as Secure Shell) is well-known as the most secure method of authenticating and encrypting access to remote Linux systems via command line. It is a secure alternative to insecure file transfers with FTP. In this paper, we investigate whether SSH is also viable as a transport layer for simultaneous API requests to similar systems. We discuss two methods used to evaluate the API performance. First, we identify the bottlenecks with respect to memory, CPU, and I/O when a burst of simultaneous SSH connection requests are initiated by the clients. We study how tuning the SSH daemon configuration parameters can improve successful concurrent connections to the remote system. Secondly, we seek to understand the performance of our existing files management APIs and ways to optimize it for remote access to HPC resources.

In this study, we also compare the performance of various available SSHv2 implementations in Python and Java, such as Paramiko [6] and ssh2-python [7], J2SSH Maverick [8] and the Linux command line client. We then select the most suitable implementation for our SSH API design. To evaluate the performance, we calculate the total time to connect to the HPC system and execute different commands (I/O and non-I/O based), for example, "ls" command, which is primarily used for listing files with the Tapis files management API. We perform load test for our APIs by simulating realistic work loads using Locust [9], a load testing tool. Locust can simulate a multi-user API access scenario with thousands of active users, which is similar to existing Tapis files management API usage.

The rest of this paper is organized as follows. In Sect. 2 we discuss the related work and motivation behind this case study. In Sect. 3 we provide background details on the general API performance expectations, introduction to Tapis Files Management API, and survey on available SSHv2 libraries. In Sect. 4, we describe the SSH backed APIs case study design. We discuss the proposed design and experimental setup such as the VM (Virtual Machine) configurations, comparison of different SSH libraries, SSH API framework, and load test setup. Finally, we conclude this paper with our research findings and discuss the scope of extending this study.

2   Related Work

In the realm of high speed bulk data transfers and file management, solutions such as GridFTP from Globus [10], glogin [11], BBCP [12], LFTP [13],

Cyberduck [14], scp [15], rsync [16] and Kerberos kFTP [18], exist. The choice of data transfer tools highly depends on the frequency of transfers and transfer time. For example, manual scp and rsync are more suitable for 1-time transfers [17], whereas with tools like GridFTP and BBCP, faster data transfers are achievable by doing multi-stream transfers [17]. Most of these transfer tools however have some limitations in terms of their cost and configuration complexity. Our study, on the other hand, leverages SSH directly, to securely login to remote host and leverages SFTP to transfer files, which involves minimal installation, and is easy to maintain. To the best of our knowledge, none of the prior studies evaluate the performance and scalability of SSH for multiple concurrent connections to the HPC resources, which makes this study one of a kind and important. With this case study we intend to build our next generation File Management APIs, which can provide high performance and scalability for accessing the HPC resources.

3   Background

3.1   General API Performance Expectations

Domain scientists and researchers work with distributed HPC systems to run their high performance computing jobs. They need to access data, which might be distributed across several systems present at different geographical locations. These users mostly use command-line utilities and APIs, and expect them to be responsive enough to view the job output and transfer files without significant delays. Interactive command line users are accustomed to system responsiveness fluctuating due to load on a shared system. It is not uncommon to have hundreds of individual users interactively logged in to a login node of a HPC system for accessing their resources.

With API access, it can be less obvious that one is using a shared system, so users may have an elevated expectation of responsiveness. In general, average responsive times for APIs vary substantially, but our anecdotal experience suggests that average response times exceeding one or two seconds can lead to a perception that the API is "slow". Leading cloud providers, such as Amazon and Google have described a similar phenomenon for web page load times, where above one or two seconds, the user experience is significantly impacted [19].

API quality can be determined from a combination of critical factors such as performance/responsiveness, availability/uptime and correctness. An API contract explicitly covers all the related implementation details and what to expect when the caller calls a function. However, the performance and correctness contract are always implicit and success of any software that uses the API largely depends on whether these expectations are met. Since remote calls over SSH are combined with other usage on the system, responsiveness is also affected by system load. SSH overhead usually represents a fractional amount of this delay. Often, API users benefit from being behind some sort of asynchronous queuing system (e.g. RabbitMQ [20]) that returns a response to the user before actually finishing the command. This can mitigate the responsiveness issue for end users.

3.2   Tapis Files Management APIs

Tapis [4] is an open source, NSF funded Application Programming Interface for hybrid cloud computing, data management, and reproducible science. Tapis leverages standards-compliant, open source technologies and community promoted best practices to enable users to manage data, execute research software, and share results with collaborators and colleagues. Tapis has been in production as the middleware that currently supports a number of community science gateways. It is a multi-tenant, cloud-native distributed system. All services within the platform run as Docker containers, orchestrated as a set of microservices. The Tapis files management APIs, which is one of the core services, allows management of data across multiple types of storage systems such as Linux, cloud (a bucket on S3), and iRODS. It supports traditional file operations such as directory listing, renaming, copying, deleting, and upload/download that are traditional to most file services. It also supports importing files from arbitrary locations, metadata assignment, and a full access control layer allowing to keep the data private, shared, or made publicly available. To fulfill the above operations, the current Tapis Files management API uses the J2SSH Maverick library's SSHv2 implementation.

3.3   SSH Libraries

Th choice of SSH library during API design can have a significant impact on the overall API performance, specifically for handling burst of concurrent requests. For these reasons, we evaluate different SSH implementations in this study and choose the most suitable library for SSH API development. Some of the available SSHv2 implementations in Java and Python are listed below:

- J2SSH Maverick is a complete Java implementation of the SSH2 client. We conduct performance benchmark studies using this library as it is an integral part of existing Tapis files management service.
- Paramiko is a Python implementation of SSHv2 protocol. It has been widely used in automation applications such as Ansible [23].
- ssh2-python is a new SSH library written in Python which is based on the libssh2 C library. Based on prior research, ssh2-python shows improved performance in session authentication and initialization. It is almost 17 times faster than Paramiko in performing heavy SFTP reads [24].

4   SSH API Case Study

With the distributed nature of HPC computing, there is a pressing demand for developing highly responsive file management APIs, with performance expectations that can efficiently support several concurrent users. The aim of this case study is to investigate how to develop such APIs by answering research questions below:

4.1   Research Questions

- RQ1: Is SSH a viable transport mechanism for API access to HPC resources?
- RQ2: Can we improve the performance and scalability of APIs to support multiple concurrent users by studying SSH as a protocol?

4.2   Research Design

It is not uncommon to have several concurrent users accessing the HPC resources with the Tapis files management APIs. Several web portals and CLI users access the shared HPC resources concurrently and expect the APIs to be responsive. In order to determine whether we can design a SSH backed API that meets the performance and responsiveness expectations, we need to demonstrate the feasibility of using SSH as a transport mechanism. In this study, we propose to evaluate the performance of parallel SSH connections to remote systems using bursts of simultaneous connections and continuous sustained connections over time. Benchmarking the SSH API performance by simulating multi-user request loads is a critical part of this case study. In order to demonstrate the improvements in handling concurrent SSH requests at the server, we conduct tests by modifying the default values of MaxStartUps and MaxSessions in the sshd_config file on the server. We measure the number of successful SSH connections established when a burst of concurrent requests are made by the clients during each test run. This data best describes the number of concurrent user requests that can be handled successfully at a given time for a given load. Similarly, by measuring the performance metrics "time to connect" and "time to execute commands", for commands such as "ls" and "uptime", on the remote system during a burst of simultaneous connections and continuous sustained connections over time, we can determine if SSH APIs are responsive. In the following sections, we describe the experimental setup and proof of concept SSH API framework and summarize our findings for the research questions above.

4.3   Experimental Setup

For the proposed experiments we set up three virtual machines and evaluate SSH API performance under different loads.

VM Configurations. Tests are launched from a single client VMWare virtual machine–referred to as *SSHClient*–with 2 CPU cores and 8GB of memory running CentOS 7.6 Linux. Each test then connects to one of two different server virtual machines; one of them is a VMWare virtual machine–referred to as *Taco* here–which has 2 CPU cores and 2 GB of memory, running CentOS 7.6 Linux. The other one is a Jetstream [21] Openstack virtual machine–referred to as *Jetstream* here–which has 2 CPU cores and 4 GB memory, running CentOS 7.5 Linux operating system. We selected these VMs because they are relatively small in size and represent what a developer might readily have access to. We used VMWare because it is TACC's standard VM deployment system, and Jetstream because it has a different network, IO, and hardware configuration.

Load Test Setup. In order to conduct load tests on our API, Locust, an open source load testing tool, is used to "swarm" the API and simulate concurrent multi-user requests. To set up Locust, we create a configuration file that defines the task of a simulated user, and what information to POST to the API. Other configurations includes setting wait times and sending information. Along with this, Locust provides a graphical interface where we could launch and see different request/response information such as minimum/maximum/average/median response times to connect to the server and run the commands.

Selecting SSH Library Implementation. As discussed, the choice of SSH library implementation for the API design affects API performance. We run benchmark tests to evaluate the API performance using two SSHv2 implementations: J2SSH and ssh2-python. We measure the total time to connect and run commands on both the VMs–"Taco" and "Jetstream"–from "SSHClient". On a successful connection, either "uptime" or "ls" (directory listing containing 10,000 files) is run and total response time is measured. The total time measured for 10, 100, and 500 concurrent requests provides a baseline for selecting SSH library implementation. From multiple test runs, almost seven times faster response times are seen with ssh2-python library on both Taco and Jetstream, executing the "uptime" command as compared to J2SSH implementation. Similarly, a ten to twelve times faster response is seen on both VMs, executing "ls" command on a successful connection with ssh2-python. Based on these evaluations, ssh2-python seems to be an appropriate choice for our prototype SSH API design.

4.4   SSH API Framework

We developed an SSH API using Python's Flask library. This study serves as a proof of concept to evaluate if SSH can be used as a viable transport mechanism for file management APIs to access HPC resources. With this API, users can securely connect to remote HPC resources and execute commands on the server. To make use of the API, a user first makes a one-time API call to save their sever connection credentials, including credential name, host name, user name, and an encrypted private key. These data get stored in a MySQL database for later use. Once credentials have been saved, the user can use the other API endpoints to execute different commands on the server. Table 1 describes the various SSH API endpoints and methods allowed. We note that the API in its current form is unauthenticated; as a part of future development, we are working on adding authentication via JSON Web Tokens (JWT) [25]. The API would use a JWT included in the request to verify that the API call is coming from an authorized user.

This API provides an abstraction for accessing the remote HPC resources without having to use the command line interface. Most importantly, the SSH API is vital in testing the reliability of the SSH daemon server's ability to handle multiple requests at once. Using the load testing tool Locust [9], we simulate realistic multi-user requests.

Table 1. SSH API endpoints

Name	GET	POST	Endpoint	Description
Home Page	X	-	sshapi/v2/	App Welcome Page
Credentials	X	X	sshapi/v2	Manage Credentials
Commands	-	X	sshapi/v2/[cred_name]	Run command via credential
Load test	-	X	sshapi/v2/load	Load test

4.5 Findings

In this section we present our findings for RQ1 and RQ2 and discuss how answering these questions helps us in developing a prototype for SSH-backed files management APIs, using ssh2-python library.

RQ1: With Locust, which is a distributed load testing tool, we test how many concurrent users, the SSH API is capable of handling. We simulate a multi-user API access scenario, where burst of SSH connection requests are made to each of the remote servers: "Taco" and "Jetstream" with the SSH API. The user behavior and task sets are defined in the locustfile.py. Locust spawns one instance of the Locust class for each simulated user. The user task calls the commands API enpoint, which connects to the remote host with the credential name defined in the POST request. Once a successful connection is established the command specified in the same POST request is executed. The min and max wait attribute values defined in the locustfile.py determine how much time the user will wait between each API call. In our test setup we have defined a single user task of calling the SSH API. Figure 1 shows the load test results obtained. The X axis shows the percentile of successful connections, whereas the Y axis shows the response time measured in milliseconds.

We observe that, for the memory and CPU resources available on the test machines, our SSH-based API performs sufficiently well until a certain threshold of requests per second (RPS). In fact, we expect that available server memory, not SSH, is the first limiting factor up to a certain threshold of requests per second (RPS). At 90 RPS, 99% of the requests finish in less than two seconds. At 50 RPS, almost 90% of the requests finish in one second, which shows that the API is responsive enough under these loads. For the most part, as the number of requests per second increased from 10 to 90, we saw a gradual increase in response time. The 60 RPS trial was the outlier, where performance was in fact worse than in the 90 RPS trial. Understanding this outlier will be part of a future study. Considering the existing loads that our current file management system API handles, we believe that being able to handle 90 RPS in less than two seconds is more than acceptable.

Figure 2 shows the average response times in seconds for both VMs, Taco and Jetstream, using the ssh2-python implementation. For each trial, total time to connect and run one of the commands, "uptime" or "ls", for directory size of 10,000 files, is computed. Performing a directory listing is one the most common use cases of the Tapis files management API and is therefore necessary to benchmark its performance. For these tests, we have created a nested directory structure, which includes 10,000 files to simulate the files listing call with heavy load. The average response time is computed for a set of 10 trials for each 10, 100 and 500 RPS. Similar average response times are observed on both Taco and Jetstream, when "uptime' and "ls" commands are executed at 10 RPS. At 100 and 500 RPS, a gradual increase in the average response time is seen for both the VMs, running either of the commands. However, the average response time does not vary much, when compared on both systems for 100RPS or less. We propose to study the variability of measurements (as defined, for example, in [26]), which can further explain the overall API stability as a part of our future study. With this study, we can conclude that SSH is viable transport mechanism for API access to HPC resources and can be integral part of our next generation Files management API design.

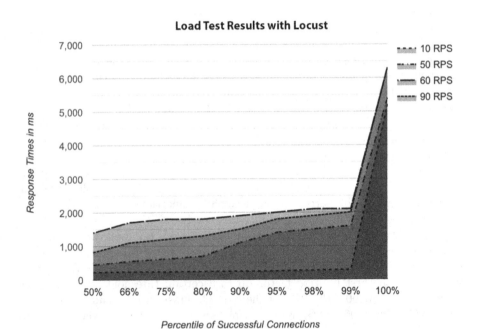

Fig. 1. Load test results for SSH API

RQ2: In order to answer our second research question, we study whether modifications to SSH daemon configuration at the server improves the scalability of the API, thereby allowing larger numbers of simultaneous connections. We made the following settings changes in the sshd_config file at both the servers:

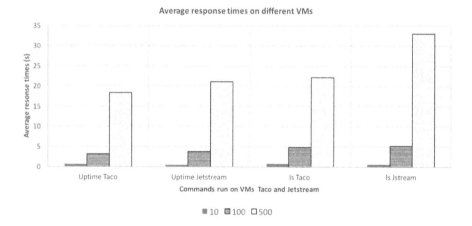

Fig. 2. SSH average response times with SSH2-Python

- MaxStartups: Specifies the maximum number of concurrent unauthenticated connections to the SSH daemon. Default is `10:30:100`, we used `3000:30:3000`, where:
  - 3000 is the number of unauthenticated connections before we start dropping
  - 30 is the percentage chance of dropping once we reach 3000 (increases linearly for more than 3000)
  - 3000 is the maximum number of connections at which we start dropping everything

  and
- MaxSessions: Specifies the maximum number of open shell, login, or subsystem (e.g. SFTP) sessions permitted per network connection. Default is `10`; we used `3000`.

With these settings, we were able to successfully connect to the server with even higher concurrent request rates. Therefore, by making these changes we were able to improve the overall scalability of the SSH APIs.

5 Conclusions

In this case study, we proposed to design a SSH-backed API towards answering two research questions: can SSH be used as a viable transport mechanism for API access to HPC resources, and can SSH performance and scalability be improved tweaking the SSH daemon parameters at the server. We tested SSH load performance in two ways: using bursts of simultaneous connections, and continuous sustained connections over time. In both cases, we observed an acceptable responsiveness from different Linux systems. This demonstrates that, in addition to its other advantages, SSH performance is sufficient for API access to HPC resources. With this study, we conclude that ssh2-python can potentially be used for our next generation Files Management API implementation.

6   Future Work

In the near future, we plan to expand the number of destination hosts to test against more diverse system configurations. We also plan to evaluate the possibility of modifying client behavior so that the server does not require sshd_config modifications. This could be done by pooling connections or taking advantage of other optimizations. We also plan to study the variability of measurements which will determine the overall performance of the SSH API for various HPC systems.

Acknowledgments. This work was made possible by grant funding from National Science Foundation award numbers ACI-1547611 and OAC-1931439. We thank the staff of TACC and Jetstream for providing resources and support.

References

1. Amazon AWS. https://aws.amazon.com
2. Google Cloud. https://cloud.google.com
3. Microsoft Azure. https://azure.microsoft.com/en-us/
4. Tapis Cloud API. https://tacc-cloud.readthedocs.io/projects/agave/en/latest/
5. Stubbs, J., et al.: Tapis: an API platform for distributed computational research. Futur. Gener. Comput. Syst. (2020)
6. Forcier, J: Paramiko: A Python Implementation of SSHv2 (2019). http://www.paramiko.org/
7. Pkittenis, ssh2-python (2019). https://github.com/ParallelSSH/ssh2-python
8. Pernavas, R.: J2SSH API. http://freshmeat.net/projects/sshtools-j2ssh
9. Locust. https://locust.io
10. Allcock, W., Bester, J., et al.: Secure, efficient data transport and replica management for high-performance data- intensive computing. In: Proceedings of the IEEE Mass Storage Conference, pp. 13–28, April 2001
11. Rosmanith, H., Kranzlmuller, D.: glogin - a multifunctional, interactive tunnel into the grid. In: Fifth IEEE/ACM International Workshop on Grid Computing (GRID 2004), pp. 266–272 (2004)
12. BBCP. https://github.com/slaclab/bbcp
13. LFTP. https://lftp.yar.ru
14. Cyberduck. https://cyberduck.io
15. SCP. https://linux.die.net/man/1/scp
16. Rsync. https://linux.die.net/man/1/rsync
17. Data transfer basics and best practises. https://princetonuniversity.github.io/PUbootcamp/sessions/data-transfer-basics/PUBootCamp_20181031_DataTransfer.pdf
18. Kohl, J., Neuman, C.: The kerberos network authentication service (V5). Request for Comments (Proposed Standard) RFC 1510, Internet Engineering Task Force, (Web site: www.ietf.org)
19. Einav Y., Amazon Found Every 100ms of Latency Cost them 1% in sales https://www.gigaspaces.com/blog/amazon-found-every-100ms-of-latency-cost-them-1-in-sales/
20. RabbitMQ. https://www.rabbitmq.com

21. Stewart, C.A., et al.: Jetstream: a self-provisioned, scalable science and engineering cloud environment. In: Proceedings of the 2015 XSEDE Conference: Scientific Advancements Enabled by Enhanced Cyberinfrastructure, 2792774, pp. 1–8. ACM, St. Louis (2015). https://doi.org/10.1145/2792745.2792774
22. Towns, J., et al.: XSEDE: accelerating scientific discovery. Comput. Sci. Eng. **16**(5), 62–74 (2014). https://doi.org/10.1109/MCSE.2014.80
23. Ansible. https://github.com/ansible
24. SSH2 Python Comparison with Paramiko. https://parallel-ssh.org/post/ssh2-python/
25. Json Web Tokens. https://jwt.io
26. Jain, R.: The Art of Computer Systems Performance Analysis: Techniques for Experimental Design Design, Measurement, Simulation and Modeling. Wiley, New York (1991)

NTP: A Neural Net Topology Profiler

Pravin Chandran$^{(\boxtimes)}$, Raghavendra Bhat, Juby Jose, Viswanath Dibbur, and Prakash Sirra Ajith

Intel Technology India Pvt. Ltd., Bangalore, India
{pravin.chandran,raghavendra.bhat,juby.jose}@intel.com,
vdibbur@gmail.com, ajithprakash77@gmail.com

Abstract. Performance of end-to-end neural networks on a given hardware platform is a function of its compute and memory signature, which in-turn, is governed by a wide range of parameters such as topology size, primitives used, framework used, batching strategy, latency requirements, precision etc. Current benchmarking tools suffer from limitations such as a) being either too granular like DeepBench [1] (or) b) mandate a working implementation that is either framework specific or hardware-architecture specific or both (or) c) provide only high level benchmark metrics. In this paper, we present NTP (Neural Net Topology Profiler), a sophisticated benchmarking framework, to effectively identify memory and compute signature of an end-to-end topology on multiple hardware architectures, without the need for an actual implementation. NTP is tightly integrated with hardware specific benchmarking tools to enable exhaustive data collection and analysis. Using NTP, a deep learning researcher can quickly establish baselines needed to understand performance of an end-to-end neural network topology and make high level architectural decisions. Further, integration of NTP with frameworks like Tensorflow allows for performance comparison along several vectors like a) Comparison of different frameworks on a given hardware b) Comparison of different hardware using a given framework c) Comparison across different heterogeneous hardware configurations for given framework etc. These capabilities empower a researcher to effortlessly make architectural decisions needed for achieving optimized performance on any hardware platform. The paper documents the architectural approach of NTP and demonstrates the capabilities of the tool by benchmarking Mozilla Deep-Speech, a popular Speech Recognition topology.

Keywords: Neural networks · Topology · Benchmark tools · openVINO

1 Introduction

Deep Neural Networks are ubiquitous in their deployment to address challenges in Vision and Speech. Neural networks are an area of increased research and development investment with novel end-to-end architectures being developed

© Springer Nature Switzerland AG 2020
W. Gao et al. (Eds.): Bench 2019, LNCS 12093, pp. 306–318, 2020.
https://doi.org/10.1007/978-3-030-49556-5_28

and deployed across several industry domains. Recently, several organizations are beginning to adapt a 'continuous modeling methodology' where the models are continuously tuned for performance in production environment through an automated-modeling infrastructure. Though there are several frameworks available to build neural net topologies, sophisticated tools to benchmark end-to-end topologies and offer insights for tuning are not available. NTP is an end-to-end benchmarking tool which addresses this gap by enabling detailed benchmarking to understand the compute and memory signature of complete neural network topology. NTP can be used to understand compute requirements for a topology as well as to identify compute hotspots, memory bottlenecks etc through run time data flow analysis.

Neural network deployments typically have two phases a) Training and b) Inference. A model is developed in training phase and is deployed for use in inference phase. The usual approach to benchmarking is to select a framework, implement a topology, optimize for accuracy and finally benchmark for performance. Topology optimizations and benchmarking is performed multiple times to arrive at an acceptable architecture. Inference is performed after an acceptable model is developed. Inference stage optimizations like pruning, quantization etc. normally requires additional retraining. Overall, a time consuming effort.

Training is typically done in compute farms with access to high performance compute hardware. Inference however is mostly done on platforms which can promise real-time performance, at low cost and power, which often requires inference specific benchmarking and optimizations. NTP addresses these challenges by enabling a researcher to quickly check the performance impact with different configurations like layer sizing, quantization, pruning etc. NTP is currently targeted to address the benchmarking requirements in Inference phase. However, there is no conceptual limitation in the tool preventing its usage in training phase. In addition to compute and memory benchmarking, the tool also allows its users to determine performance metrics like latency, queries per second etc.

Several frameworks exists for building neural networks like TensorFlow [2], Caffe [3], MXNet [4], PyTorch [5], and OpenVINO [6], to name a few. Currently NTP supports TensorFlow, PyTorch, and Intel OpenVINO as underlying framework and allows workloads to run across different hardware platforms like Intel x86 CPU, NVidia GPU, Intel Movidius, Intel GPU and Intel FPGA. NTP however does not support integration with hardware simulation platforms.

NTP allows users to easily construct complex neural-networks as workloads and interface with compatible benchmarking tools for metrics collection. Compute, memory and network bottlenecks are easily analyzed to enable effective decision making towards optimizing a topology for best performance.

2   Survey of Current Profiling Tools

A survey of current profiling tools is presented in this section. Compared to NTP, all these tools lack in more than one area like: a) Lack of ease of model creation b) Limited support for end-to-end profiling c) High effort pre-requisites like availability of framework/hardware specific implementations d) Lack of support for collecting detailed benchmark metrics e) Lack of support for performance comparison across different target hardware f) Lack of support for performance comparison across different frameworks for a given neural network etc.

Certain frameworks like TensorFlow [2] provide native support for layer-wise execution-time profiling, but lacks support for extracting detailed benchmark metrics and performance insights. DeepBench [1] is targeted to benchmark neural network libraries (kernels) across different hardware. DeepBench profiles common operations for throughput and latency at kernel-level. While kernel-level benchmarks help determine which hardware gives best performance for a chosen kernel, they cannot fully comprehend topology level bottlenecks especially the data movement cost and hence lack capability to help facilitate topology tuning. Tools like DAWNBench [7] and its successor MLPerf [8] support end-to-end topology benchmarking for actual implementations of selected ML problems and provides metrics like training and inference cost. Tools like DLInfBench [9] allows benchmarking of speed and peak memory across frameworks. Again, support is limited to a set of pre-selected topologies as with earlier tools (Table 1).

Table 1. Comparison of benchmark tools.

Tools	Hierarchy	Topology creation	Metrics
DeepBench	Kernel	No	Execution time
MLPerf	Topology	No	Training/Inference cost
DLInfBench	Topology	No	Execution Time/Memory
NTProfiler	Topology	Yes	Refer to Table 2

Several of these surveyed tools provide a high-level score for a topology with-respect-to training and/or inference. Though high level scoring enables one to compare different topologies and rank them, it does not provide insights into critical bottlenecks that led to observed performance. Also, to initiate benchmark for a new topology in these tools, the topology needs to be first created in the selected framework and supplied to the benchmark tool which is a resource intensive task. NTP has the advantage of accepting topology definition in a simple, framework-and-hardware agnostic, format and use it across all frameworks and hardware platforms. The focus of NTP is to provide an exhaustive set of benchmark metrics to help with analysis, identification and resolution of topology and hardware bottlenecks.

NTP addresses the listed deficiencies by: a) Providing a simple markup language based interface for defining neural network topologies. b) Allowing framework selection through simple command line argument. c) Simulating the topology on selected hardware platform including hetero-hardware platforms and d) Generating detailed benchmark reports for analysis. The implementation details of NTP is presented in the following section.

3   NTP Overview

NTP is an Intel proprietary tool that takes definition of an end-to-end neural network as input, optionally builds the topology corresponding to the definition on the chosen framework and executes the topology by passing data in configured precision through the entire topology. During the execution, NTP collects information on hardware specific performance counters using configured benchmarking tools. NTP leverages the collection capabilities of supported bench tools to observe and summarize performance metrics. Also additional metrics like throughput is collected to provide detailed insights into parameters that deteriorate performance (Fig. 1).

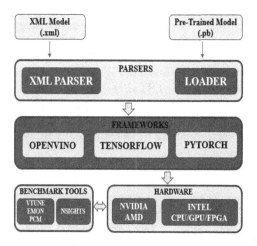

Fig. 1. Overview of Neural Net Topology Profiler

A brief description of NTP flow is provided in this section. Overview of NTP architecture is shown in Fig. 2. To support a wide range of topologies, NTP supports

1. Topologies defined in open formats like ONNX or framework-native formats like TensorFlow pb.
2. Topologies defined using Markup language definition in proprietary XML format.

When pre-trained model is provided, the Model Loader directly reads it and passes it to relevant framework. When XML format is used, NTP automatically builds framework specific model and passes the same to the chosen framework. The XML parser handles the XML processing and generates a neural network graph corresponding to the topology description. The Parser module extracts each tag in the input XML file to obtain attributes of different layers and to identify benchmarking markers. A framework independent internal graph is built by NTP which is then converted to a framework specific model. The execution is done in the context of chosen framework and NTP relies on capabilities of the chosen framework for execution.

The parser for TensorFlow models, for instance, supports 40 commonly used TensorFlow layers and additional layers can be easily added to handle new topologies containing such layers. Parser stage results in a framework specific model, irrespective of whether the architecture was specified in XML format or provided as pre-trained model.

3.1 Topology Definition

Practical neural networks will have several neural network layers combined together to address a specific problem. Networks will also contain non-neural network functions like MFCC calculation for pre-processing, beam decoders for post-processing, memcopy, format conversions etc. NTP allows these functions also be included as inlays for a realistic end-to-end performance benchmark. Example of a simple topology is shown in Fig. 2. Each layer contains one or more primitives (Ex: Prim1) like CNN, LSTM etc and inlay functions. NTP provides flexibility to benchmark the entire topology or specify layers-of-interest. For targeted benchmarking, layers-of-interest can be set using start and end 'markers'. A snippet of the xml corresponding to DeepSpeech is provided in Fig. 3B under Sect. 4.

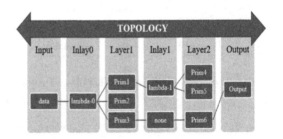

Fig. 2. Graphical description of sample neural net topology. Non-neural network layers are included as Inlays along with NN primitives to allow end-to-end benchmarking.

3.2 Benchmark Tools and Metrics

NTP is integrated with a set of benchmarking tools and appropriate tool is chosen based on hardware on which profiling is done. Choice of benchmark tool is also made through marker update in the XML. Currently, tools like VTune, Amplifier etc. offered as part of Intel Parallel Studio, NVidia NSight and command line tools like PCM, EMON etc. are supported. Users can configure and select a specific benchmark tool to be used to determine memory and compute signature of the workload. NTP relies on the ability of selected benchmarking tool to support features like Start, Stop, Pause and Resume for targeted metrics collection. For instance, if VTune Amplifier is used, the tool issues interrupt requests at specific intervals and collects Interrupt Service Routine (ISR) records like process ID, thread ID, instruction pointer, memory resources allocated and released etc. Later, information is summarized and mapped to neural network operations in a post-processing step. Markers allow for easy collection of benchmark metrics for individual layer or layer groups, independent of capabilities of the framework. The lowest hierarchy level that can be chosen for analysis is kernel level or higher. For instance, in case of topologies with fused kernels, the tool will not be able to provide a breakdown of operations inside the fused-kernel.

The list of metrics supported by Intel Benchmark tool for CPU hardware is listed in Table 2. NTP automates all the tasks related to benchmarking and generates analysis reports to facilitate quantification of topologies across applicable vectors like layers, topology, frameworks and hardware etc.

Table 2. Benchmark Metrics supported by NTP

Options	Description
CPU	CPU Utilization
DRAM	DRAM Bound, Latency
Cache	L1/L2/L3 Bound
Interface	Bandwidth Utilization
Roofline Analysis	CPU/Memory Utilization
Hotspots	Routines with high CPU usages
Vectorization	Advisory on vectorization

3.3   Framework and Hardware Support

NTP facilitates topology benchmarking on popular frameworks running on a wide range of hardware platforms without the need for framework/hardware specific implementation. For instance, when framework chosen is TensorFlow, it leverages TensorFlow's native hardware support for executing a topology on CPU and NVidia GPU.

It is also integrated with Intel OpenVINO framework and can fully leverage heterogeneous compute capability of the framework by accepting pre-trained models from frameworks like TensorFlow. OpenVINO currently supports Intel CPU, GPU, GNA, Intel Movidius, FPGA etc. For hardware like Movidius, the support is extended to use a resource-pool of movidius sticks for further acceleration. OpenVINO accepts pre-trained models from popular frameworks like TensorFlow®, Caffe® etc. and can perform additional optimization like constants folding, quantization, layer fusion etc to improve overall performance. In hetero-mode, a workload will allow users to leverage multiple hardware accelerators to meet performance/cost/latency targets. Based on user intent and hardware-support for the constituent kernels, the workload will be automatically partitioned into different subgraphs and each subgraph will be run on its chosen hardware. In addition to eliminating the effort needed to implement a workload for different hardware platforms, OpenVINO also enables NTP to support optimal utilization of available hardware resources.

Ease of model creation, control over benchmark layers, support for inlays, access to a wealth of benchmark metrics, and support for multiple hardware platforms etc. facilitate users to build, analyze, compare and in-turn optimize neural net topologies in a quick and efficient manner. The capabilities described so far will be demonstrated using a case-study in the following section.

4   UseCase: Mozilla DeepSpeech

This section demonstrates NTP capabilities as applied to an Automated Speech Recognition workload: Mozilla Deep Speech [10]. As a general disclaimer, the comparison plots presented in this paper are illustrative to demonstrate NTP tool capabilities. This should not be taken as absolute numbers for respective comparisons. DeepSpeech is a character level speech-to-text model that takes Mel Frequency Cepstral Coefficients (MFCC's) extracted from speech utterance as input and generates textual transcription. The topology (Fig. 3A) has few fully connected layers (FC), bi-directional LSTM (BI-LSTM) and a final CTC beam search decoder for removing duplicate characters.

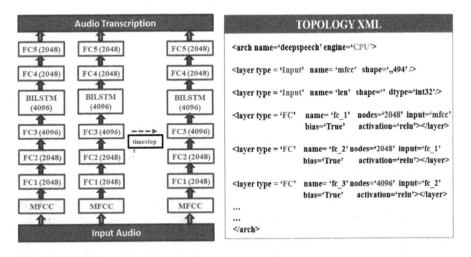

Fig. 3. A. Mozilla DeepSpeech topology B. NTP-XML snippet depicting syntax for initial set of layers

A snippet of input XML for initial few layers of DeepSpeech is presented in Fig. 3B. Layer name is used to uniquely identify layer and connect different layers to create the topology graph. Topology optimization would simply need updates to the XML. As discussed earlier, the choice of XML is primarily to allow users to quickly define a neural network topology and simulate it without the need for framework/hardware specific implementations. The ease of model creation allows for fast iteration over multiple configurations to compare and contrast the hardware implications

From Fig. 3B, it can be seen that several topology parameters like layer type, number of nodes for a given layer etc. are all easily specified and updated through the xml. In addition, batching information, data precision, hardware engine, benchmark tool are also accepted as user arguments. Since NTP is a topology exploration and optimization tool, it also supports a topology to executed for performance benchmarking even before actual training. This is done by building a topology model and supplying random weights and biases to the constituent layers. For inputs, synthetic dataset in required format (dimension, batch size, precision, range) is generated and fed to the model. Empirical tests have been run on all topologies discussed in this paper to validate that the performance reported by NTP is well aligned with the performance observed from framework-specific implementations of the topology. For cases where pre-trained model is available, layer weights and biases from the model is directly used.

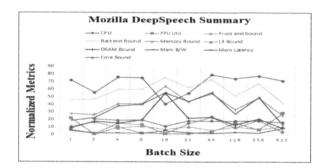

Fig. 4. DeepSpeech metrics summary

Due to tight integration with Intel benchmarking tool-suite for CPU profiling, NTP can provide both high level summary as well as facilitate deep dive into details-of-interest. High level summary of different benchmark metrics for DeepSpeech topology is plotted in Fig. 4. Depending on kernel-type, kernel-dimensions, input dimensions, memory requirements, cache status etc., each layer runs with a unique execution signature. This is captured and summarized by the tool while data flows through the architecture. Using this information, a tool user can easily a) Optimize the topology to better run the available hardware and/or b) Understand the hardware requirements for a topology and make effective decisions to configure the same.

A set of benchmark metrics for different batch sizes is shown in Fig. 4. The co-relation between various metrics and their combined impact on performance can be deduced from such a view. For instance, CPU utilization drops when DRAM bottleneck increases around batch size of 16 which is where the hardware stops offering real-time performance. DRAM utilization increases due to memory hungry nature of BI-LSTM layer as will be described in following sections. As a consequence of this observation, optimization of the BI-LSTM was done leading to a performance boost of close to 6X.

4.1 Layer Comparison

Execution times of individual layers of the topology can be summarized and compared using layer-wise comparison feature of NTP as shown in Fig. 5A.

LayerWise Runtime Profile (% of total)		
LAYER	RunTime	PeakMemory
FC1	1.0 %	25MB
FC2	0.3 %	25MB
FC3	0.5 %	50MB
BI-LSTM	97.5 %	200MB
FC4	0.4 %	25MB
FC5	0.1 %	25MB
MISC	0.2 %	50MB
TOTAL	100%	200MB

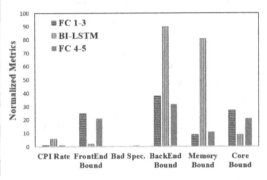

Fig. 5. A. Mozilla DeepSpeech benchmark B. Layerwise benchmark metrics

From above figure, BI-LSTM layer contributes to majority of the runtime and as well as memory consumption. FC layers of this topology do not heavily depend on cache or external memory. However BI-LSTM pulls most of its data/weights from external memory and significantly slows down overall execution.

In-depth analysis of layers can be done using NTP's targeted benchmarking capabilities. To demonstrate this, the topology was bench-marked as three segments. (Segment1: FC1-3 = FC1 + FC2 + FC3, Segment2: BI-LSTM, Segment3: FC4-5 = FC4 + FC5). From the benchmark data in Fig. 5B, it can be seen that the FC-Layers are Front-End/Core bound while the BI-LSTM is Backend/Memory bound translating to large runtimes.

4.2 Topology Comparison

To quantify the performance impact of parameters like layer sizing, precision etc, relevant parameters can be easily updated in the XML and resultant topologies compared across critical performance metrics. For illustration, DeepSpeech topology [10] was used as reference and two other variants of the topology were generated by changing node counts as shown in Table 3. As described in earlier sections, changes are required only in the input XML, which enables topology modification and hence analysis at an accelerated pace.

Table 3. Topology comparison: Three variants of DeepSpeech topology is shown to demonstrate topology comparisons during hyper-parameter tuning.

Layer	Topology1	Topology2	Topology3
FC1	256	256	2048
FC2	256	256	2048
FC3	256	256	4096
BILSTM	256	4096	4096
FC4	256	256	2048
FC5	29	29	29

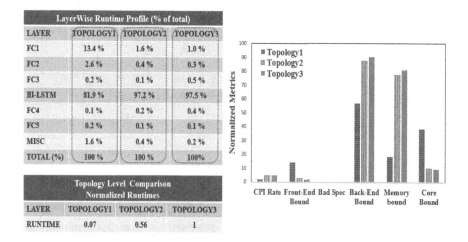

Fig. 6. Topology comparison using NTP A. Runtime comparison B. Benchmark metrics comparison

Percentage run-time contribution from different layers for execution on CPU is shown in Fig. 6A. For topology-1, majority of the time (81.9 %) is spent in execution of the BI-LSTM layer. The percentage tends to increase further to 97% if the number of LSTM nodes increases (Topology2, Topology3). Several benchmark metrics can be used to compare topology designs as illustrated in Fig. 6B. It can be seen that the topologies are all Memory/Backend bound. In addition to being memory intensive, BI-LSTM layer cannot be parallelized to the same level as other primitives like CNN. Utilization drops with increase in threads for BI-LSTM layer due to even higher memory contention leading to further reduction in CPU utilization. As a result, topology would not benefit significantly from multi-threading either. This memory hungry nature of BI-LSTM seems to be the key performance bottleneck for this topology. And the topology will yield better performance on hardware with better memory capacity and bandwidth.

4.3 Hardware Comparison

Comparison of a topology across different hardware is demonstrated in this section. FPGA's are massively parallel and have lot of on-chip memory and bandwidth when compared across several hardware classes and can be a hardware choice for this topology. To offload execution to a supported accelerator, the choice of hardware alone needs to be updated in NTP run. A comparison of deepspeech runtime signatures on CPU vs FPGA is shown in Fig. 7A below, In addition to significant speedup, LSTM contribution to the total runtime also shows some reduction signifying efficiency. In Heterogeneous hardware mode (HETERO), the BI-LSTM layer is executed on FPGA and remaining layers on CPU. Data at interface of LSTM layer is much larger in size compared to primary input/output of the topology and this results in slightly lower performance compared to pure FPGA run.

LayerWise Runtime Profile (% of total)			
LAYER	CPU	FPGA	HETERO
FC1	1.0 %	1.0 %	19.6 %
FC2	0.3 %	1.3 %	5.9 %
FC3	0.5 %	2.5 %	9.7 %
BI-LSTM	97.5 %	90.2 %	28.6 %
FC4	0.4 %	2.2 %	7.2 %
FC5	0.1 %	2.6 %	1.5 %
MISC	0.2 %	0.2 %	27.5 %
TOTAL	100%	100%	100 %

LayerWise Runtime Profile (% of total)		
LAYER	TENSORFLOW	OPENVINO
FC1	1.0 %	0.5%
FC2	0.3 %	0.3%
FC3	0.5 %	12.4%
BI-LSTM	97.5 %	85.5%
FC4	0.4 %	0.4%
FC5	0.1 %	0.1%
MISC	0.2 %	0.8%
TOTAL (%)	100%	100%

Topology Level Comparison Normalized Runtimes			
LAYER	CPU	FPGA	HETERO
RUNTIME	159.6	1	3.2

Topology Level Comparison Normalized Runtimes		
LAYER	TENSORFLOW	OPENVINO
RUNTIME	3.32	1

Fig. 7. A. Hardware runtime comparison B. Framework runtime comparison

4.4 Framework Comparison

Comparison of performance across frameworks is also commonly performed by hardware platform providers, as well as, framework developers to ensure that the framework chosen is well optimized for given hardware. NTP allows users to seamlessly switch between supported frameworks. A comparison between execution times for DeepSpeech topology on TensorFlow vs OpenVINO is shown in Fig. 7B. Deployment teams can also benefit from any potential improvements that are framework specific. OpenVINO is Inference-only framework and hence is significantly light-weight compared to TensorFlow. Further it performs inference specific optimizations on topologies like layer-fusion leading to improvement in observed performance.

5   Other Observations

Several other topologies have been tested using NTP to demonstrate the scalability of NTP to a broad set of topologies. Current list of topologies tested include a) DeepSpeech b) Resnet50 c) GNMT etc. Several kernels were exercised across these topologies including, Fully Connected layer, LSTM, Convolution Layer, Activation Layer (Sigmoid, Tanh, Relu) in addition to basic operations (Add, Multiply, Slice, Concatenate) etc.

In Resnet50, for example, OpenVINO's model optimizations resulted in 30% reduction of layers as batch-normalization layers were fused with convolution layers which translated to significant performance improvement compared to native execution on Tensorflow. CPUs and GPUs have been observed to perform poorly compared to FPGA's for bandwidth dominated topologies. However as NTP depends on underlying benchmarking tools to provide detailed metrics, lack of support for some metrics in certain hardware will result in insufficient coverage for hardware like FPGA. As described in earlier sections, current deployments have different training and inference environment due to difference in performance, memory, power, bandwidth, latency requirements of the hardware used for these tasks. Topology level analysis helps with identification of optimal configuration for inference hardware, in-addition to architectural insights for topology optimization. By enabling fast diagnosis of performance/memory bottlenecks with least efforts, NTP aims to help researchers arrive at right set of model parameters and/or hardware configurations at faster pace compared to traditional methods.

6   Conclusion

We have presented a topology profiling tool in this paper to help holistically address challenges associated with neural net model development, profiling and tuning. The tool allows for accurate estimation of performance bottlenecks and facilitates quick iterations to optimize the network. We believe this would significantly accelerate the model development, optimization and deployment process for neural network inference. In future, this analysis data can be fed directly into an 'continuous modeling' environment for targeted tuning. Also the tool can be plugged to a Design of Experiments (DoE) setup to automatically determine best configuration for running heterogeneous-compute workloads.

References

1. DeepBench, Baidu. https://github.com/baidu-research/DeepBench
2. Abadi, M., et al.: TensorFlow: large-scale machine learning on heterogeneous systems. Software available from tensorflow.org (2015). https://www.tensorflow.org
3. Yangqing, J., et al.: Caffe: convolutional architecture for fast feature embedding. arXiv:1408.5093 (2014). https://caffe.berkeleyvision.org
4. Chen, T., et al.: MXNet: a flexible and efficient machine learning library for heterogeneous distributed systems. arXiv:1512.01274. https://mxnet.apache.org/
5. Paszke, A., et al.: Automatic differentiation in PyTorch (2017). https://pytorch.org/
6. OpenVINO, Intel Corporation. https://github.com/opencv/dldt
7. Coleman, C., et al.: DAWNBench: An End-to-End Deep Learning Benchmark and Competition, NIPS ML Systems Workshop (2017). https://github.com/stanford-futuredata/dawn-bench-entries
8. MLPerf, MLPerf Benchmark Suite. https://mlperf.org/
9. DLInfBench. https://github.com/nicklhy/DLInfBench
10. Hannun, A., et al.: Deep speech: scaling up end-to-end speech recognition (2014). arXiv:1412.5567

MCC: A Predictable and Scalable Massive Client Load Generator

Wenqing Wu[1,2], Xiao Feng[1,2], Wenli Zhang[1], and Mingyu Chen[1,2,3(✉)]

[1] State Key Laboratory of Computer Architecture, Institute of Computing Technology, Chinese Academy of Science, Beijing, China
{wuwenqing,fengxiao,zhangwl,cmy}@ict.ac.cn
[2] University of Chinese Academy of Sciences, Beijing, China
[3] Peng Cheng Laboratory, Shenzhen, China

Abstract. The network load generators are widely used by network researchers to analyze link bandwidth, evaluate network performance and test device capabilities. Data center and IoT networks are quickly evolving and we desire to get a load generator that can precisely generate flow-level workload with high-throughput. Often researchers choose software-based generators because of their flexibility and open-source nature. However, despite the emerging of different solutions, existing software-based flow-level generators have difficulty in generating millions of concurrent TCP connections or achieving one-microsecond precision of packet inter departure time (IDT) which can undermine the correctness of experiments.

In this paper, we present a new network load generator, called Massive Client Connections (MCC). MCC is a client load generator which means it performs flow-level load simulation. We separate the control plane from the data plane and design a two-stage timer mechanism to get higher precision. To take full advantage of multicore processors, we utilize the shared-nothing multi-threaded model. Our evaluation demonstrates that MCC generates network load conforming to expected distribution with one-microsecond precision. Moreover, MCC shows definite scalability of throughput in multicore systems. And it is capable of generating more than three million concurrent TCP connections with ten CPU cores.

Keywords: Network load generator · Predictability · Scalability

1 Introduction

During the process of testing and developing new network elements, such as equipment, protocols, applications regarding both the production and research area, researchers and practitioners rely on the load generator to inject a vast number of packets into a network in a controlled way [15]. It is vital to predict the behavior of the computer network and how it will run in realistic scenarios. In this paper, we concentrate on simulating the network load in data center and

© Springer Nature Switzerland AG 2020
W. Gao et al. (Eds.): Bench 2019, LNCS 12093, pp. 319–331, 2020.
https://doi.org/10.1007/978-3-030-49556-5_29

IoT network. This means we need a synthetic load generator that is capable of generating millions of concurrent network load with high precision [12].

When referring to a load generator, our first concern is the level of load simulation. Because of the reliability of TCP, interactions above layer 4 require a state machine maintained in the system. Hence a load generator is stateful if it acts as one or more TCP clients and evaluates the performance of the system under test. Otherwise, a load generator is stateless which can only evaluate limited metrics, such as bandwidth and packet loss. According to the classification model in [17], load generators can be classified into the following three types according to the abstraction level.

- Packet-level load generators. They do not maintain TCP state machine but typically forge packets starting from layer 2 to upper layers. Generators such as MoonGen [14], pktgen [1], Pktgen-DPDK [4] fall into this category.
- Flow-level load generators. Generators of this category generate packets organized as flows. They are capable of simulating the client-server interaction that is closer to realistic TCP traffic.
- Application-level load generators. They simulate the behavior of a specific application layer network such as HTTP protocol. Siege [9], Surge and wrk [5] fall into this category.

Table 1. Existing load generators

Category	Generators	Stateful	Advantages	Limitations
Hardware-based	Sprient [7]	No	Precise, High speed	Expensive (>$100,000)
	OSNT [16]	No	Precise, High speed	Expensive (>$2,000)
	BRUNO [10]	No	High throughput	Limited usage scenarios
Software-based	MoonGen	No	High throughput	Only layer 2 support
	Iperf [8]	Yes	Cross-platform	No concurrency support
	D-ITG [11]	No	Scalable	Millisecond precision
	Surge	Yes	Layer 7 support	Low throughput
	wrk	Yes	Flexible, scriptable	Poor Scalability

To simulate workload in data center and IoT scenarios, we need a stateful network load generator. Both flow-level load generators and some TCP-based application-level load generators are stateful according to the explanation above. Table 1 summarizes the advantages and limitations of the state-of-the-art load generators. Hardware-based load generators require commodity hardware to run. Usually, this category of generators brings better performance. And they are typically more precise. However, they are expensive because of FPGA design and associated hardware. And few of them achieve stateful load generation. Most of the time, researchers prefer software-based generators, not only for economic reasons but mainly for their flexibility. For example, they can be easily modified and extended for specific research purposes [17]. MCC is also a software-based solution. It is developed for three explicit goals:

- Generating million-scale concurrent TCP connections.
- Sending packets with one-microsecond precision.
- Scaling in multicore systems.

In this paper, we make three key contributions. Firstly, we separate the control plane from the data plane in the load generation process. Secondly, we propose a two-stage timer mechanism to obtain a higher precision of IDT. Compared to the traditional application layer timing method, the error of the two-stage timer mechanism has dropped below $1\,\mu s$ and the K-L divergence decreases by more than 90%. Thirdly, we design a shared-nothing multi-threaded model, making it possible for MCC to scale in multicore systems. According to experiments in Sect. 4, MCC provides about 3 times higher throughput than previous stateful solutions and shows almost linear scalability in multicore systems before reaching the line rate.

The remaining part of this paper is organized as follows. Section 2 introduces the background and motivation of our work. Section 3 describes the design and implementation details. Section 4 presents the evaluation results. Finally, Sect. 5 concludes this paper.

2   Background and Motivation

We first review the major limitations of existing generator implementations and proposed solutions. We then discuss our motivation towards a predictable and scalable network load generator.

2.1   Imprecise Packet Inter Departure Time

Existing flow-level load generators have difficulty in generating network load with microsecond precision. For it involves the correctness of the test system itself [17], the generator is supposed to bring load as expected by users. However, previous software-based solutions fail to simulate the flow-level network load precisely. To transmit packets, the conventional generators naturally apply the BSD socket API and timing functions provided by the Linux kernel. Which meets the convenience and portability, but also brings imprecision problems. In [18], Paredes et al. quantitatively point out that running applications with strict real-time requirements like load generator in Linux, which is designed for general purpose, will introduce large deviations.

According to related works, the problem results mainly for three reasons. First, the scheduling policies in the operating system will aggravate the precision of timing functions [18]. For example, commonly used sleep() does not provide a one-microsecond precision guarantee, especially when the operating system performs the frequent process or thread scheduling. Then POSIX blocking I/O interfaces are not suitable for time-sensitive occasions [19]. For instance, select() introduces at most $20\,\mu s$ error when dealing with timed I/O events. The third reason is that the stack in Linux kernel imposes non-negligible processing overhead [17]. Which poisons the precision of timing operations running in the application layer.

The essence of the imprecision problem is that the operating system itself tightly couples the packet generation in the control plane with the packet transmission in the data plane, while the flow control in Linux TCP only involves the transmission process in the data plane [14]. Thus, load generators based on Linux socket API inevitably introduces the overhead of performing control plane operation. This leads to the inconsistency between the actual packet transmission time and the expected time [20].

2.2 Ossified Load Generation Path

Performance is another challenge faced by software-based load generators. As mentioned before, most of the stateful load generators depend on the stack in the Linux kernel. Yet the heavy stack not only flaws the precision of IDT but results in the inefficiency of load generation process. Firstly, generators implemented with BSD socket API suffer the overhead of system call, that is, the program undergoes frequent user/kernel mode switching [22] when forging high-concurrent network load. Furthermore, the efficiency of load generators built with kernel's stack can be weakened by memory copy. In addition, the heavy stack is hard to modify and apply the new features. As a result, it is laborious to optimize the load generation path.

The use of a high-speed I/O framework such as the DPDK [6] helps to deal with the inefficiency problem. This model has inspired many new software-based load generator implementations. They obtain extremely high transmission rate and low latency at the expense of the ability to use the kernel's stack. For example, the Pktgen-DPDK which is the re-implementation of pktgen gets great improvement of throughput. However, due to the lack of stack, DPDK-based generators only support stateless load generation or simulation of simple TCP connections. Fortunately, there is a trend on moving the network stack up to the user level and bypassing the kernel recently. So we could make use of user-level TCP stack to generate stateful network load.

2.3 Poor Utilization of Multicore CPUs

Existing software-based load generators show poor utilization of multicore architecture [21]. It limits the performance increase of generators. multicore CPUs have been ubiquitous in data centers and even in mobile devices. Nevertheless, previous solutions have difficulty in gaining definite performance improvement in multicore systems. The experiment in [22] proves that ab [3] gets limited performance gains with the increase of CPU cores. Additionally, the network has kept up growing in size, complexity, and number of its users [15]. Massive network load is needed when researchers evaluate and optimize the performance of network products with the rapid development of the Internet. Good scalability in multicore systems will not only lead to the capability of massive load generation but also help to meet needs in different scenarios.

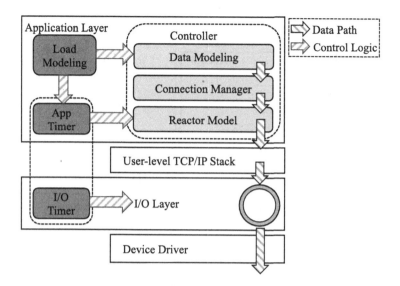

Fig. 1. Load generation model of MCC

Now, the motivation of our work is clear. Can we design a stateful load generator capable of generating connections with extremely high concurrency? How much of a performance improvement can we get if we build such a system? Can we get good scalability in multicore systems? Can we get a traffic model consistent with the input pattern? To answer these questions, we implement MCC, a predictable and scalable massive client load generator.

3   Design and Implementation

In this section, we first present the design of MCC's core components of load generation model. Next, we introduce MCC's user-space load generation path. Then we describe the two-stage timer mechanism. Finally, we explain how MCC scales in multicore systems by introducing our shared-nothing multi-threaded model.

Figure 1 shows the architecture of MCC's load generation model. The whole model consists of two parts indicated by arrows with different fillings. One is the data path. The other is the control logic. Load Modeling plays a role in modeling the distribution of traffic. The Controller consisting of three sub-modules controls the behavior of concurrent TCP connections. Data Modeling is the process of determining the payload of packets according to the result of Load modeling. For example, the data module fills the payload with HTTP header fields when carrying out HTTP benchmarking. The Connection Manager is responsible for managing TCP connections. To manage high-concurrent connections efficiently, we adopt Reactor non-blocking pattern here. Which is based on the epoll-like event framework provided by user-level stack. During the generation process,

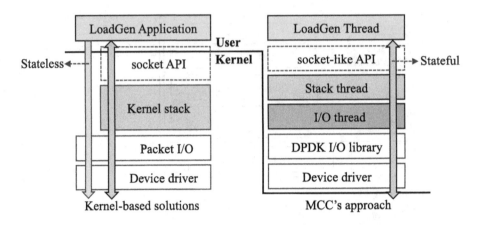

Fig. 2. Comparison of kernel-based solution and MCC

data is delivered to the TCP stack via the Reactor model. Then stack encapsulates data into a packet and submits it to the I/O layer. For the purpose of achieving one-microsecond IDT, we design a two-stage time mechanism to reach one-microsecond precision.

3.1   User-Space Load Generation Path

MCC runs completely in userspace so that we are able to optimize the full path of load generation expediently. Figure 2 presents the difference between MCC and kernel-based solutions. Stateless generators directly send Ethernet packets with the I/O library in layer 2. While stateful load generators rely on network stack to maintain the TCP state machine. Rather than using socket API provided by Linux kernel, MCC is built on top of user-level TCP stack powered by DPDK. As a result, all of the MCC's core components run in user space, including load generation, stack processing, and packet I/O. Which makes it possible for us to improve the efficiency of the whole load generation path. For example, to eliminate timing error caused by packet processing in TCP stack, we create a dedicated I/O thread at the end of the data path, which brings precise control of transmission operation.

3.2   Two-Stage Timer Mechanism

MCC achieves predictable network load generation with our proposed two-stage timer mechanism. As explained before, conventional stateful generators fail to transmit packet precisely with the single application layer timer offered by the operating system. MCC can achieve precise control of I/O operation. To do this, we layout two timers with different granularity in application and I/O layers respectively. Because of this, MCC is able to separate the control plane from the data plane and move the time-sensitive control logic to the end of

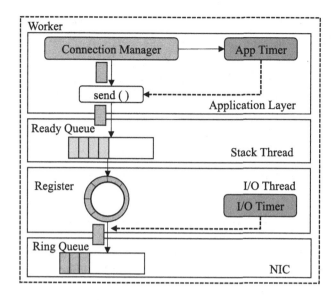

Fig. 3. Architecture of two-stage timer mechanism

the data path. As is shown in Fig. 3, the APP Timer controls the statistical properties of network load and the transmission behavior of flows on a one-second scale, such as the average bandwidth of the traffic within 10 seconds, or which TCP connections send data in the next second. The I/O Timer is a packet-level controller that adjusts the packet inter departure time (IDT) on a one-microsecond scale.

Application Layer Timer. To eliminate the overhead caused by CPU's scheduling strategy, we adopt an approach of polling to implement the application layer timer. As is shown in Fig. 4, the user adds events by calling user API (e.g. sched(time, func), where a 2-tuple (timestamp, function) represents a timed task). The Task Set is maintained with *multi_map* in C++ STL. The underlying implementation of *multi_map* is a red-black tree, which helps to reduce the overhead of inserting and deleting operations. The event loop checks if any events have timed out by comparing the timestamp of RB-tree's root with the current clock. The corresponding callback function will be executed if the timestamp of any task expires. In the actual experiment, the application layer timer supports I/O operations with a maximum precision of $10\,\mu s$ and non-I/O operations with $1\,\mu s$.

I/O Layer Timer. In order to eliminate timing error introduced by network stack, we add a novel I/O timer under the stack. As is shown in Fig. 3, we add an intermediate queue, called Register between stack's Ready Queue and NIC's Output Queue for the purpose of sending packets at the specified time. It is

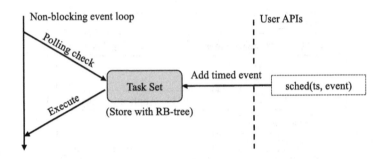

Fig. 4. Polling model of application layer timer

implemented with a lock-free queue for the sake of avoiding overhead caused by synchronization operations. When encapsulated, the pointer of the packet will be inserted into Register, then the I/O layer timer will send the packet to NIC according to the information such as IDT of given load pattern. To do this, we make a few changes to the code of user-level stack's I/O module. We create a dedicated thread under the TCP stack. The I/O thread itself runs in polling mode and continuously checks the clock in the system. If the preset timer has expired, a packet is taken from Register and sent out. In this controllable I/O model, the processing delay of the network stack is completely eliminated. The experiment in Sect. 4 showcases that this approach can bring the timing precision of up to $1\,\mu s$, which is quite close to the limit that software can achieve.

3.3   Shared-Nothing Multi-threaded Model

We design a shared-nothing multi-threaded model to take full advantage of the multicore processor. We apply quite many optimization technologies to maximize the scalability of MCC. As is shown in Fig. 5, Worker threads carry out basic load generation logic described before. Thanks to user-level stack, we are able to utilize shared-nothing data structures such as per-core listening queue and per-core file descriptors. To reduce context switching between threads, we bind each load generation thread and corresponding stack thread to a specific CPU core. To better manage Worker threads, we create a Distributor thread responsible for distributing tasks and gathering state information and statistics. We also make use of the advanced features of the hardware platform. For example, we turn to RSS [2] of modern network adapters, so that packets of the same flow will be directed to the same receive queue in NIC. And each queue is bound to a specific CPU core to cut down operations across different cores. These optimizations help to mitigate the overhead caused by context switching and avoid Cache pollution. Thus, MCC is capable of extending in multicore platforms without sacrificing precision.

Message Passing Model. We use the message passing model for the communication between the Distributor and Workers. The overhead introduced by

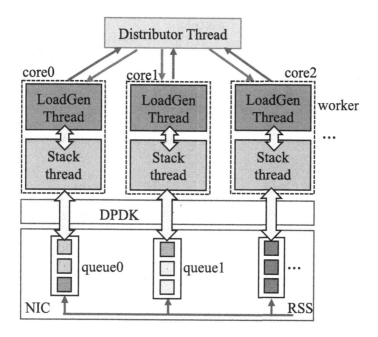

Fig. 5. Shared-nothing multi-threaded model

inter-thread communication is likely to aggravate the efficiency of load generators and even becomes a performance bottleneck, so it is necessary to minimize
the cost of inter-thread communication. We choose the message passing model
upon consideration. Compare with the method like shared-memory, the message
passing model discards the assumption that threads have a global memory view.
It views communication between threads from the perspective of distributed
systems. Therefore, synchronization primitives, such as lock, atomic operation,
and memory barrier are not needed. In addition, it is also easy to scale in the
multi-threaded model. Actually, two queues are set between the Distributor and
each Worker. One for distributing load generation tasks, see Task Queue in the
Fig. 6, the other for feeding back statistics and state information is called Result
queue. The operations in relation to the queues are encapsulated into "push"
and "pull" in MCC.

This section introduces the load generation model and the multi-threaded
design of MCC. Particularly, the two-stage timer mechanism is one of the most
important features. Which provides packet-level timing precision. The multi-
threaded model further expands the performance of MCC, thereby achieving
the goal of generating ultrahigh throughput network load.

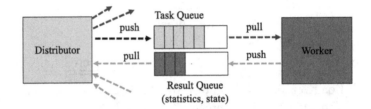

Fig. 6. Message passing model between Distributor and Workers

4   Evaluation

The goal of MCC is to generate massive network load obeying expected distribution and achieve performance scalability in multicore systems. In this section, we evaluate how well MCC meets these goals. We use a machine with one 12-core CPU (Intel(R) Xeon(R) CPU E5645 @ 2.40 GHz), 48G RAM, and an Intel 82599ES 10GbE NIC to run load generator as a client, and a same type of machine as a server.

4.1   Scaling in Multicore Architecture

As mentioned above, MCC is able to simulate the stateful network load. In this part, We compare MCC with wrk when acting as an HTTP benchmark tool. Considering wrk also supports multi-threaded model, we compare the throughput of MCC and wrk under the different number of CPU cores when they request a 64B HTML file. Two more CPU cores are used for I/O thread and Distributor in each experiment. The server side is an HTTP server built with user-level stack's BSD-like socket API. Figure 7 presents the result of requests per second (RPS). The performance of MCC scales almost linearly with the increase of the number of CPU cores before reaching the line rate. Furthermore, MCC provides about 3 times throughput that of wrk with the same number of cores in the actual experiment.

4.2   Precision of Different Timers

To verify the precision of MCC, we evaluate the influence of different timers when load generators simulate constant bit rate (CBR) traffic. We compare the effect of each timer by enabling different timers in each experiment. In fact, we measure the average packet inter departure time and calculate the standard deviation. The results are shown in Table 2, within which the "Linux" signifies that the load generation application is built on top of the Linux kernel stack. Naturally, Linux only provides application layer timers. Statistics in the table indicate that stack processing in Linux kernel introduces 20 μs timing error. It is about 3 μs for the user-level stack. According to the results, MCC is able to generate network load with one-microsecond precision thanks to the two-stage timer mechanism.

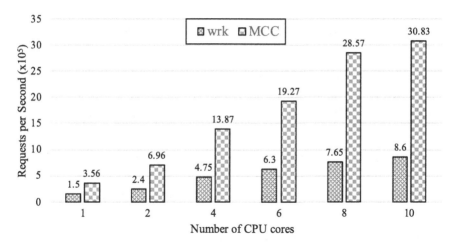

Fig. 7. Performance of generators as a function of CPU cores

Table 2. Precision of generators when simulating CBR traffic

	Timers	Set IDT	Average IDT	Standard deviation
Linux	sleep()	100 μs	201.93 μs	6.53
	App timer	100 μs	99.74 μs	0.63
	App timer	10 μs	33.83 μs	1.98
MCC	App timer	10 μs	9.52 μs	0.67
	App timer	1 μs	3.37 μs	0.24
	App timer+I/O timer	1 μs	1.03 μs	0.04

4.3 Predictable Load Generation

With the help of controllable network I/O, MCC is able to generate load corresponding to specific distributions. Some work on Internet load models declares that traffic distributions in both data center and wide area network (WAN) have self-similar characteristics [13]. The Poisson process can simulate this self-similarity in a shorter time scale. Therefore, our concern is how well MCC generates the Poisson distribution load in this part. We replicate an average packet rate of 100,000 packets per second, which is the Poisson process flow with an average IDT of 10 μs. Figure 8 shows that MCC can generate traffic quite close to the analytical Poisson distribution when enabling both App timer and IO timer.

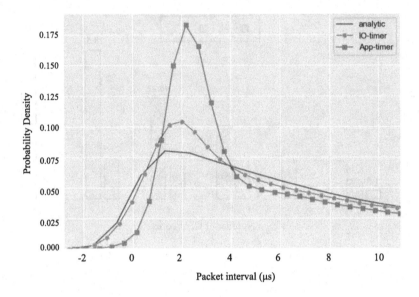

Fig. 8. Poisson load generation with timers in different layers

5   Conclusion

MCC is a predictable and scalable massive load generator designed for multi-core architecture. We highlight the imprecision of software-based stateful load generators which may influence the reliability of the test system. By introducing a two-stage timer mechanism, MCC is able to separate the control plane from the data plane and generate network load with one-microsecond precision. To generate network load with ultrahigh rate, MCC is built on top of the user-level stack and shows about 3 times throughput that of the kernel-based wrk. Finally, the shared-nothing multi-threaded model makes it possible for MCC to win good scalability in multicore systems.

MCC is open-source and can be found at https://github.com/acs-dcn/MCC. In the future, we will expand MCC to distributed systems to generate much more network load. In addition, we plan to perfect MCC to support more application layer protocols to meet more needs.

Acknowledgments. This work is supported by National Key Research and Development Plan of China No. 2017YFB1001602.

References

1. Pktgen. https://www.kernel.org/doc/Documentation/networking/pktgen.txt
2. RSS: Receive Side Scaling. https://docs.microsoft.com/en-us/windows-hardware/drivers/network/introduction-to-receive-side-scaling
3. ab: Apache Bench. http://httpd.apache.org/docs/2.4/programs/ab.html

4. Wiles, K.: Load generator powered by DPDK (Pktgen-DPDK) (2015)
5. wrk. https://github.com/wg/wrk/
6. Intel DPDK: Data Plane Development Kit. http://dpdk.org/
7. Sprient. https://www.spirent.com/Products/TestCenter/Platforms/Appliances
8. Iperf. https://github.com/esnet/iperf
9. Siege. https://www.joedog.org/siege-home/
10. Antichi, G., Di Pietro, A., Ficara, D., et al.: Bruno: a high performance traffic generator for network processor. In: 2008 International Symposium on Performance Evaluation of Computer and Telecommunication Systems, pp. 526–533. IEEE (2008). https://docs.microsoft.com/en-us/windows-hardware/drivers/network/introduction-to-receive-side-scaling
11. Avallone, S., Guadagno, S., Emma, D., Pescapè, A., et al.: D-ITG distributed internet load generator. In: Proceedings of the First International Conference on the Quantitative Evaluation of Systems, QEST 2004, pp. 316–317. IEEE, (2004)
12. Wette, P., Karl, H.: DCT2Gen: a traffic generator for data centers. Comput. Commun. **80**, 45–58 (2016)
13. Park, K., Willinger, W.: Sele-Similar Network Traffic and Performance Evaluation. Wiley, New York (2000)
14. Emmerich, P., Gallenmüller, S., Raumer, D., Wohlfart, F., et al.: MoonGen: a scriptable high-speed packet generator. In: Proceedings of the 2015 Internet Measurement Conference, pp. 275–287. ACM (2015)
15. Patil, A.G., Surve, A., Gupta, A.K.: Classification of UTGen synthetic load generator. In: 2016 Conference on Advances in Signal Processing (CASP), pp. 280–285. IEEE (2016)
16. Antichi, G., Shahbaz, M., Geng, Y., Zilberman, N., et al.: OSNT: open source network tester. IEEE Netw. **28**(5), 6–12 (2014)
17. Botta, A., Dainotti, A., Pescapé, A.: Do you trust your software-based load generator? IEEE Commun. Mag. **48**(9), 158–165 (2010)
18. Paredes-Farrera, M., Fleury, M., Ghanbari, M.: Precision and accuracy of load generators for packet-by-packet traffic analysis. In: 2nd International Conference on Testbeds and Research Infrastructures for the Development of Networks and Communities, TRIDENTCOM 2006, p. 6. IEEE (2006)
19. Primorac, M., Bugnion, E., Argyraki, K.: How to measure the killer microsecond. In: Proceedings of the Workshop on Kernel-Bypass Networks, pp. 37–42. ACM (2017)
20. Saeed, A., Dukkipati, N., Valancius, V., et al.: Carousel: scalable traffic shaping at end hosts. In: Proceedings of the Conference of the ACM Special Interest Group on Data Communication, pp. 404–417. ACM (2017)
21. Baumann, A., Barham, P., Dagand, P.E., Isaacs, R., et al.: The multikernel: a new OS architecture for scalable multicore systems. In: Proceedings of the ACM SIGOPS 22nd Symposium on Operating Systems Principles, pp. 29–44. ACM (2009)
22. Jeong, E.Y., Wood, S., Jamshed, M., Jeong, H., et al.: mTCP: a highly scalable user-level TCP stack for multicore systems. In: 11th USENIX Symposium on Networked Systems Design and Implementation (NSDI 2014), pp. 489–502 (2014)

Scientific Computing and Metrology

Apache Spark Streaming, Kafka and HarmonicIO: A Performance Benchmark and Architecture Comparison for Enterprise and Scientific Computing

Ben Blamey$^{(\boxtimes)}$ ⓘ, Andreas Hellander ⓘ, and Salman Toor ⓘ

Department of Information Technology, Division of Scientific Computing,
Uppsala University, Uppsala, Sweden
{Ben.Blamey,Andreas.Hellander,Salman.Toor}@it.uu.se

Abstract. Many scientific computing applications generate streams where message sizes exceed one megabyte, in contrast with smaller message sizes in enterprise contexts (order kilobytes, often XML or JSON). Furthermore, the processing cost of messages in scientific computing applications are usually an order of magnitude higher than in typical enterprise applications. Frameworks such as Apache Spark offer high throughput processing of streams with such 'enterprise' characteristics, as well as scalability, with high resilience and many other desirable features. Motivated by the development of near real-time image processing pipelines for roboticized microscopy, we evaluate the suitability of Apache Spark for streams more typical of scientific computing applications, those with large message sizes (up to 10 MB), and heavy per-message CPU load, under typical stream integrations. For comparison, we benchmark a P2P stream processing framework, *HarmonicIO*, developed in-house. Our study reveals a complex interplay of performance trade-offs, revealing the boundaries of good performance for each framework and integration over a wide domain of application loads. Based on these results, we suggest which are likely to offer good performance for a given load. Broadly, the advantages of Spark's rich features makes its performance sensitive to message size in particular, whereas the simplicity of HarmonicIO offers more robust performance, and better CPU utilization.

Keywords: Stream processing · Apache Spark · HarmonicIO · High-throughput microscopy · HPC · Benchmark · XaaS · HASTE

The HASTE Project (http://haste.research.it.uu.se/) is funded by the Swedish Foundation for Strategic Research (SSF) under award no. BD15-0008, and the eSSENCE strategic collaboration for eScience. Computational resources were provided by the Swedish National Infrastructure for Computing via the SNIC Science Cloud (SSC) [13], an OpenStack-based community cloud for Swedish academia.

W. Gao et al. (Eds.): Bench 2019, LNCS 12093, pp. 335–347, 2020.
https://doi.org/10.1007/978-3-030-49556-5_30

1   Introduction

Several stream processing frameworks have gained wide adoption over the last decade or so. Apache Flume is designed for the analysis of server application logs. Apache Spark improves upon the Apache Hadoop framework [1] for distributed computing, and was later extended with streaming support [18]. Apache Flink [5] was later developed primarily for stream processing. These frameworks boast excellent performance, scalability, data security, processing guarantees, and efficient, parallelized computation; together with high-level stream processing APIs (augmenting familiar map/reduce with stream-specific functionality such as windowing). These features are attractive for scientific computing – including imaging applications and simulations in the life-sciences.

Previous studies have shown that these frameworks are capable of processing message streams on the order of 1 million or more messages per second, but focus on enterprise use cases with textual rather than binary content, and of message size perhaps a few KB. Additionally, the computational cost of processing an individual message may be relatively small (e.g. parsing JSON, and applying some business logic). By contrast, in scientific computing domains messages can be much larger (order of several MB, in medical imaging and systems biology applications [4]). In other scientific computing applications, message sizes can be smaller [10].

Due to the different design priorities for streaming frameworks, a single benchmark will not be adequate to cover various features. However, an alternative approach is to use a standard use case to compare different frameworks. The presented study highlights the needs of scientific communities, importance of streaming frameworks for scientific workloads and the difference in the inherent nature of the scientific datasets as compared to the enterprise context.

We selected Apache Spark for this study because of its popularity, and to allow comparison to earlier studies. Its core *RDD* API [17] allows for deterministic re-computation in cases of error and node failure, various high-level APIs which make such details transparent to the application developer. Apache Spark can scale successfully to 1000 s of nodes [16]. Spark Streaming was a later addition, leveraging the batch functionality for a streaming context by creating a new batch every few seconds (the batch interval). As with batch operations, data is further subdivided into partitions for distribution and scheduling.

Our motivating use case is the development of a cloud pipeline for the processing of streams of microscopy images. Existing systems for working with such datasets have largely focused on offline processing: our online processing (processing the 'live' stream), is relatively novel in microscopy. Electron microscopes generate high-frequency streams of large, high-resolution image files (message sizes 1–10 MB), and feature extraction is computationally intensive. This is typical of many scientific computing use cases: where files have binary content, with execution time dominated by the per-message 'map' stage. Our pipeline consists of a single 'map' operator. Thereby, we investigate how well the performance of enterprise stream processing frameworks (such as Apache Spark) translates to loads more characteristic of scientific computing, for example, microscopy image stream processing, by benchmarking under a spectrum of conditions representative of both. We do this by varying both the processing cost of the map stage, and the message size to, expand on previous studies. For comparison, we measured the performance of HarmonicIO [14] – a research prototype with a which has a P2P-based architecture, under the same conditions. This paper contributes:

- A performance comparison of an enterprise grade framework (Apache Spark) for stream processing to a streaming framework tailored for scientific use cases (HarmonicIO).
- An analysis of these results, and comparison with theoretical bounds – relating the findings to the architectures of the framework when integrated with various streaming sources. We quantify performance under different application loads.
- Benchmarking tools for Apache Spark Streaming, with tunable message size and CPU load per message – to explore this domain as a continuum.
- Recommendations for choosing frameworks and their integration with stream sources, especially for atypical stream processing applications, highlighting some limitations of both frameworks especially for scientific computing use cases.

2   Background: Stream Processing of Images in the HASTE Project

High-throughput [15], and high-content imaging (HCI) experiments are highly automated experimental setups which are used to screen molecular libraries and assess the effects of compounds on cells using microscopy imaging. Work on smart cloud systems for prioritizing and organizing data from these experiments is our motivation for considering streaming applications where messages are relatively large binary objects (BLOBs) and where each processing task can be quite CPU intensive. In the HASTE project[1] – a collaboration between Uppsala University, Stockholm University, Vironova AB and AstraZeneca, we are investigating methodology for near real-time filtering and control of image streams from such HCI platforms.

Online analysis of the microscopy image stream allows both the quality of the images to analyzed (highlighting any issues with the equipment, sample preparation, etc.) as well as detection of characteristics (and changes) in the sample itself *during the experiment.* Industry setups for high-content imaging can produce 38 frames/second with image sizes on the order of 10 MB [8]. These image streams, like other scientific use cases, have different characteristics than many enterprise stream analytics applications: (a) messages are binary (not textual, JSON, XML, etc.), (b) messages are larger (order MBs, not bytes or KBs), and (c) the initial map phase can be computationally expensive, perhaps dominating execution time.

---

[1] http://haste.reserach.it.uu.se.

Our goal is to create a general pipeline able to process streams with these characteristics (and image streams in particular). Apache Spark Streaming (ASS) has many of the features needed to build such a platform, with rich APIs suitable for scientific applications, and proven performance for small messages with computationally light map tasks. However, it is not clear how well this performance translates to the regimes of interest to the HASTE project. This paper explores the performance of ASS for a wide range of application characteristics, and compares it to a research prototype streaming framework HarmonicIO.

3   Existing Benchmarking Studies

Several studies have investigated the performance of Spark, Flink and related platforms. However, these studies tend use small messages, with a focus on sorting, joining and other stream operations. Under an experimental setup modeling a typical enterprise stream processing pipeline [6], Flink and Storm were found to have considerably lower latencies than Spark (owing to its micro-batching implementation), whilst Spark's throughput was significantly higher. The input was small JSON documents for which the initial map – i.e. parsing – is cheap, and integrated the stream processing frameworks under test with Kafka [7] and Redis [12] making it difficult to get a sense of maximum performance of the streaming frameworks in isolation. In their study the data is preloaded into Kafka. In our study, we investigate ingress bottlenecks by writing and reading data through Kafka *during the benchmarking*, to get a full measurement of sustained throughput.

Other studies follow a similar vein: [11] used small messages (60 bytes, 200 bytes), and lightweight pre-processing (i.e. 'map') operations: e.g. grepping and tokenizing strings, with an emphasis on common stream operations such as sorting. Indeed, sorting is seen as something of a canonical benchmark for distributed stream processing. For example, Spark previously won the GraySort contest [16], where the frameworks ability to shuffledata between worker nodes is exercised. Marcu et. al. (2016) offer a comparison of Flink and Spark on familiar BigData benchmarks (grepping, wordcount), and give a good overview of performance optimizations in both frameworks.

HarmonicIO, a research prototype streaming framework with a peer-to-peer architecture, developed specifically for scientific computing workloads, has previously shown good performance messages in the 1–10 MB range [14]. To the authors' knowledge there is no existing work benchmarking stream processing with Apache Spark, or related frameworks, with messages larger than a few KB, and with map stages which are computationally expensive.

4   HarmonicIO

HarmonicIO [14] is a peer-to-peer distributed processing framework, intended for high throughput of medium and large messages. HarmonicIO's smart architecture will favor P2P message transfer, but fall back to a queue buffer when necessary to absorb fluctuations in input or processing rate. Messages are processed in a simple loop: pop a message from the master queue (if any exists) otherwise wait to receive a message directly from the streaming source over TCP; process it; and repeat. Per-node daemons aggregate availability information at the master, from where clients query the status of available processing engines. The master node manages the message queue.

We chose HarmonicIO for its simple P2P architecture. Its APIs are a simple abstraction around TCP sockets (in contrast to Apache Spark). Its container-based architecture provides a convenient way for scientists to encapsulate complex (and often fragile) software with a variety of dependent libraries, models and datasets. Docker containers are a useful 'unit' of scientific computing code. Being a research prototype, it lacks many features of more mature frameworks error handling and guaranteed delivery. The simplicity of the implementation makes it easily adoptable and extensible; and configuration is much simpler than Apache Spark.

5   Theoretical Bounds on Performance

For a range of message sizes and CPU costs of the map function, we consider the theoretical performance of an 'ideal' stream processing framework which exhibits performance equal to the tightest bound, either network or CPU, with zero overhead; across this domain. In this article we investigate how close the frameworks under study can approach these bounds over our domain (Fig. 1).

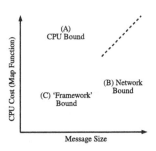

Fig. 1. Schematic of parameter space for this study, showing the processing cost of the map function, and the message size.

A - Small message size, large processing cost - CPU Bound: For sufficiently large processing cost in relation to message size, performance will be CPU bound. Relative performance of the frameworks in this region will be determined by their ability to utilize CPU, and minimizing processing overheads. This regime would be typical of scientific computing applications involving e.g. a simulation step as part of the map stage.

B - Large message size, small processing cost - Network Bound: For sufficiently large message size, performance will be network bound. In this region, relative performance between frameworks will be determined by the network topology and overheads. This regime would be typical for scientific computing applications involving relatively simple filtering operations on binary large objects (BLOBs), such as filtering of massive genomics datasets [3].

C - Small messages, small processing cost: In this regime processing frequency should be high. This region will expose any limitations on the absolute maximum message frequency for the particular integration and thus may be 'framework bound'. Well-performing frameworks may be able to approach the network bounds; with very high frequencies. This regime would be typical for the type of enterprise applications studied in previous benchmarks.

A-B Boundary Region - Large messages, large processing costs: Near this boundary (indicated by the dotted line), processing frequency will be low. The large message size means that network speed will bound the overall frequency, whilst high processing costs means that CPU load will also bound the message frequency. Theoretically, the exists a boundary where these two bounds are equal. Overheads in network communication and CPU load will influence exactly where this lies.

6   Methodology

Varying message size (100 bytes – 10 MB), and CPU cost for processing each message (0–1 s per message) allowed us to sample the performance of the studied streaming frameworks over a parameter space with settings ranging from highly CPU-intensive workloads to highly data-movement intensive workloads - capturing use cases typical of both enterprise and scientific computing.

The microscopy use case is a particular focus: message (image) sizes 1–10 MB, with a CPU cost profiled at around 100mS for very simple analysis (consistent with [14]) – CPU cost would depend on the specific features being extracted, and could be significantly higher. We measure maximum sustained frequency (i.e throughput, messages per second) at each point (message size, CPU), for HarmonicIO, and each of the Spark stream source integrations explained below:

Spark + TCP Socket: TCP sockets are a simple, universal mechanism, easy to integrate into source applications, with minimal configuration.

Spark + Kakfa: Kafka is a stream processing framework in its own right: Kafka producers write messages onto one end of message queues, which are processed by Kafka *consumers*. Kafka is commonly used in conjunction with Spark Streaming in enterprise contexts, to provide a resilient and durable buffer, allowing Spark applications to be restarted without interrupting the streaming source. We deploy a single Kafka server as this most resembles the HarmonicIO deployment. The newer *Direct DStream* integration approach with Kafka is used in this study. Under this integration, messages are transferred directly from the Kafka server to Spark workers.

Spark + File Streaming: Under this approach, Spark will process new files in each batch interval. We configure an NFS share on the streaming source node. This allows direct transfer of file contents from the streaming source node, to the processing machines – similar to the TCP socket approach used in HarmonicIO. We do not use HDFS, a distributed filesystem intended replicated storage of very large (append-only) files – many GBs; TBs, this makes it inappropriate for the files used in this study, which are at most 10 MB. Indeed, other distributed filesystems wouldn't offer us the P2P message transfer. Nor did we not use Cassandra, a distributed wide-column store, as we exceed the "single digits of MB" being suggested as a sensible limit [2].

7   Experimental Setup and Benchmarking Tools

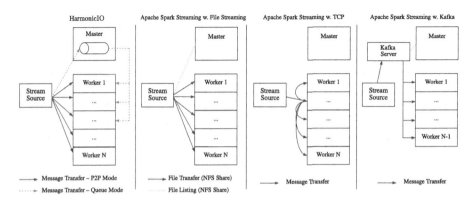

Fig. 2. Architecture / Network Topology Comparison between the frameworks and streaming source intregrations – focusing on major network traffic flows. Note that with Spark and a TCP streaming source, one of the worker nodes is selected as 'receiver' and manages the TCP connection to the streaming source. Note the adaptive queue- and P2P-based message processing in HarmonicIO. Neither the monitoring and throttling tool (which communicates with all components) are shown, nor is additional metadata traffic between nodes (for scheduling, etc.).

To explore the (message size, CPU cost per message) parameter space we developed benchmarking tools[2] for Spark and HarmonicIO, able to process synthetic messages, and generate synthetic CPU load. Figure 2 shows the various pipelines showing of HarmonicIO, and Apache Spark Streaming with file, Kakfa and TCP based integrations. The arrows show the busy network communication. For each setup, 6 stream Processing VMs were used, each with 8 VCPUs and 16 GB RAM (1 master, 5 workers). For the streaming source VM we used a 1 VCPU, 2 GB RAM instance. These resources are similar to the experimental setup of [16], where 40 cores were used. The maximum network bandwidth monitored using

---

[2] Available at: https://github.com/HASTE-project/benchmarking-tools.

`iperf` was 1.4Gbit/s. Ansible scripts used to deploy the cluster are at: https://github.com/HASTE-project/ansible-benchmarking.

Below, we describe the details of the experimental setup for each framework, and the approach used for determining the maximum frequency message throughput.

7.1   Apache Spark

Messages are generated by a streaming source application, consisting of the CPU pause (as a string), padded up to the specified message size, so that both parameters (CPU load and message size) can be controlled by the throttling application, via a REST API. Inside the Spark application, we used the `getThreadCpuTime()` method of the `ThreadMXBean`[3] from JavaSE, which returns the total time spent executing by the thread in both user and system mode (excluding blocked and waiting times), polling this until the 'CPU load' parameter from the message has elapsed. Hence, we simulate a CPU-intensive message processing step, revealing the CPU overhead of the different frameworks.

To determine the maximum throughput for each (fixed (message_size, CPU cost) pair, we adopt the approach of gradually increasing the message frequency until a bottleneck is detected somewhere in the pipeline, then a binary search to find the maximum. A monitoring and throttling tool, monitors our streaming source application and the spark application, through a combination of queries to Spark's REST APIs and real-time log file analysis. A simplified version of this algorithm is as follows:

1. Streaming begins at a pre-defined low initial frequency.
2. After 13 batch intervals, the fractional of maximum load is estimated from various metrics.
3. The frequency is scaled up (always increasing by at least 1 Hz), based on the estimated load.
4. This continues until the metrics indicate that the maximum frequency has been exceeded.
5. A binary search to find the maximum message frequency, i.e. the greatest integer frequency where processing remains stable.

The scaling factors used for the initial geometric progression are chosen based on the load, to avoid completely overloading the framework (and crashing it), whilst increasing towards maximum frequencies in a timely fashion. This process is repeated for the (message_size, CPU cost) parameter sweep. We used a batch interval of 5 s, and a micro-batch interval of 150 mS. Experimenting with other values had little impact on throughput. For the Spark File Streaming investigation, files are shared on the streaming server with NFS. Maximum throughput is reached when a bottleneck occurs somewhere in the system, as detected by the throttling tool: (a) ASS taking too long to process messages, (b) a network

---

[3] https://docs.oracle.com/javase/7/docs/api/java/lang/management/ThreadMXBean.html

bottleneck at the stream source, (c) for file streaming, ASS is taking too long to perform a directory listing.

7.2 HarmonicIO

For HarmonicIO, the maximum throughput is determined by measuring the time to stream and process a predefined number of messages for the given parameters. We created a separate benchmarking application for HarmonicIO, which reads messages in our format. As with Spark, metadata describing the amount of CPU load is embedded in each message.

8 Results

Table 1. Maximum Message Processing Frequencies (Hz) of Apache Spark (under TCP, File streaming, and Kafka integrations), and HarmonicIO; in that order. These results are visualized in Fig. 3. There is no data for Spark + TCP for message sizes of 1 MB or more, as it did not perform reliably in this domain. The highest message frequency in each case is shown in bold. † 0.0 denotes nil CPU load.

CPU Cost	Message Size (bytes)							
1.0 secs	14, **43**	11, **44**	12, **41**	13, 38	15, **40**	-, **41**	-, 17	-, 11
	7, 39	7, 40	7, 39	8, **40**	8, 39	7, 37	6, **29**	4, **16**
0.5 secs	30, 39	31, 43	32, 39	30, 42	31, 39	-, 35	-, 18	-, 12
	23, **79**	24, **78**	26, **73**	24, **76**	21, **78**	20, **54**	11, **30**	6, **17**
0.2 secs	85, 41	83, 44	81, 39	82, 43	88, 37	-, 40	-, 18	-, 12
	88, **185**	92, **172**	92, **192**	90, **185**	72, **166**	49, **121**	12, **28**	7, **15**
0.1 secs	182, 41	180, 41	164, 40	162, 38	156, 36	-, 35	-, 15	-, 13
	201, **277**	208, **238**	210, **263**	207, **312**	163, **227**	63, **128**	12, **32**	7, **16**
0.05 secs	336, 39	326, 42	327, 40	351, 38	306, 43	-, 33	-, 16	-, 12
	466, 454	**463**, 416	**471**, 357	438, **454**	277, **333**	55, **128**	12, **34**	6, **15**
0.02 secs	884, 42	859, 35	904, 37	838, 37	402, 42	-, 37	-, 20	-, 12
	1K, 555	**1K**, 500	**1K**, 454	**1K**, 500	587, **500**	61, **125**	10, **32**	6, **16**
0.0 secs †	**0.32M**, 32	**86K**, 40	22K, 40	5K, 38	504, 42	-, 34	-, 15	-, 12
	49K, 625	63K, 625	**35K**, 625	**6K**, 555	598, 500	54, **125**	12, **33**	7, **16**

The maximum frequencies achieved by each framework (and stream integration setup), according to message size and per-message CPU load, are show in Fig. 3 and Table 1. A subset of these results is presented again in Fig. 4 and Fig. 5, where results for particular CPU loads are shown in relation to CPU and network-theoretical bounds. The results in summary:

Apache Spark Streaming with TCP: This integration achieves very high frequency when message size and CPU load are small, consistent with previous

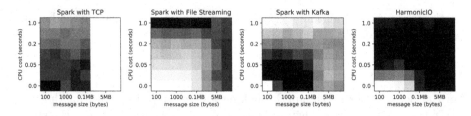

Fig. 3. Performance of the frameworks and stream integrations over the domain under study. The shading shows the message frequency as a fraction of the best performing framework at that position – lighter areas indicate lower message frequency. Compare with Fig. 1. There is no data for Spark + TCP for message sizes of 1 MB or more, as it did not perform reliably in this domain.

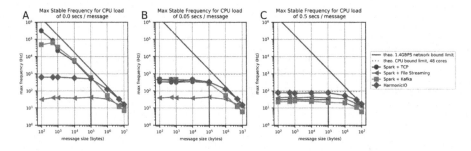

Fig. 4. Maximum stream processing frequencies for Spark (with TCP, File Streaming, Kafka) and HarmonicIO by message size; for a selection of CPU cost/message.

studies. For 100 byte messages without CPU load; the pipeline was able to process messages at frequencies approaching 320KHz, meaning around 1.6M messages were processed by Spark in a 5 s batch. This can seen in the extreme lower-left of Fig. 3, and the results shown in Fig. 4A. But performance degraded rapidly for larger message sizes, and under our benchmarks, it couldn't reliably handle messages larger than 10^5 bytes at any frequency.

Apache Spark Streaming with Kafka: This streaming pipeline performed well for messages less than 1 MB, and CPU loads less than 0.1 s/message, at the bottom-left of Fig. 3. Away from this region, relative performance degrades.

Apache Spark Streaming with File Streaming: This integration performed efficiently at low frequencies – in regions tightly constrained by network and CPU-theoretic bounds (the top and right of Figs. 1 and 3, and the results for higher message sizes in Fig. 4).

HarmonicIO: Fig. 3 shows this was the best performing framework for the broad intermediate region of our study domain, for medium-sized messages (larger than 1.0 MB), and/or CPU loads higher than 0.05 s/message. It matched the performance of file-based streaming with Apache Spark for larger messages and higher CPU loads.

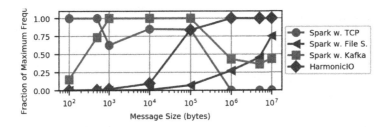

Fig. 5. Maximum frequency by message size, for Spark (with TCP, File Streaming, Kafka) and HarmonicIO, for nil CPU load; normalized as a fraction of the best performing framework for the particular parameter values.

9 Discussion

Maximum message throughput is bound by network and CPU bounds, which are inversely proportional to message size and CPU cost respectively (assuming constant network speed, and number of CPU cores; respectively). The relative performance of different frameworks (and stream integrations) depend on these same parameters. Figure 3 shows that all frameworks also have specific, well-defined regions where they each perform the best. We discuss these regions in turn, moving outwards from the origin of Fig. 3.

Close to the origin, theoretical maximum message throughput is high, Fig. 4A, Spark with TCP streaming is able to outperform Kafka for at very high frequencies. Both configurations involve some form of message forwarding (as shown in Fig. 2.), so throughput is bound at half the network link speed (half for incoming messages, half for outgoing). Consequently, Fig. 4A shows that Spark with neither Kafka nor direct TCP can approach the theoretical network bound.

Moving further from the origin, into the region with CPU cost of 0.2–0.5 s/message and/or medium size (1–10 MB) – HarmonicIO performs better than the Spark integrations under this study. It exhibits good performance – transferring messages P2P transfer yields good use of bandwidth (when the messages are larger than 1 MB or so). Similarly, when there is considerable CPU load, its simplicity obviates spending CPU time on serialization, and other overheads (under the Kafka integration, some of the 48 cores are used by the Kafka server).

HarmonicIO achieved a maximum message transfer rate of 625 Hz, hence performing poorly for the smallest, lightest messages (see Fig. 3). Figure 4A clearly shows this frequency bound – making it unsuitable for enterprise use cases with high message frequencies. For large messages, and heavy CPU loads, this integration is able to approach closely to the network and CPU bounds – its able to make cost-effective use of the hardware. For the very largest messages, and the highest per-message CPU loads, the network and CPU bounds are very tight, and overall frequencies are very low (double digits). In these regions HarmonicIO performs similarly to Spark with File Streaming. Both approaches are able to tightly approach the network and CPU theoretic bounds – as shown in Fig. 4.

Where the message frequency is theoretically bounded to double-digit frequencies, Spark's File Streaming integration is very efficient, and is the best performing framework at very high CPU loads (the top of Fig. 3). Each worker directly fetches the files it needs from the streaming source machine, making good use of network bandwidth. The implementation polls the filesystem for new files, which no doubt works well for quasi-batch jobs at low polling frequencies – order of minutes, with a small number of large files (order GBs, TBs, intended use cases for HDFS). However, for large numbers of much smaller files (MBs, KBs), this mechanism performs poorly. For these smaller messages, network-bound throughput corresponds to message frequencies of, say, several KHz (see Fig. 4). There frequencies are outside the intended use case of this integration, and the filesystem polling-based implementation is cumbersome for low-latency applications. At the time of this study, the `FileInputDStream` was not intended to handle the deletion of files during streaming[4].

10   Conclusions

In summary, for very small messages (and lightweight processing), Spark with Kafka performs well (as does Spark with TCP streaming). For quasi-batch processing of very large files (at large polling intervals), Spark with file streaming integration performs well. These are the two typical enterprise stream analytics contexts: low-latency, high-frequency processing of small messages, and high-latency quasi-batch file-based processing of large message batches such as log files. In the middle region – messages 1–10 MB, and CPU intensive processing of small messages (>0.1 s/message) HarmonicIO is able to outperform the Spark streaming approaches benchmarked in this study.

This study has confirmed Spark's excellent performance, consistent with earlier studies, albeit for use cases with small message size, and low message processing cost – and quasi-batch loads at low frequencies. But, we find that these 'islands' of excellent performance do not generalize across the wider domain of use cases we studied. It was difficult for Spark to achieve good performance in the 1–10 MB message size range (typical of microscopy image analysis, for example), with the integrations chosen for this study. By contrast, HarmonicIO performs well in this region, with good hardware utilization at low frequencies – whilst not matching Spark for maximum frequency for the small message/cheap map function use case. Its simplicity (and comparative lack of features) makes its performance less sensitive the parameters of the application load.

This paper has quantified the performance of Spark integrations, in comparison to HarmonicIO; and theoretical bounds. Our results show the importance of choosing a stream source integration appropriate for the message size and required frequency. We hope our findings prove useful to designers of stream processing applications, especially atypical workloads – including microscopy image processing.

---

[4] Now implemented, see: https://issues.apache.org/jira/browse/SPARK-20568.

References

1. Apache Software Foundation: Apache Hadoop. http://hadoop.apache.org/ (2011)
2. Apache Software Foundation: Cassandra Limitations. https://cwiki.apache.org/confluence/display/CASSANDRA2/CassandraLimitations (2019)
3. Ausmees, K., John, A., Toor, S.Z., Hellander, A., Nettelblad, C.: BAMSI: a multicloud service for scalable distributed filtering of massive genome data. BMC Bioinform. **19**(1), 240 (2018). https://doi.org/10.1186/s12859-018-2241-z
4. Blamey, B., Wrede, F., Karlsson, J., Hellander, A., Toor, S.: Adapting the secretary hiring problem for optimal hot-cold tier placement under Top-K workloads. In: 2019 19th IEEE/ACM International Symposium on Cluster, Cloud and Grid Computing (CCGRID). pp. 576–583, May 2019. https://doi.org/10.1109/CCGRID.2019.00074
5. Carbone, P., Katsifodimos, A., Ewen, S., Markl, V., Haridi, S., Tzoumas, K.: Apache Flink^{TM}: stream and batch processing in a single engine. Bull. IEEE Comput. Soc. Techn. Committee Data Eng. **36**(4), 28–38 (2015)
6. Chintapalli, S., et al.: Benchmarking streaming computation engines: storm, flink and spark streaming. In: 2016 IEEE International Parallel and Distributed Processing Symposium Workshops, pp. 1789–1792. IEEE (2016)
7. Kreps, J., Narkhede, N., Rao, J., et al.: Kafka: a distributed messaging system for log processing. In: Proceedings of the NetDB, pp. 1–7 (2011)
8. Lugnegård, L.: Building a high throughput microscope simulator using the Apache Kafka streaming framework (M.sc. Thesis) (2018)
9. Marcu, O.C., Costan, A., Antoniu, G., Pérez-Hernández, M.S.: Spark versus flink: understanding performance in big data analytics frameworks. In: 2016 IEEE International Conference on Cluster Computing (CLUSTER), pp. 433–442, September 2016. https://doi.org/10.1109/CLUSTER.2016.22
10. National Energy Research Scientific Computing Center: Characterization of the DOE Mini-apps. https://portal.nersc.gov/project/CAL/designforward.htm, June 2014
11. Qian, S., Wu, G., Huang, J., Das, T.: Benchmarking modern distributed streaming platforms. In: 2016 IEEE International Conference on Industrial Technology (ICIT), pp. 592–598, March 2016. https://doi.org/10.1109/ICIT.2016.7474816
12. Salvatore Sanfilippo: Redis (2009). https://redis.io/
13. Toor, S., et al.: SNIC Science Cloud (SSC): a national-scale cloud infrastructure for Swedish academia. In: 2017 IEEE 13th International Conference On E-Science (e-Science), pp. 219–227. IEEE (2017)
14. Torruangwatthana, P., Wieslander, H., Blamey, B., Hellander, A., Toor, S.: HarmonicIO: scalable data stream processing for scientific datasets. In: 2018 IEEE 11th International Conference on Cloud Computing (CLOUD), pp. 879–882, July 2018. https://doi.org/10.1109/CLOUD.2018.00126
15. Wollman, R., Stuurman, N.: High throughput microscopy: from raw images to discoveries. J. Cell Sci. **120**(21), 3715–3722 (2007). https://doi.org/10.1242/jcs.013623
16. Xin, R.: Apache Spark the fastest open source engine for sorting a petabyte, October 2014. https://databricks.com/blog/2014/10/10/spark-petabyte-sort.html
17. Zaharia, M., et al.: Resilient distributed datasets: a fault-tolerant abstraction for in-memory cluster computing. In: Proceedings of the 9th USENIX Conference on Networked Systems Design and Implementation, pp. 2–2. NSDI 2012, USENIX Association, San Jose (2012)
18. Zaharia, M., et al.: Apache spark: a unified engine for big data processing. Commun. ACM **59**(11), 56–65 (2016). https://doi.org/10.1145/2934664

Benchmark Researches from the Perspective of Metrology

Kun Yang$^{(\boxtimes)}$, Tong Wu, Qingfei Shen, Weiqun Cui, and Guichun Zhang

Division of Electronic and Information Technology, National Institute of Metrology,
Peking, China
{yangkun,wut,shenqf,cuiwq,zhgch}@nim.ac.cn

Abstract. This paper discusses some problems the benchmark researches should pay attention to from the perspective of Metrology. Metrology is about the science of measurement, and it is considered as the foundation of industry development, for you have to measure it before you know what level it reaches. Metrology has a series of mechanisms to ensure the attributes of the measurement results, including Accuracy, Traceability, consistency and legality. Benchmark is widely used to evaluate the information technology products and helps the users to choose the products they need, and if absorbing the ideas of Metrology research during the designing, developing and application procedures of the benchmark, the quality of the measurement result of the benchmark will be improved greatly and become more authoritative.

Keywords: Benchmark · Metrology · Accuracy · Traceability · Consistency · Legality

1 Introduction

As is said by the chairman of Tencent Company that the future is dealing with big data on the cloudy computing platform by AI technology. The booming development of Big data, Cloud computing, and AI technology promote the social development and make people's lives much easier and smarter. In order to meet the tremendous application requirements in above areas, A lot of tools or products in above areas are provided for the users, for example, some big data open source projects as Hadoop, MapReduce, Hive, ClouderaImpala, NoSQL database, Spark and GraphLab, and different AI frames as TensorFlow, Caffe and PyThorch. While faced with so many choices, the users often feel confused to make a proper decision if there is no an appropriate benchmark to evaluate those tools or products. And the tools developers and products manufacturers also need a benchmark to learn their tools or products so as to improve their products or introduce them to their users. This situation gives rise to great pressure on benchmark corresponding specific areas.

Benchmark is critical to the development of related industries for the following two reasons:

W. Gao et al. (Eds.): Bench 2019, LNCS 12093, pp. 348–359, 2020.
https://doi.org/10.1007/978-3-030-49556-5_31

1) **To the users:** it provides an approach to help the users to understand a specific tool or product and make it possible to compare it with others, which can help the users to make a better choice according to their requirement indeed.

2) **To the manufacturers:** benchmark helps them to find out the advantages and disadvantages of their products, and finally they can optimize their performance by tuning with a clear target.

Many researchers devote themselves to develop benchmarks that can evaluate products objectively and fairly in specific area, and some principles are generalized on how to develop a good benchmark. Some of features that a good benchmark should own are put forward by [1] based on the point of view of [2] as following:

1) **Representative:** Big data, Cloudy Computing and AI are widely used in many field, it is prohibitively costly and time consuming to create a comprehensive benchmark suitable for all those fields. So it is a great challenge to improve the field coverage of the benchmark while keeping it easy enough. The representative of a benchmark should be reflected by the workload, the testing data and the software stack of it.

2) **Portability:** Benchmarks are used not only to evaluate the portraits of a specific product, but also to compare different products. So the benchmark chosen should be able to run on different platform with the same algorithm, so as to yield the same output to the same input.

3) **Scalability:** The benchmarks for Big data, Cloudy Computing and AI need huge amount of data, while it is impossible to obtain real data sets for they are treated as important trade secrets. So the benchmarks should provide scalable data sets and workloads according to the portraits of the product to be measured.

4) **Comprehensibility:** A good benchmark should be easy to understand, deploy and evaluate, and the result of evaluation can used to direct the evaluation, improvement and optimization of the measured product.

These basic principles mentioned above are followed by a lot of benchmark researchers when designing and develop a benchmark applied in a specific field. Are those principles enough for a good benchmark? This paper provide a new perspective to review the creation of a good benchmark, and puts forward some principles it should followed from the perspective of the perspective of Metrology which focuses on the quality of the measurement result.

2 Related Work

For the importance of promoting industrial development, many benchmarks are provided in Big Data, Cloud Computing and AI fields. They are illustrated as following:

BigBench [3] is an offline and End-to-End Big Data benchmark to be used for DBMS and MapReduce systems, which is based on TPC-DC and adds some data types of semi-structure and non-structure.

CloudSuite [4] is a suite of benchmarks used for Scale-out workloads, which can be used for machine learning task running on Hadoop frame and data services based on Yahoo Cloud service standards.

HiBench [5] is a suite of benchmarks put forwarded by Intel for MapReduce applications, which mainly includes some micro benchmarking programs, workload related machine learning or Cloud services, and HDFS benchmark.

CALDA [6] is a benchmark for Hadoop and RDBMS system. It provides a series of workloads for data analysis and its evaluation targets include index creating time, search time and system loading time.

YCSB [7] is a benchmark for NoSQL which focuses on the performance and scalability of Cloud service system. It is mainly used to test pressure, such as the throughput when the database under testing is reading, or writing or updating concurrently.

AMP [8] Benchmarks is a Big Data benchmark being used for real-time analysis applications which is put forwarded by UC Berkeley AMP Lab. It is mainly used to test the system response time of a series of relation queries under different data size.

LinkBench [9] is a customizable and scalable benchmark for social graph database, which is developed based on real social network Facebook. Its evaluation targets mainly include the delay and throughput when querying and updating the system in real time.

CloudBM [10] is a benchmark for Cloud data management system which is put forward by Renmin University of China. It provides a set of performance evaluation indicators by taking Telecom business as background.

A series of AI benchmarks are proposed as follows. Fathom [11] provides eight deep learning workloads implement with TensorFlow. DeepBench [12] consists of four operations involved in training deep neural networks. BenchNN [13] develops and evaluates software neural network implementations of5 high-performance applications from the PARSEC Benchmark Suite. DNN-Mark [14] is a GPU benchmark suite that consists of a collection of deep neural network primitives. Tonic Suite [15] presents seven neural network workloads that use the DjiNN service. DAWNBench [16] is a benchmark and competition focusing on end-to-end training time to achieve a state-of-the-art accuracy level, as well as inference time with that accuracy.

Most benchmarks above either are designed for specific application fields or software stack or lack reasonable grounds for choosing workload. Aiming to overcome the limits mentioned above, [17] proposes a scalable benchmarking methodology that uses the combination of one or more classes of units of computation performed on different initial or intermediate data inputs to represent diversity of big data and AI workloads. And following this methodology, [17] presents a unified big data and AI bench−+3.mark suite—BigDataBench 4.0, which is publicly available from http://prof.ict.ac.cn/BigDat aBench.

Currently, most benchmark researches focus on the implementation at the methodology level and application level, while pay little attention to the quality of the evaluation results. Are these results accurate and stable enough? What factors affect the results, and how to evaluate them so as to reflect them in the results? Comprehensive and objective evaluation results have more authoritative to be used in some serious situations such as arbitration or trading, are easier to be trusted by users, and can help understanding the object under evaluation deeply. How to obtain comprehensive and objective benchmark evaluation results? Some methods and opinions are suggested from the perspective of Metrology in the following sections and some examples in our researching work are also provided along to illustrate the methods and opinions mentioned here.

3   The Perspective of the Metrology

Maybe "Metrology" is unfamiliar to many people, and should be introduced and explained first.

What is Metrology: Metrology is about the science of measurement, and it is considered as the foundation of industry development, for you have to measure it before you know what level it reaches. It focuses on the preserving and reproducing of the measurement units, the technologies of accurate measurement and the uncertainty assessment of the measurement result. Its final goal is ensuring the units to be unified and the measurement result to be accurate and reliable. There are some features the measurement results should have from the perspective of Metrology, including Accuracy, Traceability, consistency and legality. And Metrology has a series of mechanisms to ensure these features. Besides the features mentioned above, Metrology also requires the measurement results to be stable and repeatable. The features mentioned here will be illustrated as follows in order to help understanding them.

A. Accuracy
As a basic feature of Metrology, accuracy is used to characterize the proximity of the measured value to the true value. Strictly speaking, Accuracy means that not only the measurement value but also the uncertainty of that value are need to be provided when giving a measurement result. Measurement uncertainty is a parameter associated with measurement result, being used to characterize the dispersion of the measurement results. Usually, it is expressed as standard deviation σ (or $k\sigma$) or half width of a given confidence interval.

B. Consistency
The consistency means the consistency of the measurement units and measurement results. There are a series of units defined in SI international unit system, which is widely used in worldwide, such as Meter, Kilogram, Ampere, Kelvin, Lumen, Second and Moore. SI units and derived units related with them should be prior choice during measuring. Measurement results consistency means as long as the relevant measurement requirements are met, the Measurement results should be consistent with the given uncertainty no matter they are carried out by anyone, at anytime, at anywhere, by using any method or any instrument.

C. Traceability
The measurement value must come from a single source, otherwise, it is bound to cause technical and application confusion and result in serious consequence. Each unit in SI system has a unified and clear definition, based on real object before and based on physical constants recently. There is a measurement basic standard saving or reproducing a specific unit in one country, and all measurement value related to that unit can be traced to that measurement basic standard so as to make the measurement technology and people's understanding unified relatively and guarantee the accuracy and consistency of the measurement result.

D. Legality

Metrology aims to ensure the units to be unified and the measurement result to be accurate and reliable, which should be guaranteed by not only technical means but also law and regulations, especially for those measurement activities being important for national welfare and people's livelihood, such as those in society safety, medical health care, environmental protection and trade settlement fields. Some law and regulations are enacted to regulate the measuring processes, the choice of methods or instruments and the processing methods of the measurement results, so as to guarantee the measurement results rigorous and reliable.

In the following section, some of our researches and practices about benchmark will be introduced from the Metrology perspective.

4 Our Research and Practice

Cloud Computing is charged by usage amount, that means its measurements involve trade settlement, so it is urgent to create a reliable, stable and scalable benchmark for it from the perspective of the Metrology. We develop a suit of Metrology test tools for calculation performance of Cloud Computing unit, which include 30 sets of workloads and corresponding test data set. These workloads selected and developed based on the principle of stable, repeatable and representative. The details of the test tool suit are listed in the following Table 1:

Table 1. Workload list.

SN	Type	Description	SN	Type	Description
1	Integer	Script execution	16	Floats	International chess
2	Integer	Unzip	17	Floats	Gomoku chess
3	Integer	Encryption & decryption	18	Floats	Matrix conversation operation
4	Integer	Program compilation	19	Floats	Fourier transform
5	Integer	Optimized logic	20	Floats	Polynomial optimization
6	Integer	XML handling	21	Floats	Fluid collision
7	Integer	PDF generation	22	Floats	Quantum mechanics
8	Integer	Image processing	23	Floats	Fluid mechanics
9	Integer	Document processing	24	Floats	Bio/molecular mechanics
10	Integer	Video processing	25	Floats	Structural mechanics
11	Integer	Gene sequence search	26	Floats	Computational electromagnetic
12	Integer	Physical quantum mechanics	27	Floats	Quantum chemistry
13	Integer	Discrete event simulation	28	Floats	Weather forecast
14	Integer	Path finding algorithm	29	Floats	Ray tracing
15	Floats	Go chess	30	Floats	Feature recognition

As illustrated in Table 1, 14 of the 30 workloads are for integer calculation performance of CPU and the left 16 workloads are for floating point performance. Except for these workloads and corresponding test data set, a tool system that controls the testing procedure is also developed. It includes two parts, one runs on client side mainly used to control the workloads, return result records and report the result, the other runs on server side mainly used to interact with the software and hardware on the server under test. There are two versions for the server side, one is for single core and another is for multi-core.

The final evaluation result is obtained by synthesizing all the evaluation result of each workload above. It is meaningless of the result of each workload and impossible to compare with each other, so a baseline server is set up, and the evaluation result of each workload for this baseline server is recorded, and the ratio of the evaluation result of one workload for a server under test and that for the baseline server is treated as evaluation result of the workload for the server under test. Then 30 evaluation result will obtained by the 30 workload mentioned above. And the final evaluation result will be obtained as follows:

$$S = (X_1 \times X_2 \times \ldots \times X_n)^{\frac{1}{n}} \tag{1}$$

In (1), n equals 30 and xi means the evaluation result of each workload according to the method introduced above.

We aim to evaluate the calculation performance of cloud computing units, while as known to all, there are many factors affect the evaluation result, such as the configuration, the network station, the environment and so on. In order to find out the stability and repeatability of our benchmark in a relatively stable and controllable environment, we use it to evaluate a local server from Tide Company. The evaluation result is illustrated in Table 2 as follows:

Table 2. Test result of the local server.

SN	Repeat-ability for single core	Repeat-ability for multi-core	Uncertainty for single core	Uncertainty for multi-core
1	0.12%	1.28%	0.030	0.182
2	0.34%	0.57%	0.704	0.405
3	0.01%	0.21%	0.004	0.033
4	0.08%	0.25%	0.030	0.045
5	0.06%	0.35%	0.156	0.291
6	0.04%	0.66%	0.013	0.104
7	0.17%	0.35%	0.067	0.072
8	0.02%	0.26%	0.014	0.083
9	0.06%	0.28%	0.017	0.043
10	0.13%	0.27%	0.033	0.036

(continued)

Table 2. (*continued*)

SN	Repeat-ability for single core	Repeat-ability for multi-core	Uncertainty for single core	Uncertainty for multi-core
11	0.02%	0.24%	0.021	0.118
12	0.17%	0.27%	0.088	0.070
13	0.07%	0.23%	0.019	0.033
14	0.03%	0.23%	0.008	0.029
15	0.08%	0.24%	0.046	0.068
16	0.27%	0.28%	0.422	0.161
17	0.01%	0.22%	0.006	0.071
18	0.09%	0.23%	0.025	0.037
19	0.02%	0.20%	0.013	0.053
20	0.03%	0.28%	0.012	0.062
21	0.03%	0.27%	0.024	0.105
22	0.07%	0.26%	0.043	0.074
23	0.01%	0.28%	0.003	0.059
24	0.04%	0.30%	0.021	0.075
25	0.05%	0.28%	0.027	0.077
26	0.01%	0.24%	0.006	0.086
27	0.01%	0.26%	0.007	0.102
28	0.02%	0.22%	0.020	0.083
29	0.10%	0.24%	0.040	0.047
30	0.09%	0.34%	0.109	0.172
Final	0.04%	0.18%	1.190	1.806

Each result listed in Table 2 above for each workload is based on 25 times tests. It costs 3 h for each time, and the server under test is rebooted and to be ensured in normal working station, which guarantees the reliability of the evaluation result. From the result in Table 2, the Repeatability for single core and multi-core are both less than 1%, and the conclusion that our benchmark is stable and reliable.

We can find out by further analysis that the result of single core is much stable than that of multi-core. The processing capability of single core is weaker than that of multi-core, while multi-core has much more complex programs about linkages and threads to control, which affects its stability greatly, so its repeatability result is worse. The repeatability of the results is evaluated by (2) and the uncertainty of the results is evaluated by (3) as follows:

$$s(q_k) = \sqrt{\frac{\sum\limits_{k-1}^{n} (q_k - \bar{q})^2}{n-1}} \tag{2}$$

$$s(q_k) = \sqrt{\frac{\sum\limits_{k-1}^{n} (q_k - \bar{q})^2}{n}} \tag{3}$$

Where $s(q_k)$ is the repeatability value, q_k is evaluation value of current time, $\bar{q}$ is the average of n times, and n is the times of measurement.

After ensuring the reliable and stability of our benchmark, we further use it to evaluate the cloud computing units. Ali cloud and Tencent cloud are chosen as our testing objects for they are very popular and representative in industry. There are many factors affect our evaluation result including equipment inherent factors, environmental factors, memory factors and network factors. All the affects that these factors bring to the result should be evaluated, and Due to the space limitation, we only introduce part of our work.

For the calculation performance of shared cloud server is not guaranteed and the repeatability result is not so good, so we choose exclusive cloud server, and the result of exclusive Tencent cloud server is illustrated as following Table 3.

Table 3. Test result of exclusive tencent cloud serve.

SN	Repeat-ability for 2-core 4 GB	Repeat-ability for 4-core 8 GB	Uncertainty for 2-core 4 GB	Uncertainty for 4core 8 GB
1	1.34%	3.52%	0.55	1.39
2	1.91%	5.63%	5.13	13.96
3	1.33%	3.38%	0.6	1.48
4	1.30%	3.40%	0.72	1.82
5	2.41%	5.61%	8.07	17.28
6	1.43%	2.86%	0.66	1.28
7	2.09%	3.25%	1.27	1.92
8	1.38%	3.07%	1.38	2.96
9	1.51%	3.24%	0.68	1.42
10	1.57%	2.71%	0.62	1.04
11	2.04%	3.76%	3.41	5.93
12	1.89%	3.43%	1.48	2.58
13	1.10%	2.79%	0.46	1.15
14	1.17%	2.43%	0.42	0.85

(continued)

Table 3. (*continued*)

SN	Repeat-ability for 2-core 4 GB	Repeat-ability for 4-core 8 GB	Uncertainty for 2-core 4 GB	Uncertainty for 4core 8 GB
15	1.36%	2.50%	1.22	2.11
16	0.97%	4.79%	2.05	9.25
17	1.29%	2.92%	1.3	2.77
18	0.68%	1.78%	0.31	0.78
19	1.57%	2.44%	1.31	1.9
20	1.00%	2.13%	0.67	1.36
21	1.86%	3.95%	2.37	4.67
22	1.81%	3.26%	1.63	2.73
23	0.96%	3.15%	0.63	1.95
24	1.20%	2.41%	0.94	1.76
25	1.53%	2.68%	1.33	2.22
26	1.16%	2.36%	1.33	2.53
27	1.76%	2.28%	2.27	2.75
28	0.93%	2.01%	1.14	2.3
29	0.92%	2.72%	0.54	1.52
30	1.42%	2.36%	2.48	3.8

From the result in Table 3, a conclusion can be made that with more cores, the repeatability is worse.

In order to evaluate the difference between shared and exclusive cloud server with the same number of cores and the same size of memory, we carry out 5 times tests on shared and exclusive Ali cloud server of 2-core 4 GB and of 16-core 32 GB respectively, and the evaluation result for each server is the average of the 5 times. The final result is illustrated in the following Table 4.

Table 4. Difference evaluation result for share and exclusive cloud server of Alibaba.

SN	Difference evaluation value for share and exclusive cloud server of 2-core 4 GB	Difference evaluation value for share and exclusive cloud server of 16-core 32 GB
1	7.38%	9.06%
2	12.01%	17.40%
3	7.74%	7.61%
4	7.10%	7.89%

(*continued*)

Table 4. (*continued*)

SN	Difference evaluation value for share and exclusive cloud server of 2-core 4 GB	Difference evaluation value for share and exclusive cloud server of 16-core 32 GB
5	13.86%	32.71%
6	7.39%	7.85%
7	8.61%	6.78%
8	7.70%	11.39%
9	7.25%	9.30%
10	7.21%	7.57%
11	9.03%	17.50%
12	8.13%	15.46%
13	7.75%	8.49%
14	6.95%	10.32%
15	7.39%	5.61%
16	13.70%	6.92%
17	5.09%	3.58%
18	4.38%	4.63%
19	9.55%	5.10%
20	6.85%	3.67%
21	9.65%	6.36%
22	4.32%	2.53%
23	5.93%	1.12%
24	9.61%	1.70%
25	7.79%	1.59%
26	10.39%	0.97%
27	7.59%	0.29%
28	8.67%	5.18%
29	6.42%	3.97%
30	11.61%	0.29%

The Difference evaluation values illustrated in Table 4 is calculated as follows:

$$R = \left| \frac{A}{B} - 1 \right| \times 100\% \qquad (4)$$

In (4) above, R is the result listed in the table, A and B are evaluation result of our benchmark for specific share and exclusive cloud server respectively. From the results in Table 4, the repeatability for the cloud server of the same configuration is bad, which means there is a huge difference between the calculation performance of share cloud servers and that of the exclusive servers. This proves the instability of the shared CPU assigned by the network server.

5 Conclusion

From the examples above, Metrology provides a suit of ideas and technical means to evaluate the measurement result, it focuses on all the factors that affect the measurement result and attempts to qualify those affects, at the same time it provide a way to evaluate the reliability and stability of a benchmark, after all, in an environment where the influencing factors are controllable, the only factor affecting them is the benchmark itself.

With the development of the technology, the measurement results of benchmark maybe are adopted in more formal and serious occasions. It is not enough only considering the benchmarks at the technical realization level, and some thoughts and methods should learn from the Metrology to assess and improve the benchmark used. By absorbing the ideas of Metrology research during the designing and developing procedures of the benchmark, the quality of the measurement result of the benchmark will be improved greatly and become more authoritative.

References

1. Zhan, J.-F., Gao, W.-L., et al.: BigDataBench: an open-source big data benchmark suite. Chin. J. Comput. **39**(1), 196–211 (2016)
2. Gray, J.: Benchmark Handbook for Database and Transaction System, 2nd edn. Morgan Kaufmann Publishers, San Francisco (1933)
3. Ghazal, A., Rabl, T., Hu, M., et al.: BigBench: towards an industry standard benchmark for big data analytics. In: Proceedings of the 2013 ACM SIGMOD International Conference on Management of Data, New York, USA, pp. 1197–1208 (2013)
4. Ferdman, M., Adileh, A., Kocberber, O., et al.: Clearing the clouds: a study of emerging scale-out workload on modern hardware. ACM SIGPLAN Not. **47**(4), 37–48 (2012)
5. Huang, S., Huang, J., Dai, J.Q., et al.: The Hibench benchmark suite: characterization of the MapReduce-based data analysis. In: Proceedings of the ICDE Workshops on Information & Software as Services, LongBeach, USA, pp. 41–51 (2010)
6. Pavlo, A., Paulson, E., Rasin, A., et al.: A comparison of approaches to large-scale data analysis. In: Proceedings of the 2009 ACM SIGMOD International Conference on Management of Data, Providence, USA, pp. 165–178 (2009)
7. Coper, B., Silberstein, A., Tam, E., et al.: Benchmarking cloud serving systems with YCSB. In: Proceeding of the 1st ACM Symposium on Cloud Computing, Indianapolis, USA, pp. 143–154 (2010)
8. http://amplab.cs.berkeley.edu/benchmark/
9. Armstrong, T.G., Ponnekanti, V., Borthakur, D., Callaghan, M.: LinkBench: a database benchmark based on the Facebook social graph. In: Proceedings of the 2013 ACM SIGMOD International Conference on Management of Data, New York, USA, pp. 1185–1196 (2013)
10. Xia, F., Li, Y., Yu, C., et al.: BSMA: a benchmark for analytical queries over social media data. Proc. VLDB Endow. **7**(13), 1573–1576 (2014)
11. Bing-Bing, L., Xiao-Feng, M., Ying-Jie, S.: CloudBM: a benchmark for cloud data management systems. J. Front. Comput. Sci. Technol. **6**(6), 504–512 (2012). (in Chinese)

12. Adolf, R., Rama, S., Reagen, B., Wei, G.-Y., Brooks, D.: Fathom: reference workloads for modern deep learning methods. In: Workload Characterization (IISWC), pp. 1–10. IEEE (2016)
13. Deepbench. https://svail.github.io/DeepBench/
14. Chen, T., et al.: BenchNN: an the broad potential application scope of hardware neural network accelerators. In: 2012 IEEE International Symposium on Workload Characterization (IISWC), pp. 36–45. IEEE (2012)
15. Dong, S., Kaeli, D.: DNNMark: a deep neural network benchmark suite for GPUs. In: Proceedings of the General Purpose GPUs, pp. 63–72. ACM (2017)
16. Coleman, C., et al.: DAWNBench: an end-to-end deep learning benchmark and competition. Training **100**(101), 102 (2017)
17. Gao, W., Zhang, J., et al.: BigDataBench: a scalable and unified big data and AI benchmark suite. arXiv:1802.08254v2 (22 November 2018)

Author Index

Ajith, Prakash Sirra   306
Aseeri, Samar   172

Bachstein, Matthew   251
Berre, Arne Jørgen   165
Bhat, Raghavendra   306
Blamey, Ben   335

Candan, K. Selçuk   234
Cao, Zheng   278
Chalhoub, Elias   295
Chandran, Pravin   306
Chen, Ge   75
Chen, Kaizhong   123
Chen, Maosen   116
Chen, Mingyu   319
Chen, Qianyun   116
Chen, Tun   116
Cheng, Lu   234
Cui, Weiqun   348
Curbelo III, Gilbert   295

Deng, Kai   75
Deng, Weixin   101
Dibbur, Viswanath   306
Djan, Dennis Mintah   187
Du, Zhihui   225

Eichhorn, Timo   165

Feng, Xiao   319
Feng, Xiaobing   51
Francalanci, Chiara   165
Fu, Li   75

Gao, Wanling   262
Gong, Tongyan   149
Guo, Minyi   101
Guo, Ruocheng   204, 234

Han, Rui   215
Hao, Tianshu   110
He, Peng   75

Hellander, Andreas   335
Hou, Pengpeng   85
Huang, Cheng   141
Hui, Yujie   32

Ibrahim, Khaled Z.   3
Ivanov, Todor   165

Jamthe, Anagha   295
Jiang, Zihan   57, 262
Jose, Juby   306

Kong, Yangyang   91

Li, Chao   101
Li, Chundian   67
Li, Guangli   51
Li, Jiansong   57
Li, Jinheng   278
Li, Yichuan   204
Li, Zeqing   215
Liang, Yande   123
Liang, Yi   123
Lien, Jeffrey   32
Liu, Huan   204, 234
Liu, Lei   51
Liu, Zifeng   215
Lobo, Tomás Pariente   165
Lu, Xiaoyi   32

Ma, Xiu   51
Meng, Xiaofeng   225
Miao, Yuxia   85
Moraffah, Raha   234
Muite, B. K.   172

Niu, Huiqian   149

Oliker, Leonid   3
Oral, Sarp   251

Packard, Mike   295
Pernici, Barbara   165
Pham, Trong-Ton   187

Raglin, Adrienne   234
Ren, Rui   278
Rodriguez, Ivan Martinez   165

Saiz, Ricardo Ruiz   165
Shapi, Roseline   295
Shen, Qingfei   348
Stubbs, Joe   295

Tai, Yang   85
Tang, Qing   225
Toor, Salman   335

Wang, Feiyi   251
Wang, Jing   101
Wang, Lei   20, 262, 278
Wang, Pengyu   101
Wang, Weiying   204
Wang, Xueying   51
Wang, Yifan   67
Wen, Xu   141
Williams, Samuel   3
Wu, Tong   348

Wu, Wenqing   319
Wu, Yanjun   85

Xiong, Xi   156
Xiong, Xingwang   141

Yang, Chen   225
Yang, Kaiyong   262
Yang, Kun   348
Yao, Ping   75
Yin, Yan   278
Yu, Jiageng   85
Yu, Minghe   20

Zeng, Chen   67
Zeng, Shaokang   123
Zhang, Guichun   348
Zhang, Wenli   319
Zhao, Chen   85
Zheng, Ziping   110
Zuo, Xiaojiang   215

Printed in the United States
By Bookmasters